The Rise of the Western Armenian Diaspora in the Early Modern Ottoman Empire

Non-Muslim Contributions to Islamic Civilisation
Series Editor: Carole Hillenbrand

Titles in the series include:

*Jewish Medical Practitioners in the Medieval Muslim World:
A Collective Biography*
Efraim Lev

The Rise of the Western Armenian Diaspora in the Early Modern Ottoman Empire: From Refugee Crisis to Renaissance
Henry R. Shapiro

edinburghuniversitypress.com/series/nmcic

The Rise of the Western Armenian Diaspora in the Early Modern Ottoman Empire

From Refugee Crisis to Renaissance

Henry R. Shapiro

EDINBURGH
University Press

Edinburgh University Press is one of the leading university presses in the UK. We publish academic books and journals in our selected subject areas across the humanities and social sciences, combining cutting-edge scholarship with high editorial and production values to produce academic works of lasting importance. For more information visit our website: edinburghuniversitypress.com

© Henry R. Shapiro, 2022

Cover image: Grigor the Illuminator Monastery, May 2014 © Henry R. Shapiro
Cover design: www.hayesdesign.co.uk

Edinburgh University Press Ltd
The Tun – Holyrood Road
12 (2f) Jackson's Entry
Edinburgh EH8 8PJ

Typeset in 11/15 EB Garamond by
Cheshire Typesetting Ltd, Cuddington, Cheshire

A CIP record for this book is available from the British Library

ISBN 978 1 4744 7960 8 (hardback)
ISBN 978 1 4744 7962 2 (webready PDF)
ISBN 978 1 4744 7963 9 (epub)

The right of Henry R. Shapiro to be identified as author of this work has been asserted in accordance with the Copyright, Designs and Patents Act 1988 and the Copyright and Related Rights Regulations 2003 (SI No. 2498).

Contents

List of Figures	vi
A Note on Transliteration, Abbreviation and Translation	viii
Acknowledgements	x

PART I MIGRATION AND REFUGEE CRISIS

1	Armenians and the 'Seventeenth-century Crisis' in the Ottoman Empire	3
2	Kemah and the 'Great Armenian Flight'	29
3	An Armenian Refugee Crisis in Ottoman Rodosto (Tekirdağ)	83

PART II INTEGRATION AND RENAISSANCE

4	Grigor Daranalts'i and the Crisis of Leadership and Infrastructure in the Early Seventeenth-century Western Armenian Diaspora	147
5	Eremia K'eōmurchean and the Foundation of the Western Armenian Intellectual Tradition in Ottoman Istanbul	197
6	Eremia K'eōmurchean and the Establishment of an Armeno-Turkish Translation Movement in Ottoman Istanbul	261
	Conclusions: Legacies of the Great Armenian Flight	288

Bibliography	293
Index	315

Figures

(All photographs taken by the author unless otherwise noted)

1.1	Map of Ottoman Anatolia	2
1.2	Map of Greater Armenia and Cilicia as conceived by the Armenian delegation to the 1919 Paris Peace Conference	7
2.1	Map of Kemah and its vicinity	28
2.2	Modern-day town of Kemah as seen from Ani Fortress ruins	30
2.3	Grigor the Illuminator Monastery	34
2.4	Armenian tombstone of (1042) 1593	35
2.5	Avag Monastery	36
2.6	Monastery of the Sepulchre of the Nine Saints, Tʻordan Village (Doğan Köyü)	37
2.7	Monastery of the King	37
3.1	Rodosto (contemporary Tekirdağ)	84
3.2	*Sicil* from 1605 banning 'bastard (*harâmzâde*) Armenians' from living in Muslim neighbourhoods of Rodosto (RŞS 1545, 69a)	109
4.1	Hermit caves near Kemah	151
4.2	Bayburt	153
4.3	Vahanshēn (Vahşen/Çatıksu) Village, Bayburt Province	155
4.4	Kefevi Mosque, Istanbul (formerly St Nicholas Church)	157
4.5	*Sicil* from 1609 documenting Grigor Daranaḷtsʻi's visit to court (RŞS 1553, 58a)	163
4.6	St Makar Monastery, Cyprus	165

4.7 Pages of autograph copy of Grigor Daranałts'i's *Chronicle*
     (J 1069, 180b–181a) 169
4.8 Ruins of the fortress above Sis (modern-day Kozan, Adana) 171
5.1 Akn (Kemaliye) 201
5.2 Genealogical chart for Sultans Osman, Orhan and Murad, prepared in the eighteenth century by Step'anos Dashtets'i
     (M 1786, 37a) 217
5.3 St Grigor the Illuminator Church in Tophane, Istanbul (modern structure) 237
6.1 Genealogical chart from autograph copy of Eremia's Armeno-Turkish translation of Moses Khorenats'i
     (V 411, 1b–2a) 277

A Note on Transliteration, Abbreviation and Translation

All Ottoman Turkish transcriptions are made in accordance with the standard employed in the history departments of Turkish universities. This standard contrasts with that found in literature departments, as it prioritises readability for those fluent in Modern Turkish.

For all Armenian transcriptions I made use of the Classical Armenian transcription alphabet found at the beginning of Robert W. Thomson's *Moses Khorenats'i: History of the Armenians* (Cambridge, MA: Harvard University Press, 1978). I chose this transcription alphabet because it is the most comprehensible for readers who do not know Armenian. I sometimes use the commonly employed variants of well-known names, such as Moses, instead of transcribing.

Armeno-Turkish represents a particular challenge for transcription. All of the Armeno-Turkish sources that I employed required use of a Western Armenian transcription alphabet – as opposed to the Classical one that I used for Armenian sources – in order to convey the correct Turkish pronunciation. Thus, I used the transcription alphabet printed at the beginning of the Turkish version of Kevork Bardakjian's *Reference Guide to Modern Armenian Literature* (Istanbul: Aras, 2013) for all transcriptions of Armeno-Turkish texts.

Armenian manuscripts are designated according to the abbreviation system found in Bernard Coulie, 'Collections and Catalogues of Armenian Manuscripts', *Armenian Philology in the Modern Era: From Manuscript to Digital*, Valentina Calzolari (ed.) (Leiden: Brill, 2014). Citation practices for Classical Armenian books differ from that for Turkish books; for the sake of greater consistency and clarity, I listed primary sources in Armenian by their author instead of editor.

All transcriptions and translations from Armenian (Classical and Modern), Turkish (Ottoman and Modern), Armeno-Turkish and other languages into English are my own, with the exception of quotations from the chronicles of Moses Khorenats'i and Agat'angełos, where I relied on the translations of Robert W. Thomson.

Acknowledgements

This book originated as a dissertation in the History Department at Princeton University. I am grateful to my advisers at Princeton – Molly Greene and Michael Cook – for their consistent encouragement of this project from its inception to the present. Other Princeton professors who offered kind advice and encouragement include Şükrü Hanioğlu, Heath Lowry and Daniel Sheffield, from whom I also gained invaluable language instruction in Ottoman Turkish paleography, Ottoman chronicles, and Classical Persian literature.

Outside of Princeton the professor who has most supported this project is Sebouh Aslanian of UCLA. He has been very generous to me, sitting on my dissertation committee, sharing advice and inviting me to conferences at UCLA. I am very grateful to him for his encouragement of this project and I have always been edified by our ongoing dialogue. His forthcoming book, *Global Early Modernity and Mobility: Port Cities and Printers in the Armenian Diaspora, 1512–1800*, will address diaspora formation and the spread of Armenian print on a global scale in the early modern period.

My training as an Armenologist largely took place in Yerevan, Armenia, where I spent two years conducting research. I would like to thank the director, Vahan Ter-Ghevondyan, and all of the staff of the Mesrop Mashtots' Institute of Ancient Manuscripts (Matenadaran), where I would spend my afternoons transcribing and translating. I am also indebted to Tatevik Manukyan for introducing me to the study of Armenian manuscripts and helping me to develop my paleography skills. Gayane Ayvazyan kindly read my research about Eremia and provided helpful feedback. Shushan Hambaryan

Ghazaryan, Garnik Harutyunyan, Anna Ohanjanyan and Anoush Sargsyan also answered many questions. I am very grateful to Lusine Mooradyan for Eastern Armenian conversation practice. I have also consulted with Marc Nichanian many times over the years and he has always been ever so generous with his advice and comments.

In addition to Yerevan, my other homes of the past decade have been Istanbul and Jerusalem. In Istanbul I regularly made use of the Center for Islamic Studies (İSAM) Library and I am grateful to Mustafa Birol Ülker and all the other staff there for always helping me kindly. I would also like to thank Feridun Emecen of 29 May University for welcoming me into his graduate seminars on Ottoman documents and chronicles.

In Jerusalem I am grateful first and foremost to the Polonsky Academy of the Van Leer Jerusalem Institute for giving me an academic home after I finished my Ph.D. In particular, I would like to thank Shai Lavi, Sanda Fuchs and the librarian Bayla Pasikov for their kind support, as well as Ümit Kurt for comradery. I taught courses on early modern Islamic empires and the Classical Armenian language in the Department of Islamic and Middle Eastern Studies at the Hebrew University of Jerusalem and I am indebted to Reuven Amitai, Hillel Cohen, Eyal Ginio and Miriam Goldstein for welcoming me to the university.

I must offer very special thanks to Michael Stone for his generous hospitality during my time in Jerusalem. Visits and conversations with him were both delightful and edifying, and I am truly grateful that he encouraged me to teach Classical Armenian at the Hebrew University.

Various friends and colleagues have read this book in its entirety or in part. They include Reuven Amitai, Alex Balistreri, Evangelia Balta, Thomas Carlson, Caroline Finkel, Vladimir Hamed-Troyansky, Metin Kunt, Marc Nichanian, Aslı Niyazioğlu, Ayşe Özil, Erin Pinon, Ani Shahinean, Michael Stone, Lev Weitz, Ali Yaycıoğlu and Fikret Yılmaz. It was very generous of them to take the time to read the whole manuscript or a chapter, and I benefited immensely from their generous feedback. It was particularly kind of Metin Kunt to read my entire draft; sadly, our correspondence about this book turned out to be my last contact with this most debonair, erudite and genteel of professors. Other scholars with whom I have consulted recently on particular questions include Levon Avdoyan, Peter Cowe, Salih Değirmenci, Sevan Deirmendjian, Rachel Goshgarian, Selim Güngörürler, Khachik

Harutyunyan, Polina Ivanova, Daniel Ohanian, Michael Pifer, Zara Pogossian, Arevik Sargsyan and Vasileios Syros.

It would not have been possible to complete this book without gaining access to unpublished archival documents and manuscript pages. I have already thanked İSAM and the Matenadaran above. I would also like to thank Fr Boghos Kodjanian of the Mkhit'arean Monastery Manuscript Library in Vienna, Fr Levon Zekiyan and the priests of the Mkhit'arean Monastery Manuscript Library in Venice, as well as Patriarch Nourhan Manougian and his secretary at the Armenian Patriarchate of Jerusalem.

I have benefited from the generosity of several organisations while conducting research for this book. They include the American Research Institute in Turkey (ARIT), Fulbright, the National Association for Armenian Studies and Research (NAASR), the Cyprus American Archeological Research Institute (CAARI), the Institute of Turkish Studies (ITS), the Princeton University Department of History and the Polonsky Academy of the Van Leer Jerusalem Institute. This book would not have been possible without their kind assistance.

Portions of Chapters Three and Four of this book have either appeared or will appear in parallel publications. I would like to thank Simon Ditchfield of the *Journal of Early Modern History* and Tijana Krstic, editor of a forthcoming collection of articles, for granting permission for any overlap. These articles appear in the bibliography of this book.

Publishing with Edinburgh University Press has been a delightful experience. I am grateful to Nicola Ramsey and to the series editors Carole Hillenbrand and Myriam Wissa for all of their kind support, as well as to the three anonymous reviewers for very constructive feedback. It was most enlightened of them to allow me to include most of my primary-source translations, which I consider to be an indispensable part of this book.

This book was shaped by the three cities that have been my home for the past decade, namely Istanbul, Yerevan and Jerusalem. My own patterns of habitation have mirrored those of the Armenian authors discussed in this book. As with those writers who came before me, these three cities inspired and energised my research, and I thank all of my friends there, both academic and non-academic, for their contribution to this work.

PART I

MIGRATION AND REFUGEE CRISIS

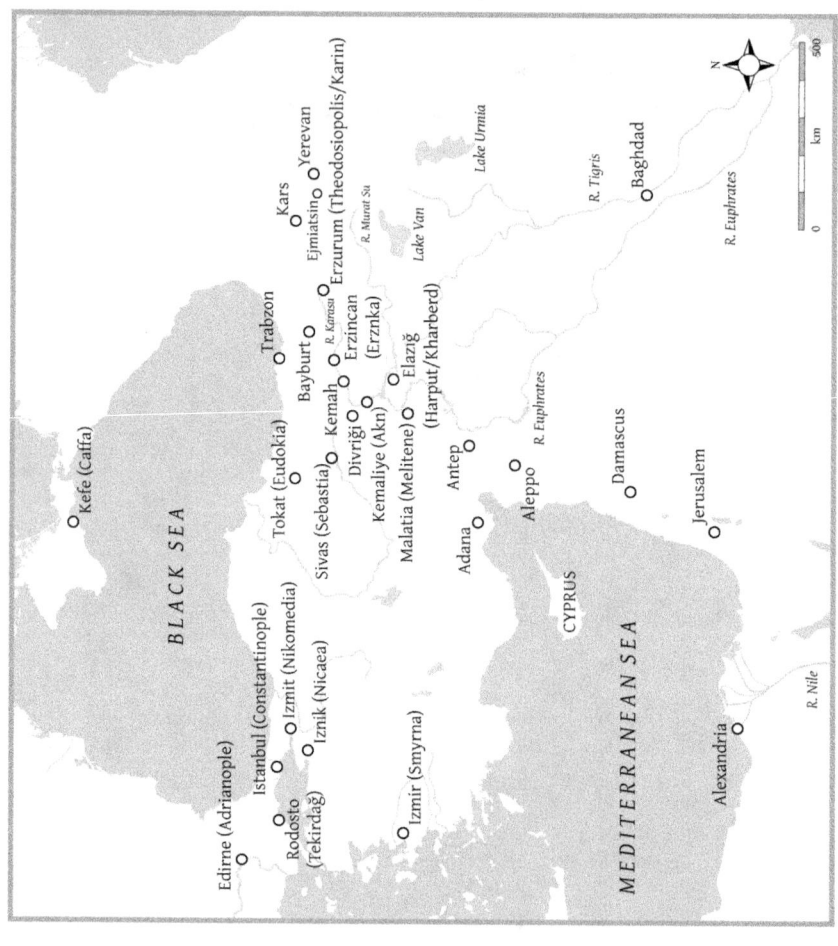

Figure 1.1 Map of Ottoman Anatolia. Credit: Stone Country Cartography.

1

Armenians and the 'Seventeenth-century Crisis' in the Ottoman Empire

In his diary entry for 18 April 1656, a twenty-year-old Armenian named Eremia recorded a murder committed by a fellow Armenian. He lamented that 'because of these Eastern Armenians who have filled up this place, there has been much destruction and tumult in this city [Istanbul] . . .'[1] These 'Eastern Armenians' about whom Eremia complained were refugees from Eastern Anatolia. Ironically, he too was a descendant of refugees from the East who had settled in Istanbul earlier in the seventeenth century. The seventeenth century in the Ottoman Empire was one of mass migrations from Eastern Anatolia westwards, migrations that profoundly impacted Armenian history, as well as the demographic landscape of the empire at large.

While much research has addressed the destruction of Armenian culture and society in the Ottoman Empire during World War I, much less attention has focused on the origins and development of the Armenian community in the early modern period. Yet it was during this era that a thriving Ottoman-Armenian social and cultural scene emerged in Istanbul and its environs in the aftermath of mass migrations that had their high point at the beginning of the seventeenth century. I call this seventeenth-century mass migrations of Armenians from Eastern Anatolia westward the 'Great Armenian Flight'.[2]

This book tells the story of how instability at the turn of the seventeenth century in Eastern Anatolia and the South Caucasus – territories sometimes called 'Greater Armenia'[3] – as well as Cilicia – a region on the Mediterranean Sea that includes the city of Adana – caused mass migrations of Ottoman subjects from historic centres of Armenian population and culture towards more secure Ottoman territories, namely, Western Anatolia, Istanbul, Thrace and beyond. At the beginning of the seventeenth century Armenians fled from Greater Armenia westwards, thereby causing a refugee crisis in multiple Ottoman urban centres, such as Istanbul, Izmit (ancient Nikomedia) and Rodosto (modern-day Tekirdağ). In time, however, these refugees adapted to life in the western parts of the Ottoman Empire. They became part of both the rural landscape in Western Anatolia and the urban landscape in the above-mentioned cities. In some urban centres – like Rodosto and Izmit – the first major settlement of Armenians was a direct result of the Great Armenian Flight. In others, like Istanbul, an existing local Armenian community was greatly augmented. In all these places the arrival of the refugees catalysed an efflorescence of intellectual and cultural life, giving rise over the course of the century to a new and vigorous 'Western Armenian Diaspora' in the Ottoman Empire, with its demographic and cultural hub in Istanbul. Although the mass migrations included Armenians, Greeks, Muslims and Jews[4] it had a disproportionate effect on Armenian cultural life in the Ottoman Empire.

The Great Armenian Flight and the rise of a Western Armenian Diaspora in the Ottoman Empire have been largely overlooked by historians because analyses of pre-modern Armenian history and Ottoman history have traditionally been distinct scholarly ventures. This book relies on both Armenian and Turkish sources to integrate these two fields. In this introduction I begin by offering readers a brief overview of Armenian history and the 'Seventeenth-Century Crisis' in the Ottoman Empire before proceeding to consider the history of Armenian literature and language in the early modern period. The book will be a journey from Eastern Anatolia to Istanbul and its environs and an exploration of how Armenian cultural life changed after the main sites of cultural production – such as manuscript copying and original literary composition – were transplanted from east to west.

The Armenians and Historically Armenian Lands

There are numerous general history books on the 'Armenians' which begin with prehistoric times and move forward to the present-day,[5] assuming ethnic and cultural continuities across centuries and even millennia. These books document a series of Armenian kingdoms that were present in the South Caucasus, Eastern Anatolia and, later, medieval Cilicia. At the very beginning of the fourth century CE the king of one of these kingdoms – the Arsacid King Trdat III (250–330 CE) – converted to Christianity after evangelisation by the Armenians' patron saint, Grigor the Illuminator (257–331 CE). In the fifth century CE, Mesrop Mashtotsʻ (362–440 CE) invented the Armenian alphabet, catalysing a wave of translations and the beginnings of a rich literary tradition that began in Late Antiquity and continues to the present day. After the fall of the Arsacids, Armenian lands were divided between empires, namely the Christian Byzantines and the Zoroastrian Sassanians and, later, the Islamic caliphates. Armenian noble houses maintained local influence under those empires but it was only about two centuries after the Islamic conquests that new Armenian kingdoms appeared, ruled by dynasties such as the Bagratunids, part of a broader revival of Iranian polities in the period called the 'Iranian intermezzo'.[6] Migrations to Cilicia led to the rise of other kingdoms, most notably that of the Rubenids, but by the end of the fourteenth century all these kingdoms had fallen and conquests in Anatolia largely brought an end to Armenian autonomy until the twentieth century, with most Armenians of the early modern period living either in the Ottoman Empire or in Safavid Persia.

This very short summary of a widespread and useful periodisation of Armenian history posits ethnic, religious and linguistic continuities from one period to the next. These assumptions, however, should not be taken for granted. Modern academic debates tend to eschew assumptions about static categories of identity, and scholars often go to extremes by emphasising fluidity, the importance of local identity over ethnicity in the pre-modern period and the social construction of ethnicity. Yet in the words of the historian Walter Pohl: 'The fact that ethnic identities were socially constructed does not mean at all that they did not exist'.[7] Ethnic identity was a prominent fact of the pre-modern world and these identities were cultivated through diverse 'strategies of distinction'.[8] Among the Armenians, these strategies included the use of the Armenian ethnonym and history-writing, in which claims of Armenian identity are often on prominent display.

The present work takes an intermediate position between emphasis on continuity and change. Armenians of the early modern period saw themselves as heirs to a literary and ecclesiastical tradition that went back to Late Antiquity and to a peoplehood that went back much further. That being said,

Armenians were in constant interaction with their environs and the diverse peoples and languages with which they came into contact constantly shaped and changed their cultural lives. While many experts on the Armenians (called Armenologists) have traditionally focused on the importance of the Armenian Church in preserving Armenian culture across centuries, the present work is far more interested in observing cultural change and exchange, following a shift in scholarly interest to cultural hybridity.[9]

By 'Armenians' I refer to those people of the seventeenth century who considered themselves Armenians and rallied around the Armenian ethnonym: most of these people associated with the Apostolic Armenian church but many were influenced by Roman Catholic missionary activities; many of these people spoke Armenian as their mother tongue but many others would have spoken another language, such as Turkish, or been multilingual; some of these people would have felt commonality with Muslim and Greek countrymen from their home cities and villages but many would nonetheless have been conscious of cultural ties binding them to Armenians throughout the Ottoman Empire and beyond – a fact which comes across unambiguously in Armenian literature of the period. In short, this work does not deny traditions and continuities, but it is interested in how these were transformed and reshaped from epoch to epoch in interaction with neighbours. The noted Armenologist Seta Dadoyan has written about the deep interaction between Armenian and Islamic cultural life in the medieval period and one aim of this work is to advance this exploration upwards into the early modern.[10]

In Late Antiquity most of the world's Armenians lived in Greater Armenia, namely Eastern Anatolia and the South Caucasus. Byzantine settlement policy of the tenth century and Seljuk Turkish conquests of the eleventh century caused migrations of large numbers of Armenians from those territories to Cilicia. Regions with historically high Armenian populations have been depicted variously on maps and in history books. Defining their limits took on great political importance in the early twentieth century, in the midst of nationalistic competition for territory in Anatolia after the dismantling of the Ottoman Empire, and Armenian nationalists often sought to lay maximalist claims to broad territories that had ancient and medieval Armenian population concentrations (see Figure 1.2). Here I emphasise the facts of historical demography and refer to Greater Armenia and Cilicia as

ARMENIANS AND THE 'SEVENTEENTH-CENTURY CRISIS' | 7

Figure 1.2 Map of Greater Armenia and Cilicia as conceived by the Armenian Delegation to the 1919 Paris Peace Conference. Source: Wikipedia Commons, https://commons.wikimedia.org/wiki/File:Armenia_in_Paris_Peace_Conference_1919.jpg

the regions remembered by early modern Armenians as the lands of their ancestors, while maintaining awareness that they were always a shared space also inhabited by Arabs, Georgians, Kurds, Syriac Christians, Turks and others across time. While the term Greater Armenia is now mostly used by Armenologists, it should be noted that premodern Muslim authors – such as Kâtip Çelebi – sometimes employed the concept in geographical writings.[11]

Medieval history did not see Armenians settling only in Cilicia; rather, Seta Dadoyan speaks of the formation of a 'Medieval Armenian Diaspora' further afield to Syria, Mesopotamia and Egypt.[12] Moreover, there were waves of Armenian settlement in the northern Black Sea regions, including Kefe (Caffa) and the Crimea, such as the one that took place in the wake of the Mongol invasions in the thirteenth century.[13] The migration discussed in this book is one of a succession of migrations of Armenians out of Greater Armenia, but it was this seventeenth-century migration that shaped the Armenian experience in the Ottoman Empire. Moreoever, while there have been wide-ranging Armenian travellers and merchants throughout history, in the seventeenth century we see Armenian merchants – most famously those of New Julfa in Safavid Iran – scattering around the world to an unprecedented degree, forming bases of trade from Europe to East Asia.[14]

Even before the rise of a Western Armenian Diaspora in the seventeenth century there was already an east/west cultural divide among Armenians. As Dadoyan has argued, 'by the end of the twelfth century, there were distinct eastern and western Armenian worlds'.[15] The arrival of the Turkic tribes in the eleventh century had already initiated a process of urbanisation of Armenians. The Great Armenian Flight was a continuation of this process, a new wave of migration and urbanisation that pushed the centre of gravity of the Armenian Diaspora of the Middle Ages away from Anatolia and towards Istanbul.

Although 'Western Armenian' would become a literary language of Armenians in the Ottoman Empire, the term Western Armenian Diaspora is not intended to highlight a linguistic unity. In modern times Armenians whose ancestors once resided in the Ottoman Empire are distinguished from Armenians with roots in Safavid Persia and the Russian Empire both by cultural difference and by the fact that they speak different standardised dialects of Armenian – Western and Eastern Armenian, respectively. As will be described below, the linguistic landscape of early modernity was not so simple, as neither of these standardised dialects existed before the nineteenth century. Armenians throughout Anatolia and the Caucasus spoke a plethora of diverse dialects, in addition to various languages other than Armenian. While most of the dialects spoken in the Ottoman Empire were part of a broader dialectical group with many similarities to Western Armenian, at the time there was no spoken standard.

Rather than highlighting language I use the term Western Armenian Diaspora to emphasise the importance of Istanbul and Western Anatolian cities and countryside in the cultural life of Armenians in the Ottoman Empire from the seventeenth century until the Armenian Genocide and, soon thereafter, the Ottoman Empire's collapse. I delineate a distinct period in Armenian history from 1600 to 1915, three centuries during which Istanbul was the Western Armenians' demographic and cultural capital. The shift of cultural centres from Greater Armenia and Cilicia to Istanbul and its environs catalysed a renaissance of intellectual and cultural productivity. Ottoman historians take Istanbul's importance for Armenian culture for granted, but the rise of Armenian Istanbul and the demographic and cultural landscape of Armenians familiar to students and scholars of the Late Ottoman Empire only came into being in the aftermath of the seventeenth-century mass migrations, opening a new chapter in the history of Ottoman cosmopolitanism.

The 'Seventeenth-century Crisis' in the Ottoman Empire

This work differs from most research on Armenians by pointing to the turn of the seventeenth century as a critical turning point in their cultural history, and thus it raises the question of the reasons for this shift. Answers can be found in debates about the 'Seventeenth-Century Crisis' in Ottoman domains. According to Ottoman historians, the main symptom of instability in Eastern Anatolia at the turn of the seventeenth century was the so-called 'Celali Revolts' (pronounced *Jelali*). The term Celali Revolts refers to a diverse series of rebellions that shook the Ottoman Empire in the late sixteenth century and throughout the seventeenth century. The rebellions reached their peak intensity between 1591 and 1611, an upheaval sometimes referred to as the 'Great Anatolian Rebellion'.[16] While discussion of the Celalis often focus on those two decades, intermittent rebellion continued in the Ottoman Empire until the eighteenth century, when it seems that local leadership was finally able to fill the void of central authority.[17]

Ottoman historians have long debated the causes of the rebellions, offering a series of explanations ranging from economic crisis to military transformations to climate change. For example, foundational research on the Celali Revolts by Mustafa Akdağ emphasised that they were not motivated by political or religious factors but rather the problems arose out of an 'economic depression'[18] which caused peasants to flee from their lands. Flight from Anatolian farmlands accelerated to its high point because of violent rebellion between 1603 and 1607, a period that he designates as the 'Period of Great Flight' (*Büyük Kaçgunluk Dönemi*). While Akdağ's insights into the nature of the revolts remain central elements of discussion about the Celalis to this day – such as his emphasis on the unclear line between the defenders of imperial order and Celali rebels[19] – his focus on economic factors as the primary cause of the revolts has been contested for decades,[20] and other scholars have long wondered if it was indeed 'population pressure' pushing peasants off the land that led to the revolts, or perhaps a 'pull' which drew them away from agricultural to other activities.[21]

The Ottoman historian Halil İnalcık certainly conceived of the Celalis' origins in terms of a pull rather than a push. İnalcık identifies the rebellions' causes as stemming from changes in Ottoman military practice. In particular he observes that, starting in the late sixteenth century, the Ottoman army had a large demand for infantrymen bearing firearms, particularly for wars against the Habsburgs. İnalcık argues that, upon being decommissioned, these troops could turn to rebellion and it is these soldiers-turned-rebels who gave rise to the Celali Revolts.[22] In short, he suggests that structural changes in the Ottoman military were the primary cause of rebellion, as masses of peasants were drawn to the life of soldiering and did not want to return subsequently to agricultural work on the land.

More recently Sam White and Geoffrey Parker have added another variable to the debate: climate change.[23] White argues that there is a correlation between the severe 'Little Ice Age-type weather events' that took place from the 1580s to the 1610s and the rise of the Celali Revolts. He sees the revolts as merely one consequence of this period of climate change, along with drought and other disruptions, all of which combined to cause real suffering for the Anatolian peasantry and a flight to the Ottoman Empire's western cities. In time, the crisis prompted adaptations in Ottoman administration, but only after a long period of violence, starvation and mass flight.[24] While White focused on the Ottoman Empire, the early modern historian Geoffrey Parker has made much broader claims, arguing that climate change in the seventeenth century destabilised societies on a global level, causing a whole series of 'involuntary migrations' similar to the Ottoman 'Great Flight'.[25]

It seems that a convergence of factors led to the Celali Revolts. Economic factors have been brought back to the fore of debate by Baki Tezcan, who has questioned İnalcık's linking of the start of the Celali Revolts with the Habsburg wars, seeking their origins instead in competitions between local magnates who had cash in hand to hire armed men thanks to increased monetisation in the late sixteenth century.[26] Compelling though Tezcan's thesis may be, neither climate change nor military transformations can be discounted as playing a role in the breakdown of the imperial order in Anatolia.

For the purposes of this book, an understanding of the effects of the revolts are more important than their causes. In *The Collapse of Rural Order in Ottoman Anatolia* Oktay Özel shifts the focus away from causes towards effects, encouraging readers to take very seriously Ottoman Turkish accounts of destruction in Anatolia. The collapse of the Anatolian rural economy was both a real and a catastrophic fact of seventeenth-century Ottoman history. Basing his research on narrative sources and tax documents for the Amasya region prepared between the years 1576 and 1643, Özel shows decisively that

> In terms of the demographic and historical-geographical aspects of this crisis in the history of the Anatolian provinces, the case of Amasya offers a prime example in which all the relevant offices of the central administration produced both qualitative and quantitative evidence for a sharp fall in the tax-paying population, for the mass desertion of rural settlements, and for the transformation of rural society in the countryside during the early seventeenth century.[27]

In short, the seventeenth-century crisis accelerated the trend towards urbanisation in Anatolia highlighted by Dadoyan, with flight away from rural settlements. While the Ottoman Empire eventually adapted to the multiple shocks – economic, military and environmental – it endured over the course of the seventeenth century, acclimation took a long time, during which the lives of countless thousands of people were either lost, ruined or drastically altered. Recognition of the depths of the hardship endured by the peasantry of Anatolia in the seventeenth century is a necessary first step in understanding Ottoman-Armenian history.

Ottoman historians have occasionally noted an influx of Armenian refugees from Eastern Anatolia at around the time of the Celali Revolts,[28] but none of them have been aware of the particularly critical impact the revolts had on Armenian communities in the East. This is primarily due to a reliance on Ottoman Turkish sources and a traditional focus of scholarly attention on the Ottoman state. It has not been the case for historians and linguists who make use of Armenian sources. For example, Y. S. Anasean makes ample use of Armenian sources to reveal the suffering of Armenian peasants at the turn of the seventeenth century and their flight westwards. He writes,

One of the immediate results of the Celali Revolts was an emigration of the Armenian population from its motherlands, a great flow of emigration, which entirely depopulated the Armenian provinces. Popular masses fleeing from their native lands emigrated by the hundreds of thousands in indescribable conditions.[29]

Similarly, in 1966 M. K. Zulalyan – a Turkish-speaking Armenian from Aleppo – wrote a book in Eastern Armenian entitled *The Celali Movement and the State of the Armenian People in the Ottoman Empire (Sixteenth and Seventeenth Centuries)*.[30] Like Anasean, he was aware of the Great Armenian Flight, writing that

> Military activities in Armenia and the Celali Movement . . . brought with them extraordinary disasters – famine and epidemic – which were taking the lives of tens of thousands of people. Under these conditions the merchant-artisan class of the Armenian people, independent of any forced resettlement, willingly emigrated from their countries – with the hope of being saved from famine, sword, epidemic and locusts – to Constantinople, Tabriz, Isfahan, Thrace, the Crimea, Russia, Poland, and other places.[31]

Thus, Armenian historians of the twentieth century were cognizant of the traumas endured by Anatolian Armenians during the Celali Revolts.[32] Their research, however, went mostly unnoticed by the broader field of Ottoman and Middle Eastern Studies because of linguistic and disciplinary barriers.[33] Moreover scholars have not yet sufficiently investigated the cultural ramifications of the mass migrations and their profound impact on the trajectory of Armenian language and literature. This study does just that by bridging the fields of Armenian and Ottoman history, using both Armenian and Ottoman Turkish sources to show how the mass migrations caused a transplantation of centres of cultural and intellectual productivity away from Greater Armenia towards Istanbul and its environs.

Armenian History-writing and Manuscript Production, 1453–1700

In order to set the stage for a detailed account of cultural history in the seventeenth century, let us now provide an overview of Armenian cultural production in both the period in question and that immediately prior. Here I will use

Armenian history-writing and manuscript production from 1453 to 1700 as an index of cultural output. We will see a major increase in manuscript and literary production in the seventeenth century which took place concomitantly with a movement of intellectual centres away from Greater Armenia and Cilicia to coastal cities of the Ottoman Empire – predominantly Istanbul – and the main ecclesiastical and economic centres of Safavid Iran.

An account of original history-writing in Armenian between 1453 and 1600 is an easy story to tell, as no major histories were produced in Armenian for more than 150 years. The only major Armenian historical work of the fifteenth century was a history of Timur by T'ovma Metsop'ets'i,[34] written in in the first half of the century. No major Armenian histories survive from the entire sixteenth century,[35] only various short narratives, chronologies and longer colophons.[36] Just as the picture with regards to historiographical production implies a downturn in intellectual production in Armenian,[37] so does the state of manuscript copying. The Armenologist Dickran Kouymjian has argued that it is possible to chart upturns and downturns in manuscript production from the thirteenth century to the nineteenth through statistical analysis of the catalogues of the main repositories of Armenian manuscripts in Armenia, Europe and Israel. In spite of the vagaries of productivity and ebbs and flows in intellectual and material life, one would expect there to be a gradual decrease in the number of extant manuscripts moving backwards across the centuries as a result of destruction over time. For the sixteenth century, however, Kouymjian observes a drop in the number of extant manuscripts compared to the previous century. In particular, he notes that 'the half century from 1500 to 1550 represents the absolute lowest point in the production of Armenian scriptoria until printing finally replaced the manual copying of manuscripts altogether in the eighteenth century'. He goes on to note 'a steady rise in manuscript copying starting in the 1550s, rising sharply, especially after 1610, to reach the absolute historic high point of productivity in the decade ending in 1660'.[38] In short, Kouymjian's statistical analysis shows that the ebb in history-writing in the sixteenth century mirrored an ebb in manuscript copying, while both pursuits revived and reached new heights in the seventeenth century (coexisting with book-printing).

Kouymjian suggested that the wars of the Ottoman sultans Selim (r. 1512–20) and Süleyman (r. 1520–66) – both of whose armies traversed

Eastern Anatolia – probably account for this decline in productivity.[39] Whatever caused this relative paucity of manuscript production in the sixteenth century, the reasons for the seventeenth-century renaissance in productivity are easier to discern. In the East the forced population transfer of Armenians from Julfa in the Caucasus to a suburb of the Safavid capital of Isfahan gave rise to the New Julfa trade networks and created a class of patrons for book-copying and original writing, while the Treaty of Zuhab (*Kasr-ı Şirin Antlaşması*) of 1639 between the Ottoman and Safavid empires finally put an end to the intermittent wars between the Ottomans and Persians in Eastern Anatolia and the Caucasus, catalysing an upswing in trans-imperial trade. In the Ottoman Empire the arrival of the Armenian refugees from the Great Flight in its coastal cities would provide the context and stimulus for the rise of a rich new Western Armenian intellectual life. Consideration of the major historians of the seventeenth century reveals that the centres of history-writing had moved away from Anatolia and Cilicia to the Ottoman Empire's coastal cities – including Rodosto, Istanbul and Kefe – on the one hand, and to Safavid Persian ecclesiastical and trade centres in Persia and the Caucasus, on the other.

The great seventeenth-century Armenian historians of the Ottoman Empire are Grigor Daranaltsʻi, a *vardapet* (learned priestly rank in the Armenian ecclesiastical hierarchy) who wrote in the first half of the seventeenth century in Rodosto; Eremia Kʻeōmurchean, the Istanbul-Armenian diary writer quoted at the beginning of this work and a polymath who wrote in the mid to late seventeenth century; and Minas Amdetsʻi, who was a bishop and later patriarch in Jerusalem at the turn of the eighteenth century. All three of these authors had roots in Anatolia. Grigor personally participated in the Great Flight, escaping from Anatolia to Istanbul. His life and chronicle will be the topic of Chapter Four.[40] Though born in Istanbul, Eremia's grandfather was a refugee from the Celalis, and Eremia wrote with an awareness of his Anatolian roots.[41] Eremia is by far the greatest and most prolific Armenian author of the seventeenth century and his life and corpus are the topics of Chapters Five and Six. In general, Greek, Armenian and Muslim authors described the same reality in culturally different ways, but Eremia is important because in his corpus readers see Ottoman historiographical culture entering the Armenian literary tradition. Finally, Minas was a native of Diyarbekir who composed a lengthy unpublished personal diary rich with historical data.⁴² In addition to these major historians, the Ottoman city of Kefe in the Crimea also produced several minor historians, including Martiros Ḻrimetsʻi,⁴³ among others.

Safavid centres in the East also produced major historians in the seventeenth century. By far the greatest of the authors working in Safavid Persia was Aṙakʻel of Tabriz, who wrote a history of events from 1602 to 1662 in the Armenian holy city of Ējmiatsin.⁴⁴ As will be seen, Grigor Daranaḻtsʻi documented the momentous impact of the seventeenth-century crisis on Armenians living in the Ottoman Empire and it can be said that Aṙakʻel of Tabriz pursued a similar task with a focus further east, documenting Celali outrages in the Caucasus, the forced migration instituted by Shah Abbas and ecclesiastical history in Ējmiatsin. His life's work was continued by one of his students, Zakʻaria Kʻanakʻeṙtsʻi, who wrote a history that was highly influenced by Aṙakʻel's model.⁴⁵ The seventeenth-century Safavid Empire also produced an Armenian history of a completely different nature (and lower linguistic register) than the work of the aforementioned churchmen, namely the 'journal' of Zakʻaria Aguletsʻi.⁴⁶ Zakʻaria was a merchant, not a churchman, and through his journal one can carefully follow the long trans-imperial travel routes of early modern Armenian merchants.

Finally, seventeenth-century Armenian history-writing and manuscript copying also took place in centres outside of the Ottoman Empire and Safavid Persia, and over the course of the seventeenth century some ancient Armenian centres of religious life and learning revived. One major creative Armenian literary centre outside of the Islamic world was Poland. The travelogue of Simēon of Poland is one example of a major work written by a Polish-Armenian,⁴⁷ and though his work is technically a travelogue it nonetheless constitutes one of the most important Armenian historical sources of the early modern period. The Ottoman Empire's attempts to conquer Poland under Sultan Osman II also catalysed a flurry of literary activity. An author named Yovhannēs Kamenatsʻi produced a 'History of the Khotʻin War'⁴⁸ in a relatively high register of Classical Armenian, by the standards of the time, depicting Osman II's failure within the literary framework of classical tragedy.⁴⁹ A work on the same theme was also produced by Armenian Christians in the Kıpçak Turkish dialect written with Armenian letters.⁵⁰ Finally, increased transit and trade across the Ottoman-Safavid borderlands after the signing of the Treaty of Zuhab in 1639 stimulated greater economic prosperity and a revival in the ancient Armenian religious centres of Ējmiatsin and Bitlis during the seventeenth century, as well as the rise of the Armenian neighbourhood of New Julfa near Isfahan as a major ecclesiastical centre for the first time. All three of these locations became centres of education and intellectual production, where Armenians wrote works on chronology, religion, philosophy, logic and grammar.[51]

In sum, while the fifteenth and sixteenth centuries represent a period of greatly lowered production of history-writing and manuscript copying among the Armenians, the seventeenth century sees a major increase in productivity in both spheres, but with the most important centres of intellectual production shifting away from Greater Armenia and Cilicia mainly to the western parts of the Ottoman Empire and to centres of trade and ecclesiastical life in Safavid Persia. This book will focus on the resurgence of Armenian history-writing and literature in Ottoman centres.

Linguistic Transformations in Early Modern Armenian

Let us now consider the language in which contemporary Armenian historians wrote. Classical Armenian – called *grabar* in Armenian – remained the literary standard throughout the seventeenth century, but it was not the same Classical Armenian of prior periods. In a process comparable to the enshrinement of fifth-century BCE Attic as the gold standard of Greek prose composition for subsequent centuries, the Classical Armenian language of the fifth-century CE became the standard literary language of Armenian authors of the medieval and early modern periods. But just as many authors writing in Greek could not imitate the complex syntax of Thucydides, most Armenian authors writing in the late medieval and early modern periods were unable to mimic the prose styles of Late Antique Armenian classics. Gradually, a syntactically simplified Classical Armenian became the universal literary language of Armenian clergy (though it continued to change in subtle ways that have not been systematically studied). While the Armenians of medieval Cilicia developed an alternative literary language – called 'Middle Armenian' – this language was never standardised to the same degree as *grabar*. Rather, 'the Middle literary Armenian [language did] not have a stabilised norm and it [appeared] in different literary versions'.⁵² Middle Armenian had an influence on early modern Armenian authors but it was usually a secondary one compared to the dominance of *grabar*, which remained the language of ecclesiastical education throughout the period under investigation. Authors could modulate between Middle Armenian and *grabar* depending on literary context.

While *grabar* primarily, and variants of Middle Armenian secondarily, were the literary registers available to Armenians of the early modern period neither were spoken languages. Rather, spoken Armenian had always been characterised by a diversity of dialects, with great variations between regions and sometimes even from village to village. Armenian linguists categorise the great diversity of Armenian dialects into three groups – western, eastern and '*grabar*-form' – according to the way in which the present and past imperfect tenses are conjugated.⁵³

The extent of Armenian's dialectic diversity does not have parallels in all languages. For example, the Armenian philologist Hrachʻya Acharyan notes in his classic *History of the Armenian Language* of 1951 that 'contemporary Turkish [in the Republic of Turkey] . . . does not present in such an extreme form dialects which are distinct from one another'.⁵⁴ Rather, even before Atatürk's Language Reform, variants of Turkish in the Ottoman Empire were mutually intelligible to a much higher degree than was true of Armenian dialects or, to offer an alternative example, the great diversity of Persian dialects. This plethora of Armenian dialects is an ancient phenomenon and there had always been an interaction between local vernaculars and the literary language.

While acknowledging an interaction between vernaculars and the formal literary languages of all periods of Armenian literature, it is clear that linguistic changes accelerated in the seventeenth and eighteenth centuries. In the seventeenth century Armenian authors began to increase their use of spoken dialects in writing alongside Classical Armenian. This development took place long before the standardisation of Eastern and Western Armenian as modern Armenian literary languages in the nineteenth century. The Soviet Armenian linguist S. L. Lazaryan describes the transformation as follows in his *Concise History of the Armenian Language*:

> In the development and refinement of the Modern Armenian language (*ashkharhabar*) definite advancement is observable from the end of the

seventeenth century. From that period comprehensible dialectic elements penetrate sharply into literature. The Modern Armenian language accepts an abundance of dialectic elements. Authors and historians appear who craft their works using more or less of dialects and the traditions of the old literary language. In works written in this period we encounter many linguistic elements, some of which – becoming more widespread in the future – would spread and establish the component elements of the Armenian national language [Eastern and Western Armenian].[55]

This linguistic transformation was observed and noted by Armenians in the late seventeenth century; it was not an entirely unconscious transformation. In his history of the Armenian language, Marc Nichanian notes that in 1674 the Armenian author Hovhannēs Holov explicitly distinguished between three kinds of Armenian, namely, *grabar*, 'vulgar Armenian (*vulgaris*)' and the 'civil language (*civilis*)', defining the latter as a mix of the former two particularly employed in commercial transactions between Armenians who spoke different dialects.[56] Sebouh Aslanian identifies Holov as 'one of the key architects of the literary version of modern vernacular Armenian'[57] because he was the first Armenian to print a book entirely in colloquial Armenian in 1675.

In short, the resurgence of Armenian history-writing which took place in the seventeenth century was accompanied by great linguistic flux, with authors amply mixing *grabar*, Middle Armenian and a broad diversity of dialects. I would suggest that in the seventeenth century stable dialects had not yet developed in cities in the western parts of the Ottoman Empire; rather the Armenian refugees and their descendants were speaking a diversity of Anatolian dialects, swamping out whatever original dialects had been spoken by the smaller Armenian populations of western cities before the Great Armenian Flight. In the course of the eighteenth century, when Armenians' demographic situation became more settled, stable dialects evolved in western cities such as Istanbul and Rodosto. Finally, with the rapid expansion of print culture in Istanbul in the nineteenth century, the Istanbul dialect's grammar became the basis of a standardised literary language – Western Armenian – while Turkish-infused aspects of its pronunciation and much of its vocabulary[58] were rejected and replaced with a diversity of 'pure' Armenian alternatives, with some drawn from Classical Armenian while others were contrived.[59]

Alongside these transformations in the Armenian language in the seventeenth century went the development of an alternative literary language for Armenians in the Ottoman Empire: Armeno-Turkish, or Turkish written in the Armenian alphabet. Many Armenians in the Ottoman Empire spoke mainly Turkish and communication between Armenians speaking different dialects could be difficult. Thus, when Armenian authors wanted to reach a broad audience, they often wrote in the Turkish language using the Armenian alphabet. The tradition of writing Armeno-Turkish poetry goes back to medieval Anatolia but the development of Armeno-Turkish prose-writing accelerated rapidly in the seventeenth century after the Great Armenian Flight.

Summary of Chapters

This book is the story of the resurgence of Armenian cultural life in the aftermath of mass migration, based on archival documents in Ottoman Turkish and on prose and poetry written both in Armenian (in its fluctuating variants) and in Armeno-Turkish. The book has two parts. In the first part, I will describe in detail the evidence for a mass migration of Armenians from Eastern Anatolia to Western Anatolia, Istanbul and Thrace. Because of the chaotic nature of these migrations, I have chosen to focus on one migration, that of Armenians from Kemah, in the province of Erzincan, to Rodosto (Tekirdağ), a small port city near Istanbul. Thus, the first part of this book consists of two case studies. In Chapter Two, I describe the Kemah region and its significance for early modern Armenians, based on Armenian chronicles, Modern Armenian-language geographical and monastic reference books, published Ottoman Turkish tax records and my own personal travels. Then I move on to both a general and a localised description of the Celali Revolts and the Great Flight as recounted in Armenian primary sources of the seventeenth century, showing how the economy and security of the region collapsed as a result of the Celali Revolts, prompting mass flight from both Kemah and the general region. In Chapter Three I follow the Kemah Armenians in their flight. I am fortunate, as the second Armenian bishop of Rodosto, the above-mentioned author Grigor Daranaltsʻi, was himself a Kemah refugee who left a first-hand account of the Armenians' arrival in Rodosto. Moreover, a complete series of Ottoman Turkish court records exists for Rodosto covering the period from the late sixteenth century all the way until the nineteenth. Thus, it is possible to describe the Armenians' arrival using both Armenian narrative sources and Ottoman Turkish court records concerning Armenian refugees.

The Kemah-Rodosto case studies were chosen for several reasons. Firstly, the sheer quantity of Ottoman Turkish archival sources from Rodosto – including sixteenth-century cadastral surveys and both sixteenth- and seventeenth-century court records – allows for the collection of large amounts of raw data about Rodosto, its economy and its Armenian community. Moreover, the existence of Grigor Daranalts'i's chronicle allows for a rich comparison between an Armenian narrative source and Ottoman Turkish archival material. It is likely no coincidence that a Kemah Armenian would be the first refugee to write a major chronicle of his life and times in the aftermath of the Great Flight. As will be explained, Erzincan and nearby Kemah were religious and intellectual centres in the Middle Ages and Kemah remained a destination for holy pilgrimage until 1915. After the migrations westward, some of the first major authors and intellectuals who became productive in Istanbul and its environs – including Rodosto – were either Kemah Armenians, like Grigor Daranalts'i, or among their descendants, like Eremia K'eōmurchean. It is the important role of Kemah Armenians in building a new Western Armenian intellectual life that makes the study of this particular migration both possible and worthwhile.

In the second half of this book, focus shifts from migration and refugee crisis to analysis of intellectual history. I will offer a detailed account of the life and works of two Kemah-Armenian authors, Grigor Daranalts'i in Chapter Four and Eremia K'eōmurchean in Chapters Five and Six. Both authors were exceptional and idiosyncratic men, but study of their biographies and literary self-presentations can provide insights into broader social and cultural transformations.

In Chapter Four I will show that Grigor was a political leader and infrastructure-builder whose chronicle was very much a political testament. He lived in a time of religious tension characterised by the 'confessionalisation initiatives of various sociopolitical groups jockeying for power in the seventeenth century'.[60] Scholars such as Tijana Krstic and Marc David Baer have respectively analysed competitions between Orthodox and Catholic Christians, as well as Ottoman state initiatives to encourage conversion to Islam and Islamicise public space.[61] This chapter will consider the place of the Armenians in this raucous 'jockeying', documenting their efforts to rein in heterodox practices and obtain sacred spaces. Analysis of Grigor's chronicle will provide a means of showing how one Armenian priest played a critical role in settlement, community and infrastructure-building among the Armenian refugees. The early seventeenth century was a period of crisis management and infrastructure-building, during which time the first generation of Armenian refugees from Anatolia literally built the foundations for subsequent social and cultural life in the Western Armenian Diaspora with stone and mortar.

Whereas Grigor Daranaḷtsʻi was more of a politician and less of an intellectual, Eremia Kʻeōmurchean was the first prolific author and intellectual of the Western Armenian tradition in early modern Istanbul. In his works readers see the result of three influences which shaped Western Armenian intellectual life for its more than three centuries of development in the Ottoman Empire: the influence of ancient and medieval Armenian literary traditions; interaction with the Islamic intellectual life of the Ottoman capital; and a flourishing of new literary genres – such as the increased popularity of first-person narratives and travelogue – which arose in diverse literary traditions across the early modern Mediterranean Basin. Eremia befriended and collaborated with Western European consuls and local Muslim intellectuals alike in Istanbul, simultaneously serving as a conduit of information exchange between Europe and the Ottoman Empire as well as between Armenian Christians and Muslim intellectuals within the empire. His life and corpus in Armenian will be the subject of Chapter Five, while his translations from Armenian into Armeno-Turkish will be the topic of Chapter Six.

With Eremia's death in 1695 one can say with confidence that the Western Armenian Diaspora known to historians of the late Ottoman period had truly been born. It was characterised by a rich literary and manuscript culture in Istanbul, the rise of an independent and influential ecclesiastical centre in the Armenian Patriarchate of Constantinople, the presence of a substantial minority of Roman Catholic Armenians, the increasing importance of Armenian merchants in the economic life of Istanbul, and the development of distinctly Western Armenian modes of literary expression, namely extended prose works in Armeno-Turkish, none of which had been evident in Istanbul before 1600. Of course, this society would continue to develop in upcoming centuries, being further influenced in the eighteenth century by the Mkhitʻ-areans – an Armenian Catholic religious order famed for their intellectual production – by westernisation and modernisation efforts in the nineteenth century and the trauma of genocide in the twentieth century. The subsequent development of Western Armenian literary life would take place, however, among Armenians who largely descended from the refugees of the seventeenth century, and latter-day literary and intellectual achievements would build upon foundations and precedents going back to the age of Eremia.

The early modern Ottoman Empire's cosmopolitan landscape was shaped by several mass migrations. Examples include the forced migrations (called *sürgün* in Ottoman Turkish) of non-Muslim merchants and tradesemen to Istanbul ordered by Mehmed II after his conquest of the Byzantine capital,[62] and the arrival of the Sephardic Jews in Istanbul, Salonika and other Ottoman cities after their expulsion from Spain in 1492. The arrival in Istanbul and Western Anatolia of Armenian refugees from the Celali Revolts at the turn of the seventeenth century is a largely overlooked migration that would have a similarly great impact on the cultural and economic life of the empire and its capital for the following three centuries of its history. Let us begin our examination of this migration and its impact by turning to our first geographical case study, the Anatolian city of Kemah, Erzincan.

Notes

1. Eremia Kʻeōmurchean, *Ōragrutʻiwn Eremia Chʻēlēpi Kʻeōmurcheani*, Mesrop Nshanean (ed.) (Jerusalem: Tparan Srbotsʻ Yakobeantsʻ, 1939), p. 155.
2. I adapt this term from the Turkish 'Büyük Kaçgunluk Dönemi', or 'Period of Great Flight', discussed in the work of the Ottoman historian Mustafa Akdağ. See Mustafa Akdağ, *Türk Halkının Dirlik ve Düzenlik Kavgası: Celâlî İsyanları* (İstanbul: Yapı Kredi, 2009).
3. I use the term 'Greater Armenia' in contrast to Cilicia, and thus inclusive of territories both west and east of the Euphrates River (both *Mets Haykʻ* and *Pʻokʻr Haykʻ*).
4. See Yaron Ben-Naeh, *Jews in the Realm of the Sultans: Ottoman Jewish Society in the Seventeenth Century* (Tübingen: Mohr Siebeck, 2008), p. 351.

5. A good example of this approach to Armenian history is George A. Bournoutian, *A History of the Armenian People*, Vols I–II (Costa Mesa: Mazda Publishers, 1993).
6. See Alison Vacca, *Non-Muslim Provinces under Early Islam: Islamic Rule and Iranian Legitimacy in Armenia and Caucasian Albania* (Cambridge University Press, 2017).
7. Walter Pohl, 'Archeology of Identity: Introduction', in Walter Pohl and Matthias Mehofer (eds), *Archeology of Identity* (Vienna: Austrian Research Academy, 2010), p. 12.
8. Walter Pohl, 'Telling the Difference: Signs of Ethnic Identity', in Walter Pohl and Helmut Reimitz (eds), *Strategies of Distinction: The Construction of Ethnic Communities, 300–800* (Leiden: Brill, 1998).
9. The Armenian historian Sebouh Aslanian has been a prominent voice advocating for such a shift in recent years. See Sebouh David Aslanian, 'The Marble of Armenian History: Or Armenian History as World History', *Études arméniennes contemporaines* 4 (2014): 129–42; and 'From Autonomous to Interactive Histories: World History's challenge to Armenian Studies', *An Armenian Mediterranean: Words and Worlds in Motion* (New York: Palgrave Macmillan, 2018), pp. 81–126.
10. Seta B. Dadoyan, *The Armenians in the Medieval Islamic World: Paradigms of Interaction, Seventh to Fourteenth Centuries*, Vols I–III (London: Routledge, 2011–14).
11. See Kâtip Çelebi, *Kitâb-ı Cihânnümâ li-Kâtib Çelebi* I (Ankara: Türk Tarih Kurumu, 2009), p. 410.
12. Dadoyan II, 255.
13. Dadoyan III, 99.
14. The authoritative work on early modern Armenian trade networks is Sebouh David Aslanian, *From the Indian Ocean to the Mediterranean: The Global Trade Networks of Armenian Merchants from New Julfa* (Berkeley: University of California Press, 2011).
15. Dadoyan, II, 258.
16. William J. Griswold, *The Great Anatolian Rebellion, 1591–1611* (Berlin: Klaus Schwarz, 1983).
17. Suraiya Faroqhi, *Coping with the State: Political Conflict and Crime in the Ottoman Empire, 1550–1720* (İstanbul: Isis Press, 1995), p. 88.
18. Akdağ, 14.
19. Ibid.

20. M. A. Cook, *Population Pressure in Rural Anatolia: 1450–1600* (Oxford University Press, 1972), p. 31.
21. Faroqhi, *Coping with the State*, pp. 88–9.
22. Halil İnalcık, 'Military and Fiscal Transformation in the Ottoman Empire, 1600–1700', *Archivum Ottomanicum* 6 (1980): 283–337.
23. Griswold first suggested the potential importance of climate change, but it was not a theme that he developed. See Griswold, *The Great Anatolian Rebellion*, p. xix.
24. Sam White, *The Climate of Rebellion in the Early Modern Ottoman Empire* (Cambridge University Press, 2011), p. 276.
25. Geoffrey Parker, *Global Crisis: War, Climate Change, and Catastrophe in the Seventeenth Century* (New Haven: Yale University Press, 2013), p. 102.
26. See Baki Tezcan, *The Second Ottoman Empire: Political and Social Transformation in the Early Modern World* (Cambridge University Press, 2010), p. 10.
27. Oktay Özel, *The Collapse of Rural Order in Ottoman Anatolia: Amasya 1576–1643* (Leiden: Brill, 2016), p. 183.
28. For example, Bruce Masters, *The Origins of Western Economic Dominance in the Middle East: Mercantilism and the Islamic Economy in Aleppo, 1600–1750* (New York University Press, 1988), pp. 84–7; Rhoads Murphey, 'Population Movements and Labor Mobility in Balkan Contexts: A Glance at Post-1600 Ottoman Social Realities', in Melek Delilbaşı and Özer Ergenç (eds), *Southeast Europe in History: The Past, the Present, and the Problems of Balkanology* (Ankara University Press, 1999), p. 92; Ronald C. Jennings, 'Zimmis (non-Muslims) in Early 17th Century Ottoman Judicial Records: The Sharia Court of Anatolian Kayseri', in *Studies on Ottoman Social History in the Sixteenth and Seventeenth Centuries: Women, Zimmis and Sharia Courts in Kayseri, Cyprus and Trabzon* (Istanbul: Isis Press, 1999), p. 351; and Özel, *The Collapse of Rural Order in Ottoman Anatolia: Amasya 1576–1643*, p. 123.
29. Y. S. Anasean, 'T'urk'akan tirapetut'yunĕ Hayastanum XVII darum', in *Manr erker* (Los Angeles: Armenian American International College, 1987), p. 508.
30. M. K. Zulyalan, *Jalalineri sharzhumĕ ew hay zhoḷovrdi vichakĕ ōsmanyan kaysrut'yan mej (XVI–XVII darer)* (Yerevan: Haykakan SSH GA Hratarak-ch'ut'yun, 1966).
31. Zulyalan, p. 56.
32. For an English overview of seventeenth-century Armenian history that draws on the above-mentioned research, see Edmond Schütz, 'An Armeno-Kıpchak

Document of 1640 from Lvov and its Background in Armenia and in the Diaspora', in György Kara (ed.), *Between the Danube and the Caucasus: Oriental Sources on the History of the Peoples of Central and South-Eastern Europe* (Budapest: Akademiai Kiado, 1987).

33. One Armenologist left a small body of work that has been more influential in the field of Ottoman history because he wrote in Turkish. See Hrand Andreasyan, 'Bir Ermeni Kaynağına Göre Celâlî İsyanları', *İstanbul Üniversitesi Edebiyat Fakültesi Tarih Dergisi* 13 (1963): 27–42; 'Abaza Mehmed Paşa', *Tarih Dergisi* 13 (1967): 131–42; 'Celâlilerden Kaçan Anadolu Halkının Geri Gönderilmesi', in *İsmail Hakkı Uzunçarşılı'ya Armağan* (Ankara: Türk Tarih Kurumu, 1976), pp. 45–53.

34. See T'ovma Metsop'ets'i, *T'ovma Metsop'ets'i patmagrut'yun*, L. Khach'ikean (ed.) (Yerevan: Magałat', 1999); and *T'ovma Metsobets'i's History of Tamerlane and his Successors*, Robert Bedrosian (trans.) (New York: Sources of the Armenian Tradition, 1987).

35. Though major original histories were not being composed, older histories were being copied. For discussion of manuscript copying of histories in Bitlis and Van in the sixteenth century see Robert W. Thomson, 'Bitlis and Armenian Histories', in Richard G. Hovannisian (ed.), *Armenian Baghesh/Bitlis and Taron/Mush* (Costa Mesa: Mazda Publishers, 2001); and Nersēs Akinean, *Baleshi dprots'ě 1500–1704: Npast mě hayots' ekełets'woy patmut'ean ew matenavn grut'ean* (Vienna: Mkhit'arean Tparan, 1952).

36. For example, Avedis K. Sanjian, *Colophons of Armenian Manuscripts, 1301–1480: A Source for Middle Eastern History* (Cambridge, MA: Harvard University Press, 1969), pp. 221–4.

37. The dearth of history-writing in the sixteenth century does not imply a lack of literature and folklore. See Peter Cowe, 'The Armenian Oikoumene in the Sixteenth Century: Dark Age or Era of Transition?', in Kathryn Babayan and Michael Pifer (eds), *An Armenian Mediterranean: Words and Worlds in Motion*, (New York: Palgrave Macmillan, 2018), pp. 133–60.

38. Dickran Kouymjian, 'Dated Armenian Manuscripts as a Statistical Tool for Armenian History', in Thomas J. Samuelian and Michael E. Stone (eds), *Medieval Armenian Culture: Proceedings of the Third Dr. H. Markarian Conference on Armenian Culture* (Philadelphia: University of Pennsylvania, 1982), p. 429.

39. Thomas A. Carlson's research similarly shows how levels of violence led to decreased composition of historical writing in fifteenth-century Iraq. See Thomas A. Carlson, *Christianity in Fifteenth-Century Iraq* (Cambridge University Press, 2018).

40. Grigor Daranaḷtsʻi, *Zhamanakagrutʻiwn Grigor vardapeti Kamakhetsʻwoy kam Daranaḷtsʻwoy*, Mesrop Vardapet Nshanean (ed.) (Jerusalem: Tparan Aṙakʻ Atʻoṙotsʻ S. Yakobeantsʻ, 1915).
41. For an English-language account of Eremia's life and corpus, see the introduction of Eremia Kʻeōmurchean, *Eremya Chelebi Kömürjian's Armeno-Turkish Poem: The Jewish Bride*, Andreas Tietze and Avedis K. Sanjian (trans.) (Wiesbaden: Harrassowitz, 1981).
42. J 1316; *Grand Catalogue of St James Manuscripts* IV, Norayr Bogharean (ed.) (Jerusalem: Armenian Convent Printing Press, 1964), pp. 564–5. For a summary of the diary's contents, see Eremia Kʻeōmurchean, *Ōragrutʻiwn Eremia Chʻēlēpi Kʻeōmurcheani*, Mesrop Nshanean (ed.) (Jerusalem: Tparan Srbotsʻ Yakobeantsʻ, 1939), pp. ciiiv–cxliv. For two general studies about his chronicle see Roberta Ervine, 'Patriarch Minas Amtʻecʻi and His *Diary*', in Nicholas Awde (ed.), *Armenian Perspectives* (Richmond: Curzon, 1997); and Karapet Amatuni, *Minas vrd. Amdetsʻi patriarkʻ Yerusaḷēmi (1630–1704 noymb 24)* (Vienna: Mkhitʻarean Tparan, 1984). I have a digital copy of Minas's chronicle and am currently working on a study of it.
43. Martiros Ḷrimetsʻi, *Martiros Ḷrimetsʻi: Usumnasirutʻyun ew bnagrer*, A. A. Martirosyan (ed.) (Yerevan: Haykakan SSṘ GA Hratarakchʻutʻyun, 1958).
44. Aṙakʻel Davrizhetsʻi, *Aṙakʻel Davrizhetsʻi girkʻ patmutʻeantsʻ*, L. A. Khanlaryan (ed.) (Yerevan: Haykakan Khah GA Hratarakchʻutʻyun, 1990), p. 103; Aṙakʻel Davrizhetsʻi, *Aṙakʻel of Tabriz: Book of History*, George A. Bournoutian (trans.) (Costa Mesa: Mazda Publishers, 2010).
45. Zakʻaria Kʻanakʻeṙtsʻi, *Patmutʻiwn: Kondak surb ukhtin Yohannu Vanitsʻ*, Armen Virabyan (ed.) (Yerevan: Heḷinakayin Hratarakutʻyun, 2015); *The Chronicle of Deacon Zakʻaria of Kʻanakʻeṙ*, George A. Bournoutian (trans.) (Costa Mesa: Mazda Publishers, 2004).
46. *Zakʻaria Aguletsʻu ōragrutʻyunē*, S. V Ter-Avetisyan (ed.) (Yerevan: Armfani Hratarakchʻutʻyun, 1938); *Journal of Zakʻaria of Agulis*, George A. Bournoutian (trans.) (Costa Mesa: Mazda Publishers, 2003).
47. *Simēon dpri Lehatsʻwoy uḷegrutʻiwn*, P. Nersēs Akinean (ed.) (Vienna: Mechitharisten, 1936); *The Travel Accounts of Simēon of Poland*, George A. Bournoutian (trans.) (Costa Mesa: Mazda Publishers, 2007).
48. Yovhannēs Kamenatsʻi, *Patmutʻyun paterazmin Khotʻinu*, H. Asasyan (ed.) (Yerevan: Haykakan SSṘ GA Hratarakchʻutʻyun, 1964).
49. For a description of Armenian colophon authors' debates regarding Sultan Osman II's deposition, see Henry R. Shapiro, '17. Yüzyıl Osmanlı-Ermeni

Sosyal ve Entelektüel Tarihine Aralanan Yeni bir Pencere: Ermenice Elyazması Kolofonlar', *Toplumsal Tarih* 265 (January 2016): 41–3.

50. E. Schütz, *An Armeno-Kipchak Chronicle on the Polish-Turkish Wars in 1620–1621* (Budapest: Akademiai Kiado, 1968).

51. Paolo Lucca, 'Philology, Documentary Research, and Channels of Cultural Diffusion from the Seventeenth to the Nineteenth Century', in Valentina Calzolari (ed.), *Armenian Philology in the Modern Era: From Manuscript to Digital Text* (Leiden: Brill, 2014), pp. 421–3.

52. G. B. Jahukyan, *Hay barbaṙagitut'yan neratsut'yun (vichakagrakan barbaṙagitut'yun)* (Yerevan: Haykakan SSH GA Hratarakch'ut'yun, 1972), p. 193.

53. S. Ḷ. Ḷazaryan, *Hayots' lezvi hamaṙot patmut'yun* (Yerevan: Erevani Hamalsarani Hratarakch'ut'yun, 1981), pp. 295–6. See also Ar. Ḷaribyan, *Hay barbaṙagitut'yun: Hnch'yunabanut'yun ev dzevabanut'yun* (Yerevan: Haykakan SSṘ Petakan Heṙaka Mankavarzhakan Institut, 1953), pp. 47–56.

54. Hrach'ya Achaṙyan, *Hayots' lezvi patmut'yun*, Vol. II (Yerevan: EPH Hratarakch'ut'yun, 2013), p. 363.

55. Ḷazaryan, pp. 322–3.

56. Marc Nichanian, *Âges et usages de la langue arménienne* (Paris: Éditions Entente, 1989), p. 273.

57. Sebouh Aslanian, 'Print and Port-to-Port Mobility: Censorship and Letters of Excommunication in the Work of Oscan's Press in Livorno and Marseille', unpublished chapter in forthcoming book entitled, *Global Early Modernity and Mobility: Port Cities and Printers in the Armenian Diaspora, 1512–1800*, p. 24.

58. For an example of the Turkish-infused nineteenth-century Istanbul-Armenian dialect, see Hrach'ya Achaṙyan, *Polsahay angir banahyusut'yun* (Yerevan: EPH Hratarakch'ut'yun, 2009).

59. Achaṙyan, *Hayots' lezvi patmut'yun* II, pp. 470–2.

60. Tijana Krstic, *Contested Conversions to Islam: Narratives of Religious Change in the Early Modern Ottoman Empire* (Stanford University Press, 2011), p. 174.

61. Marc David Baer, 'The Great Fire of 1660 and the Islamization of Christian and Jewish Space in Istanbul', *International Journal of Middle East Studies* 36, 2 (2004): 159–81; and *Honored by the Glory of Islam: Conversion and Conquest in Ottoman Europe* (Oxford University Press, 2011).

62. See Halil İnalcik, 'The Policy of Mehmed II Toward the Greek Population of Istanbul and the Byzantine Buildings of the City', *Dumbarton Oaks Papers* 23/24 (1969/1970): 229–49.

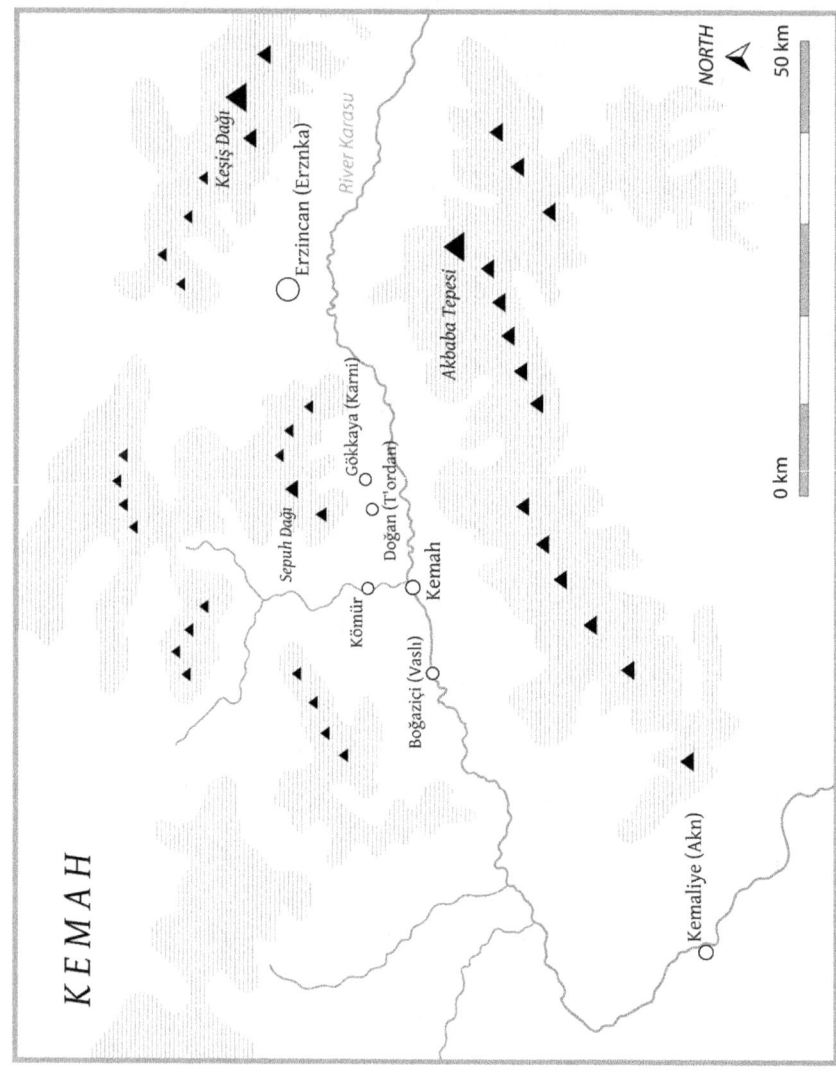

Figure 2.1 Map of Kemah and its vicinity. Credit: Stone Country Cartography.

2

Kemah and the 'Great Armenian Flight'

The Tigris and Euphrates Rivers are most famous for nourishing the great ancient Mesopotamian civilisations: the Sumerians, Assyrians and Babylonians. But long before the Euphrates River reaches the ruins of Babylon, long before it nourishes agriculture in the lands called the Fertile Crescent, the river arises from the confluence of the Karasu (Western Euphrates) and Murat Su (Eastern Euphrates) Rivers in the Anatolian province of Elazığ. The Karasu River has a long trajectory before it transforms into the Euphrates, arising on the Dumlu Mountain in Erzurum Province and flowing through the Erzincan Province, where it passes the small town of Kemah. Although the Karasu River receives less treatment in world history books than the Euphrates River that it helps to form, it too played a role all on its own in nourishing an ancient civilisation, for which Kemah (see Figure 2.2) was once an important military and religious centre.

This chapter will introduce one of the two key cities of this study: Kemah, currently in Erzincan Province, Turkey, explaining its historical and religious significance for Armenians of the early modern period. Then, after briefly discussing the Celali Revolts according to several Ottoman Turkish sources, it will describe the economic collapse, famine, war and rebellion that would plague Eastern Anatolia at the turn of the seventeenth century, as recounted by contemporary Armenian primary sources – including major histories, travelogues, colophons, short chronicles and poetry – most of which are new to research on Ottoman history. While Ottoman Turkish chroniclers did not focus on the plight of the Christian peasantry, instead centring their narratives on the state, Armenian sources document the rebellions' effects on Armenian

Figure 2.2 Modern-day town of Kemah as seen from Ani Fortress ruins.

peasants and townspeople. This chapter will conclude by providing extensive literary evidence of a Great Armenian Flight – to adapt Mustafa Akdağ's term to the present study – of Ottoman Armenians from chaos in the East towards Western Anatolia, Istanbul and Thrace, and even as far afield as Egypt, Poland and the Crimea. Temporal focus will be on 1598 through to 1608, the peak years of the Celali Revolts.

The 'Valley of Monasteries' (*Vâdî-i Vank*): Kemah and its Environs

The origin of the name 'Kemah' (*Kamakh*, in Armenian) is debated, with some Armenian scholars suggesting that it is a variant of the name of the ancient city Kummakhan, which is mentioned in a Hittite inscription. Others suggest that the name derives from the Armenian word (*kmakhk'*) – meaning skeleton – identifying Kemah as the site of the burial ground of the Armenian Arsacid kings who ruled Armenia from the first to the fifth century CE.[1] Clearly these suggestions are all conjectural, as other Armenologists have proposed that the name derives from the Armenian word for the asp tree (*kałamakh*), which are plentiful in the region.² In any case, the name most likely derives from an Armenian word, adopted by local Muslims in the Ottoman period. Despite waves of place-name changes from Greek and Armenian into Turkish throughout the twentieth century, the town retains its old name in the modern Republic of Turkey.³

The town of Kemah lies just about 50 km southwest of Erzincan and one reaches it from Erzincan by travelling through the Karasu River Valley. It is best remembered in Armenian history because its ancient fortress, Ani, was a key stronghold of the Armenian Arsacid kings (not to be confused with the more famous city of Ani located near Kars). According to Armenian chronicles, part of the Arsacid treasury was located in Ani along with – as mentioned – their burial ground, until a Persian incursion in 369 CE, during which the Persians 'captured the fortress of Ani and seized all the royal treasures in it, even the bones of the kings'.⁴ The date of the foundation of Ani's fortifications is unknown but they were in place by at least the second century CE. Before the Armenian kingdom's acceptance of Christianity Ani was a Zoroastrian religious and cultural centre, home to a temple to the father of the gods Aramazd. Ani receives frequent mention in the Classical Armenian chronicles, often in connection with this temple, which is sometimes also referred to as a temple of Zeus.⁵ By the twelfth and thirteenth centuries CE the Armenian sources gradually cease to refer to Ani and begin to mention the town of Kemah which formed beneath the Ani fortress's ruins.⁶

Kemah is located in the ancient Armenian province of Daranałik‛, and for this reason Armenians from Kemah and its vicinity were usually referred to as *Daranałts‛i* during the Ottoman period. Close by, to the northeast of Kemah, lie the heights of Mount Sepuh, a tall mountain about 3,000 m in height.⁷ Below Mount Sepuh lie the village of T‛ordan and the Caves of Manē, important sites associated with Grigor (Gregory) the Illuminator (257–331 CE), who Classical Armenian chronicles describe as the evangelist of the Armenian people. In the seventeenth century the classical chronicles of Moses Khorenats‛i and Agat‛angełos were well known to Armenian priests, shaping their conceptions of Armenian history. Their narratives can help us to understand how seventeenth-century Armenians imagined Kemah and its religious history.

According to Moses Khorenatsʻi, Grigor retired and passed away on Mount Sepuh. Thus, the Province of Daranaḷikʻ receives frequent mention in his chronicle, which describes Grigor's life at length. Moses Khorenatsʻi writes

> In the seventeenth year of Trdat's reign we have found that our father and parent in the gospel, Gregory, sat on the throne of the holy apostle Thaddaeus. After illuminating the whole of Armenia with the light of divine knowledge, banishing the darkness of idolatry and filling all regions with bishops and teachers, in his love for the mountains and solitude and a secluded life with tranquility of mind to speak to God without distraction, he left his own son Aristakēs as his successor and remained himself in the province of Daranaḷikʻ in the mountain 'Caves of Manē'.[8]

Khorenatsʻi later adds that

> Saint Gregory lived in seclusion in the Cave of Manē for many years and on his death was transposed to the ranks of the angels. Shepherds found him dead and buried him in the same place without knowing who he was. It was indeed fitting that they who were the ministers of our Savior's birth [cf. Luke 2:13] should also be the servants of his disciple's burial. [Saint Gregory's relics] were hidden for many years by divine providence you might say, like Moses of old [cf. Deut. 34.6], lest they become the object of a cult to the half-converted barbarian nations. But when the faith had become firmly established in these regions, after a long time Saint Gregory's relics were revealed to a certain ascetic called Garnik, who took them and buried them in the village of Tʻordan.[9]

Agatʻangeḷos, describes an earlier visit by Grigor to the Province of Daranaḷikʻ in order to spread Christianity and to destroy the temples there:

> ... [Gregory] hastened to the other regions of the whole territory of Armenia that they might there sow the word of life. He came to the province of Daranaḷikʻ in order to destroy the altars of those falsely called gods, where in the village of Tʻordan there was a famous temple of the glorious god Barshamin. First they destroyed this and smashed his image; they plundered all the treasures, both of gold and silver, and distributed them to the poor. And the whole village with its properties and territories they devoted

to the name of the church. And here too they set up a copy of the all-saving sign.[10]

Grigor the Illuminator was also said to be responsible for the destruction of the temple in the fortress of Ani, as Agatʻangełos subsequently states:

> ... [Grigor] went to the fortified site of renowned Ani, the site of the royal burial ground of the Armenian kings. There they destroyed the altar of the god Zeus-Aramazd, called father of all the gods. And there they set up the Lord's sign, and the town with its fortress they devoted to the service of the church.[11]

Juxtaposing these testimonies of Moses Khorenatsʻi and Agatʻangełos, we see that Tʻordan, a small village just 20 km away from Kemah, had originally been the site of a temple to the god Barshamin, but legend has it that it subsequently became the depository of Grigor the Illuminator's relics some time after his death. Grigor likewise destroyed the famous shrine of the Armenian goddess Anahit that had been present in Erzincan, a site that the Roman geographer Strabo described as having special importance for the Armenians at the beginning of the first century CE,[12] as well as the shrine to Zeus-Aramazd at Ani-Kemah. The Classical Armenian chronicles narrate that the modern-day Turkish Province of Erzincan was home to multiple ancient Armenian holy sites that were toppled and replaced by Christian ones in the fourth century CE. The actual history of this transition was likely far more complex, but this is how it would have been remembered by educated Armenians of the Ottoman period.

In the Middle Ages a series of Armenian monasteries were built on Mount Sepuh and throughout the regions of Kemah and Erzincan. The monasteries of Mount Sepuh were associated with sites connected to Grigor the Illuminator. Many of these monasteries remained active until 1915, and in the mid-twentieth century their histories were carefully compiled by an Armenian priest from Erzurum of the Mkhitʻarean Order, Hamazasp Oskean, in his book *The Monasteries of High Armenia*.[13]

One of these monasteries, built directly on a foothill of Mount Sepuh, bore three names: the Monastery of St Grigor the Illuminator, the Monastery of Sepuh and the Cave of Manē (see Figure 2.3). This monastery

Figure 2.3 Grigor the Illuminator Monastery.

is a considerable hike uphill from the nearest village, Karni. Karni, renamed Gökkaya by the Turkish state, lies 24 km northeast of Kemah. High above the village, the monastery offers a clear view of Mount Sepuh's peak, and it became a pilgrimage site because it is supposed to have been built at the location of the tree where Grigor the Illuminator died.

According to tradition, a monastery was first established on the site of the Illuminator's passing in the fourth century CE, but Oskean is careful to note that it is not possible to confirm when exactly the monastery was first built. The oldest reference to it in Armenian literature is a colophon of 1201, showing that it had already been erected by the twelfth century at least.[14] It is currently called the *Çengelli Manastır*, or 'Hooked Monastery', by the local villagers and it still stands to this day in a half-ruined state. It is still possible to find Armenian tombstones in the woods around the path from Karni to the monastery, and I found one dated to (1042) 1593 (see Figure 2.4).

Downhill, closer to the village of Karni, lies the Avag (Great) Monastery, which also went by the name St Thaddeus and Bartholomew (see Figure 2.5).

Figure 2.4 Armenian Tombstone of 1042 (1593).

As with the Grigor the Illuminator Monastery, tradition attributes this monastery's foundation to the fourth century. The earliest reference to the Avag Monastery cited by Oskean, however, is a colophon from 1227, implying that the monastery was already built and flourishing by the thirteenth century.[15]

Figure 2.5 Avag Monastery.

The Avag Monastery still stands in ruins and the villagers in Karni refer to it by its Armenian name to this day.

The ancient Armenian village of T'ordan still exists, though the Turkish government has renamed it Doğan Köyü. It lies between Karni and Kemah, and to this day it is dominated by the ruins of the Monastery of the Holy Cross, also called the Sepulchre of the Nine Saints (see Figure 2.6). It bore the second name because the relics of nine of Armenia's most important saints – including Grigor the Illuminator and King Trdat the Great, who Armenians traditionally believe to have proclaimed Armenia a Christian kingdom – were said to have been held there. Oskean does not explicitly mention the latest possible date of construction of the church and he does not seem to have uncovered any early colophons which refer to it. He only mentions a single colophon of 1450, which proves that the monastery was in place by the fifteenth century.[16]

The Monastery of the King, or Vaslı Monastery (see Figure 2.7), stands next to the Karasu River near to the village of Vaslı, renamed Boğaziçi Köyü

Figure 2.6 Monastery of the Sepulchre of the Nine Saints, T'ordan Village (Doğan Köyü).

Figure 2.7 Monastery of the King.

by the Turkish state in lieu of its original Greek name. The village lies approximately 12 km west of Kemah. The Monastery of the King differs from the three previous structures in a key regard. While the other monasteries under discussion remained active Armenian ecclesiastical centres until 1915 this church was abandoned by Armenians in the early seventeenth century because of Celali violence.[17]

These four monasteries are only a few of the many more Armenian churches and monasteries that fill the valleys, hills and villages around Kemah. During the late medieval period – particularly the thirteenth and fourteenth centuries – the monasteries around Erzincan and Mount Sepuh constituted a vibrant Armenian cultural and literary centre. In the thirteenth century the Armenian author Yovhannēs Erznkats'i studied and lived on Mount Sepuh. He wrote works of advice literature, a commentary on a Classical Greek grammar and even two treatises influenced by Islamic *futuwwa* regulations.[18] In the late thirteenth and early fourteenth centuries the Armenian poet Kostandin Erznkats'i wrote Armenian poetry influenced by Persian literary imagery, showing an awareness of the great Persian classic, the *Shahname*.[19] It was also in Erzincan that one of the first examples of Armeno-Turkish – Turkish literature written in the Armenian alphabet – was produced, in a late thirteenth-century poetical work.[20] Under Seljuk and Ilkhanid rule Armenian religious life thrived in the monasteries of Erzincan, Kemah and its environs, and literary and cultural dialogue developed between local Muslims and Armenian Christians.[21]

Kemah was controlled by several different Muslim principalities before being taken by the army of the Ottoman Sultan Selim I (r. 1512–20) from the Safavids after the Battle of Çaldıran in 1514. As was their practice, the Ottomans subsequently prepared a cadastral survey of the region (*tapu tahrîr defteri*) in 922 (1516), along with a regulation manual (*kanunnâme*).[22] Multiple tax surveys of the region were repeated throughout the sixteenth century; they were studied by İsmet Miroğlu, who shows that the Ottoman tax collectors registered both the Armenian villages and the Armenian monasteries. For example, they registered the village and monastery of T'ordan distinctly, describing the monastery there as *Vank-ı Tortan* – the Armenian word for monastery, *vank'*, and the Classical Armenian town name T'ordan joined with a Persian particle called an *izafet* (*-ı*). The tax collectors noted that the monks there produced wheat and barley. Always recording the Armenian place names to the best of their abilities, the tax collectors listed the Avag Monastery as *Vank-ı Evak,* noting that in addition to wheat and barley, the monastery also produced millet and fruits and it possessed a mill.[23] Either struck by the abundance of monasteries in the region, or recording the local name, the Ottoman tax collectors designated one valley northwest of Kemah as the *Vâdî-i Vank* – or 'Valley of Monasteries' – a typical Ottoman Turkish name consisting of the Arabic word for valley (*vâdî*) joined with the Armenian term for monastery (*vankʻ*) by a Persian *izafet*. Under the Ottomans, the ancient Armenian fortification of Ani was in active use.[24] During the reign of Sultan Süleyman (r. 1520–66) the Ottomans placed an inscription on one of the fortress's gates noting its conquest in the time of his father, Sultan Selim.[25]

The Ottoman tax collectors of the sixteenth century were certainly aware of the monasteries of Daranaḷikʻ and of their religious importance to the local Christians. Likewise, educated Ottoman Armenian clergy knew the region's history well, as Armenian scribes continued to copy and study Classical Armenian chronicles and to reproduce geographical works about Armenia throughout the early modern period. For instance, the thirteenth-century *vardapet* Vardan Areveltsʻi describes the province of Daranaḷikʻ, Kemah and Mount Sepuh in his geographical treatise, remarking on their religious and historical significance.[26] Vardan's treatise was repeatedly recopied in seventeenth-century Armenian manuscript *zhoḷovatsoy* – a manuscript 'collection' containing multiple diverse texts, like Arabic *majmûʻa* – and thus his work undoubtedly served to propagate the ancient conception of historical Armenia among Armenians in the Ottoman Empire.[27] Likewise the seventeenth-century author Yakob Karnetsʻi wrote a history of his home town of Erzurum, in which he also describes the province of Daranaḷikʻ and its holy places, showing a deep awareness of the region's importance for Armenian Christian history.[28]

In contrast, Muslim historians of the Ottoman period took little interest in Armenian history, with only a few scattered exceptions. Evliya Çelebi – the famed author of a voluminous travelogue in Ottoman Turkish – made explicit use of an Armenian source, a currently unknown work relating the 'legendary history' of various cities in Eastern Anatolia, Western Iran and Mesopotamia.[29] As will be discussed later in more detail, the Muslim scholar Müneccimbaşı

Ahmed Dede Efendi included a section on ancient and medieval Armenian history in his late seventeenth-century Arabic-language universal history.[30] Earlier in the seventeenth century, Kâtip Çelebi wrote a renowned geographical work, the *Cihânnümâ*, in which he describes the concept of 'Armenia' (*Ermenistan*) and the regions of 'greater' and 'lesser' Armenia. Kâtip Çelebi considered the former to consist of the provinces of Van, Kars and Erzurum, while Adana and Maraş (Cilicia) constituted the latter.[31]

In spite of these exceptions, I'm not aware of a single Muslim author who took interest in the particular impact of the Celali Revolts on the Ottoman Empire's Armenian communities. Rather, the selected authors described above were interested in questions about the ancient history of the Armenians and the geography of their lands, asking questions of 'who' and 'where', but not considering the Armenians as a variable of contemporary history. It seems that historians and geographers interested in broad spans of history and space might sometimes discuss the Armenians, while chroniclers of contemporary affairs would ignore them. Even Evliya Çelebi makes no reference to Armenian sources or lore in his description of Kemah. Rather, he begins his account by vaguely stating that 'it is the edifice of the Caesars in the days of old'.[32] In this way he passes over more than a millennium of Armenian history, moving on to mention Kemah's various Muslim rulers up to the Ottoman sultans. He describes several local villages, as well as Kemah Castle. Though Evliya demonstrates keen awareness of the Kemah region's cheese, salt and linen,[33] he does not describe its monasteries or its ancient Armenian past. Likewise, Kâtip Çelebi mentions Kemah in his *Cihânnüma* and he was aware that part of its surrounding region was known as the 'Valley of Monasteries' (*Vâdî-i Vank*), but his historical conception of the place begins with Sultan Bayezid (r. 1389–1402).[34]

At the turn of the seventeenth century, law and order broke down in Kemah and its environs as a result of wars with Persia and the Celali Revolts, producing a Great Flight of both Muslims and Armenians from the region. Having provided a description of Kemah's history and monasteries, this chapter will now turn to primary source descriptions of the Celali Revolts in Eastern Anatolia. While the Ottoman sources take great interest in the Ottoman state's campaigns against the Celalis, they show almost no interest in the plight of Ottoman-Armenians. Armenian sources, on the other hand, give priority to the suffering of their fellow Armenians and thus offer a new perspective on the period which has important repercussions for Ottoman history.

Eastern Anatolia at the Turn of the Seventeenth Century According to Ottoman Turkish Sources

Description of the Celali Revolts exists in multiple genres of Ottoman Turkish, including the chronicle tradition, archival documentation, folklore and the travelogue of Evliya Çelebi. These sources have already been used extensively by Ottoman historians to study the period. Nonetheless, examination of a few samples of contemporary Ottoman Turkish writing on the Celalis is necessary to show how they differ from the Armenian narrative source material. I have chosen four representative – but in no way comprehensive – examples of a diverse nature: accounts of the Celalis contained in Kâtip Çelebi's Ottoman Turkish *Digest* (*Fezleke*); the military officer Topçular Kâtibi 'Abdülkâdir Efendi's chronicle; an account of the exploits of the grand vizier Kuyucu Murad Paşa; and the travelogue of Evliya Çelebi.

Kâtip Çelebi discusses the Celali Revolts extensively in his historiographical works, particularly his Ottoman Turkish *Digest*, which has been one of the main primary sources for research on the uprisings in English, Turkish and Armenian. For Kâtip Çelebi, as for most seventeenth-century chronicle-writers composing in Ottoman Turkish or Arabic, the driving force of the narrative is the Ottoman state: the rise and fall of sultans, grand viziers and grand muftis; wars and military campaigns; and affairs of state. Of course, the range of topics addressed was broader, but the state was the consistent focus of narrative attention. The *Digest* is organised in strictly chronological fashion, listing events (and the deaths of prominent individuals) for each year from 1591 until 1655.[35]

Kâtip Çelebi describes the origins of the Celalis in connection with the Ottoman Wars against the Habsburgs in Hungary (1593–1606),[36] stating that the problems began during the reign of Sultan Mehmed III (r. 1595–1603). He writes

> Because the soldiers of Islam did not repose in their native lands, the vilest of the peasantry of Anatolia found their country empty. They followed the

path of looting and plundering, and in that way every vagabond came to possess a horse and outfit of clothes. For every group there would arise a captain. With armor and weapons ready, cavalry and infantry were spreading out in groups throughout the lands. They pillaged, plundered, and committed violations of honor.[37]

After this general introduction, Kâtip Çelebi proceeds to describe the histories of particular Celali chiefs, beginning with Kara Yazıcı, and continuing with Deli Hasan, Kalenderoğlu, Tavil and others. The *Digest* is a critical source for seventeenth-century Ottoman history and it was used by subsequent Ottoman authors, including the first official Ottoman chronicle writer, Naima. In the course of his bureaucratic career, Kâtip Çelebi travelled and saw first-hand the difficult situation in Eastern Anatolia, about which he also comments in other works,[38] and he was also interested in Byzantine history.[39] Nonetheless, Kâtip Çelebi's corpus does not offer specific treatment of the contemporary histories of Ottoman Armenians or other Christian communities at the turn of the seventeenth century.

Kâtip Çelebi is widely regarded as having been one of the greatest intellectuals of the seventeenth-century Ottoman Empire. Another chronicler of the period, Artillery Secretary (*Topçular Kâtibi*) 'Abdülkâdir, offers a less lofty perspective on the Celali Revolts, drafting a chronicle based largely on his own experiences in a humbler register of Ottoman prose. Like Kâtip Çelebi's, his account is filled with the details of the comings and goings of Ottoman armies. He also shows interest in the plight of the Anatolian peasantry and the Celali Revolts' effects on them. He writes, for example, that

> In the Anatolian provinces, the Celali bandits rebelled. Among the inhabitants of the provinces, no one remained. In highlands and mountains they settled, from fear of the Celalis. The towns and cities lay in ruins. Most of the peasantry (*re'âyâ*) were coming to the capital with cries [of woe].[40]

'Abdülkâdir's work is replete with such references to the Great Flight of Anatolian peasants from Eastern Anatolia westwards,[41] but as was the case with other Ottoman Muslim authors, the internal histories of Christians lay beyond his area of interest.

Another genre of Ottoman historiography was the *gazavatnâme*, or war epic. A manuscript found in Istanbul's Süleymaniye Manuscript Library provides an account of the martial exploits of Sultan Ahmed I's grand vizier 'Kuyucu' Murad Paşa, including his famed campaign to rid Anatolia of the Celalis in 1606–8. Murad Paşa's campaigns were notoriously bloody, so much so that he won the nickname 'well-digger', or *kuyucu*, in reference to the mass graves he would build for defeated Celalis. Nonetheless, he was deemed a hero by many Ottoman authors, both Muslim and also Armenian.

The author of this *gazavâtnâme* wrote in high Ottoman Turkish prose interspersed with poetry and Qu'ranic verses. His focus is far narrower in scope than that of the major chronicles mentioned above, constituting a eulogy to the grand vizier. Like other chroniclers of the period, the author of the *gazavâtnâme* was aware of the destruction wreaked on Anatolia by the Celalis. He writes that 'so many prosperous provinces became ruined, homes to owls and crows, thus the provinces of Anatolia came to this state'.[42] Moreover, he describes in detail the formation of Celali bands at the beginning of the seventeenth century and their skirmishes with various Ottoman commanders. Ultimately, however, it was only the 'soldiers of Islam (*'asâkir-i İslâm*)' under their 'victory-marked commander (*serdâr-ı nusret-şi'âr*)' Kuyucu Murad who succeeded in breaking the Celalis and driving their survivors off to Safavid Persia.[43] As with the previously discussed chroniclers, the history of the Armenians of Anatolia, for whom Kuyucu's campaigns made such a critical impact, was not a topic of interest for the author of this panegyric to Grand Vizier Kuyucu Murad.[44]

The above-mentioned chroniclers are but a few among many, but they provide examples of various treatments of the Celali Revolts within the historical genre. Evliya Çelebi provides yet another perspective on the Celali Revolts and their consequences in his *Seyahatnâme*, or travelogue. Numerous references to the Celalis are scattered throughout Evliya's work, and they vary in nature. One of Evliya's primary interests was to describe cities, towns and castles, and on multiple occasions he notes that citadel defences were either reinforced or demolished because of the Celali threat. Concerning a small fort near Manisa, for instance, Evliya notes that 'Zağanos Paşa demolished the castle here and there . . . so that it might not belong to the Celali Kara Yazıcı'.[45] Evliya also describes how the elites of Amasya hid their valuables in the caves below Amasya Castle in order to protect them from Celalis during the times of Kara Yazıcı and Kara Saʿîd,[46] and he recounts a man's complaints about losing thousands of sheep due to Celali plundering.[47] He also provides lengthy historical narratives about particular Celalis leaders, such as the rebel Abaza Hasan.[48] In short, Evliya Çelebi provides numerous details about how the Celali Revolts caused changes to cities and castles and about suffering and defense strategies in his *Seyahatnâme*. Nonetheless, his accounts do not provide much further insight into the effects of the Celali Revolts on Ottoman Christians in general, or Armenians in particular.

In sum, Ottoman Muslim authors tend to focus on Ottoman military history, the comings and goings of viziers, and battles. At times, they show awareness of the sad plight of the Ottoman peasantry. As mentioned, ʿAbdülkâdir writes that 'among the inhabitants of the provinces, no one remained . . . the towns and cities lay in ruins', and the author of the *Gazavâtnâme* of Kuyucu Murad describes the provinces of Anatolia as a depopulated 'homes to owls and crows'. Indeed, Ottoman intellectuals and bureaucrats were generally aware of the peasantry's difficult plight in the early seventeenth century,[49] but they do not note that the Celali Revolts were a particularly significant event in Ottoman-Armenian history. To understand the importance of this period for Ottoman Armenians, it is necessary to broaden the source base beyond the Ottoman Turkish chronicles and to turn to the extensive Armenian language narrative accounts of the period, almost none of which have been used by Ottoman historians until now.

War, Rebellion, Scarcity, Famine and Cannibalism in Eastern Anatolia According to Armenian Literary Sources

In contrast to Ottoman Turkish material reviewed in the previous section, multiple genres of Armenian literature of the seventeenth century took keen and special interest in the Celali Revolts' effects on the lives of Armenian Christians in Anatolia in the first decade of the seventeenth century. This section begins by summarising discussions of the Celalis in travel-writing and major (long-form) chronicles before analysing colophons, short chronicles and poetry. Finally, attention will turn back to Kemah with Grigor Daranaḷtsʿi's accounts of the Celali Revolts' effects on his home region. The sources discussed here represent but a fraction of Armenian accounts of the

Celalis, chosen because they demonstrate the omnipresence of the topic across genres, and because all of the authors mentioned were either first-hand witnesses to the revolts or gained information about them from an eyewitness.

Travelogues and major chronicles

The most important Armenian travelogue of the seventeenth century with relation to the theme of this study is undoubtedly that of Simēon of Poland, who travelled extensively throughout the Ottoman Empire, mostly between 1608 and 1618, in the immediate aftermath of the first phase of the Celali Revolts that caused the Great Flight. As he travelled from city to city in Anatolia, Simēon frequently commented on the effects of the Celali Revolts on the local Armenian populations. In his description of Tokat, he writes that

> There were eight Armenian churches [in Tokat], learned and knowledgeable priests, [and] sweet-voiced expert [singers]. And one *vardapet,* Malak'iay, was a local, and [there were] 500 Armenian households. But they said that before there had been 1000 households [*hâne*], some of which the Celalis dispersed, others of which they killed.[50]

In other words, half of Tokat's Armenian population had been destroyed.

In Sivas Simēon notes that an even higher percentage of the Armenian community had been lost: 'They say that there were 2000 [Armenian] households [*hâne*], but now [there are] 600: the others have been scattered and dispersed'.[51] Meanwhile, he records that 'the Celalis had destroyed Bingöl and Ēnkēl [modern Eğil, near Diyarbekir] [along with] all its province'.[52] Upon arrival at the fortress of Manushkut, Simēon notes that

> On the [mountain] slopes [there were] Armenian cottages, which they were restoring. And they said that the Celalis had destroyed them and scattered the Armenians. Now this Kurdish lord loves very much the Armenians, on account of which he has gathered them. Everyone is coming to his place, and they are making buildings. They don't fear anyone.[53]

Simēon also described how Kayseri had become depopulated and ruined, but unlike the village below Manushkut, conditions were not ripe for resettlement. He writes that

[Kayseri] has inns (*han*), a covered market (*bedesten*), stores, an outdoor market (*çarşı pazar*) and goldsmiths, but few men appear in [the city]. They do not come and revive (*şenlik*) it because, on the one hand, the Celalis destroyed it, and, on the other hand, because of the tyranny (*zulüm*) of the *emir*'s servants (*avn*).[54]

Even Bursa, a former Ottoman capital, had been sacked by the Celalis in 1607 and, from a nearby mountain peak, Simēon saw that 'half of the city was destroyed and burned and [rendered] uninhabited by the Celalis'.[55]

In addition to his descriptions of depopulation and destruction in many and far-flung Armenian population centres of Anatolia, Simēon also shows that the Celali rampages were affecting trade and pilgrimage networks far from the Celalis' actual geographical range of activity. During the Ottoman Period Ankara was famous for its special mohair wool, *sof*. Simēon notes this, stating that 'All the townsmen of [Ankara] are *sof*-dealers. Good *sof* goes from there and spreads throughout the entire world'. He also notes, however, that 'the Celalis had destroyed and looted [Ankara]',[56] and in a separate section of his work he shows how this disrupted trade. While in Italy, Simēon heard a story about how the *sof* merchants there caused controversy by trying to pass off sheep's wool as mohair. To defend their attempted fraud, the merchants apparently confessed that

> Mohair (*tiftik*) is not to be found in our land because the Celalis have ruined and destroyed that land. Some of the goats they killed; others they took away with them. For this reason you found such forgery in our goods (*erzak*).[57]

The Celalis also created serious problems for the Armenian Church hierarchy far away from Eastern Anatolia. Simēon describes how the Armenian Patriarchate of Jerusalem entered into terrible debt during the reign of Patriarch David (r. 1583–1615) because of the Celali rampages:

> In [Patriarch David's] time the Celalis came forth. The roads were bound up. Some of the people were impoverished, others died. Pilgrims did not come to Jerusalem, [and] on account of this debts multiplied and oppression (*zulüm*) increased. The debt became 40,000 *kuruş*.[58]

Pilgrims were a major source of revenue for the Armenian patriarchate and because of the Celali disruption the patriarchate went bankrupt. The Patriarchate of Jerusalem's financial situation prompted grave concern among Armenian churchmen.

Major Armenian chroniclers of the seventeenth century also describe the chaos unleashed on Ottoman-Armenians as a result of the Celali Revolts and wars with Safavid Iran. Prominent among them is Grigor Daranalts'i, a native of Kemah. Grigor provides an Ottoman/western perspective of the crisis and its history based in large part on his own personal experiences, which he records years later in the 1630s.

Grigor Daranalts'i begins his chronicle with a narrative history of the Celalis, describing the exploits of some of their leaders.[59] For example, of Kara Yazıcı he writes,

> In the year 1046 (1597), a certain rebel named Yazıcı came forth among them and incited many to rebel with him. He gathered countless forces and spoiled many provinces. First, he established himself in a durable fortress in Edessa [Urfa] for a year and a half. Many commanders came with numerous forces from the king. They waged war with Edessa many times, but they were not able to take it.[60]

Later, when Yazıcı died, his brother Deli Hasan took command. The rebellion then spread to Sivas, where Hasan's Celalis were victorious in battle against an Ottoman general. According to Grigor, '[The Ottoman general] entered into the citadel, and [the Celalis] entered the city and unsparingly killed both Armenians and Turks,[61] and they did not have mercy on anyone'.[62]

After describing Kara Yazıcı and Deli Hasan's violent rampages, Grigor continues to discuss various Celali leaders, describing the annual looting of Eastern Anatolian cities, battles between the Celalis and Ottoman armies and the incursions of Shah Abbas of Persia. Grigor's various descriptions of the Celalis are too numerous and extensive to receive full treatment here, but it suffices to say that the Celali Revolts had such an impact on his life and times that their history prefaces his chronicle and they continually reappear throughout its pages.

The Celali insurrection and the incursions of Shah Abbas were not the only disasters to befall Eastern Anatolia during Grigor's time. Grigor also describes natural catastrophes facing the Anatolian peasantry of the early seventeenth century. For example, he writes that

> In 1048 (1599) the land became dry. From the end of May until the start of winter, it did not rain in the land anywhere. All the seeds dried up, and the water of irrigation also grew frigid. There was a great affliction for man and beast.[63]

As an implied result of the drought, Grigor states that

> And in the next year, it was 1600, there was extreme famine everywhere, and many were dying from the extremity of the famine, and their corpses were falling in the villages, in the cities, and road passes, and there was no one to bury them. There was a certain priest of Erzincan – from the village Sholay – named Yenovkʻ, when we were in the city of Kars, and he explained to us that 'When I went out from Erzincan to Erzurum, I saw thirty men who had died, as they had fallen from hunger on the roads'. [There] was still more suffering in that year and the beginning of the coming [one]. And a somar of wheat, which is four bushels, went up to eight *kuruş*, and it was not to be found anywhere, so that many were living on grass, turned black, and died.[64]

As will be seen, such tales of drought, famine and scarcity were commonplace in other seventeenth-century Armenian sources.

While both Siměon and Grigor provided western views of the Celali Revolts from their experiences living in the Ottoman Empire, other authors wrote from an eastern vantage in the Caucasus, which had become secure Safavid territory by 1639 with the signing of the Treaty of Zuhab and the end of the Safavid-Ottoman Wars. Aṙakʻel of Tabriz, for example, wrote a long chronicle in the Armenian holy city of Ējmiatsin documenting events from 1602 to 1662. Though he is most famous for his account of the Ottoman-Persian wars and of Shah Abbas's forced deportations of Armenians to Isfahan, where they founded New Julfa – an event which we pass over here because of its thorough treatment elsewhere[65] – he also discusses the Celalis. Aṙakʻel's account is based largely on eyewitness testimonies.

Aṙakʻel provides an entire chapter on the problems in Eastern Anatolia at the beginning of the seventeenth century, entitled 'Concerning the Appearance of the Celalis and Extreme Famine and Man-eating Wolves, and

Other Extortions which Arrived in the Land'.⁶⁶ In this chapter Aṙakʻel provides a list of the most notorious Celali leaders, starting with Kara Yazıcı's assault on Urfa.⁶⁷ His stories of Celali attacks upon Christians focus on the region of Ējmiatsin and Yerevan, where he himself lived and could listen to survivors' reports. It is clear that Aṙakʻel relied on oral histories for this section because he occasionally begins narratives with statements such as 'as they described to us . . .' and 'witnesses recounted to me . . .'⁶⁸

Aṙakʻel's tales of Celali depravations around Yerevan in 1605 to 1606 emphasise the terrible tortures they inflicted on the local population in order to find stores of provisions and treasure. For example, at the beginning of his chapter on the Celalis he describes the exploits of a certain Topal Osman Paşa:

> Osman Paşa gathered to him many ruffians. He made an army of thousands and held as his outpost the village Karpʻi [NW of Yerevan], there he settled. That winter, he wintered there. He sent his forces to the neighboring districts and villages to bring food for them and their livestock. The men who went and entered the settlements were not content with that which was sufficient, so that after procuring enough, they cast their hands on excess. Seizing men they were hanging them, some by the feet, others by the arms, and some by both. Mercilessly they were beating them with sticks, until they were senseless, as if they had died. And some also died from the torture. They were cutting the ears off some [people], and they were making others turn [to the side], hitting [them] in the nose with arrows. With such evil tortures they were tormenting them to reveal their stores of wheat and barley, the caches and holding-places of their treasures and goods.⁶⁹

Aṙakʻel thus describes the torture and pillage of Yerevan's local peasantry. He also documents attacks on the local monasteries and churches in order to ransack their treasuries. For example, he recounts how Celalis came to the famous Hovhannavankʻ near to the town of Karpʻi:

> Some of the Celalis went to this illustrious [place] of pilgrimage, Yohanavankʻ. Upon seeing them, all the residents of the monastery fled, but they seized a feeble and sick friar and demanded that he show the caches and holding-places. And for three days they hung the friar by his arms, beating him. And since he did not show them any holding-place, the Celalis became

angry like ferocious beasts. Lowering him from his arms, they hung him by the testicles and tortured him very badly. And he, having no recourse, showed them the cache. Entering inside the cache, they robbed and pillaged everything. Then they killed the friar, and they threw him into a pit of the monastery.[70]

In addition to providing many such tales of Celali crimes against the peasants and clergy around Yerevan, Aṙakʻel also includes stories of the famine of 1607–8. The horrors that resulted from this famine – including tales of cannibalism – were heard by Venetian diplomats far away in Istanbul.[71] Like several other seventeenth-century Armenian authors it seems that Aṙakʻel took particular relish in recounting the gruesome details. In his chapter on the Celalis, Aṙakʻel recounts the gradual adoption of cannibalism by starving peasants:

> . . . because there was no bread, they began to eat animals, oxen and sheep. And when the religiously sanctioned animals ran out, they began to eat impure animals: horse, mule, donkey, and other impure animals, until [they were eating] dogs and cats, and whatever was falling into their hands, on account of a need for food. And as the famine became even more intense, they began to eat the dead. They were not burying them, but they were eating them, because the famine reigned over the land. And many [people] in many places were seizing living people, and they were eating them.[72]

Aṙakʻel provides more tales of kidnapping, cannibalism and enslavement at the hands of the Celalis. There is no need to describe his stories in any more detail here, except to note that Aṙakʻel is the key source for Armenian lore about the effects of the Celali Revolts in the South Caucasus.

Colophons and 'short chronicles'

The above-mentioned major chronicles and travelogue are crucial sources for understanding the human suffering and destruction caused by the Celali Revolts, especially upon the Ottoman Empire's Armenian Christian population. But the Celalis' impact on Ottoman Armenians does not leave its traces in only one genre. After chronicles, the next most important Armenian source for the impact of the Celali Revolts is manuscript colophons. Colophons were notes written at the end of manuscripts – of diverse genres of texts – listing the name of the scribe and usually including a prayer for his family and patrons. They are an invaluable historical source for the period because they often included accounts of current events and history – sometimes in prose, sometimes in verse – which could span several pages.[73] Compared to other literary cultures of the early modern Mediterranean, the Armenians tended to write more extensive colophons and they provide a commentary on the history of the Ottoman Empire from a class of subjects usually unheard by Ottoman historians: Armenian clergymen.

Countless seventeenth-century Armenian colophons remain extant to this day. Some of them are available only in unpublished manuscript form; others are contained in various published colophon compilations; while yet others are accessible in the catalogues of the main Armenian manuscript libraries of the world, such as the Mesrop Mashtots' Institute of Ancient Manuscripts (Matenadaran) in Yerevan, the Mkhit'arean Order's libraries in Vienna and Venice and the Armenian Patriarchate of Jerusalem's St James Library. References to the Celali Revolts abound in seventeenth-century colophons and there are too many of them to allow for comprehensive treatment here. Nonetheless, a selection is provided here to show how the Celalis are discussed in this previously unutilised source for Ottoman history.

One Armenian colophon of this period – composed in 1609, directly after the decade of Celali onslaughts of 1598–1608 – is a poetic lament written by a scribe named Azaria Sasnets'i. Azaria was from Sason – in the modern-day Turkish province of Batman – and thus wrote with an Ottoman/western orientation as opposed to a Safavid Persian one. His lament is, in fact, a short history of the Celali Revolts in verse that focuses on the insurrection in Anatolia, as opposed to the campaigns of Shah Abbas which are frequently described in colophons from Iran and the Caucasus. Azaria begins his history of the Celalis with Kara Yazıcı and Deli Hasan and their rampages in Anatolia. Azaria writes that

> . . . gathering many forces,
> he became their commander,
> he who was called Yazıcı.
> Nourished in Severak,

taking up arms there,
this was the beginning of the Celalis,
bringing the destruction of the world.
From there they rushed before Urfa,
with 40,000 cavalry,
besieging the city,
he surrounded it for two months.
And after [some] days he entered,
and he took the fortress there,
decapitating its grandees,
and sitting in their place.[74]

Azaria's poem continues in a similar manner, documenting the campaigns against the Celalis and their battles with Ottoman armies. Like the chronicle writers, Azaria also mentions the famine that, according to him, was a direct result of Celali looting:

Yazıcı departed in the spring,
And he went to Sivas,
he took the city,
gathering much booty.
Taking the whole country captive,
he seized property and goods,
on account of which there was a great severe famine,
and bread was nowhere to be found.
One pound of bread was 10 [pieces] of gold,
and no one could find it,
because they had burned all the fields,
and they carried off its produce with them.[75]

At times, Azaria's poem reaches depths of pathos in his description of Celali outrages. At one point he even evokes sympathy for the Ottoman general Hasan in the face of the Celali commander Deli Hasan's unrestrained lawlessness:

Seizing the wife [of the Ottoman commander Hasan Paşa],
they brought her to Hasan Beğ [Deli Hasan],

and he rejoiced upon seeing her,
taking her with him to his tent.
He kept the woman for many days,
profaning and dishonoring her,
he sent her back disgraced,
to wound her husband.
And she, thus put to shame,
reached her husband in Tokat,
when Hasan Paşa saw her,
the color of his face changed.[76]

Like the chroniclers and other colophon writers Azaria complements his historical narrative with general commentary on Celali activities against the local peasant population. For example, he writes that

... they were called the Celalis,
destroying villages and cities,
taking men and women captive.
they did not spare orphans or widows,
putting both rich and poor to the sword,
having no mercy on the elderly or children,
taking their livestock and possessions.
They were so merciless,
cruel, their hearts turned to stone...[77]

There is no other Armenian colophon of the period quite like Azaria's in its narrative focus and pathos.

While Azaria's colophon provides many pages focusing exclusively on the Celalis, shorter references to them abound in numerous other colophons, with frequent emphasis on attacks against Armenian Christians. For example, M. K. Zulalyan appends his book with a short collection of early seventeenth-century colophons and he includes an entry from 1602–4 about the looting of Sivas by Kara Yazıcı. It describes how Yazıcı 'unsparingly killed many Christians and took their children captive'.[78] Likewise in a colophon of 1606 the scribe complained that priests, in particular, were being taken captive.[79] As in all the Armenian literature of the period, famine, scarcity and stories of cannibalism are discussed. The same colophon notes that 'we heard that some [people] ate the meat of men'.[80] One scribe from Van lamented in 1606 that 'a liter of oil is three *kuruş*!'[81] But Christians were not only victims in the colophons. While admittedly rare, the scribes sometimes relished small victories against the bandits. One colophon of 1604 records that 'Lord Martiros rescued this Gospel; he took it from the hands of the Celalis!'[82]

In their works on the New Julfa merchant networks, Edmund M. Herzig and Sebouh Aslanian provide a partial translation of a colophon of 1608. Both of their works present only a portion of the colophon, focusing on Shah Abbas's forced movement of Armenians from the region between Shirakavan and Kars[83] in order to illuminate the history of New Julfa. The colophon's scope, however, is much greater, emphasising that Armenians of the first decade of the seventeenth century endured two major traumas which had long-lasting impacts: the incursions of Shah Abbas into the Caucasus and Eastern Anatolia and the Celali Revolts, and the colophon author describes both in his colophon. In addition to his descriptions of Shah Abbas, the author also adds that

> Again the land of Ararat became abandoned. A band of brigands, who they call 'Celali', came from the Turkish side and settled there, and they committed many crimes of iniquity against the few [people] who remained. Going by night, they were looking and searching, wherever a man might be found. Coming across one, they would kill him and take his children captive. They were looting houses and churches, to the point that they spread famine over the land. Then, they became cannibals. Seizing a bishop from Mōḷnoy Monastery, they roasted him and ate him.[84]

This author was particularly mesmerised and haunted by tales of the 1607–8 famine. In addition to the barbeque described above, the same author also provides this gruesome anecdote:

> And there was extreme famine everywhere, so much that they were taking the dead from graves and eating them. Parents were eating their children, according to the prophet, who said that 'The hands of merciful women cooked their children' (Lam. 4:10), and they ate them. On fast days they were eating dog and cat and every impure animal. The frenzy and madness of the belly

made them forget reason, and they became like beasts, laying an ambush they were hunting one another. When a mother would leave the house, the family members were slaughtering the child. When the mother came [home], they were putting cooked meat before her. She would eat it unknowingly, and then she would leave searching for and asking for her child. Very much distressed the family members were not saying [that], in fact, it was [the child] whose meat you ate. Finding rotting bones on the street they were rubbing them with the palms [of their hands] and eating them, and then they were dying. Mourning in heaven and lament on the earth! O mountains and hills, together with the beasts, animals and all of the birds, raise a cry, as there has not been such a famine, which we have seen, since a pound of flour is three *kuruş*. In the city of Erzurum they were selling the meat and oil of men. When the governor of the city learned of it, he had the men strangled, those who were doing this, but he was not able to stop it.[85]

Such descriptions of cannibalism are likely exaggerated horror stories written by a traumatised population. They are widespread in seventeenth-century Armenian literature and they also appear in some Muslim sources of the period.[86] Viewed in aggregate, the Armenian colophons of the early seventeenth century reflect the themes of the major chronicles: the Ottoman-Persian Wars and Shah Abbas's famous deportations, the rise of the Celalis, famine, scarcity, and all of these disasters' effects on the Armenian populations of Eastern Anatolia and the Caucasus.

Another group of texts which also discusses early seventeenth-century Ottoman history is the so-called 'short chronicles', most of which consist of chronological lists. The previously mentioned geography writer from Erzurum, Yakob Karnets'i, wrote a notable 'short chronicle' which differs in character from the more common chronologies, as it was a biography of his father, a priest named Gēorg. Gēorg was the son of an Armenian merchant named Mirakʻ who was born in 1583 in a village named Keḷi, which lay in the vicinity of Erzurum. His biography provides a critical complement to the Armenian-language accounts of early seventeenth-century history described above, because it shows the effects of instability upon an Armenian family, as described in the course of a narration about his father's upbringing. Yakob writes that

Gēorg was a twelve year-old youth, and he had read six canons of the Psalms and the whole of [the poem] *Jesus Son*.[87] And pious Mirakʻ rejoiced at the boy's reading and bought for him *Jesus Son* and a hymnal. [Mirakʻ] was continually going around in the buying and selling of commerce, going to Erzurum and to Yamitʻ [Diyarbekir]. And in that time a rebellion from the impure race of Kurds and many Celalis came forth, who were plundering each others' lands, and they were continually looting and robbing. In the passes of the roads and in the mountains many were hunting and killing, as is still their custom. Up to two and three times they plundered and ruined the land of Keḷi and Balva, as the Ottomans were not so mighty, they conquered all the land, so that it was abandoned by the kings. On account of which, year by year, destruction began and a high price for bread. And pious Mirakʻ departed and went to Erzurum, and he bought silk and goods (*esbab*), and wheat, so that he might bring it home, and he went to Hamitʻ to sell his wares with many friends. And when they arrived in the country of Hanterdzu, many forces of the Medes [i.e., Kurds] arrived over them and they killed them all with swords and took away all their possessions. Sad news of their cry came [and] reached Keḷi. And the owners of the dead came out with their families, and Gulinar [the wife of Mirakʻ] came with her four children to Erzurum to complain to the *paşa*, so that perhaps he might have mercy on the families of the deceased and find their goods. The *paşa* sent many troops, and they did not find them. And [of] those who came, some went to their own countries, and half remained here. And the mother of Gēorg said, 'Children, our land is expensive, let's remain here [in Erzurum] one year, and then let's go [back home].' And on account of this they remained here. And young Gēorg was continually going to church, and the elder priest Lord Mktrichʻ saw Gēorg to be successful and diligent in learning, [and] he took him on as a pupil. And he called his mother and adopted him. And the mother of Gēorg said, 'a promise, which is for God', and with joy she took the boy by the hand and gave him to Lord Mktrichʻ, saying 'before God I deliver Gēorg to you, as in antiquity Hannah gave Samuel to the priest Eli, I also give him to you' [1 Sam. 1:1–2:11]. And Gēorg remained at the feet of Lord Mktrichʻ and officiated the Psalms and all the hymns. And the mother of Gēorg married off the girls, and death took her with her two sons. And only Gēorg remained, and day by day famine was descending, when it was the year fifty and five (1606). The famine became so extreme in all of the land, that men were eating dog, cat, and men, as Lord Gēorg himself would describe, as many straits came over him.[88]

Gēorg survived these 'straits' and was ordained a priest in 1611. He married, and his son Yakob would go on to become a noted seventeenth-century Armenian author and local historian of Erzurum. Rather than discussing the chaos of early seventeenth-century Anatolia in abstract terms, this text uniquely shows how it impacted the lives of a single Armenian family, as Yakob's grandfather was killed in the midst of instability and his grandmother and father settled in Erzurum as refugees. Yakob's father remembered the horrors of famine and cannibalism in Erzurum and recounted the tales to his son.

Stories about the Celalis, scarcity and famine resonate throughout the Armenian colophons and 'short chronicles' of the early seventeenth century, often providing a less formalised picture than the major chronicles. The chronicle authors had to contextualise tales of the Celali Revolts within a grand narrative. The colophon authors, however, could take relish in the joy of rescuing a Gospel or recount the gruesome horrors of cannibalism without concern for a broader narrative discourse. Likewise, Yakob, in his short biography of his father, could show how his father's youth was defined and shaped by the instability of the times without needing to fit his poignant tale within a framework of political or ecclesiastical history.

Poetry and verse

As many of the colophons were written in verse this section overlaps to some degree with the previous one. But looking beyond the verse colophons, there were many Armenian poets, troubadours and bards who sang and composed songs and poems throughout the seventeenth century. Most of their works – such as the numerous songs of Armenian '*ashuł*' (Turkish, *aşık*) minstrels[89] or the diverse verses of a monk from Lim Island on Lake Van, Nerses Mokatsʻi[90] – largely stand outside the theme of this chapter. Sometimes, however, the harsh historical realities of the times did reverberate in poetical works, often in the context of the poet's references to his own biography.

Two poets whose works describe the Celali Revolts at length were Stepʻanos and Yakob, both Armenians from Tokat who extolled the beauty and glories of the city before it was destroyed by Celali incursions. Writing about Kara Yazıcı's sacking of his hometown in 1602, Step'anos describes it as a 'paradise'.[91] Of the Celali assault, he writes that

> [The Celalis] destroyed and demolished
> that settlement [Tokat], the whole city.
> Three times they plundered it,
> until they had plucked it clean.
> Praiseworthy city of Tokat,
> which is very close to Koman,
> in which [lies] the tomb of Yohann
> the golden-mouthed *vardapet*.
> Many are its beautiful hamlets, filled with good things,
> filled with vineyards, fields and gardens (*bahçe*),
> abundant in water, plants, and vegetables,
> [Tokat] was like the Garden of Eden.[92]

Like Step'anos, Yakob praises Tokat's past glories at great length in his poem. Referring to Tokat by its Greek name Eudokia, Yakob writes that

> You, dear Eudokia
> [you were] like Egypt,
> you were filled with treasure and fabric (*kumaş*)
> like the throne of a great king.
> Lovely is your position
> in the bottom of two valleys,
> you turn your back on the precipice,
> and you look upon the face of a plain.
> From you gushes the water of springs
> in the four corners of your expanse,
> sweet for the thirsty,
> sprinkling wet the fields.
> There are churches in you,
> working astonishing miracles,
> its servants were rejoicing,
> they were taking pride in the glories of its saints.

> In you there were good houses
> high-walled prosperous palaces,
> decorated belvederes,
> windows for relaxation [bay windows].
> There were four strongholds in you
> which they named *bedestan*,
> the treasures of all were there,
> of the Armenians, the Turks, and the Romans.[93]

But Tokat's glories came to a sudden end with the Celali incursion. Yakob writes that

> Exalted city of Eudokia,
> the Celalis cast the evil eye upon you.
> Coming against you from four directions,
> they suddenly besieged you.
> On that day, evil and tribulation
> shook everyone.
> Tears and sighing entered [their] lamentation.
> 'woe' they were screaming unanimously.
> At that time [the Celalis] were killing the elderly,
> they were decapitating the youths,
> and your beautiful children,
> they separated them from their parents.[94]

Thus, two Armenian scribes from Tokat describe both their city's glories and its sudden destruction in tragic lamentation.

In sum, the Celali Revolts are discussed across genres by almost every major Armenian author of the seventeenth century. Whereas Ottoman-Turkish historiography emphasises the political and military aspects of the period's history, Armenians focused on the human tragedy the revolts unleashed upon their population. The Armenian authors also consistently and frequently complained of famine and scarcity that wreaked havoc on peasant populations throughout Eastern Anatolia in the first decade of the seventeenth century.

Armenian Views on the Causes of the Celali Revolts

As noted in the previous chapter, questions about the root causes of the Celali Revolts continue to be debated in the field of Ottoman history. Since Armenian sources have not yet been used in addressing this debate, it would be worthwhile to briefly consider Armenian authors' comments about the origins of the chaos that broke forth so violently at the turn of the seventeenth century. Two authors – among several – who comment explicitly on the causes of the Celali Revolts are the previously mentioned poet Azaria Sasnets'i and the chronicler Grigor Daranalts'i.

In his poetic history of the Celali Revolts, Azaria offers the following testimony about their origins:

> . . . this land was filled with countless evils,
> fulfilling the word of the Lord,
> which warned us beforehand.
> Nation moved over nation,
> bringing destruction to one another's lands,
> and the kings became very wicked,
> contracting false oaths with one another.
> Commands arose from them,
> taking bribes for judgements,
> they scorned the innocent [and] just,
> and they advanced rascals.
> Giving provinces (*sancaks*) to *paşas*,
> they went with mirth,
> and after a few days they passed on,
> giving that place again to others.
> And going they drove him away [Kara Yazıcı],
> taking him from his throne (*taht*),
> he became very shaken,
> reckoned despicable by all.
> On account of this he rebelled,
> he made himself autonomous from his king,
> amassing many forces around him,

he made himself independent.
The king heard of his repute,
sending many forces to him,
but he destroyed all of them,
not fearing the king.
Continually he grew stronger.
And his cavalry grew stronger,
as he gave them booty as gifts,
and promising the glory of greatness.[95]

Taking the rise of Kara Yazıcı as a paradigm, this verse analyses the origins of the Celali Revolts through several frameworks. It begins with biblical language, borrowing from Jesus's predictions of the end of time, when 'nation will rise against nation' (Matthew 24: 7). Moreover, it complains of the ill-treatment of the just, alluding perhaps to the cornerstone of Ottoman political theory, the 'Circle of Justice', which was predicated on the state's just treatment of the peasantry who lay at the basis of the economic and military order.[96] Mostly, however, it dwells on administrative dysfunction, casting primary blame for the rise of the Celalis there. Azaria complains of how quickly – 'after a few days' – governors who had attained their positions through bribing the court lost their posts, leaving men of rank aggrieved and despised.

This description of the rise of the Celalis correlates with research on the Ottoman bureaucracy in the seventeenth century. The turn of the seventeenth century was a time of deep structural transformation within the Ottoman state, both at the centre – most notably in changes in the upbringing and method of succession of heirs to the Ottoman throne[97] – and in the provincial administration. In *The Sultan's Servants* Metin Kunt describes three main transformations in provincial administration that occurred concomitantly with the gradual decline of the *timar* system, which was a kind of prebend for compensating Ottoman officials and officers: more widespread assumption of high ranking positions in provincial administration by central government officials; an expansion in administrative units from district (*sancak*) to the larger province (*eyalet*); and the rising importance of households and household patronage.[98] Along with these main structural changes, other patterns of administration diverged from previous norms, one of which was a demonstrable decrease in the duration of *sancakbeyi* appointments, a phenomenon that receives extensive criticism in the Ottoman Turkish advice literature of the period.[99] Thus, Azaria's attribution of the rise of the Celalis to corrupt bribers who come to the provinces with appointments from the centre and served only short periods before being forced to find new positions, resonates both with advice literature – most notably Koçi Bey – and with contemporary research on Ottoman history.

Grigor Daranalts'i similarly lays the blame for the rise of the Celalis on administrative incompetence, explicitly criticising the ineptitude of the Ottoman sultan Mehmed III (r. 1595–1603). Grigor writes that

> ... in 1044 (1595) Sultan Murad died, who had reigned for twenty-one years, and his son sat [on the throne], Sultan Mehmed, now in our [life] time, [and] like his father he does not have care or concern about the prosperity of the land. He was so deranged, and he was so drunk and dulled by mind-numbing wine, that he was not conscious of his own state (*hal*) and not the peril of the land, as the prophet says that 'You had us drink the wine of senselessness' (Ps. 59: 5), and Isaiah says 'Woe on you, you who have become drunk and not from wine' (Is. 28: 1). There was almost no king and no sovereign and no head and overseer of the lands, but there was only a wicked name over every country of his rule. [All] rights of legal arbitration and inquiries and dispensation of justice for the deprived had disappeared. And all the Celalis and rebellions took place in his days, who wreaked plenty of destruction and [destroyed] all the land of Asia, which now is called Anatolia, so that we who survived their sword became refugees and sojourned in this land from that time on, until we had forgotten our [homeland]. Four scourges took place one after the other over all the lands: Famine and death and the sword and being eaten by wild beasts, so that there was much cannibalism. [The lands] from Erzurum up to Kars and to the region of Yerevan were filled [by these scourges], and from there, they spilled to Constantinople and to everywhere, being spread and dispersed. And on account of Sultan Mehmed's heedlessness, Shah Abbas, the king of the Persians, destroyed many castles and cities of the land, and many provinces. In the course of one year, because the lands were abandoned, he took everything. It was in the year 1052 (1603). And this Sultan Mehmed was

weak and neglected the lands, [with the result that] all the governors and judges and troops and soldiers and many of the common troops and peasants were oppressed by unjust privations and seizures of property. And the governors were oppressed by the unjust judgement of the king and of the viziers, who were distributing the governance of provinces and conquests and judgeships for bribes. And even before [the new governors and judges] had reached their posts, they removed them from office and replaced them with someone else. And when the latter came, the one who had come first would not permit him to enter and to sit in his place, and the two were fighting with one another over the position. And they were conscripting troops, they were levying from the common peasants and they were becoming a great army. In this way they all became rebels from the king; they became Celalis. They were like big and little fishes, which were swallowing one another, according to the word of Habakuk (Hab. 1: 14–15), and they were destroying each other without foreign enemies, but they became enemies to one another and to their countrymen. Becoming wicked in this way, they destroyed all the land of Anatolia. The will of God permitted all of this, on account of our going astray, so that many lands became uninhabited, and ruins abounded. Wolves and beasts became ferocious, and they became rebels against men: forsaking animals, they were eating men.[100]

This passage shows that Grigor Daranalts'i attributes the origins of the Celali Revolts primarily to the failings of one individual, Sultan Mehmed III, while also observing more systemic administrative failings. Grigor's comments about Mehmed III put too much blame on one individual to resonate with contemporary understandings of Ottoman history, which emphasises broader transformations, be they economic, military or climatic. Moreover, the Celali Revolts continued long after Mehmed III's reign and thus we cannot blame his administration for a century of disorder. Nonetheless, Grigor's complaints about corruption, 'unjust extortions and seizures of property' and bribery overlap with other criticisms of Ottoman administration of the time. This was, after all, a period in which the state was forced to balance the books of increasing military expenditure while one of its main instruments of compensation – the *timar* – was simultaneously falling into irrelevance.[101] Grigor's observation that 'they were levying [troops] from the common peasants' also resonates with historical reality, as 'the rise of the *sekbans*' – the musket-bearing infantrymen who became notorious for their service to Celali leaders – was a phenomenon of the late sixteenth century.[102]

In spite of these resonances, neither Grigor nor Azaria's descriptions of the rise of the Celalis advance our understanding of the revolts' origins to any great degree because they were too inclined to interpret the revolts as a product of the sultan's personal failings and rampant corruption, without being fully conscious of multi-variable structural changes taking place in the Ottoman Empire at large. Thus, the Armenians' testimonies provide some scattered support for various modern interpretations of the Celali Revolts but reliance on them in no way settles the debate. Modern research on the Celali Revolts suggests that they had several causes,[103] the results of a convergence of economic transformations, changing ways of warfare, and perhaps also climate change which coalesced to give rise to wide-ranging rebellion and instability.

Although the Armenian sources do not offer revolutionary new insights into the causes of the Celali Revolts, their study leads us in a different direction altogether, indicating a previously unnoticed variable in the demographic, cultural and social development of early modern Ottoman society. The seventeenth-century Armenian literary tradition repeatedly makes reference to an Armenian demographic shift. Viewed in aggregate, it points in a very definite geographical direction – westwards – highlighting a flow of Armenian refugees from Eastern Anatolia towards Istanbul and its environs. These migrations would ultimately catalyse the formation of a vibrant new Ottoman Christian culture in the coastal cities of the Ottoman Empire.

The Great Armenian Flight: Testimonies of Armenian Migration

Just as tales of Celali rampages, war with Persia, scarcity and famine reverberate throughout seventeenth-century Armenian literature, another theme is also omnipresent: mass flight. Almost all of the authors mentioned above describe migration as a common response to the hardships of life in Eastern Anatolia at the turn of the seventeenth century.

In his verse-history of the Celalis, Azaria states that

Armenia's foundation collapsed
it was destroyed through and through.

> It began in 1040 (1591),
> until 1060 (1611),
> many misfortunes were seen,
> the Armenians' world was erased.[104]

Some verses later the scribe adds,

> Everyone was put to flight,
> dispersed and scattered from country to country,
> Istanbul became very full,
> from there all the way until Poland they spread.[105]

Similar references to the Armenians' mass flight abound in colophons. For instance, one of the previously discussed colophons described the Great Armenian Flight as a product of famine:

> Then . . . the Armenian people were scattered from the area of the famine to Persia, to Assyria, and to Georgia until they reached Chorchē, Abhazia, and Kefe. Father despised son, mother [despised] daughter, brother [despised] brother. Men left their wives, women forgot the misery of their children. Not only [in] one or two particular countries [were they dispersed], but everywhere – beginning from the gates of the Huns and Alans and from the Caucasus Mountains until Pontos and Ephesus and Cappadocia, and until Damascus and Sis and Mesopotamia. All of Armenia became scattered and dispersed.[106]

In one of his manuscript colophons, Grigor Daranalts'i – who participated in the Great Flight – wrote that

> Armenia was overturned and corrupted from its foundation, like in the days of the Flood [of Noah], it was depopulated and destroyed, [something] which we saw with our [very own] eyes. And on account of this we were exiled and we have no rest. Thanks and glory to the Holy Trinity, now we are in the holy city of Jerusalem.[107]

Grigor was not alone in providing personal testimony of his own flight in colophon form. Another example is a colophon from 1603, which describes how a manuscript was begun in Sivas in 1601 but, because of the Celali incursions, the scribe was forced to flee. He finally finished it in Khizan (near Bitlis) two years later.[108] The Armenologist Gohar Grigoryan very recently published analysis of a Gospel copied in Istanbul in 1607 by a Celali refugee from Tokat.[109]

In addition to the colophon scribes, the major chronicle and travelogue authors also left extensive testimony of the Great Armenian Flight from Eastern Anatolia westward. Throughout his travelogue Siměon of Poland remarks on the numerous Armenian refugees that he encountered all over the Ottoman Empire. For example, he explicitly writes that all 200 of the Armenian households of Egypt were refugees from the Celali Revolts.[110] Siměon repeatedly offers general laments about the Armenians' sad plight, writing that 'Wherever you might go, you will find Armenians. They have spread and scattered across the face of the world like dust'.[111]

Grigor Daranalts'i also offers multiple accounts of the Great Armenian Flight in the course of his chronicle.

> And in [Sultan Ahmed's] time, the Celalis were covering the land of Anatolia like snow. From [the time of] Sultan Murad they began the combustion of sparks of fire and in the time of his father, Sultan Mehmed, all the land was devoured by the fire of the flames of the Celalis, so that there was no place of peace anywhere, but only in Constantinople and in the country of Thrace, which is called Rumelia. On account of which all of the country, Armenians and Turks, gathered here [in Constantinople and Thrace] and dispersed until Belgrade, until the land of Moldova and of the Goths and of all the Scythians.
>
> And the Red Hat [i.e., Safavid Persia] reigned from [their] regions, and until the borders of Theodopolis [Erzurum] it ruled in tyranny. Istanbul and Rumelia and the land of Egypt remained inhabited territory, [they] alone being under the command of the [Ottoman] kingship.[112]

Elsewhere Grigor also states that

> In this time we are in a state of pilgrimage and emigration in a foreign land, being scattered and spread like dust flowing over the land by the wind of sins, in Istanbul and in Anatolia and in Thrace, which is *Rumelia*, and in the remote land of the Goths and until Egypt, being among depraved peoples

> ... Not all the men of one country are dwelling in one place, but some [here] some [there], like our countrymen [from Kemah], the men of a few villages here [in Rodosto] and in Istanbul and [like] the people of Divriği, making settlement around Alov, and others being in a state of helter-skelter.[113]

Aṙakʻel of Tabriz also provides descriptions of the Armenians' mass migration at the beginning of the seventeenth century. For instance, in his chapter on the Celalis he writes that

> And in this time the Armenian people were dispersed and scattered, and they went each to a region to find a place to stay and live. Some [went] to Rumelia, others to Moldavia; some to Poland, others to Kefe; some to the coast of the Black Sea, others to Tabriz, Ardabil, and their provinces. As a result, of the Armenian people, so many are strangers (*garip*) in the above-mentioned lands; they went in this time and for this reason [the Celalis and famine]. And Shah Abbas the king drove and took so many of the Armenian people, many Christians, to the land of Isfahan and Farahabad; they all came in this time, when the Shah took them.[114]

Like Grigor, Aṙakʻel describes early seventeenth-century Anatolia as if it were the site of a massive tempest, sending Armenians running and fleeing both eastward and westward.

In addition to the colophons, travelogues and chronicles, tales of the Great Armenian Flight also appear in poetry. The above-mentioned Stepʻanos of Tokat writes that upon the Celali incursion, the Armenians of that city fled en masse:

> This word of Scripture took place
> of the holy prophet Moses,
> they persecuted one thousand
> two myriads were put to flight.
> They fled with haste and speed
> and they were not looking back,
> until they went to Loṙtʻpelin,
> then snow fell on the ground.
> The city's residents, bidding "adieu,"
> they abandoned home and place,

> leaving they fled, one to a fortress,
> some to the hills, many to the mountains.
> Some lost one another,
> and they were not able to find [each other again].
> Others, barefoot and bare-headed,
> they walked around in a pillaged [state].
> Some didn't find bread for a month,
> and they were eating the grass of the mountains,
> while others were eating their good things.
> Looking from afar, they were weeping.[115]

Step'anos also documents his own flight, writing that

> When evil suddenly came
> Black Yazıcı to Tokat,
> he scattered everyone like dust,
> he hurled everyone to various places.
> Some went to Istanbul,
> one to Bursa; [another to] Edirne,
> many went to Rumelia,
> the house of the Franks, Moldavia, Poland . . .
> And as for me, I Step'anos,
> scurrying I escaped to Kefe,
> indigent, emigrant, refugee, stranger (*garip*),
> or like a boat on the sea.[116]

Stepa'nos' counterpart, Yakob of Tokat, also documents the Great Armenian Flight, writing that

> The city's noble residents
> clergy and lay,
> Armenian, Roman, and Muslim
> dispersed to mountain and valley.
> Some, escaping, entered into a fortress,
> half fled to the mountains, hiding [there],
> they cast away all their possessions,
> barely taking their children, they escaped.

Those gleaming virgin girls
who had not seen the sun,
face uncovered [and] barefoot in the mountains
she was straying from her family.
All at once your [Tokat's] inhabitants
were all dispersed and scattered.
They emigrated to foreign lands,
to Frankistan and Persia.[117]

Step'anos notes that he fled to Kefe, a city in the Crimea, as a result of the Great Flight. There he continued to work as a scribe, priest and teacher, passing the ecclesiastical and literary traditions of Tokat on to his students. Step'anos had a student named Martiros of the Crimea who also described the Great Flight in the course of one of his poems, a historical verse about the Armenian history of the Crimea. Martiros writes,

When it was 1050 (1601)
Great misfortunes happened to this land
the middle-territories, which they call the land of the Greeks,
nearly from Istanbul until Persia.

Ignoble bandit-men came forth
they gathered like-minded rascals,
increasing day by day, they multiplied greatly,
they were called Celalis, the world-destroying.

They pillaged the land wherever they went,
indescribable crimes were committed by them.
The deeds and actions which they dared [to commit]
it is impossible to count all the things that happened.

Among other incidents of punitive anger
Armenia drank these bitter dregs,
departing from their own motherland
[the Armenians] were scattered and dispersed by land and sea.

On that day of the anger of divine wrath
many of our people went to Kefe,

having left their motherland, they stayed there,

having escaped from [their] persecutors, they gave thanks to the Lord.[118]

Martiros was a man of erudition and esteem, and he served as the Armenian Patriarch of Jerusalem. The story of Step'anos and Martiros shows how the Great Armenian Flight produced intellectual transplantations away from intellectual centres in Greater Armenia, such as Tokat, towards Ottoman coastal cities, in this case Kefe.

The Celali Revolts in Kemah and the 'Valley of Monasteries'

This chapter began with focus on one case study and the time has come to turn our sights back to Kemah and the 'Valley of Monasteries'. Grigor Daranalts'i provides specific testimony about the history of his home town at the turn of the seventeenth century, documenting banditry, famine and flight.

Grigor records Celali activities in the region of Kemah as early as 1591, and banditry and clashes between the Celalis and Ottoman troops would continue to plague the region intermittently throughout the last decade of the sixteenth century.[119] At the very beginning of the seventeenth century conditions worsened. Grigor writes that in 1602

> ... [Celalis] went with fifty thousand cavalry and stationed themselves in suffering and afflicted, pitiful Erzincan. They looted it and brought unmentionable troubles and afflictions. They stayed there for two and a half months, and they were so inflamed and so enraged ... They destroyed many places: Erzincan, Kemah, Divriği, and other nearby districts, and wherever they went, they plundered everyone ... And there was no justice or righteous judgements of God in exchange for their evils, which they committed on the afflicted, the suffering Armenian people and the common Turks.[120]

Thus, in addition to the general instability caused by banditry, Grigor explicitly states that Kemah was 'destroyed' and 'plundered' in 1602. Not a year would pass before another group of Celali bandits came and settled in Erzincan in 1603.[121]

At the beginning of the seventeenth century, Mount Sepuh and the 'Valley of Monasteries' did not remain untouched. It has already been mentioned that the Monastery of the King was pillaged by the Celalis and abandoned by the Armenians. The other monasteries described at the beginning of this chapter were not permanently abandoned until 1915 but their monks were sometimes forced to give food and money to the Celalis. Moreover, some monasteries of Mount Sepuh endured shorter periods of abandonment in which the monks were temporarily evacuated.

Grigor describes how, in 1596, he came to his home town of Kemah from Bayburt, where he was a student, and visited the monasteries of Mount Sepuh. He writes that in the summer season, 'the brigands set out for the mountains, and they were living off the monasteries'. In particular he describes an occasion when 'a Kurd named Khulakhsuz went with seven friends to the Illuminator [Monastery] for food'. Grigor explains that later, after leaving, Khulakhsuz promised a bounty if some Kurds would go back to the monastery to kill the monks. Sometime later seven Kurds came again to the monastery saying that 'we've come to kill you'. Thankfully these Kurds were not the Celalis' most vicious killers and it was possible to dissuade them from their plan. The monks fed them, gave them a blessing upon request, and then they left peacefully.[122] It seems that the monasteries and their monks were recognised as holy figures across faiths, even for Celalis, as indicated by their request for the monks' blessing. Thus the monasteries of Mount Sepuh were sometimes able to survive the vagaries of the period with food, payments and prayers in the early years of the revolt.

Eventually, however, the region became so dangerous that the monks were forced temporarily to abandon Mount Sepuh. In a long section at the end of his chronicle, Grigor describes the religious significance of Mount Sepuh and its monasteries, noting both their association with Grigor the Illuminator and, in the case of the T'ordan Monastery, its roots as a pre-Christian holy site. He emphasises that they were important pilgrimage sites for Armenians, noting that the region around Erzincan and Kemah had so many monasteries and churches that 'they called it the Province of Churches',[123] a similar phrase to the Ottoman tax collectors' nickname, *'vâdî-i vank'*. He writes that 'All [the monasteries] are worthy of adoration and worship, and they are a second Jerusalem and new Sion'.[124] But later he adds that 'now in this bitter and brutal time, these miraculous holy places have become dark and they lay deserted'.[125]

Grigor narrates that a certain Armenian holy man lived at the Monastery of the Illuminator, 'until the insurrection and the uprising of the Celalis and the destruction of villages and the persecution of mankind'.[126] Later

> when from fear of the brigand Kurds they called the monks, and [the monks] went near the villages, he [the holy man] was not wanting to leave the monastery, but by day he was staying in a cave, and he was watching it from afar and lighting the lights and incense of all of the churches and praying at their gates.[127]

This passage shows that the Celali threat forced the monks to evacuate the Illuminator Monastery, but even at times of abandonment someone was watching over it.

In short, Kemah and its holy sites lay victim to Celali banditry and general chaos and instability for at least twenty years, during the last decade of the sixteenth century and the first decade of the seventeenth century. Though the Ottoman state won some victories against the Celalis – such as during the grand vizier Kuyucu Murad Paşa's campaign of 1609 – it was unable to impose lasting stability in Eastern Anatolia, and both banditry and famine continued to plague the populations of Kemah and Erzincan even after his campaign. Like Armenians from throughout the South Caucasus and Eastern Anatolia, Kemah's Armenians responded with mass flight. As Grigor wrote, some even 'fled naked'. Although an Armenian population remained in the Kemah region until 1915, the impact of the Celali Revolts could still be seen centuries later. The Armenian travel author Garegin Sruandzteants' passed through the Kemah region in the late nineteenth century and he wrote that 'Numerous hamlets and ruined villages are visible, and they remind us of the *great emigration of Armenians,* who were transplanted from this region to Tekirdağ [and] the cities and villages of Gallipoli'.[128] To this day diverse ruins in the region reinforce the impression that some sites were abandoned centuries ago, while others were inhabited by Armenians until 1915.

Summary

This chapter has shown that the Ottoman Turkish literary tradition – including chronicles, travelogues and panegyrics – differs fundamentally in its presentation of early seventeenth-century Ottoman history when compared with Armenian sources. Muslim authors writing in Ottoman Turkish tended to identify with the state, and for them the history of the Celali Revolts was the history of sackings, battles and politico-military appointments. For the Armenians, however, the focus shifts to the suffering of the Armenian Christian peasantry. They dwell on the particular damage wreaked on Greater Armenia, the human cost of war, scarcity and famine. Tales of suffering – some perhaps clichéd and embellished, others probably quite accurate – reverberate across genres of Armenian letters, from chronicles to colophons to poetry.

Turkish secondary literature has observed the Great Flight of Ottoman peasants westward, but as a result of the above-mentioned discrepancy it has not highlighted the disproportionate effect this flight had on the Ottoman Empire's Armenian subjects. It is thanks to the Armenian primary sources that we become aware of a Great Armenian Flight which forced Armenian Christians to flee from their historical demographic and cultural centres in Greater Armenia to western regions of the Ottoman Empire not historically home to large Armenian populations.

Thus, we are now indebted to the Armenian primary sources for highlighting a critical event in Ottoman history: a massive demographic shift of Armenians from Greater Armenia to Istanbul, Thrace, and even as far afield as Egypt and Poland. But the Armenian sources provide relatively less testimony about what happened to the Armenians after their arrival in the western parts of the Ottoman Empire. We sometimes know their destinations, but there were hundreds of different migrations occurring chaotically at the same time, and it is usually impossible to follow the histories of specific Armenian communities after they fled and settled in new homelands. Here it is proposed that, just as the Armenian sources have cast light on a previously unnoticed event in Ottoman history, perhaps Ottoman Turkish archival sources might fill in this lacuna in the Armenian historical narrative.

The next chapter follows the Kemah Armenians in their flight. The plight of the Kemah Armenians has been chosen in order to simplify a chaotic situation by focusing on one migration among hundreds, following, so to speak, one thread in a disordered ball of yarn. Grigor Daranalts'i informs us that the Kemah Armenians established a settlement in Rodosto, and he provides some basic testimony about their first arrival. Let us now see if the Ottoman

Turkish Archive can provide us with more detail and complement Grigor's narrative account with new facts and a different perspective. The Armenians fled westwards, after all, because it was secure Ottoman territory where the apparati of the Ottoman state continued to function properly. Thus it is likely that record of the Armenian refugees' arrival should remain extant in the Ottoman Archives of Istanbul, which preserves an abundance of diverse documentation from the turn of the seventeenth century.

Notes

1. For a general introduction to Armenian history during the Arsacid period see Nina Garsoian's chapter in Richard G. Hovannisian (ed.), *The Armenian People From Ancient to Modern Times*, Vol. I (London: Palgrave Macmillan, 1997).
2. T'.Kh. Hakobyan, et al., 'Kamakh', *Hayastani ew harakits' shrjanneri telanunneri bararan* II (Yerevan: Yerevani Hamalsarani Hratarakch'ut'yun, 1988), p. 913.
3. See also İlhan Şahin, 'Kemah', *İslam Ansiklopedisi* 25 (Ankara: Türkiye Diyanet Vakfı, 2002), p. 219.
4. Moses Khorenats'i, *History of the Armenians*, Robert W. Thomson (trans.) (Cambridge, MA: Harvard University Press, 1978), p. 282. On the Persians' capture of Ani see also *The Epic Histories Attributed to P'awstos Buzand (Buzandaran Patmut'iwnk')*, Nina G. Garsonian (trans.) (Cambridge, MA: Harvard University Press, 1989), p. 157.
5. Moses Khorenats'i, p. 152. For a study of Armenian religious life before Christianity see James R. Russell, *Zoroastrianism in Armenia* (Cambridge, MA: Harvard University Department of Near Eastern Languages and Civilization, 1987). While I use the term 'Zoroastrian' to describe Armenian religious life in the Arsacid Period the reader should consult with Russell for a more nuanced understanding of the interaction between Hellenistic and Persian religious currents among Armenians in Late Antiquity.
6. Hakobyan, *Hayastani ew harakits' shrjanneri telanunneri bararan* II, p. 913.
7. T'.Kh. Hakobyan, et al., 'Sepuh', *Hayastani ew harakits' shrjanneri telanunneri bararan* IV (Yerevan: Yerevani Hamalsarani Hratarakch'ut'yun, 1998), p. 574.
8. Moses Khorenats'i, p. 248.
9. Moses Khorenats'i, pp. 249–50.

10. Agatʻangeḷos, *History of the Armenians*, R. W. Thomson (trans.) (Albany: State University of New York Press, 1976), p. 323.
11. Ibid., p. 325.
12. Ibid., pp. xxxviii–xl.
13. Hamazasp Oskean, *Bardzr Haykʻi vankʻerě* (Vienna: Mkhitʻarean Tparan, 1951).
14. Oskean, pp. 31–4. See also Hamza Gündoğdu et al., *Kültür Varlıkları ile Kemah* (Ankara: Kariyer Matbaacılık, 2009), pp. 67–9.
15. Oskean, pp. 3–5. See also Gündoğdu, pp. 65–6.
16. Oskean, pp. 29–31. See also Gündoğdu, pp. 59–61.
17. Michel Thierry, 'L'église martyriale triconque de Vasli (Haute Arménie)', *Revue des Études Arméniennes* 25 (1994–5): 257.
18. See Rachel Goshgarian, '*Futuwwa* in 13th-century Rum and Armenia: Reform Movements and the Managing of Multiple Allegiances in Medieval Anatolian Urban Centers on the Periphery of the Seljuk Sultanate', in A. C. S. Peacock and Sarah Nur Yıldız (eds), *The Seljuks of Anatolia: Court and Society in the Medieval Middle East* (London: I. B. Tauris, 2013), pp. 236–8. For further research on this period, see also classic articles by Levon Khachikyan, e.g., L. Khachikyan, 'Mongols in Transcaucasia', *Journal of World History* (1958): 98–125.
19. See Theo van Lint, 'Kostandin of Erznka: An Armenian Religious Poet of the XIII–XIVth Century', Dissertation of University of Leiden, 1996. See also Goshgarian, pp. 242–4.
20. Goshgarian, pp. 244–6.
21. For further discussion of cultural and intellectual life in medieval Erzincan and Kemah see Seta B. Dadoyan, *The Armenians in the Medieval Islamic World: Paradigms of Interaction, Seventh to Fourteenth Centuries*, Vol. III (London: Routledge, 2014).
22. For a transcription, see İsmet Miroğlu, *Kemah Sancağı ve Erzincan Kazası (1520–1566)* (Ankara: Türk Tarih Kurumu Basımevi, 1990), pp. 196–8.
23. Miroğlu, pp. 58–9.
24. For a detailed description of the Ani Fortress ruins see T. A. Sinclair, *Eastern Turkey: An Architectural and Archaeological Survey II* (London: Pindar Press, 1989), pp. 415–22. Although generally quite comprehensive in his survey, Sinclair did not describe the above-mentioned monasteries, noting only with respect to the Illuminator Monastery that 'The present state of the buildings is unknown. They probably survive in various states of rooflessness and dilapidation'.
25. Gündoğdu, p. 29.

26. See Vardan Arewelts'i, *Ashkharhats'oyts' Vardanay vardapeti*, Hayk Pērpērean (ed.) (Paris: Arak's, 1960), pp. 44–8.
27. Two examples – out of many – of seventeenth-century copies of Vardan Arevelts'i's geographical treatise are contained in the Mashtots' Institute of Ancient Manuscripts (Matenadaran) in Yerevan, Armenia, namely M 1903, 282a–292a, a collection from 1600; and M 2292, 70a–92b, a collection from 1624.
28. *Manr zhamanakagrut'yunner XIII–XVIII darer* II, V. A. Hakobyan (ed.) (Yerevan: Haykakan SSṚ Gitut'yunneri Akademiayi Hratarakch'ut'yun, 1956), pp. 551–2. See also *Erzeroum ou topographie de la Haute Arménie: texte armenien de Hakovb Karnetsi (XVII siècle)*, K. Kostaneants and M. Frederic Macler (eds) (Paris: Imprimerie Nationale, 1919).
29. See Robert Dankoff, '"Mığdisi": An Armenian Source for the Seyahatname', in Hakan Karateke and Hatice Aynur (eds), *Evliya Çelebi Seyahatnamesi'nin Yazılı Kaynakları* (Ankara: Türk Tarih Kurumu, 2012), p. 67.
30. A. N. Ter-Ḷevondyan, 'Eremia Ch'elepin orpes Munajjim Bashii aḷbyurnerits' mekě', *Haykakan SSṚ Gitut'yunneri Akademiayi Teḷekagir* 7–8 (1960): 143–51.
31. Kâtip Çelebi, *Kitâb-ı Cihânnümâ li-Kâtib Çelebi* I (Ankara: Türk Tarih Kurumu, 2009), p. 410. For a discussion of Armenia in medieval Islamic geographical literature see Alison Vacca, *Non-Muslim Provinces under Early Islam: Islamic Rule and Iranian Legitimacy in Armenia and Caucasian Albania* (Cambridge University Press, 2017), pp. 43–77.
32. *Evliyâ Çelebi Seyahatnâmesi*, 2/194.
33. *Evliyâ Çelebi Seyahatnâmesi*, 2/195.
34. Kâtip Çelebi, *Cihânnüma*, p. 423.
35. See Orhan Şaik Gökyay, 'Kâtip Çelebi: Hayatı, Şahsiyeti, Eserleri', *Kâtip Çelebi: Hayatı ve Eserleri Hakkında İncelemeler* (Ankara: Türk Tarih Kurumu, 1957), pp. 43–5.
36. See Caroline Finkel, *The Administration of Warfare: The Ottoman Military Campaigns in Hungary, 1593–1606* (Vienna: VWGÖ, 1988).
37. Kâtip Çelebi, *Fezleke-i Kâtip Çelebi* I (İstanbul: Ceride-i Havadis Matbaası, 1286/1869–70), p. 289. See also Kâtip Çelebi, *Fezleke [Osmanlı Tarihi (1000–1065/1591–1655)]*, Vol. I, Zeynep Aycibin (ed.) (İstanbul: Çamlıca, 2016), p. 379.
38. See Orhan Şaik Gökyay, 'Düstûrü'l-amel', *İslâm Ansiklopedisi* 10 (İstanbul: Türkiye Diyanet Vakfı, 1994), pp. 50–1.

39. Kâtip Çelebi, *Târih-i Kostantiniyye ve Kayâsire*, İbrahim Solak (ed.) (Konya: Gençlik Kitabevi Yayınevi, 2009).
40. 'Abdülkâdir (Kadrî) Efendi, *Topçular Kâtibi 'Abdülkâdir (Kadrî) Efendi Tarihi (Metin ve Tahlîl)* I, Ziya Yılmazer (ed.) (Ankara: Türk Tarih Kurumu, 2003), p. 458.
41. Among other examples, see also 'Abdülkâdir (Kadrî) Efendi, pp. 344 and 352.
42. Süleymaniye Manuscript Library, Istanbul, Esad Efendi 2236, 6a.
43. Esad Efendi 2236, 22b–23a.
44. For more about this manuscript see András J. Riedlmayer, 'Ottoman Copybooks of Correspondence and Miscellanies as a Source for Political and Cultural History', *Acta Orientalia Academiae Scientiarum Hungaricae* 61.1/2 (2008): 207; and Ayşe Pul, 'Kuyucu Murad Paşa'nın Anadolu'da Celâlilerle Mücadelesine Dair bir Osmanlı Kaynağı', *Uluslararası Sosyal Araştırmalar Dergisi* 5.20 (2012): 206–12.
45. *Evliyâ Çelebi Seyahatnâmesi*, 9/32. For similar examples, see also *Evliyâ Çelebi Seyahatnâmesi*, 9/25 and 29.
46. Ibid, 2/95. See also Anna S. Tveritinova, *Türkiye'de Kara Yazıcı-Deli Hasan İsyanı (1593-1603)*, Ali Haydar Avcı (ed.) (Ankara: Barış, 2012), p. 111. And for similar examples see *Evliyâ Çelebi Seyahatnâmesi*, 9/20 and 51.
47. *Evliyâ Çelebi Seyahatnâmesi*, 4/358.
48. Ibid., 5/122–129.
49. E.g. *Koçi Bey Risaleleri*, Seda Çakmakçıoğlu (ed.) (İstanbul: Kabalcı Yayınevi, 2007), pp. 62–3.
50. *Simēon dpri Lehats'woy ułegrut'iwn*, P. Nersēs Akinean (ed.) (Vienna: Mechitharisten, 1936), p. 187. See also *The Travel Accounts of Simēon of Poland*, George A. Bournoutian (trans.) (Costa Mesa: Mazda Publishers, 2007), p. 168. Please note that almost all studies of Simēon's work – including Bournoutian's translation – are based on Akinean's critical edition, as until recently the original manuscript was lost.
51. *Simēon dpri Lehats'woy ułegrut'iwn*, p. 188. See also *The Travel Accounts of Simēon of Poland*, p. 169.
52. *Simēon dpri Lehats'woy ułegrut'iwn*, p. 189. See also *The Travel Accounts of Simēon of Poland*, p. 170.
53. *Simēon dpri Lehats'woy ułegrut'iwn*, p. 196. See also *The Travel Accounts of Simēon of Poland*, p. 175.
54. *Simēon dpri Lehats'woy ułegrut'iwn*, p. 326. See also *The Travel Accounts of Simēon of Poland*, pp. 272–3.

55. *Simēon dpri Lehats'woy ułegrut'iwn*, p. 35. See also *The Travel Accounts of Simēon of Poland*, p. 60.
56. *Simēon dpri Lehats'woy ułegrut'iwn*, p. 332. See also *The Travel Accounts of Simēon of Poland*, p. 277.
57. *Simēon dpri Lehats'woy ułegrut'iwn*, p. 86. See also *The Travel Accounts of Simēon of Poland*, p. 98.
58. *Simēon dpri Lehats'woy ułegrut'iwn*, p. 273. See also *The Travel Accounts of Simēon of Poland*, p. 235.
59. Brief sections of Grigor's account of the Celalis have been translated into Turkish. See Hrand D. Andreasyan, 'Bir Ermeni Kaynağına Göre Celâlî İsyanları', *Tarih Dergisi* 17–18 (1962-3): 27–42.
60. Grigor Daranałts'i, pp. 24–5.
61. The medieval and early modern Armenian word for Turk was 'Tachik' (տաճիկ), not Turk. Etymologically, this word has a Semitic root (طوء/'to move') and an Aramaic variant (ṭayyāyā/pl. ṭayyāyē) was used to refer to Arab Bedouins in the Late Antique Period. The word later was adopted in Middle Persian, whence it acquired the Persian suffix 'chik'. Presumably, the Armenian word is a Middle Persian or Parthian borrowing, and its meaning gradually shifted from reference to the nomadic Arabs – who are called Arabs in early modern Armenian texts – to Muslims in general, and finally to Turks. I am grateful to Michael Cook and Lev Weitz for their generous feedback and suggestions concerning this word's etymology and history. See also the entry 'Tachik' in Hrach'ya Achaṙyan, *Hayerēn armatakan baṙaran* (Yerevan: Yeravani Hamalsarani Hratarakch'ut'yun, 1926).
62. Grigor Daranałts'i, p. 26.
63. Ibid., p. 35.
64. Ibid., pp. 35–6.
65. The authoritative work on the New Julfa Armenians is Sebouh David Aslanian, *From the Indian Ocean to the Mediterranean: The Global Trade Networks of Armenian Merchants from New Julfa* (Berkeley: University of California Press, 2011).
66. Aṙak'el Davrizhets'i, *Aṙak'el Davrizhets'i girk' patmut'eants'*, L. A. Khanlaryan (ed.) (Yerevan: Haykakan Khah GA Hratarakch'ut'yun, 1990), p. 103. See also *Aṙak'el of Tabriz: Book of History*, George A. Bournoutian (trans.) (Costa Mesa: Mazda Publishers, 2010), p. 86.
67. *Aṙak'el Davrizhets'i girk' patmut'eants'*, pp. 107–8, See also *Aṙak'el of Tabriz: Book of History*, pp. 90–2.

68. E.g. *Aṙakʻel Davrizhetsʻi girkʻ patmutʻeantsʻ*, p. 109. See also *Aṙakʻel of Tabriz: Book of History*, p. 93.
69. *Aṙakʻel Davrizhetsʻi girkʻ patmutʻeantsʻ*, p. 103. See also *Aṙakʻel of Tabriz: Book of History*, p. 86.
70. *Aṙakʻel Davrizhetsʻi girkʻ patmutʻeantsʻ*, p. 104. See also *Aṙakʻel of Tabriz: Book of History*, p. 87.
71. Sam White, *The Climate of Rebellion in The Early Modern Ottoman Empire* (Cambridge University Press, 2011), p. 183. Seventeenth-century Armenian sources offer frequent reference to drought, the weather and famine, supplying a fascinating complement to White's research in the Ottoman Archives.
72. *Aṙakʻel Davrizhetsʻi girkʻ patmutʻeantsʻ*, p. 109. See also *Aṙakʻel of Tabriz: Book of History*, p. 93.
73. For an introduction to Armenian colophons as a source for late medieval and early modern history see Avedis K. Sanjian, *Colophons of Armenian Manuscripts, 1301–1480: A Source for Middle Eastern History* (Cambridge, MA: Harvard University Press, 1969), pp. 1–41; Tom Sinclair, 'The Use of the Colophons and Minor Chronicles in the Writing of Armenian and Turkish History', *Journal of the Society of Armenian Studies* 10 (1998): 45–53; Anna Sirinian, 'On the Historical and Literary Value of the Colophons in Armenian Manuscripts', in Valentina Calzolari (ed.), *Armenian Philology in the Modern Era: From Manuscript to Digital* (Leiden: Brill, 2014); and Henry R. Shapiro, '17. Yüzyıl Osmanlı-Ermeni Sosyal ve Entelektüel Tarihine Aralanan Yeni bir Pencere: Ermenice Elyazması Kolofonlar', *Toplumsal Tarih* 265 (January 2016): 41–43.
74. *Hayeren dzeṙagreri XVII dari hishatakaranner (1601–1620 tʻvakanner)* I, Vazgen Hakobyan (ed.) (Yerevan: Haykakan SSH Gitutʻyunneri Akademiayi Hratarakchʻutʻyun: 1974), p. 439.
75. Ibid., p. 440.
76. Ibid., pp. 441–2. For contrasting accounts of this incident, see Grigor Daranaḷtsʻi, pp. 28–9 and also Tveritinova, pp. 122–3.
77. Ibid., p. 438.
78. Zulalyan, p. 228.
79. Ibid., p. 231.
80. Ibid.
81. Ibid., p. 232.
82. Garegin Sruandzteantsʻ, *Tʻoros Aḷbar* II (Istanbul: G. Baḷtatlean, 1884), pp. 374–5.

83. See Edmund M. Herzig, 'The Deportation of the Armenians in 1604–1605 and Europe's Myth of Shâh 'Abbâs I', *Pembroke Papers: Persian and Islamic Studies in Honor of P. W. Avery*, Charles Melville (ed.) (University of Cambridge Centre for Middle Eastern Studies, 1990), pp. 63–4; and Aslanian, pp. 33–4.
84. *Hayeren dzeragreri XVII dari hishatakaranner (1601–1620 t'vakanner)* I, p. 288.
85. Ibid., p. 289.
86. For example, a similar story about starving familes slaughtering their children because of the 1607 famine also exists in a seventeenth-century Muslim sheykh's Arabic history. See Ş. Receb-üs Sıvâsî, *Hidâyet Yıldızı: Şems-ed-dîn-i Sıvâsî Hazretlerinin Menkıbeleri* (İstanbul: Seçil Ofset, 2000), p. 85.
87. Classic work by the twelfth-century Armenian author Nerses Shnorhali. See Nerses Shnorhali, *Yisus ordi* (Yerevan: Apolon Hratarakch'ut'yun, 1991). This work was printed multiple times during the seventeenth century.
88. *Manr zhamanakagrut'yunner XIII–XVIII darer*, 246–7.
89. See Hasmik Sahakyan (ed.), *Hay ashuḷner (XVII–XVIII darer)* (Yerevan: Haykakan SSṚ GA Hratarakch'ut'yun, 1961).
90. See Nerses Mokats'i, *Banasteḷtsut'yunner*, A. G. Dolukhanyan (ed.) (Yerevan: Haykakan SSH GA Hratarakch'ut'yun, 1975).
91. Ḷ Alishan (ed.), *Hayapatum* (Venice: S. Ḷazar, 1901), p. 605.
92. Alishan, *Hayapatum*, p. 606.
93. Ibid., pp. 608–9.
94. Ibid., p. 609.
95. *Hayeren dzeragreri XVII dari hishatakaranner (1601–1620 t'vakanner)* I, pp. 437–8.
96. For more about the 'circle of justice' see Linda T. Darling, *A History of Social Justice and Political Power in the Middle East: The Circle of Justice from Mesopotamia to Globalization* (London: Routledge, 2013).
97. See Leslie P. Peirce, *The Imperial Harem: Women and Sovereignty in the Ottoman Empire* (Oxford University Press, 1993).
98. Metin Kunt, *The Sultan's Servants: The Transformation of Ottoman Provincial Government, 1550–1650* (Columbia University Press, 1983), p. 95.
99. Ibid., pp. 70–1.
100. Grigor Daranaḷts'i, pp. 13–15.
101. Kunt, pp. 79–80.

102. Baki Tezcan, *The Second Ottoman Empire: Political and Social Transformations in the Early Modern World* (Cambridge University Press, 2010), pp. 141–5.
103. For a visual representation of the situation's complexity, see Oktay Özel, 'The Reign of Violence: The Celalis, 1550–1700', in Christine Woodhead (ed.), *The Ottoman World* (London: Routledge, 2012), p. 192.
104. *Hayeren dzeṙagreri XVII dari hishatakaranner (1601–1620 tʻvakanner)* I, p. 448.
105. Ibid., p. 449.
106. Ibid., p. 289.
107. *Hayeren dzeṙagreri XVII dari hishatakaranner (1621–1640 tʻvakanner)* II, Vazgen Hakobyan (ed.) (Yerevan: Haykakan SSṘ Gitutʻyunneri Akademiayi Hratarakchʻutʻyun: 1978), p. 54.
108. Zulalyan, p. 228.
109. Gohar Grigoryan, 'Two Armenian Manuscripts in Switzerland (with an annotated translation of a newly-found abridgement of the Commentary of Canon Tables attributed to Stepʻanos Siwnecʻi)', *Le Muséon* 133 (2020): 97–8.
110. *Simēon dpri Lehatsʻwoy uḷegrutʻiwn*, p. 217. See also *The Travel Accounts of Simēon of Poland*, p. 193.
111. *Simēon dpri Lehatsʻwoy uḷegrutʻiwn*, p. 41. See also *The Travel Accounts of Simēon of Poland*, p. 64.
112. Grigor Daranaḷtsʻi, p. 18.
113. Ibid., p. 476.
114. *Aṙakʻel Davrizhetsʻi girkʻ patmutʻeantsʻ*, p. 109. See also *Aṙakʻel of Tabriz: Book of History*, pp. 92–3.
115. Alishan, *Hayapatum*, pp. 605–6.
116. Ibid., p. 608.
117. Ibid., p. 609.
118. Martiros Ḷrimetsʻi, *Martiros Ḷrimetsʻi: Usumnasirutʻyun ew bnagrer*, A. A. Martirosyan (ed.) (Yerevan: Haykakan SSṘ GA Hratarakchʻutʻyun, 1958), pp. 150–1.
119. E.g. Grigor Daranaḷtsʻi, pp. 28–9, 32.
120. Ibid., pp. 37–8.
121. Ibid., p. 41.
122. Ibid., pp. 77–8.
123. Ibid., p. 510.
124. Ibid., p. 513.

125. Ibid., p. 518.
126. Ibid., p. 507.
127. Ibid., pp. 507–8.
128. Sruandzteants', *Erker* II, p. 352, emphasis added.

3

An Armenian Refugee Crisis in Ottoman Rodosto (Tekirdağ)

The present chapter provides an introduction to Ottoman Rodosto (Tekirdağ) and describes the arrival of Armenian refugees from Anatolia – mainly Kemah and its vicinity – as recounted by Ottoman Turkish court records (*şer'iyye sicilleri*) and the written testament of the second Armenian bishop of Rodosto, Grigor Daranalts'i. An Armenian community did not exist in Rodosto until the arrival of Celali refugees, and I describe in detail the struggles they faced as refugees upon their initial arrival, as well as their gradual efforts to build new lives, which involved the establishment of Armenian churches and an Armenian neighbourhood. Thereafter, I consider several Ottoman cities – namely Istanbul, Izmir, Rodosto, Balıkesir and Izmit – suggesting that the vast majority of Armenians in Western Anatolia, Istanbul and Thrace, who constituted the new Western Armenian Diaspora in the seventeenth century, were the descendants of Celali refugees. In short, the refugee crisis in Rodosto is but one example of a much broader demographic shift of Armenians from Greater Armenia to western parts of the Ottoman Empire.

Rodosto (Tekirdağ) at the Turn of the Seventeenth Century

To this day Rodosto – which now goes solely by the Turkish name Tekirdağ – is a quaint coastal town in Thrace approximately 140 km from central Istanbul (see Figure 3.1). A settlement has been present there since antiquity and it is mentioned both by Herodotus and Xenophon under the name Bisanthe. The name Rodosto – written *Rodosçuk* in the Ottoman Turkish documents – was predominant in Ottoman times, though both seventeenth-century Armenian and Ottoman Turkish sources note that it was sometimes

Figure 3.1 Rodosto (contemporary Tekirdağ).

called *Tekfurdağı*, meanings 'king's mount' in Turkish. The word *tekfur* likely derives from the Armenian word for 'king' and it was commonly used by the early Ottomans to refer to Byzantine lords. The city receives scant reference in the seventeenth-century Ottoman chronicle tradition, though it was sometimes mentioned as a way station on the journey from Gallipoli to Istanbul[1] and perusal of the chronicles also reveals that a boat could be taken from Istanbul to Rodosto's port as a short cut on the journey to Edirne.[2] The occasional references to Rodosto in the Ottoman chronicles fail to convey its critical role in provisioning seventeenth-century Istanbul.

Rodosto's use as an alternative port for Istanbul gave it great economic importance in the early modern period. Its granaries stored grain produced in Thrace, which could be sent for sale and consumption in Istanbul, while iron from Samokov and rice from Plovdiv in Bulgaria were also shipped to Istanbul via Rodosto.[3] Evliya Çelebi – whose range of interests was broader than the Ottoman chroniclers – noted the importance of its port. In his description of 'paradise-like Tekirdağ' he writes that ships from 'the ports of Egypt and all the coasts of the Black Sea and of the Mediterranean' come to Rodosto and that their goods can reach Edirne in two days.[4] Rodosto lay on a branch of the famous Roman Via Egnatia, which extended from Istanbul to the Adriatic Sea,[5] and near to the military road from Istanbul to Belgrade (via Edirne) that was used by Ottoman troops marching to the Hungarian front during the campaigns of 1593–1606.[6] At the turn of the seventeenth century Rodosto was secure Ottoman territory that could supply provisions to the capital city and to troops marching on campaign,[7] far from the disruption of wars with the Hapsburgs or Persians or the rebellion in the East.

By the beginning of the twentieth century, Rodosto's population was primarily composed of Greeks, Turks and Armenians, with a population of 19,000 Greeks, 14,000 Turks and 7,600 Armenians.[8] As was the case in nineteenth-century Istanbul, Rodosto's three main spoken languages were Greek, Turkish and Armenian, and many of its inhabitants were to some degree trilingual. Henri Verneuil (née Ashot Malak'ean) – a dean of twentieth-century French suspense cinema and a Rodosto native – recalls that when he arrived as a child refugee in Marseilles in 1924, his father tried to find a house to rent by walking up and down the port inquiring in Greek, Turkish and Armenian.[9] At the turn of the twentieth century Rodosto's Armenian community was vibrant, possessing several churches and schools and even a local magazine.[10] Little evidence of this remains today, but memory of the Armenian past has been preserved in Western Armenian local history and also in fiction, most notably the Bulgarian-Armenian diplomat Sevda Sevan's historical novel *Rodosto, Rodosto . . .*[11] There are twentieth-century local histories of Rodosto in Greek, Modern Turkish and Western Armenian, focusing on their own community's past, neighbourhoods and buildings.[12]

In the seventeenth century Rodosto's ethnic, linguistic and religious diversity was richer than these three communities' introverted memories imply. Largely forgotten are the ethnically Georgian (*Gürcü*) and Russian (*Rus*) concubines (*câriye*), the Bulgarians (*Bulgar*), the Albanian Christians (*Arnavut*), the gypsies (*Çingene*), the Catholics (*Latin*), both semi-nomadic and settled Turkmen (*Yürük*)[13] and the Jewish (*Yahûdî*) tax-farmers, whose names appear so frequently in the Rodosto court records of the early seventeenth century. But stone lasts longer than both people and memory. Three nineteenth-century Armenian tombstones are currently in storage in the backyard of the Tekirdağ Archaeology and Ethnography Museum, and farmers continue to unearth fragments with Armenian writing all over the region, often duly reporting them to museum authorities who photograph and record them.[14] Moreover, the Jewish cemetery of Rodosto remains largely intact. It is only a short walk away from the modern bus station and contains many tombstones in Judaeo-Spanish (Ladino). More importantly for our purposes, the Ottoman Turkish court records of the Prime Ministerial Archives in Istanbul preserves the names, religions and oftentimes the ethno-linguistic groups of all these peoples and more, recorded along with their legal business and a date.

Rodosto provides an ideal case study for the Great Armenian Flight for several reasons. Firstly, there was not a significant Armenian community in Rodosto until the turn of the seventeenth century. This is strongly implied both by sixteenth-century Ottoman Turkish cadastral surveys of Rodosto (*tahrîr defterleri*), and by the Ottoman Turkish court records (*şer'iyye sicilleri*), for which notebooks (*defter*) survive from the mid-sixteenth century (1546/953) until the beginning of the nineteenth century (1808/1222). Within this broad expanse of time there is an unbroken series of notebooks for the turn of the seventeenth century, providing records of cases at Rodosto's Islamic court both before and after the Armenian emigrants' arrival.

Both the Rodosto cadastral surveys and a selection of court records have already been studied by Turkish scholars. A study of Rodosto's court records of 1546–53 notes almost no mention of Armenians, suggesting that 'it is tempting to conclude that the Armenian settlement probably came into being after the mid-sixteenth century; however, further studies on court records must be implemented before a definitive conclusion can be made'.[15] A thorough study of urbanisation in Rodosto in the sixteenth and seventeenth centuries by Hacer Ateş notes that there is no mention whatsoever of Armenians in the sixteenth-century cadastral surveys. Ateş did pinpoint the Armenians' arrival to Rodosto to the turn of the seventeenth century and she charted the city's seventeenth-century demographic shifts.[16] Ateş merely observes these shifts, however, and does not document the story of the Armenians' contentious arrival or explain the demographic shock's broader implications for the field of Ottoman history. This chapter does precisely that, focusing on the period of the Armenians' first arrival in Rodosto, between 1595 and 1611, and also examining later records from 1620–2 and 1629–32.

Another sharp difference in this chapter's treatment of Rodosto is its reliance on a major Armenian narrative source in conjunction with the Ottoman Turkish court records, namely the *Chronicle of Grigor Daranałts'i*, written by Rodosto's second Armenian bishop. This chronicle survives in a sole manuscript copy – located at the Armenian Patriarchate of Jerusalem – which was transcribed and published by Mesrop Nshanean in 1915.[17] It is the confluence of a complete set of court records spanning the period both before and after the Armenians' arrival, combined with the narrative testament of an eyewitness to the Armenians' settlement that makes Rodosto an ideal case study for the Great Armenian Flight. Conclusions made on the basis of analysis of sources about Rodosto in Armenian and Ottoman Turkish will then be broadened by comparison with demographic data about Armenians in other Ottoman cities of Western Anatolia that were also destinations for Celali refugees.

The Armenians' Arrival According to Grigor Daranałts'i

Grigor Daranałts'i first came to Rodosto in 1607, only two days after the arrival of the man newly installed as Rodosto's first Armenian bishop, Yakob. Grigor recounts their meetings as follows:

> ... it was in 1056 (1607), when we came and went up to Little Ĕratōz (Rodosto), which now is called *Dağı* (Tekirdağ), on account of its being near a small mountain, and *Vardapet* Yakob was here, having come from Istanbul with edicts of the grandees and with an order of the king, Sultan Ahmed, and with the supporting aid of Halil Paşa, who was at that time the Janissary *Ağası*, and he was a local and a close relation of *Vardapet* Yakob. He brought an order and legal verdict (*emir* and *fetva*), as here were newly come people, all from our land and from our villages [Kemah], many were our people [Armenian]. He had taken an order to lead all of these people, especially for the construction of a church, a house of prayer. And at the time we met, he had been [here] two days. And when we met one another, he embraced us with much rejoicing, just as a father grows tender over his beloved son, so did he grow tender over us ... .[18]

The passage clearly states that Yakob was formally commissioned both to lead the newly arrived Armenians in Rodosto and to build their first church. Grigor later also writes that 'when [Yakob] built [the church] it was 1056 (1607), and he remained nine months after the construction. He passed away on June 18, 1057 (1608), and he was buried in his own handiwork, within the portico of the church, with three other priests'.[19]

With regards to the state of the newly arrived Armenian refugees, Grigor writes that

> Here [in Rodosto] there was no place to stay, as everyone was newly arrived and they [the Armenians] were in the houses of the Turks and Rum, entering under tight and difficult and narrow roofs they were dwelling. Two households and three households were dwelling with one another in one house, according to the word of prophecy of Nerses the Great, who says that 'They go out from wide and spacious houses and they go and enter under a tight and difficult and narrow roof.' Scarcely could they find lodging for a *vardapet* in an Armenian household.[20]

In addition to these general statements about the Armenians' lack of homes and lodging, and their cramped living conditions, Grigor recounts a series of clashes between the newly arrived Armenians, the Ottoman authorities and Rodosto's Greek natives.

Immediately after describing his first meeting with Yakob, Grigor narrates an argument among the Armenian priests of Rodosto that led directly to confrontation with the local Ottoman officialdom. According to Grigor, a certain priest named Nalash Lazar claimed precedence over his local peers, a claim which his fellows rejected. A fight broke out, and ultimately the priests gave Nalash a beating. In vengeance, Nalash chose to slander the Rodosto Armenians to the judge (*kadı*) of the local Islamic court, claiming that he learned from private confessions that the Armenian men were 'profaning the Muslim women and servant girls of the city'.[21] In response to this claim, Grigor writes that the *kadı* became enraged, exclaiming,

> Woe upon that Muslim or local non-Muslim (*yerli gâvur*), who after three days lets an Armenian man or couple in their house, for rent or without charge. Cast them out of your homes and drive them from the city and from all your borders.[22]

In response to this order, the newly arrived Armenians were thrown out of their new homes, and they 'filled the streets of the city and far outside it'.[23] Daranalts'i laments that

> After these misfortunes, torrents of rain descended from the sky and it was muddy and cold, [there was] fear [and] dread of plunderers and looters, and we were like sheep wandering and falling abandoned into the hands of murderous wolves. We did not know what to do. Many said that . . . 'Since a so-called priest acted in this way – he betrayed such a multitude to death – we do not need such a faith. Tomorrow at dawn let's go to the court, let's turn to the laws of Muhammad and to apostasy from our native faith and let's be like them [the Muslims].'[24]

Grigor writes that he and the other priests were able to convince the Armenian refugees to change their minds and to remain Christian. But around that time there were some Rodosto Armenians who did choose conversion, as will be seen later in this chapter. Grigor chooses to pass over their stories.

After averting mass apostasy, the Armenian priests of Rodosto then began seeking means to convince the *kadı* to rescind his order. They visited the 'grandees of the city',[25] and though lacking the means to give a bribe they won sympathy by offering to work in their vineyards. Grigor recounts that the grandees interceded on the Armenians' behalf with the judge, censuring him for making such an order on the testimony of just one witness.

All of this took place in 1607, immediately after Grigor's first visit to Rodosto. The Rodosto Armenian community's next trial would come in 1609, when the Ottoman state made an attempt to send the refugees in Istanbul and its environs back to Anatolia. Daranalts'i describes how soon after the return of Kuyucu Murad Paşa from his successful campaign against the Celalis at the beginning of 1609, the state sent messengers around Istanbul to proclaim in the sultan's words that 'In three months, all those who came from Anatolia, every race and people, see to your preparations, so that you might be ready (*hazır*). I am making a forced migration (*sürgün*), [and] I will send all to their native places'.[26] This order prompted widespread attempts at evasion, with some Armenians gaining permission to remain in Istanbul because they were working on the construction of the Sultan Ahmed Mosque.

The Rodosto Armenians fared far better than those of Istanbul, gaining a mass exemption. Daranaḷtsʻi recounts that

> They did not move a single man from his place in our Rodosto on account of agriculture. Going [to Istanbul], [the Rodosto Armenians] requested [the following] writ from the vizier: 'Grant us a time of pardon until autumn, when we will gather the produce of our labors in the soil. Whatever we have we have deposited in the ground. We don't have any money, all our earnings are in the soil.' On account of this they took a writ, and delaying they were forgotten and remained.[27]

The Rodosto Armenians were able to gain a similar exemption, on the basis of precedent, when the state again attempted to deport refugees back to Anatolia in 1635, thanks in part to the intervention of a lady at court on their behalf.[28]

The next major episode in Grigor's chronicle regarding the Rodosto Armenians relates to a frequent theme in seventeenth-century Armenian literature: Greek-Armenian animosity. According to Grigor's narrative, in December 1620 a Greek girl married an Armenian man. This, it seems, was an unacceptable marriage in the eyes of Rodosto's Greek community. Grigor claims that he did not allow them to get married in church 'on account of fear of deceitful and perverse races', and thus the couple married at home instead.[29] As a result of the marriage, a dangerous and destructive dispute quickly erupted between the Greek (often called 'Romans' in the Armenian text) and Armenian communities of Rodosto. According to Daranaḷtsʻi,

> The Turkish people, seeing that [the mixed marriage] is a great evil in the eyes of the Greeks, began to jest and mock, ridiculing the entire race of Romans. [The Greeks], not being able to bear the ridicule and taunting, rose in the night [under] a clear and limpid moon, [and] going to the gardens of the Armenians, they destroyed all the trees [of] up to sixteen gardens. After that they returned [and] united with the local Turks and incited them against us, [saying] that 'We and you are of this place, but they [the Armenians], alien and foreign, came [and] took our patrimony, our fields, gardens, and all our land, and they do not give one cent in taxes. Now, come with unanimity, drive them from our country, so that it may be our patrimony again.' And with such an evil unanimity they became allies in evil: fifty grandees of the

Turks wrote a letter (*mestûr*) and sealed it (*mühür*), and they gave it into the hands of the Romans. They sent sixty people to Istanbul to protest to the Caesar [Sultan] about the Armenians.[30]

According to Grigor the Rodosto Armenians were able to defend themselves with effective evasive manoeuvres at the Ottoman court. In particular, he explained that the Armenians had allies there, including a beloved courtier of Sultan Osman II who was of Armenian origin. Moreover, he writes, the grand vizier at the time was the 'adopted brother'[31] of the Armenian courtier, and thus when the Rodosto Greek delegation arrived before the vizier, he 'frothed with anger at them and tore up the letter (*mestûr*)'.[32] As for the Greek girl, Grigor writes that the Rodosto Greeks seized her and brought her to the *kadı* to become a Muslim, yelling that 'It's better she be a Turk than an Armenian'.[33] In order to be with his beloved, the Armenian youth also converted to Islam, and Grigor recounts that the couple ran away together as soon as the lad recovered from his circumcision. Grigor concludes the story by pondering on the Fall of Troy: how for one girl, a great city and people perished. He writes that 'in this our city [Rodosto] our Armenian race was almost destroyed as well, but the solicitude of God and His visitation did not permit it'.[34]

The next Rodosto-Armenian crisis recounted in Grigor Daranałts'i's chronicle is depicted as an act of injustice by a state official. He describes how 'a certain sergeant (*çavuş*) kidnapped a Roman child'.[35] The Greek bishop sent a letter to Grigor, requesting that he help the Greeks now, since 'today it is us, [but] tomorrow it will be you',[36] and thus the Greeks and Armenians went together to the *kadı* and won the boy's release. The resentment caused by this victory, however, led to backlash. According to Daranałts'i,

> All of them [the Turks] resolved with unanimity on evil for the Romans and Armenians, that they take their revenge and shake off the bitterness of poison on the Armenians and the Greeks. And at that troubled time of agitations, suddenly from the influence of evil came an inspector (*teftişçi*) with many forces over the evil assembly of lawless [men], and storming them they complained firstly against the Romans, that they took a Turk, [and] they made him an Armenian and infidel (*gâvur*). And they Turkified a deacon, and the leader of the Romans, who they called Yankarak, they hung him,

and they were demanding the Roman bishop, so that they might kill him, [but] he had recently passed away to God. And after that, they turned upon our church, complaining that so long [ago] they built the church without basis (*temelsiz*) by bribes. [They were] saying this and other things, until they took an order to destroy it. There you would have seen that like a swarm of locusts they ran altogether, a multitude of atheists, over the poor church to destroy it . . .[37]

It is with this rather convoluted story that Grigor describes the destruction of Yakob's Archangel Church, the first Armenian church of Rodosto, in 1629.

This act of destruction would begin a long process in which the Rodosto Armenian community would seek both to seize existing churches and to build new religious spaces, a process that led to further conflict between Rodosto's Greek and Armenian communities. According to Grigor, some Turks felt badly for the Armenians after the loss of their church, and they suggested that they take a church from the Greeks – who supposedly had twelve churches in Rodosto – and give it to the Armenians. The Armenians were ultimately able to procure the St Yovhannēs Church for themselves from the Greeks in 1629, after organising a fundraising campaign in order to bribe Ottoman officials, a process in which Grigor played a leading role.[38] But according to the twentieth-century Rodosto historian Sargis G. P'ach'achean, the Armenians were not satisfied with this church because it was in a Greek neighbourhood, and thus they gradually began to build the Holy King (Redeemer) Church on the location of the destroyed Archangel Church.[39] It seems that Grigor may have exaggerated the number of Orthodox churches in Rodosto, or perhaps he included churches and monasteries in the general region. In either case, his numbers are difficult to reconcile with the testimony of Evliya Çelebi, who wrote that 'in total there are seven infidel churches [in Tekirdağ] . . . The Rum churches are few but they are seemly . . .'[40]

Finally, the last major issue discussed in Grigor's chronicle that explicitly relates to the Rodosto Armenians was the question of communal leadership. Note has already been made of Yakob's order to lead the Armenian refugees. Grigor also provides the story of his own rise to leadership over the Rodosto Armenian community, claiming that he assumed official leadership of the Rodosto Armenians in 1609. After recounting a long series of conflicts with the Armenian Patriarch in Constantinople, he concludes his narrative by stating that

> After a few days they sent an intermediary [from the patriarch], [saying] 'Let him come, so that you may reconcile, and we will grant him Rodosto with all its Armenians. One thousand *stak*[41] per year he will always give . . .' And taking us they brought us to St Sargis Church, near to the patriarch. When we saluted, this time he accepted our salute with love, and we kissed one another and sat down. And he wrote a writ of term, and leaving we bid him well. And taking the writ we went to the Topkapı [neighborhood]. And after a few days we left and came to Rodosto, our second homeland, and we stayed here for a while.[42]

While Grigor refers to himself as a *vardapet* and the modern Armenian secondary literature calls him an Armenian community leader, it is clear that he had the power to ordain priests, and thus he should be referred to as Rodosto's bishop.[43] Grigor's tenure as Rodosto's Armenian bishop would formally last until his death in 1643.

Neither Yakob nor Grigor's appointment documents appear among the Rodosto court records. Nevertheless it is likely that this documentation did exist, given many precedents known from research on the Ottoman Empire's Orthodox Christian hierarchy. For example, the Rodosto court records include a warrant of authority for the Orthodox bishop of Rodosto in an imperial order dated to 23 Cumâdelûlâ 1017 (4 September 1608).[44] Tom Papademetriou's work on the Greek Orthodox Church in the fifteenth and sixteenth centuries presents analyses of many such diplomas of privileges (*berats*) and emphasises that ecclesiastical leadership in the early modern Ottoman Empire entailed not only spiritual oversight of Christians but also financial responsibilities to the state.[45]

In sum, Grigor narrates that Rodosto's first Armenian bishop, Yakob, was appointed in 1607 to lead the newly arrived Armenian refugees, mostly from Kemah, and to build a church. A short time after Yakob's death, Grigor was appointed leader of the Rodosto Armenians by order of the Armenian patriarch in Istanbul, and his authority was purportedly backed up by official documentation. Grigor describes ongoing conflict between the Armenian and Greek communities of Rodosto, conflict mediated by Ottoman officials and the sultan's court in Istanbul. These conflicts were decided via bribes and with allies, usually Ottoman officials with some Armenian ancestry. Grigor states that the Greeks, on the other hand, sometimes appealed to the Turks on the basis of their common indigenous land rights to Rodosto vis-à-vis the newly arrived Armenians. Finally, he emphasises the great hardship that the Armenian refugees faced upon their first arrival in Rodosto, particularly their lack of lodgings and need to rent from Greeks and Turks, and the long struggle they waged to procure sacred spaces.

Grigor's account should not be accepted without question, however, particularly given the outlandish nature of some of his stories and his own role in Ottoman Armenian church politics. In the next two sections, I will consider the same time period from a completely different perspective, that of the records of the Rodosto Islamic court between 1595 and 1611, the years when the Armenians first arrived in the town, followed by investigation of records from 1620–2 and 1629–32. By comparing Grigor's narrative with the testament of the Rodosto court records, common themes and divergences will emerge.

The First Arrival and Settlement of Rodosto Armenians According to Rodosto Islamic Court Records (*Şer'iyye sicilleri*): 1595–1611

Before analysing records of the Rodosto Islamic court a note of warning is in order about the nature of this source genre. It has been argued that modern scholars' lack of familiarity with, for instance, strategies employed by claimants before the judge or how different segments of society used the courts at different rates can lead to distorted understandings of communities under investigation using court records.[46] Such warnings are undoubtedly warranted and attention must certainly be given to the court registers' historical contexts and regional variation of legal practice. For example, Ronald Jennings's study of sixteenth- and seventeenth-century Cyprus court records strongly implies that the Orthodox Christians must have retained an alternative legal system for themselves post-conquest,[47] given that the vast majority of the island's population at the time was non-Muslim, while the percentage of court records involving only non-Muslims was low, wavering between eight per cent and seventeen per cent in the registers covering the years 1580–1637.[48] It is clear that court records alone would leave researchers with a distorted view of non-

Muslim society in Ottoman Cyprus. That being said, overgeneralised warnings of caution are unhelpful because they apply to almost any pre-modern primary source, all of which bear their own particular intricacies and must be carefully considered in context. This author considers it justified to rely on the court records for data about facts on the ground as long as they are checked against other primary sources and carefully considered in light of their context, both historical and textual.

Preliminary note should also be given with regards to how it is possible to distinguish Greeks, Armenians and other Christians from one another in court records. For Muslims, it is usually impossible to make such distinctions along linguistic or ethnic lines, because epithets implying Islamic faith are used for almost all Muslims no matter what their provenance or mother tongue.[49] In the Rodosto court records of the first decade of the seventeenth century, however, the general term *zimmi* was not used for non-Muslims in general, but only for Christians bearing Greek names, unless there was additional qualification. Armenians, Bulgarians, Albanians and other Christians were almost always listed according to their ethno-linguistic group, not by use of the general term *zimmi*. The Rodosto court's scribes seem to have considered the archetypal non-Muslim to have been Greek, probably because they were the largest non-Muslim group in the region and since they were indigenous. The scribes distinguished between all other groups, however, making it very easy to differentiate Armenians from Greeks in the Rodosto court records. Moreover, non-Muslims appear in the Rodosto court records frequently to resolve internal affairs. While there may have been other legal forums for Christians, it is clear that the Islamic court was a forum that was frequently employed by Greeks and Armenians alike, along with Muslims and a diversity of other peoples. Nearly every page of a typical notebook from the Rodosto court contains at least one *sicil* entry involving only Christians.

Few Armenians appear in sixteenth-century Rodosto court records, but Kemah Armenians slowly began to arrive at the very end of the century. Each of these early documents offers a valuable glimpse of the vanguard in an important demographic shift. In the course of the first decade of the seventeenth century cases concerning Armenians become more frequent. While I use a chronological approach to consider the first Armenian refugees in Rodosto, the increased quantity of documentation that appears in 1605 allows for a shift to consideration of common themes, such as conversion, sartorial violations, surety (*kefîl*) for Armenian refugees, Armenians' occupation and housing and the refugees' tax-status.

The first Kemah Armenians before the Rodosto court

While it has been noted above that the sixteenth-century cadastral surveys of Rodosto make no mention of Armenians or any Armenian neighbourhoods it would be wrong to state absolutely that there were no Armenians living in Rodosto. None of the sixteenth-century *defters* studied in this investigation lacked mention of Armenians, but reference to them is quite scant in early *defters*. For example, documents covering the years 994–5 (1585–7)[50] contain more than 1,700 distinct documents, but only one of them mentions Armenians. Moreover, the single case in which Armenians are mentioned is unclear about their place of origin. According to the document, the porters of the Rodosto port complained because Armenians were unloading goods from ships without permission and the porters demanded that they be registered or forbidden access.[51] Were these Armenians some of the few locals who lived there before the Great Flight, were they early arrivals from Anatolia working illegally at the docks, or were they coming off the boats from Istanbul? The answers to these questions are unknown.

Likewise, documents covering the years 1004–5 (1595–7)[52] contain only one mention of an Armenian in a document written sidewise on the bottom margin of a page. That case involved a convert to Islam named Mustafa, who states that 'I had been an infidel from the Armenians . . . Glory be to God, I became a Muslim'.[53] No mention is made, however, of his provenance. It is unclear whether he was a local Rodosto Armenian or an early refugee.

In the following *defter*, however, records of both Armenian and Muslim refugees from Kemah begin to appear. Documents covering the years 1005–7 (1597–9)[54] contain four cases about Armenians.[55] Unlike the previous two ambiguous cases, however, the provenance of the refugees is sometimes explicitly stated. For example, one court record written at the beginning of the month of Rebî'ü'l-evvel in 1007 (October 1598) introduces an Armenian who appeared before the court explaining that he was 'formerly from the residents of the town named Vasil, bound to the district of Kemah in the province of Anatolia, [but] now is settled in the city of Rodosto . . .'.[56] This man from Vaslı – near to the Monastery of the King discussed in Chapter Two – appeared before the court to officially renounce his Armenian fiancé, stating that he had changed his mind and anyone who wanted could marry her. These documents are significant because the Western Armenian secondary literature on Rodosto explicitly states that the Kemah Armenians arrived in 1605,[57] soon before Grigor Daranalts'i. These court records, however, prove that some Armenian refugees settled several years before, at the end of the sixteenth century.

The next *defter* contains only one case involving an Armenian. The document, dating from the end of Ramazân 1007 (April 1599) records a case about a missing Armenian youth. The first witness to his disappearance was the youth's father, Menok, 'from the residents of the town named Kemah in the province of Erzurum'. Menok is recorded as testifying that four months prior a Jewish woman named Kalahi invited his son to her house in order to pay him to convey a letter to her husband Yagob in Galipoli. 'Since that time he [the Armenian youth] has been lost . . . we think that he was murdered in their house'.[58] The document also contains the testimony of Kalahi and various local Muslims regarding the circumstances of the youth's disappearance, all agreeing that the youth disappeared on the road after leaving Kalahi's house and departing on the journey for Galipoli with his pay and the letter. As is usually the case in Ottoman court registers, no verdict is provided.

Documents covering the years 1008–9 (1599–1601)[59] contain four cases involving Armenians about debts and financial issues,[60] while those covering the years 1009–10 (1601–2)[61] contain seven entries.[62] One of them describes an Armenian who is unable to pay his debts but is granted a three-month extension on repayment.[63] Three others concern a Kemah Armenian who passed away, leaving a very small estate worth ten *kuruş* and no heir to claim it.[64]

By far the longest and most significant of the cases recorded in this *defter*, however, describes a tense dispute between a group of five Armenian labourers (*ırgat*) and local Ottoman constables (*subaşı*). This document, dated Sâfer 1010 (August 1601), includes the testimony of several parties, beginning with the Armenian labourers. They testified that

We, a group of Armenians, were laying down in a room (*oda*) near to the bathhouse (*hamâm*) of the late Mehmed Paşa. After the evening prayer, the above-mentioned constable Hüseyin with a group of men raided our room. 'Open the door,' they said. When from fear we did not open it, with their arms and pipes they broke off a few stones of the brick building above the door, and they entered. 'Where is the money?' they said. They beat us and they drove us out. That day we had taken 4500 *akçe* from *cebeci* Hasan Bali, and he took all of that money from our hands and put us in jail. What is our sin? We demand our right (*hakkımız*).

In response to this accusation, constable Hüseyin states that he was out on patrol that night when he saw two people running away from him. Hüseyin claims that he followed the two to the Armenians' room and that this was why he asked them to open the door. But he says that the Armenians claimed that the fugitives weren't among us and that no one had entered. 'I arrested one or two of them,' constable Hüseyin claimed, 'but I didn't take any money.' But another witness, constable Mehmed, contradicted a key part of Hüseyin's testimony. While agreeing that they were chasing two men who had run off, he notes that Hüseyin took 180 *akçe*, though he declared no knowledge of the remaining sum the Armenians claimed to have lost. The document ends by officially registering the following statement:

> The Muslims whose names are written in appendage, say that the above-mentioned Hire Mehmed is always a cause of intrigue (*bâ'is-i fesâd*) and an originator of sedition (*bâdî-i fitne*). Henceforth, we don't want him to be a constable (*subaşı*) in our town.

They also declared that the other constable, Hüseyin, had 'tormented many Muslims without reason', and that they did not want him in the town either.[65]

This case is important for understanding Armenians' arrival in Rodosto for several reasons. Firstly, it describes a group of Armenian labourers who seem to be living in one ad hoc room (*oda*) together, similar to the 'rooms for single men (*bekar odaları*)' common in Turkey today. This living situation corresponds with the housing crisis described by Grigor. Moreover, it reinforces Grigor's description of the hardships endured by the Armenian refugees upon arrival in Rodosto by documenting wrongful entry, theft, beating and imprisonment of Armenians by two Rodosto constables. Finally, it concludes in a way that is atypical for an Ottoman *sicil*. While normally the verdict is withheld in these documents and the modern reader is unable to discern the results of the case, this document explicitly declares that the Muslims present at court sympathised with the Armenians and outlawed the rogue constables. In this instance the Islamic court proved to be a successful means of recourse for the victimised Armenian refugees, who at the very least were able to see their persecutors fired and disgraced, even if no mention is made about retrieval of the money they lost.

There are numerous cases involving Armenians in subsequent Rodosto court registers. For instance, in documents covering the years 1010–12 (1602–4)[66] there are nine such entries.[67] Moreover, there are also cases about Muslims from Kemah who might be formerly Armenian converts to Islam.

One document in the *defter* mentions a group of Muslims named 'Ali bin Müslü and Mehmed bin Abdullâh and Süleymân bin Abdullâh and Mustafa bin Abdullâh from the district of Kemah in the region of Erzurum in the Anatolia Province'. At first glance this document seems to be about Muslims from Kemah who emigrated to Rodosto along with their Armenian countrymen. In 1609, when Sultan Ahmed issued his proclamation sending emigrants back to Eastern Anatolia, two camps left Istanbul: one composed of Armenians led by Grigor and one composed of Muslims. Neither the Great Flight nor the return edicts were phenomena that affected only one religious community. Upon second glance, however, it seems likely that three of these Muslims might have been converts to Islam. It is well attested in Ottoman historical secondary literature that converts to Islam were often listed as 'bin Abdullâh'. Were these three Muslims brothers the sons of a father named Abdullâh or were they converts to Islam? It is impossible to tell. In any case, Ali must have been a Muslim from Kemah who migrated to Rodosto with his Armenian compatriots. He serves as a reminder that the refugee crisis in Rodosto described here was not only an Armenian phenomenon.

This document describes a case of theft. A certain Muslim named Dervîş Çelebi went to Istanbul, and while he was gone he allowed Mustafa to sleep in his house. Mehmed and Ali asked Mustafa if Dervîş Çelebi had money, and they convinced him to be an accomplice in theft. Mustafa informed them when Derviş Çelebi's wife, Fatma, left the house, and they robbed it. Mustafa says that 'afterwards, when I requested my share, they said "we buried it in the ground, not here, let's go to the islands, there we'll give it".' Because they didn't give his share upon demand, Mustafa reported them to Fatma, also noting that Süleymân had no knowledge of the plot (mention of him implies that they were probably brothers). The document ends by recording that Ali and Mehmed denied everything. In sum, it is the tale of down and out refugees from Kemah, preying upon an elite Rodosto Muslim and his wife.[68]

Another document from the notebook may also involve a convert. It documents a dispute between an Armenian named Kiram and a Muslim named Keyvan bin Abdullâh. Kiram testifies that 'Keyvan hit my head without reason, and he wounded me'. In retort Keyvan claimed that 'I told Kiram to come serve me. When he didn't come, I hit his head'.[69] This description prompts several questions. Firstly, what is the source of Keyvan's sense of entitlement? Does his contempt for Kiram derive from his status as a poor Christian refugee? Or was Keyvan a convert to Islam who had some old relationship with Kiram that cannot be discerned from the text? Or had Kiram made some promise or commitment that goes unmentioned? As is often the case with *sicils*, such questions must go unanswered.[70]

One page of the notebook records another group of Armenians who are robbed by a Muslim. The case is quite similar to that between the Armenian labourers and the two constables described above. It begins by listing the names of four Armenians (though the group of Armenians is larger than these four), and it states that

> They [the Armenians] said that 'tonight after the evening prayers a [Muslim] resident of Rodosto named Kara Hasan raided our rooms and took our money by force. He said, "I am the tax-collector", and he tormented us (*cevr ü cefâ*). We demand action according to the *sharia*.' To inquire into the circumstances he was invited but not found, and it was registered that he raided the above-mentioned Armenians' rooms contrary to custom.[71]

While the document about Mehmed, Mustafa and Ali's bungled theft depicts the Kemah refugees as preying upon the local elite, this case and the previous one imply that the Armenian refugees were particularly vulnerable to theft and abuse. As in modern times, refugees can disproportionately be both perpetrators and victims of crime.

Discussion of these early documents should end with mention of two short records. One document about a minor debt refers to a certain 'Markon son of Mardiros from the region of Sivas in the province of Anatolia'.⁷² While the case's topic is mundane, this document, along with other such examples in later notebooks and Grigor's own testimony remind us that Armenians and Muslims from other nearby regions of Eastern Anatolia joined the refugees from Kemah in their migration to Rodosto. Also significant is a document in which some Muslims provide surety, or *kefîl*, for Kemah Armenians.⁷³ To settle in a neighbourhood it was often required that someone of standing guarantee the decency and behaviour of the newcomers. In this particular document, the Muslims are 'ibn Abdullâh', implying that they may have been converts. More documents of this nature appear in subsequent notebooks.

So far these court cases have provided scattered glimpses into the earliest arrival of the Kemah Armenians in Rodosto: images of beatings, theft and alleged murder, along with more mundane cases about broken engagements, surety and debt. Henceforth records for subsequent years about Armenians in the Rodosto court are more reliably abundant. In particular, a surge begins with documents covering the years 1014–15 (1605–7),⁷⁴ jumping from only three cases about Armenians in the previous notebook⁷⁵ up to twenty cases,⁷⁶ with an average of approximately twenty cases about Armenians per *defter* in documents covering the years 1014–19 (1605–11).⁷⁷ The fact that this surge in the number of records about Armenians begins in 1605 is significant, as the timing corresponds exactly with the mass arrival of Kemah Armenians mentioned in the Western Armenian secondary literature and noted by Grigor. With more court cases at our disposal, it is now possible to turn to a more thematic and comparative approach to the documents, beginning with a study of cases about Armenian converts to Islam.

Armenian converts to Islam

The earliest document found relating to an Armenian convert is about the aforementioned Mustafa, mentioned in a marginal note contained in the *defter* covering the years 1004–5 (1595–7).⁷⁸ His provenance and back story are, however, impossible to discern. The earliest reference to a convert from among the Kemah Armenians was recorded in Ramazân 1013 (January–February 1605). It involves a debt dispute that mentions a certain 'Hasan bin Abdullâh who now works as a laborer (*ırgatlık*) in the town of Rodosto [but] is from the town named Toşin bound to the Kemah district in the Erzurum region in the province of Anatolia'. Normally Hasan's epithet 'bin Abdullâh' would be insufficient to prove that he is a convert, let alone an Armenian convert, but in this case his provenance is clear because the debt dispute is between Hasan and a Christian, 'Evak son of Nigol, the above-mentioned Hasan's paternal uncle'.[79] 'Avag' is a common Armenian name and Hasan's father was therefore an Armenian Christian. The same *defter* contains another document about a dispute between two brothers. The document describes the first brother by stating that 'when he was an Armenian, his name was Sarkiz son of Melak, but upon being honoured by the glory of Islam his name became Ahmed'.[80] The second brother, however, remained a Christian. These two cases suggest that conversion led to financial disputes and litigation among the families of Armenian refugees.

The tales of such converts are scattered among the subsequent notebooks. Documents from 1014 (1605–6),[81] for instance, contain the testimony of the son of a convert who related how his father was a native of Kemah who accepted Islam in Edirne and assumed the name Bayrâm.[82] The next *defter* contains yet another dispute between brothers, one named Murâd bin Abdullâh, the other two being explicitly listed as Armenian Christians.[83] Moreover, the same *defter* contains another entry with an error, in which the scribe forgets for a moment the brotherhood of all Muslims and drafts a surety (*kefîl*) agreement between a Muslim named Mehmed bin Ramazân and 'an *Armenian* named Sefer bin Abdullâh who works as a labourer in the town of Rodosto'.[84] To explicitly designate the convert's ethnic background in a document of this nature was a faux pas by the scribal conventions of the time. This was clearly a sloppy scribe, as he accidently referred to an Armenian Christian as 'an Armenian named Arslan *bin* Babacan' in another surety record on the previous page, contradictory language since 'bin' was only supposed to be used for Muslims.[85] The religious identity of the people involved is unambiguous, however, as Christians could only provide surety for other Christians, not Muslims. One other such error was found in the notebooks under investigation, showing that memory of converts' origins lay below official discourse.[86]

The norms of the Ottoman *kadı* court scribes – who usually did not specify the ethnicity of Muslims – contrasts with scribes of other periods of Islamic history. It was not uncommon, for instance, to refer to ethnically Armenian Muslims as 'Armenians' in Fatimid Egypt.[87]

Some documents in subsequent notebooks consist merely of two-line notices of conversion, listing Armenians' original names, the date of conversion and their new Muslim names.[88] In multiple instances married Armenian women converted to Islam before the court, and in such instances their husbands were offered conversion or divorce.[89] In all of the documents examined in this study, the husbands remained Christian and preferred divorce, and this sometimes resulted in financial litigation over dowries and property.[90] The use of the Islamic court as a route to divorce for Christian women is well attested in Ottoman historical literature.[91]

In addition to the benefits of an easy route to divorce, a new name, some money and new clothes, and membership in the religion of the ruling class, conversion could also be employed as a legal strategy. A document written in 1607 describes the case of a certain Christian named Sâfir – having taken the name Mehmed upon conversion to Islam – who owned two Muslim concubines, Cânfedâ and Fatma. Sâfir purchased Cânfedâ first in Edirne and then he purchased Fatma in Rodosto, from where he was planning to depart by ship. But before he could leave, suspicion was aroused about his religious identity and he was seized by a local constable and brought to court. Mehmed admitted that he was a Christian when he purchased the concubines and that he converted to Islam upon seizure.[92] He lied and claimed to have left the concubines in the home of a Muslim, but both Cânfedâ and Fatma testified against him, saying that he left them in an Armenian home. As is customary in *sicils*, no ruling is mentioned. In this case conversion to Islam was a legal strategy employed to save him from punishment for purchasing Muslim women. Mehmed may also have been using a Muslim identity beforehand in order to purchase the concubines. If so, Sâfir/Mehmed's case is reminiscent of Late Ottoman stories of crypto-Christians who operated with two identities, alternating between a Muslim and Christian identity according to the needs of the moment.[93]

In Sâfir/Mehmed's case as well as in divorce documents, motivations for conversion are not difficult to understand. But far more often the *sicil* records are ambiguous, and the question of motivation lies in the realm of speculation. One record from Şevvâl 1016 (January–February 1608) documents a squabble surrounding a certain youth, named Ahmed bin Abdullâh, who had converted to Islam twenty days earlier. His father, an Armenian named Murâd, ran afoul of the local Ottoman authorities because he tried to take back his son and 'wanted to make him an Armenian' again, though he was prevented by the local Muslims. The document includes testimony recounting that 'the above-mentioned Murâd gathered guards (*yasakçı*), showed up, and stormed the above-mentioned Ahmed's room. Saying, "he's my son", he wanted to take Ahmed'. The ensuing fight took place right before Ahmed's circumcision (*sünnet*), and it seems that Ahmed's father wanted to kidnap him before the ceremony could be completed. The only explanation given for the young Ahmed's conversion was that an elder Ahmed testified that he was the 'reason' (*sebeb*) for the youth's conversion. Was the young Ahmed converted forcefully by the elder Ahmed? Had he truly come to believe in Islam, or did he have some practical reason for defying his father and becoming a Muslim? The *sicils* provide no answer, only a glimpse into inter-familial strife and interreligious tension in early seventeenth-century Rodosto.[94]

While the court records provide explicit cases of conversion, usually without insight into the mind of the convert, Grigor's chronicle complements them by suggesting possible motivations. In addition to the above-mentioned stories of evicted Armenians who contemplated conversion out of frustration with the hardships they faced as refugees, and of the Armenian youth who converted in order to stay married to his convert wife, Grigor also relates stories of several other Christians who converted willingly, much to his disapproval. He complains, for instance, of a Greek woman who converted for financial reasons,[95] and he was infuriated with some Julfan merchants who were converting to Islam in order to marry Turkish women.[96] In general, Grigor understood well that Islamic laws regarding the relations between the sexes presented temptations – dangerous and sinful temptations in his eyes – for both Armenian men and women. In one passage Grigor angrily exhorts that 'Our Holy Gospel does not allow [men] to possess women for a fee, or to take many women, or to leave them easily according to *their* [Islamic] laws'.[97] He continues by lashing out against Armenian men who told their women they had the right to divorce. Grigor's narratives of conversion differ from those we encounter in the *sicils* in that he usually related stories of conversion for didactic purposes or in order to condemn and not to chronicle pragmatic conversions by Rodosto Armenians, who were all technically members of his pastoral flock.

It is noteworthy that conversion documents for Kemah Armenians first appear in early 1605, exactly when the surge of Armenian refugees described by Grigor and the Western Armenian secondary literature began to arrive. Documents about converts are relatively common in early *defters* examined in this study that cover the years 1605–11, but mention of converts is conspicuously absent from documents of later periods, i.e. 1620–2 and 1629–32. Along with Grigor's testimony, this implies that a wave of conversion followed the Armenians' first arrival, prompted primarily by the hardships of building a new life. After the Rodosto Armenian community integrated itself into the local economy and society the situation stabilised and conversion became rarer.

Sartorial violations

In addition to records of conversion, the Rodosto court records also contain some complaints about Armenians' sartorial violations. The Ottomans intermittently enforced dress regulations for its diverse communities and litigation about dress often appear in Ottoman court records. One document records that although an Armenian named Sargis wore white headgear and a beard, 'he was not a Muslim [but] an Armenian'.[98] Another registers that 'while it was forbidden to wear a white turban',[99] a certain Armenian broke the rule in the middle of Safer 1016 (June 1607). To wear white was significant, as the Janissaries wore white headgear,[100] and another *sicil* explicitly condemns an Armenian for dressing like a Janissary, noting that he wore 'a turban on his head in Janissary fashion'[101] at the beginning of Rebî'ü'l-evvel 1017 (June 1608). When asked by the court to explain his choice of dress, the Armenian stated that a Muslim named 'İmrân Çelebi had dressed him in that way.

Records of such sartorial violations are not unusual in Ottoman Turkish *sicils*, but these three documents are worthy of note because of their context. As is the case for conversion documents, records of sartorial violations do not appear in the court records for 1620–2 and 1627–32. This suggests that some Armenians chose to dress like Muslims and Janissaries as part of their efforts to integrate into their new lives in the western regions of the Ottoman Empire. When the refugee crisis of the early seventeenth century subsided, however, such assimilation efforts became either unnecessary or unnoted by the court. While such a small sample can only suggest this interpretation, it is substantiated more fully in a story recounted by Grigor regarding his own half-brother.

Grigor arrived in Istanbul in 1605. He described that the city was crowded with Armenian refugees, noting that some had arrived two years before while others had arrived with him. He wrote that 'many also came afterward and scattered to Anatolia and Rumelia, to all the cities until Belgrade, the land of Moldavia, and to Poland'.[102] Grigor was residing at the St Nicholas Church, currently the Kefeli Mosque in Istanbul, when someone informed him that his brother had arrived and wished to see him. When Grigor met his brother Markos, he initially could not recognise him, as they had not seen each other in many years and Markos was wearing Muslim clothes. Grigor describes the exchange as follows:

> I asked, 'Are you an Armenian or a Turk?' He said, 'I'm an Armenian and Christian.' I said, 'By what sign might I believe you?' He took out of his pocket the payment of the holy faith, he showed a tax statement (*haraç tezkeresi*) for all the different years, and then we believed him. I said, 'What is this way you're dressed?' Weeping he said, 'From every danger – famine, Celalis, and being devoured by beasts – we were freed by the mercy of God. We came here, [but] no one made a home for us, not among [our] people, not among the foreigners [Muslims], and not among the Christians. Being abandoned, from incapacity I joined [myself] to Turks, and I am in their service.' And I said, 'Can you take leave of them?' He said, 'If you desire, I will undress and leave today. I am not for hire or a servant, but I do not have other clothes that I might change [into].' Immediately I took from my own [belongings] a dyed woolen and a leather Crimean cap. And [he], taking the clothes of the Turk, carried them away [and] gave them to his masters, and [then] he came to us.[103]

Both the *sicils* and this passage imply that conversion was not the only way of easing the poverty and hardship faced by newly arrived Armenians: partial assimilation was another option. While some Armenians became Muslims, others stopped short of changing their faith, instead opting to take on Turkish names and clothes, to live with and serve Muslims. In Markos' unusual case, his influential brother was able to give him new clothes and to rescue him from servitude, and several years after this episode Markos would become a servant of the Holy Sepulchre of Jerusalem.[104] Many other Armenian refugees who lacked such influential connections probably Ottomanified gradually in their new lives in Istanbul and Western Anatolia, with particular impact across the generations. While many Armenian villagers in Eastern Anatolia would have grown up speaking only Armenian among themselves, it is likely that many of the refugees' children grew up speaking Turkish on the streets of Istanbul and that the move to an urban context catalysed linguistic and cultural changes.[105] In late Ottoman history it was much more common for Armenians of Western Anatolia and the Balkans to be Turkophone than those of Eastern Anatolia and the South Caucasus,[106] a pattern which probably has its origins in the early modern migrations.

*Surety (*kefîl*) documents and eviction notices for Armenian refugees*

There are several types of legal surety, or *kefîl*, in Ottoman law,[107] and surety documents are very common in Ottoman court records. The most common surety documents involving Rodosto Armenians concern surety of person (*kefalet-i nefsiyye*), and most of them were probably drawn up upon the settlement of Armenians in a new neighbourhood. The custom of requiring surety for newcomers to a neighbourhood applied not only to non-Muslims and not only during times of hardship; the practice was widespread, though applied inconsistently. But as was the case with both conversion and sartorial records, the sudden appearance of various surety records for Armenians in Rodosto in the first decade of the seventeenth century is significant, as it can imply new settlement. Some surety documents were prepared by Armenians on behalf of one another,[108] while sometimes Muslims vouched for Armenians.[109] Occasionally the surety documents explicitly mentioned that the recipients in question were from Kemah, such as an early record issued on 11 Zilka'de 1010 (3 May 1602).[110] Increased mobility in early modern Europe prompted a need for letters of recommendation and early passports in order to identify and vouch for strangers.[111] Surety documents played a similar role of establishing credentials in early seventeenth-century Rodosto.

More revealing than the surety documents – which are highly formulaic and not usually explicit about their purpose – are eviction notices. For example, in 1606 a group of Greeks appeared before the Rodosto Islamic court demanding that a small group of Armenians be thrown out of their neighbourhood. They officially declared that 'in our neighbourhood five or ten Armenians have entered a house, and they are never devoid of fighting and intrigue. Henceforth we don't want them in our neighbourhood'.[112] The document ends by noting that the Armenians agreed to leave. It seems that the Armenian refugees were sometimes an unruly crowd, as documents also exist about intoxicated Armenians getting into fights,[113] wandering the streets at night drunk with knives,[114] attacking people with knives and sticks,[115] and slandering women by calling them prostitutes. A woman gave the following testimony in complaint about a drunk Armenian man: 'He slandered me by saying, "hey whore"'.[116]

Another document from 1605 ordered the eviction of all Armenians from Muslim neighbourhoods and only permitted Armenians' settlement in Christian neighbourhoods if they obtained surety. This document (see Figure 3.2) is important enough to warrant full translation:

> The Muslims whose names are written in addendum are from the elites of the town of Rodosto. Present at court, they testified that the mosque situated in the above-mentioned town was opened and that the carpets were stolen. Shops and houses were opened and their things and provisions were taken. A third night did not pass without this offence occurring [again]. Until now in our province such an unseemly act has not taken place. Now there is a great probability that among the Armenians in the Muslim neighborhoods, it is some bastards (*harâmzâde*) from the Armenian community. From now on, unguaranteed (*kefîlsiz*) men shall not stay in our town. Let the Armenian community guarantee (*kefîl*) one another, and do not let bastard Armenians who lack surety stay in our province. And by no means shall any unbelieving Armenians stay in Muslim neighborhoods; let them stay in the unbeliever neighborhoods. It was registered with the agreement of all at the end of the month of *Şevvâl* in the year 1013 (March 1605).[117]

The incident described in this document closely resembles Grigor's story about the Armenians' eviction from Rodosto, but it differs in three details.

AN ARMENIAN REFUGEE CRISIS | 109

Figure 3.2 *Sicil* from 1605 banning 'bastard (*harâmzâde*) Armenians' from living in Muslim neighbourhoods of Rodosto (RŞS 1545, 69a). Credit: Thanks to Mustafa Birol Ülker and ISAM for permission to reproduce this image.

Firstly, this document is dated to 1605, but Grigor's story took place in 1607. Secondly, the motivation for the eviction is entirely different in the two stories, being attributed to robbery in the Ottoman document. Finally, in Grigor's story the Armenians were banished from both Muslim and non-Muslim neighbourhoods, but here they are only banished from Muslim neighbourhoods, while surety is required for them to settle in Christian neighbourhoods.

Were there two such evictions, one in 1605 and one in 1607, or does Grigor embellish an older case? Did the priest Naḷash really slander the Armenians to the local judge, or was his story fictional, crafted by Grigor for political reasons? The Ottoman document provides a more likely rationale –

thievery – than Grigor's tale, and Grigor undoubtedly had a motive to distort the story. Such discrepancies aside, this document conclusively demonstrates that there was, in fact, at least one eviction of Armenians from the Muslim neighbourhoods of Rodosto.

Armenians' occupations and housing

The Rodosto court records are also highly informative about more mundane issues than those discussed above, such as the employment and housing situation of Rodosto Armenians. The cramped rooms (*odalar*) in which the newly arrived Armenians stayed were highlighted both by Grigor and in the above-mentioned tales of theft. These rooms receive mention in several other court records. In one document, for instance, a household (*hâne*) for tax purposes is officially registered for the 'new Armenians dwelling in the rooms of Hâcı Mehmed'.[118] The same rooms receive further mention in surety documents,[119] and they were sometimes the scene of violence. On one occasion, for instance, an Armenian boy living in the rooms was attacked with a knife in front of the building.[120]

Numerous documents mention the occupations of Armenians. In the court records there are multiple references to Armenian labourers (*ırgat*)[121] and farm hands (*rençper*).[122] Mention is also made of an Armenian plumber (*lağımcı*) working on a *hamâm*,[123] a tailor (*terzi*),[124] and a spinner of goat hair (*mutafçı*) who has run afoul of the local association of spinners for not gaining a proper permit.[125] Occasional mention is also made of Armenian priests (*papa*).[126] Whereas Armenians were accused in the 1580s of moving goods at the Rodosto harbour without proper registration, by the beginning of Zilka'de 1018 (January–February 1610) Armenian names are present on the official list of porters who 'carry goods to the stores when they leave the ships in the Rodosto harbour'.[127]

This list of occupations may present a case in which the court records offer a distorted picture of Ottoman-Armenian history in Rodosto, as there may have been tendencies for certain classes and professions to frequent the court more than others. The general picture presented is of an Armenian labourer population of no great wealth. There are no lists of the deceased's effects (*muhallefât*) for wealthy Armenians, as there are for wealthy Greeks.[128] Several documents depict Armenians 'in the service (*hizmetinde*)' of Muslims.[129]

One particularly sad document registers the divorce of an Armenian couple, prompted because the husband officially declared that he 'lacked the capacity to support' his wife.[130] If any Armenian elites made their way to Rodosto in the course of the Great Flight, they left less of a document trail in the Rodosto court records than humble labourers, servants and artisans.

Celalis

In addition to Grigor's chronicle and other Armenian narrative sources of the period, some Ottoman imperial orders are also quite explicit about the reason for the sudden arrival of Armenians in Rodosto. Multiple references appear to the Armenian people who 'fled from the Celali oppression in Anatolia and passed to Rumelia'.[131] One document dated to 19 Muharrem 1015 (27 May 1606) explains that

> For a few years, with the appearance of the Celalis in Anatolia, the tax-paying Armenian subjects in the provinces of Sivas, Erzurum, Kemah, Diyarbekir and in other provinces have left the towns where they have resided from of old, and they have dwelled in the villages, towns, and farms of the cavalry (*sipâhî*) and Janissaries and other men of state in your district.[132]

In addition to such stray references to the reason for the sudden arrival of Armenians, an imperial order from summer 1608 referred generally to peasants who 'left their places because of the Celali rebel invasion', and it complained that they were unregistered for taxation. The order states that they 'must be registered'.[133]

Multiple references to the Celalis also appear in court records about refugees. Most of these cases involve Muslim refugees, implying that behind the veil of scribal terminology there may have been many Muslim refugees, who, unlike the Armenians, are difficult to distinguish from native Rodosto Muslims unless explicit mention is made of their flight, since they were not forming a new community in the town. Sometimes former Celalis even settled in Rodosto and the Rodosto court was occasionally charged with researching past crimes committed in the East.

For example, one case involves a refugee from Kayseri named Yûsuf who offers testimony in Rodosto against another refugee, named El-Hâc Hasan bin Halîl. Yûsuf testifies that

When Karayazıcı's brother Hasan was a Celali in Anatolia, the above-mentioned El-Hâc Hasan, with the ruffians of the [other] above-mentioned Celali Hasan, raided our village. He held us and tortured us, and the above-mentioned El-Hâc Hasan took my 300 *kuruş*. With difficulty I was delivered from his hands.

In response El-Hâc Hasan denied all knowledge of the event, stating that

I am from the neighbourhood of Çilehane in Amasya in the Province of Anatolia. The Celalis came to our province, and I came to this province. I have no knowledge of what Yûsuf said.

It seems likely that Hasan was lying, however, as another man testified in support of Yûsuf.[134]

Another record about refugees involves a man named El-Hâc Dervîş from Kayseri who lost his Russian-born concubine and the mother of his daughter. He testified that men raided his house in Kayseri and kidnapped her, but five years later he found her again in Rodosto and initiated litigation to win her back. The concubine testified in support of him, saying that

In truth, El-Hâc Dervîş is my lord and Ayşe is my daughter from the above-mentioned El-Hâc Dervîş. When my lord's house was raided a man called Ahmed took me and imprisoned me in a granary. Later he gave me to a man named Mustafa from the Bolu district. He brought me [here] and he sold me to the above-mentioned Hasan in Rodosto.[135]

Another story involves a woman from Akşehir who fled to Rodosto when 'the Celalis torched our province'.[136] She claimed to be free, but the couple with whom she travelled to Rodosto said that they had purchased her as a concubine. A similar case involves a Russian-born convert to Islam named Yûsuf whose freedom was also contested. While one man claimed that he was a 'runaway slave (*abd-ı 'âbık*)', Yûsuf himself testified that he had been emancipated, but after receiving an official document registering his freedom, 'the Celali rebels held me and took my emancipation declaration'.[137]

One document mentions an abandoned village near Ergene (in the Rodosto region), which is explicitly granted to refugees from the Celali Revolts for settlement. A decree dated to 1 Zilka'de 1014 (10 March 1606)

describes the 'Armenian people and others who fled from the evils and oppression of the brigands on the Anatolian side'. It states that 'for more than twenty years the people of the town named Kara Hamza have been scattered and dispersed', and thus, since Kara Hamza was vacant, the refugees could settle there:

> I order that when my edict arrives, the people of the above-mentioned town who have been for so long scattered and dispersed, if their places lie empty and vacant and no one has a deed or litigation of the above-mentioned place, if there is no connection with my royal treasury or to a pious foundation, let no one trouble or molest any Armenian people or others who having reached the above-mentioned place want to settle there, let them settle. Let it be known, let the honoured emblem be trusted.[138]

Finally, the Celalis are mentioned in another class of imperial orders. While Rodosto was safe Ottoman territory, far from the rampages of the East, the stresses of the revolts occasionally reached such an acute level that the state sent imperial orders to Rodosto for assistance. In particular, the Celali assault on Bursa in 1607 caused intense panic in Istanbul, and the state sent an imperial order to Rodosto that describes in details the problems in the East and the Celali threat. It admits that the state had not possessed enough troops to deal with the crisis, and it calls on 'whoever is the felicitous sultan's servant and Janissary to come now to Istanbul (İslâmbol)'.[139]

The above-mentioned documents are just a few examples of common reference to Celali rampages and flight from the East contained in the Rodosto court records of this period.[140] Together they show that Rodosto was not left unaffected by the state's insurrection crisis and that local resources were sometimes called upon for crisis management. The Ottoman state was well aware of the refugee crisis in Rodosto and its causes, and the chaos in the East was overflowing into the Rodosto Islamic court.

Taxation

As in almost all pre-modern agricultural societies, Ottoman peasants were bound to the land and were not permitted full freedom of movement. Authorities in all fief-based states played a delicate balancing act, whereby they usually sought to extract maximal resources from their peasants, without delving into the minimal funds necessary for the peasants to subsist and to propagate agricultural activity. Examples of breakdown of this order often led to peasant flight throughout world history, from Hellenistic Egypt to the Ottoman Empire. As Chapter Two has shown, revolt and famine led to a collapse in the peasant economy of Eastern Anatolia and subsequent flight, and those who fled became tax-evaders. But, as the saying goes, life's only two inevitable factors are death and taxes. The Armenians who participated in the Great Flight succeeded in postponing both, but eventually the Ottoman tax collectors caught up with them.

It seems that in the early years of the Armenians' settlement in Rodosto they were occasionally bamboozled by unofficial tax collection. In one of the above-mentioned stories of theft, the perpetrator tried to rob Armenians by claiming to be a tax collector. The document states that 'Kara Hasan raided our rooms and took our money by force. Saying, "I'm the tax collector," he tormented us'.[141] Another example of fraudulent taxation appears in a document drafted in early *Safer* 1015 (June 1606), in which an Armenian priest (*papa*) and two monks (*keşîş*) 'from the priests of the Armenian community' come to the court to officially protest attempts to tax them illegally. They testify that 'While we from of old do not give the *cizye* and *ispence* [taxes], the above-mentioned [tax-collector] still has demanded the *cizye* and *ispence* [taxes] from us, and he has harassed us'.[142]

The *cizye* and *ispence* were both taxes taken from Ottoman non-Muslims. Christian clergymen in the Ottoman Empire often enjoyed tax exemption and in this document the Armenian priests were asking the court to enforce their special status.[143] The tax collector denied their accusations, saying that he had not and would not tax them.

Official documentation about the group responsibility of Rodosto Armenians to pay taxes begins to appear in the court records for the year 1015 (1606–7). For example, an order drafted on 16 *Şevval* 1015 (14 February 1607) orders that *cizye* be collected from the Armenian refugees, and it commands that all be registered for subsequent taxation:

> From every man (*nefer*) of the Armenian community who was residing in Sivas, Erzurum, Kemah and other districts in the province of Anatolia, but fled oppression and settled in your district, it is necessary to gather and collect

174 *akçe* per person in *cizye* for the year 1014 (1605–1606) . . . Record correctly however many Armenians are present and have the notebook signed and sealed by the local judges. Take it together with my property, which was collected, and put it in the treasury.[144]

Grigor narrates that in 1620 the Greeks complained to the Ottoman authorities that the Armenians 'do not give one cent in taxes',[145] but the documentation shows that this was undoubtedly an exaggeration. Name lists, like the one ordered above, are extant in the notebooks under investigation. For example, one such list drafted in the beginning of Rebî'ü'l-evvel 1015 (July 1606) mentions the cavalryman (*sipâhî*) responsible for collecting the Armenians' taxes and the 'names of the Armenians whose *cizye* has been gathered',[146] totaling 182 men.

Subsequent documents which explicitly state the Rodosto Armenians' yearly tax obligations are common in the notebooks under investigation.[147] At first the collection of the Rodosto Armenians' taxes was in the hands of the above-mentioned cavalryman, but later two Jewish brothers named Yagob and Musa procured a six-year tax farm (*iltizâm*) for the collection of the Armenians' taxes,[148] although they usually delegated the actual task of collecting to Muslims. Not all Armenians had the same obligations to the treasury, as documents show that some Rodosto Armenians were bound to pious establishments (*vakıf*) and paid their taxes to them.[149] In addition to the 'scattered (*perâkende*)' Armenians who formed a distinct tax category, there were also 'scattered' Muslim refugees from Anatolia who had abandoned their farms (*çift bozan*) and the court also assigned a cavalryman to collect taxes specifically from these Muslim refugees.[150]

Complaints about illegal taxation continue to appear throughout the notebooks under consideration and are not limited to the early cases already mentioned. For example, on 2 Ramazân 1018 (29 November 1609) the royal court issued an imperial decree in response to complaints from the Rodosto Armenians about being afflicted (*rencîde ve remîde*) by tax collectors who were demanding tax (*yave harâcı*)[151] from Armenians who had resided in Rodosto for less than six months, contrary to the law. The court responded in a manner favourable to the Armenians' petition, ordering that such illegal taxation not be tolerated.[152] In another instance, the Jewish tax-farmers responsible for collecting the taxes of the 'scattered (*perâkende*)' Armenians appealed to the royal court because they claimed that the Armenians were making up various 'pretexts (*ta'allül*)', including the argument that they should not pay tax for under-aged children. The court responded with several instructions regarding all of the complaints, including the clarification that tax only be taken from 'boys in puberty who have reached the age of 13 or 14 and are capable of working'.[153] Thus the state took a middle line between the complaints of the Armenians and the demands of their tax collectors with an explicit articulation of the law. The court records also contain various complaints about tax payment prevarication, along with complementary orders for timely payment.[154] Gradually an annual ritual developed, consisting of the Armenians' yearly complaints of wrongful taxation, complemented by the tax-farmers' objections to delays and prevarications, followed up by the state's attempts to mediate these conflicts with imperial orders.

Meanwhile, back in the East, the Great Flight wreaked accounting nightmares for those who remained behind. Since communities were often jointly responsible for paying taxes, the departure of any villager increased the proportional load on the remaining villagers. On 4 *Safer* 1015 (11 June 1606) the royal court issued an imperial decree that stated that a delegation of non-Muslims from Kayseri came to Istanbul complaining that 'most of the non-Muslim (*kefere*) peasants in [our] province are scattered and dispersed because of hardship and oppression', and as a result complications ensued for tax collection. The Ottoman royal court in Istanbul decreed in response that

> You who are the judges in the manner described [in the honorifics above], have officials gather and collect without deficiency the 174 *akçe* apiece from the 1800 households which adds up to 313,200 *akçe cizye* . . . of the non-Muslim subjects of the province of Kayseri in Istanbul and other regions.[155]

According to this document, many Christian households had fled from Kayseri, and the Ottoman state chose to find them and demand that they pay their fair share of the Kayseri non-Muslims' tax burden.[156] The Rodosto court records show that some of these Kayseri non-Muslims were now Rodosto Armenians who subsequently got into an argument with the cavalryman collecting these taxes. They refused to pay the local Rodosto tax, citing the imperial decree quoted above, and saying they had already paid taxes for Kayseri.[157]

This taxation tug of war between the Kayseri Armenians in Kayseri, the Kayseri Armenians who had fled westward and the local tax collector in Rodosto evolved into a protracted struggle which lasted several years. A document from the middle of *Şevval* 1017 (January 1609) describes how a man was sent all the way from Kayseri to Rodosto to collect back-taxes from Kayseri Armenians. It states that 'the Armenians who are still in Kayseri have appointed me to gather and collect the *cizye* of the Armenians who are scattered (*perâkende*) and to hand their *cizye* over to the treasury'.[158] Another imperial decree from the same year shows that, although the Kayseri Armenians did pay their back-taxes to Kayseri, local tax collectors continued to double tax them by taking Rodosto taxes and the Kayseri Armenians complained to the royal court that the local officials were 'oppressing' them.[159] To make matters even more confusing, the Kayseri Armenians were not the only sub-group of Armenians in Rodosto who were paying separate taxes. A document from 5 *Şevval* 1019 (21 December 1610) shows that tax was also being collected from Divriği Christians in Rodosto and the general region to pay for Divriği's *cizye* taxes,[160] and on 17 Ramazân 1016 (5 January 1608) an imperial decree arrived concerning similar complaints from Erzurum.[161]

According to Grigor, it was a taxation crisis like that described above which prompted the exile order of 1635. He states that the order was promulgated because both Armenian and Turkish villagers from Sivas complained to Sultan Murad IV (r. 1623–40) about their dire tax situation while he was marching to campaign in the East:

> When [Sultan Murad] arrived in Sivas, men from every side, Armenians and Turks who had remained there, raised a cry and protested to the Caesar that 'We who have remained are few and the lands are in ruin. Tax-collection has not decreased, but the men of these lands are in Istanbul and everywhere. We are not able to endure the taxation, on account of our [being] few. Either order all of them to come to their places, or give us an order to go to them.'[162]

Of course, the further depopulation of the agricultural lands of Anatolia was not in the sultan's interests and Grigor states that the sultan responded to these complaints with an edict ordering Anatolian peasants residing in Istanbul and its vicinity to return to their homelands. As with the return edict of 1609, this one seems to have had limited effect in the long run.

In sum, the Ottoman tax collectors lost little time in demanding their dues from the Rodosto Armenians, beginning already in 1606, a year after Armenians began to arrive in large numbers. The taxation landscape was complex, with some Armenians paying to their former homelands, some paying locally, and some paying to pious foundations. To add to this confusion, it seems that tax collectors frequently attempted to collect extra taxes and that the Rodosto Armenians were constantly trying various ruses to avoid paying. The Ottoman court had to adjudicate on a yearly basis between tax farmers complaining of tax evasion and Rodosto Armenians complaining of unlawful oppression.

Two perspectives on the Armenian settlement of Rodosto, 1004–19 (1595–1611)

Descriptions of the turn of the century Armenian refugee crisis presented in Grigor Daranalts'i's chronicle and in the Rodosto court records overlap in their general outlines, even if details differ. Both describe a housing shortage faced by the refugees and a need to stay in cramped rooms for rent. Both indicate that there was a surge in Rodosto's Armenian population starting in 1605. Both sources present narratives about tense intercommunal relations. Moreover, both sources also document the Armenians' banishment from Rodosto, although Grigor's story of slander by a rogue priest seems politicised compared to the court records' far more likely tale of theft, followed by a demand for surety of Armenians who were temporarily only allowed to settle in non-Muslim neighbourhoods.

Of the two sources, however, the court records provide more objective documentation about sensitive topics such as conversion and partial assimilation. The records show that some Armenian refugees were converting to Islam, using Muslim names and imitating Muslim dress, most likely as a result of the hardship of life as refugees in a new land. The court records also document stories of theft and abuse that Grigor did not mention – like the story of the Armenian labourers who were robbed by the local constables – and they provide detailed glimpses into the Armenians' complex tax status.

In sum, these two source collections overlap and complement each other. For basic facts about the timing and sequence of events, the court documents are undoubtedly more trustworthy. They were, after all, state records, written quickly by a scribe for later use by a limited group of officials. These officials described events in accordance with their scribal language and standard narrative motifs but they had little reason for deception. Grigor, on the other hand, was crafting a far more complex narrative, mixing history with personal recollection. He consciously wrote for posterity, mixing didactic messages with an effort to shape the memory of his own life and achievements. While the court records offer more trustworthy articulations of the facts on the ground, they are one-dimensional and usually provide no indications of the motives, thoughts or emotions of Armenians before the court. Grigor's narrative, on the other hand, filled with anxieties and exhortations, offers a clearer window into the internal dynamics and humanity of the refugee community that he served. His chronicle will be analysed more fully and holistically in the following chapter.

The Later History of the Rodosto Armenian Community: The Court Records of 1620–2 and 1627–32

The most striking difference between the early notebooks already discussed and the later ones addressed here is that the Armenians have ceased to be referred to by their homelands, as Kemah, Sivas, Kayseri or Divriği Armenians. Instead of referring to their provinces of origin, they are merely referred to as 'the Armenians (*Ermeni tâ'ifesi*)'. Armenians in Rodosto continued to remember the Great Flight into the twentieth century, choosing one day per year to gather at the tombstone of Grigor Daranalts'i and to celebrate his leadership during the time of migration.[163] But from the perspective of the Islamic court it seems that the Rodosto Armenians' origins had become largely irrelevant and their status regularised.

Already noted is the absence of documents about conversion and sartorial violations. One exception to this is a document drafted in 1622 referring to a convert to Islam, Ramazân bin Abdullâh, who had recently passed away, and his brother, an Armenian Christian.[164] Unlike the documents in the early notebooks, which depict recent conversions and intra-familial strife, it seems that Ramazân was an Armenian who had converted many years before and any controversy had long since passed.

A trend in documents from 1030–1 (1620–2)[165] is an increase in documents about Armenians' economic activities. Documents about property transactions involving Armenians imply that they were gradually acquiring land and rising in socioeconomic status.[166] Another possible trend is a change in the language used to refer to non-Muslims. According to a record drafted on 11 Zilhicce 1030 (27 October 1621), a certain non-Muslim named Todori owed a debt to several men including a Muslim named Mustafa. The case in and of itself is not very informative, but the ethnic designations used for the participants are unusual by the standards of the earlier notebooks. Firstly, the document begins by describing Todori's wife as 'a non-Muslim (*zimmiye*) named Andalina who is from the Armenian community'.[167] In previous notebooks, use of the term *zimmi* for an Armenian was exceedingly rare, as was the need to clarify a specific community after use of the term *zimmi*. The woman's non-Armenian sounding name and the syntax of the sentence imply that she may have been a non-Armenian Christian who married an Armenian man. Thus she may have become a member of the Armenian community later in life and there would have been a need to clarify her relationship to it. The document also refers to the men sent to collect money from Todori, however, with both the terms '*zimmi*' and '*Ermeni*' in different instances, clearly using the terms interchangeably. Does this document provide evidence of mixed marriage, or does it imply a gradual change of scribal practice for recording non-Muslims? Perhaps the mixed terminology implies a gradual normalisation of the Armenians' status in the eyes of the scribes, who had previously considered them as a non-Muslim 'other'.

Moving ahead almost another decade, documents from 1037–8 (1627–32)[168] offer further testimony of a gradual transition from crisis to normality for the Rodosto Armenian community. Whereas in 1606 a group of Greeks had appeared before the court to complain about raucous Armenians, on 27 Ramazân 1037 (31 May 1628) a respectable Armenian appeared before the court to complain about a band of Greek robbers.[169] Property transactions appear commonly,[170] as well as mundane property disputes, such as a conflict between two Armenians that arose because one of them was passing through the other's courtyard on a regular basis.[171]

The most significant documentation from this period involves taxation. In 1606 the Ottoman state had granted permission for Armenian refugees to settle in the abandoned village of Kara Hamza near Ergene. Later documentation from the summer of 1628 shows that many Armenians had, in fact, settled there, and they complained to Istanbul about improper taxation. While it seems that their revenues were allotted to Murad IV's sister, Hânzâde Sultan, the local tax collectors were attempting to take extra money. The authorities clearly sided with the Armenians, recognising that the extra taxation was 'contrary to the *sharia*', and 'clear oppression', and even noting that it was an 'invention' of a certain notorious sergeant Murad. Although Armenians in court were no longer listed according to their former homelands in the East, this tax case shows that some institutional memory of the Great Flight remained, as the document refers to the Armenians as 'the Armenians who abandoned their ancient lands and came to this country and settled in some towns and cities'.[172] It seems that this institutional memory was preserved in part because the taxation debate of the Kara Hamza Armenians was ongoing, and the above-mentioned sentence was copied over and over again.[173] It is also likely that migrants continued to arrive gradually into the region throughout the seventeenth century, but at a slower rate that did not create a new refugee crisis.

Documentation about taxation made 'in lieu of transport by pack animal (*bedel-i mekkârî*)'[174] also provides critical demographic information about the Rodosto Armenians. One document dated to 27 Receb 1037 (2 April 1628) lists the number of households eligible for this tax by neighbourhood, noting that in the entire region (*kazâ*) of Rodosto there were 190 Armenian households (*hâne*) eligible for this tax and 570 men (*nefer*) in total (in general three actual households were considered one '*avârız* household, though there is variation across time and space).[175] Moreover it notes that the combined number of Armenian and Muslim households eligible was 877.[176] In a complementary document this total of tax-eligible 'Muslim and Armenian '*avârız* households in the [Rodosto] region' is lowered to 866.[177] The '*avârız* was an annual tax collected by household. Use of '*avârız* households to make population estimates is very tricky because of variations in counting practice and the diversity of tax categories. Their numbers roughly suggest, however, the proportion of Armenians to Muslims in the general population of Rodosto in 1628 was around 1:3.5, a huge proportion if we recall that there had been no significant Armenian population at the end of the sixteenth century.

Another important new development is the appearance of the first Armenian neighbourhood. A document dated to Zilka'de 1038 (June–July 1629) describes how a seemingly crazed Ottoman soldier attacked an Armenian with his sword 'with the intention to kill'. He caused dangerous wounds, leading the Armenian to register with the court that 'if I should die, blood money [must] be demanded from the above-mentioned Osman Beğ'. But leaving aside the drama of murder and retribution, for the purposes of this study it is critical that the Armenians involved in the case were listed as being 'from the residents of the Armenian community neighbourhood (*Ermeniyân tâ'ife[si] mahallesi*) in the city of Rodosto'.[178] Thus, we see another step in the Armenians' gradual integration into the city's structure.

There is evidence in the later tax documents that implies that emigrants continued to flow from Anatolia. One imperial decree makes a dichotomy between 'scattered and local Armenians (*perâkende ve yerli*)'. Since there was no reference to local Armenians in the older documents, it seems that while the first settlers' tax status had been regularised and they had become 'local', newcomers continued to pay taxes as 'scattered Armenians'. The same document also makes reference to Orthodox Christians (*Rum*) coming from Anatolia.[179] There was no reference to *Rum* refugees in the older notebooks of two decades prior, although their participation in the Great Flight is logical given that many ravaged Anatolian cities, such as Kayseri, had Greek populations.

There are also documents in the later notebooks concerning Armenian churches. Grigor describes the destruction of Yakob's Archangel Church, the first Armenian church of Rodosto, in 1629. He later recounts how the Armenians acquired a Greek church, St Yovhannēs Church, for themselves in the same year.[180] Grigor does not describe, however, how the Armenians of Rodosto began to gradually rebuild their old church on the same grounds as the Archangel Church. We see this process unfolding in an imperial decree. In a decree dated to 20 Ramazân 1040 (22 April 1631), an investigation is carried out concerning a certain Mehmed Beğ. It was suggested that Mehmed had taken fifty thousand *akçe* from the Rodosto Armenians illegally, using their construction of a church as his excuse. Witnesses from the Armenian community, however, testified that 'With regards to the church and other matters the above-mentioned el-Hâc Mehmed Beğ has not taken from us a single *akçe* or gift contrary to the sacred law'.[181] Either Mehmed was innocent or the Armenians had chosen to protect the Ottoman official who helped them rebuild their church in exchange for a bribe.

A second document, dated to the beginning of Rebî'ü'l-evvel 1031 (September 1631), is an imperial decree issued after the Rodosto Armenians made a petition to the Ottoman state in Istanbul. According to the decree, the Armenians came to Istanbul to inform the sultan that 'their ancient churches were dilapidated . . . and they wanted to repair them', but they were prevented by some officials (*ehl-i 'örf*). The sultan's response was based in part on Islamic law, stating that if the church was built before the Ottoman conquest (*kable'l-feth*), then he ruled that the Armenians should be permitted to repair the church and officials should not interfere.[182] It is a pity that Grigor did not discuss the new church's construction in greater detail, as it is clear that behind the legal language of these documents there was a story of complex political manoeuvring. The situation is confusing because the Archangel Church had been constructed in 1607, long after Ottoman conquest. Either legal language was being employed in a vacuum or perhaps repairs were being made to the older Greek church the Armenians had acquired in 1629. In any event, the Armenians' new church, built on the location of Yakob's Archangel Church, would be named the Redeemer and survive in continuous use for almost three centuries. Finally, in the twentieth century the Tekirdağ governor's residence (*vali konağı*) was built atop the Redeemer Church's foundation,[183] and the site is currently home to the Tekirdağ Archaeology and Ethnography Museum.

Overall, the court records of 1620–2 and 1629–32 show a gradual normalisation of the situation of the Rodosto Armenians. Cases about conversion to Islam, sartorial violations and surety documents – which often implied permission to settle – have disappeared. In their stead are numerous land transactions that document the Armenians' gradual purchase of homes and farms and Rodosto's speedy growth in the early seventeenth century. There is also evidence of the formation of an Armenian neighbourhood. While it seems that Rodosto Armenians usually no longer paid taxes to the regions from which they had emigrated, their tax status remained both complex and contested, with some taxes going to the patriarch in Istanbul, some to various pious foundations and members of the royal family and others going to the state via tax farmers – a 'normal' situation for Ottoman Christian peasants. Grigor's stories about the destruction of the Archangel Church and the Armenians' procurement of a Greek one were not reflected in the court records, but documentation does appear concerning the Armenians' efforts to build the Redeemer Church. Refugees probably continued to flow from the East westwards throughout the seventeenth century, but by the 1630s the Rodosto Armenian refugee crisis had largely abated.

Evidence for Demographic Change in Five Cities: Istanbul, Izmir, Rodosto, Balıkesir and Izmit

Thus far, this chapter has demonstrated that the stories of Armenians' mass flight presented in Chapter Two can be corroborated with Ottoman Turkish archival documents. Ottoman documents show that there was a negligible Armenian population in Rodosto until the Great Flight of the late sixteenth and early seventeenth centuries. After a few years of crisis, significant numbers of Armenians gradually purchased homes and farms, acquired churches and developed an Armenian neighbourhood. In time, they became accepted as the third main community of the town, after the Greeks and Muslims.

But demonstrating that a major population shift can be documented both in Armenian sources and in the Ottoman archive is not the same as showing that the shift was an important moment in Ottoman history. Ottoman history is replete with population movements, both forced (*sürgün*) and voluntary, so much so that one author has labelled the Ottoman Empire 'A Moveable Empire'.[184] Without doubt many Armenians also remained in Eastern Anatolia after the Great Flight, as is evident from later history. Moreover, Armenian communities already existed in some Ottoman port cities, such as Istanbul and Kefe. Not all of them were new, as was the case for Rodosto. On what grounds, then, can we suggest that the Great Armenian Flight was a critical moment in both Armenian and Ottoman history?

Firstly, let's consider the extant evidence about demography for five western cities – Istanbul, Izmir, Rodosto, Balıkesir and Izmit – beginning with Istanbul. An Armenian community was undeniably present in Istanbul before the Great Flight. Leaving aside the question of Armenians in the Byzantine Empire, Halil İnalcık's publication of a 1455 survey of Istanbul (*tahrîr defteri*) shows that some Armenians were living in Galata only two years after the

Ottoman conquest in 1453.[185] Their numbers would increase later in the reign of Sultan Mehmed II, who organised forced population transfers (*sürgün*) of Armenian Christians to the new Ottoman capital as part of a larger repopulation effort for the city. During the course of his campaigns against Karaman between 1468 and 1474, Mehmed sent Armenians to Istanbul from Anatolia and, in 1475, wealthy Armenians were sent to the capital from Kefe in the Crimea.[186] Documentation concerning the Sultan Mehmed pious foundations mentions exiled Armenians from Larende, Konya, Niğde, Tokat, Amasya, Ankara, Trabzon, Istanos and Bursa.[187] Memory of Mehmed's *sürgün* policies persisted into the early seventeenth century. Grigor Daranałts'i narrates a dispute between local Istanbul-Armenian priests and refugee priests which was arbitrated by a *kadı* in the Islamic court who chided the local Istanbul Armenians' treatment of the refugees by asking, 'Infidels (*kâfir*), are *you* not exiles (*sürgün*) brought from Karaman by Sultan Mehmed?'[188]

In addition to information about Mehmed's forced population transfers, there is also Ottoman Turkish evidence directly relating to the population of Galata and Istanbul in the late fifteenth century. A report from the Topkapı Palace Archives indicates that by 1477 – after the above-mentioned population transfers – there were 372 Armenian households amidst a total 14,803 households in Istanbul, and 62 Armenian households out of a total of 1,521 households in Galata.[189] These numbers imply that at the end of the fifteenth century only about 2.7 per cent of the combined population of Istanbul and Galata was Armenian. Making population estimates on the basis of early modern Ottoman documentation is a notoriously uncertain venture. Moreover, Armenians did continue to settle in Istanbul after the deportations of Sultan Mehmed,[190] and population ratios probably shifted throughout the sixteenth century. Nonetheless, the percentage of Armenians relative to the general population suggested by these data is extremely low compared to the data for the late Ottoman Empire. In 1844, for instance, Armenians represented approximately 22 per cent of the total population of Istanbul.[191] The critical question is whether this demographic shift happened gradually or was the result of a singular event.

The travel writer Siměon of Poland states explicitly that the population shift was a product of the Celali Revolts. He arrived in Istanbul in 1608 and he wrote the following critical lines about its Armenian population:

> Scarcely eighty [Armenian] households were local households, but more than forty thousand households of strangers (*garîp*) came to Istanbul, Galata, and Üsküdar, because on the other side (*öte-yaka*) the Celalis had destroyed [everything]. All of them were persecuted, driven off, and they settled there [in Istanbul].[192]

In short, Simēon confirms the implications of the Rodosto case study: that the Celali Revolts, famine and war with Persia at the beginning of the seventeenth century created a massive Armenian population shift from Eastern Anatolia to Western Anatolia, Istanbul and Thrace. Rodosto was chosen for study, after all, because it is close to Istanbul, so trends there should reflect events taking place in the capital city. Armenians would continue to come to Istanbul throughout the seventeenth century.[193]

Unlike Istanbul, Izmir was a small city of little significance until the first half of the seventeenth century. Its transformation has been thoroughly studied elsewhere,[194] but the temporal coincidence of Izmir's rise to prominence with the Great Armenian Flight has gone unnoticed. Ottoman Turkish documentation notes only Greeks in Izmir's non-Muslim population until the end of the sixteenth century.[195] When Simēon visited Izmir in late 1610 or early 1611, however, he reported that there were 100 Armenian households.[196] The traveller Tavernier reports a population of 8,000 Armenians out of a total city population of 90,000 in 1657,[197] a population explosion which the Armenian linguist Hrach'ya Achaṙyan directly attributed to flight from the Celalis and the incursions of Shah Abbas.[198]

Tavernier's numbers were likely exaggerated, as is suggested by the estimates of other travellers made later in the seventeenth century,[199] but evidence that the Armenians of Izmir and its environs were largely the descendants of refugees from the East is not limited to unreliable population estimates. Hrach'ya Achaṙyan notes that even until the twentieth century, the Armenians of Ödemiş – 'if they have not forgotten Armenian' – were speaking the dialect of the Caucasian region of Karabağ.[200] While the Rodosto case study implies that most of the refugees arriving in the western parts of the Ottoman Empire were humble farmers and artisans, Izmir also drew Julfa merchants engaged in the silk trade at the beginning of the seventeenth century.[201] Any Armenian refugees coming to Izmir were undoubtedly in the right place at the right time to improve their lot. The subsequent story of the rise to prominence of Ottoman non-Muslims engaged in coastal trade with Europeans is well known to the field of Ottoman history.[202]

It is possible to chart changes in the population of the Rodosto Armenians with far more detail than for Izmir. The traveller Simēon also visited Rodosto, and he narrates that

> From there in three days we came to Tekirdağ. This city has a small port (*iskele*) upon a hill [*sic*]. And there was a fixed church on the sea, which a certain *vardapet* named Yakob from Zeytun built with great efforts and many donations, and he passed away and was buried in it. There were two hundred or more Armenians there, five priests, and two friars. We stayed there for two months.[203]

Simēon probably arrived in Rodosto sometime in early 1611,[204] and thus this estimate represents the earliest explicit comment on the Rodosto Armenian population. The twentieth-century Armenian Rodosto historian Sargis G. Pʻachʻachean also attempted an estimate based on information provided by Grigor Daranalts'i, suggesting that in 1606 there must have been at least 200 Armenians in Rodosto and that by 1620 they must have numbered at least 300.[205] All of these figures are very rough estimates.

Further information is available in Ottoman Turkish taxation documents. A list of Rodosto Armenian taxpayers drafted in 1606 includes the names of 182 men.[206] We have already reviewed documentation from April 1628 which explicitly listed 190 Armenian households (*hâne*) and 570 men (*nefer*) who were eligible for the *'avârız* tax.[207] Further tax information about the Rodosto Armenian community is available in Ottoman documentation prepared later in the seventeenth century. Hacer Ateş found *'avârız* documentation from 1661, 1681 and 1694, which allowed her to chart trends in the Rodosto Armenian community's demography. According to her financial documentation, there were 710 Armenian households (*hâne*) and 156 rooms (*oda*) in 1661; 249 households, 235 rooms and 83 'wanderers' (*haymanagân*) in 1681; and 243 households, 217 rooms and 83 wanderers in 1694. These numbers suggest that there were at least 3,500 Armenians in Rodosto in 1661; 2,000 in 1691; and 2,100 in 1694. Thus, it seems that Rodosto exploded as an Armenian population hub in the early-mid seventeenth century, while its Armenian population declined thereafter, probably as a result of further migrations to Galipoli, Edirne and Rumelia.[208] These numbers are staggering, given that it has been estimated from cadastral surveys that Rodosto's total combined population was only about 4,500 people at the end of the sixteenth century.[209] While Rodosto's Greek population remained fairly stable throughout the seventeenth century, tax documentation suggests that the Muslim population also fluctuated wildly, with a peak of more than 6,000 Muslims in the documentation for 1661, dropping down to around 1,000 in 1694.[210] Such taxation data cannot be used to provide precise population numbers and must be used with caution, but they suggest changes in population ratios that seem accurate in historical context.

Recent research by Mustafa Murat Öntuğ using court records shows that the situation in Balıkesir, in northwestern Anatolia, mirrors Rodosto almost exactly. There is no record of any Armenians in Balıkesir before the turn of the seventeenth century, when they arrived suddenly in flight from the Celalis. While Öntuğ did not make a precise population estimate for the early seventeenth century, he showed that the Armenian population of Balıkesir was a product of the Great Armenian Flight, and he documented the Armenians' efforts to build their first church there in the seventeenth century.[211]

For Izmit, comparable data comes from research with Armenian sources. In 1913 a local historian named Minas Gasapean wrote a book on the history of Armenian Izmit, which includes a graph of the foundation date of each village and neighbourhood's Armenian community. Almost all of them originated at the turn of the seventeenth century, with only a few founded afterwards, and none before.[212] Thus studies based on Ottoman Turkish archival research and those based on Armenian literary evidence both lead to the same conclusions: that Armenians first settled localities in Western Anatolia at the turn of the seventeenth century after fleeing from the Celali Revolts and famine. While there are various records of Armenian population transfers into Western Anatolia and Thrace during the Byzantine period,[213] it seems highly likely that those Armenians had Hellenised by the early modern period.

In short, there is scattered evidence for a demographic explosion in the Armenian populations of Izmit, Balıkesir, Rodosto, Izmir and Istanbul in the first half of the seventeenth century. There was probably a constant stream of migrants from the Eastern Anatolia throughout the century, punctuated by peaks in time of crisis. This case study has documented one such peak in the first decade of the seventeenth century, and sources suggest that there was another one in 1635 that was caused by Murad IV's campaigns.[214] This data corresponds with massive drops in the number of taxpayers (*nefer*) recorded in Ottoman Turkish data for Eastern Anatolia from the 1560s to the 1640s. In some instances, such as the *kaza* of Harput, the region-wide drop in taxpayers reached 90 per cent in less than a century.[215] While Mustafa Akdağ's Great Flight has been known to scholars for decades, Ottoman historians have not recognised that the collapse happened in the historical Armenian heartland, causing a disproportional migration of Armenians to areas that previously had small Armenian populations. These migrations accelerated a process of urbanisation that had begun centuries prior.

Manuscript Production and the Cultural Impact of the Great Armenian Flight

While all of this data suggests a demographic shift caused by refugee Armenians who arrived in the western parts of the Ottoman Empire at the beginning of the seventeenth century, this book's claims about the importance of the Great Armenian Flight for Ottoman and Armenian history do not rest upon demographic data alone. Rather than claiming the importance of the Great Armenian Flight solely on the basis of demographic data, I propose here that the migrations' importance lies in their impact on Armenian cultural and intellectual life. Let us introduce the question of Armenian intellectual production in the seventeenth century by considering Istanbul – broadly defined to include suburbs like Galata – as a centre for Armenian manuscript copying. The manuscript catalogues of the Mesrop Mashtots' Institute of Ancient Manuscripts (Matenadaran) in Yerevan, Armenia list 509 manuscripts produced in Istanbul. Of those manuscripts, fewer than ten were copied before 1600, with the vast majority being products of the seventeenth and eighteenth centuries. Of these early Istanbul manuscripts with definite copy-dates, three were composed during the second half of the sixteenth century, in 1556 (M 8968), 1562 (M 2964) and 1586 (M 10370). One began to be copied at the beginning of the sixteenth century in 1508 (M 6010), and three were older, dating to 909 (M 6202), 1398 (M 7416) and 1459 (M 8871). Besides these rare exceptions,[216] the Matenadaran catalogue data suggest that Istanbul exploded on the scene as a centre for Armenian manuscript production only at the beginning of the seventeenth century.[217]

Older artifacts are always rarer than more recent ones, so it is logical that there be more seventeenth-century manuscripts than fifteenth- or sixteenth-century ones. In this case, however, the divergence is too extreme to be explained away in this fashion. The Matenadaran contains many manuscripts from before the seventeenth century. Moreover, if we compare the dates of Matenadaran manuscripts produced in Bitlis with those produced in Istanbul – using Bitlis as a control – the contrast is palpable. The Matenadaran contains sixty-two manuscripts that were copied in Bitlis. Of them, twenty-one were composed before 1600. Whereas less than 2 per cent of the Istanbul manuscripts were written before 1600, the number jumps to 34 per cent for Bitlis. The same trend is also evident for other eastern cities. Erzincan was a booming centre for manuscript production in the medieval period – during the time of the famed poet Kostandin Erznkats'i, for instance, in the fourteenth century – and the Matenadaran houses numerous thirteenth-, fourteenth- and fifteenth-century manuscripts from Erzincan. Erzincan seems to have later faded as an Armenian intellectual centre, however, with the result that forty out of forty-six of the Matenadaran's Erzincan manuscripts were written before 1600, yielding a percentage of 87 per cent. For Sivas the total is not so extreme, with 30 per cent of the Matenadaran's Sivas manuscripts having been drafted before 1600. For Diyarbekir, the number drops to 19 per cent. But seventeenth-century Diyarbekir was an unusually vibrant, populous and wealthy Armenian centre, so much so that Simēon wrote that Diyarbekir 'is now the Athens of Armenians'.[218] Even this low figure, however, is more than ten times the percentage for Istanbul.

These numbers should be interpreted with some caution, and the Matenadaran's acquisition history deserves consideration. Nonetheless, even if we take into account the vagaries of preservation and the higher likelihood of preservation of more recent manuscripts, we see evidence that Istanbul only emerged as an important centre of manuscript production in the late sixteenth and early seventeenth centuries, the time of the Great Flight, with a veritable explosion of production at the beginning of the seventeenth century.

It is also only in the seventeenth century that many important original works began being drafted by home-born Istanbul-Armenian authors,[219] most notably Eremia Kʻeōmurchean. The 'renaissance' of Armenian literature among Istanbul Armenians in the seventeenth and eighteenth centuries was a birth, not a re-birth.[220]

Evidence from other spheres also suggests that Armenian Istanbul – as known to us from eighteenth- and nineteenth-century Armenian cultural history – was a product of the Great Flight. It is commonly held that the Armenian Patriarchate of Istanbul was established in 1461 by Sultan Mehmed II. But in an article by Kevork Bardakjian entitled 'The Rise of the Armenian Patriarchate of Constantinople', Bardakjian shows that 'the transformation of the seat of Constantinople from a vicariate into a universal patriarchate was ... an evolutionary historical process'.[221] Bolstered by the arrival of the Armenian refugees, the Armenian Patriarchate in Istanbul gradually rose from regional obscurity to become a major ecclesiastical centre in the seventeenth century, expanding to official jurisdiction over territories from Rumeli to Tokat by 1695. Bardakjian suggests that – among other factors – the Istanbul Armenian community's growing size and the rise of a class of wealthy and influential elites in the seventeenth and eighteenth centuries catalysed the Armenian patriarchate's transition from a local see to one of grander prestige and authority.[222] Istanbul only became an ecclesiastical centre of great importance in the course of the seventeenth century, after the Great Flight of Armenians from Eastern Anatolia westwards.

Another piece of evidence which suggests that Armenian Istanbul was a seventeenth-century phenomenon is the geographical conceptions of sixteenth- and early seventeenth-century Armenian authors. In the sixteenth and seventeenth century Armenian authors repeatedly refer to Western Anatolia and Istanbul as 'Greek'. In the seventeenth century the priest and poet Martiros Ḷrimetsʻi referred to most of Anatolia as 'the Greek land, nearly from Istanbul to Persia'.[223] The sixteenth-century author Karapet of Bitlis also referred to Western Anatolia as 'the land of the Greeks', and he explicitly designated the border between Armenian and Greek territory as the city of Sivas.[224] Finally, Grigor Daranaḷtsʻi also reveals his conception of geography. Grigor, writing about the aftermath of the Armenian emigrations, states that '... we were in a state of migration and pilgrimage in a *foreign land*, being scattered and dispersed like dust flowing on the earth by the wind of sins, to Istanbul and Anatolia and Thrace . . .'²²⁵

Moreover, when conflict erupted between the Rodosto Armenians and the Greeks in 1620, Grigor writes that the Greeks tried to ally with the Turks by saying that

> We and you are of this place, but they [the Armenians], *alien and foreign*, came [and] took our patrimony, our fields, gardens, and all our land, and they do not give one cent in taxes. Now, come with unanimity, drive them from our country, so that it may be our patrimony [again].²²⁶

For Grigor and other early modern Armenian authors Istanbul and its environs were 'a foreign land'.

Diverse evidence suggests that the turn of the seventeenth century was a critical turning point in Ottoman-Armenian history. Demographic data suggests a major population shift of Armenian peasants from Eastern Anatolia to Western Anatolia, Istanbul and Thrace. Istanbul explodes on the scene as a centre for Armenian manuscript production only at the beginning of the seventeenth century. The Armenian patriarchate in Istanbul only gradually gains importance as an ecclesiastical centre in the course of the seventeenth century. Most importantly, it is only in the seventeenth century that the first great Istanbul-Armenian author and intellectual would emerge: Eremia K'eōmurchean. Eremia is remembered as an Istanbul author, but we should not forget that he was the grandson of a Kemah refugee whose father was born on the road in mid-flight. Eremia's manuscript tradition records several epithets for him, including the 'Scribe', 'K'eōmurchean', the 'Philologist', 'of Byzantium' and also 'Daranałts'i',²²⁷ in reference to Kemah, the province of his grandfather.

Summary

The first part of this book has emphasised a fact previously unnoticed by the field of Ottoman history: that the Celali Revolts and famine at the turn of the seventeenth century disproportionately disrupted and impacted historically Armenian demographic and cultural centres, such as Erzurum, Erzincan and Kemah. While Chapter Two showed that the Celali Revolts, famine and the Great Armenian Flight were major themes of seventeenth-century

Armenian literature, spanning multiple authors and genres, Chapter Three demonstrated that an awareness of Armenian sources can lead Ottomanists to investigate new veins of Ottoman archival sources, such as the court records of Rodosto. With those records it was possible to provide the microhistory of an Armenian refugee crisis in Rodosto at the beginning of the seventeenth century and the first settlement of Armenians in that city. This microhistory both complements and corroborates the Armenian historical sources of the period, substantiating Armenian stories about mass flight and hardship, while also providing records of conversion, thievery and tax policy that Armenian priestly scribes were less likely to mention.

The second part of this book will present an entirely different avenue of argumentation. As has been noted, Erzincan and Kemah were vibrant Armenian cultural centres during the Middle Ages. By contrast, there is almost no evidence for a remotely comparable level of Armenian literary or manuscript production in Istanbul or Western Anatolia before the turn of the seventeenth century. All historians, when analysing their primary sources, must repeatedly consider questions of historical context, educational practices and audience. To produce a new literary work or to copy a manuscript in the mountains of Eastern Anatolia is quite different from taking reed to paper in Rodosto or Istanbul. The transfer of the centres of Armenian literary production from Eastern Anatolia to Istanbul, Thrace and generally to Western Anatolia must have catalysed, in time, a cultural transformation among Armenian intellectuals.

The following chapters will follow the intellectual production of Kemah-Armenian refugees and their descendants. Given the Kemah region's cultural importance in medieval Armenian history, it is no coincidence that two of the first great authors of the new Western Armenian Diaspora were either Kemah Armenians or their descendants. This book will now shift from a focus on migration and refugee crisis to analysis of literary production. Close examination will be made of Grigor Daranałts'i's life and chronicle (Chapter Four), followed by a study of Eremia K'eōmurchean's Armenian works (Chapter Five) and finally, Eremia's role in establishing Istanbul as a centre for translation work from Armenian into Armeno-Turkish (Chapter Six).

While the Armenian refugees who fled from Eastern Anatolia to Istanbul and its environs did not enter an entirely new cultural sphere, they made a great jump from the remote peripheries of the Ottoman Empire to its centre. The second part of this book will argue that the Great Armenian Flight and the Armenians' arrival in the coastal port cities of the Ottoman Empire catalysed a transformation in Armenian intellectual life in the seventeenth century and the formation of a new society and culture. While no major Armenian histories were written in the sixteenth century, there was an explosion of historical literary activity in the seventeenth. I argue that this surge of production was motivated by a demand for new types of Armenian literature shaped by diverse cultural influences in new urban environments.

Notes

1. E.g. *Topçular Kâtibi 'Abdülkâdir (Kadrî) Efendi Tarihi* I, Ziya Yılmazer (ed.) (Ankara: Türk Tarih Kurumu, 2003), p. 615.
2. E.g. Mustafa Sâfî, *Zübdetü't-Tevârîh'i*, İbrahim Hakkı Çuhadar (ed.) (Ankara: Türk Tarih Kurumu, 2003), p. 302.
3. Suraiya Faroqhi, 'İstanbul'un İaşesi ve Tekirdağ-Rodoscuk Limanı (16.–17. yüzyıllar)', *ODTÜ Gelişme Dergisi Özel Sayısı* (1979–80): 151.
4. *Evliyâ Çelebi Seyahatnâmesi*, Seyit Ali Kahraman, Yücel Dağlı and Robert Dankoff (eds) (İstanbul: Yapı Kredi Yayınları, 2011), 8/347.
5. İlber Ortaylı, 'Rodosto (extension en Marmara de la Via Egnatia) au XVIe siècle', *The Via Egnatia under Ottoman Rule: 1380–1699* (Rethymnon: University of Crete Press, 1996), pp. 193–202.
6. Caroline Finkel, *The Administration of Warfare: The Ottoman Military Campaigns in Hungary, 1593–1606* (Vienna: VWGÖ, 1988), pp. 63–4.
7. E.g. Prime Ministerial Ottoman Archives (Başbakanlık Osmanlı Arşivi): Rodosçuk Şer'iyye Sicilleri (RŞS) 1554, 5b, containing a court record which documents the gathering of provisions at the Rodosto port for soldiers heading on campaign in 1608.
8. Hacer Ateş, 'Tekirdağ', *İslâm Ansiklopedisi* 40 (İstanbul: Türkiye Diyanet Vakfı, 2011), p. 362.
9. Henri Verneuil, *Mayrig*, Elise Antreassian Bayizian (trans.) (New York: St Vartan Press, 2006), p. 14.
10. *100 Yıl Önce Türkiye'de Ermeniler* I, Osman Köker (ed.) (İstanbul: Birzamanlar Yayıncılık, 2008), pp. 12–13.
11. Sevda Sevan, *Ṙodosto, Ṙodosto ...*, Margarit T'erzyan (trans.) (Yerevan: Sovetakan Groḷ, 1989).

12. Sargis G. P'ach'achean, *Yushamatean: Ṙotost'ots'i hayerun: 1606–1922* (Beirut: Tonikean, 1971); Nikiforos Kalaitzidis, *I eparchia Raidestou apo tin alosi tis Konstantinoupoleos eos ti Mikrasiatiki Katastrofi (1453–1922)* (Thessaloniki: Mygdonia, 2007); Hikmet Çevik, *Tekirdağ Tarihi Araştırmaları* (İstanbul: Ahmet Sait Basımevi, 1949).
13. See M. Tayyib Gökbilgin, *Rumeli'de Yürükler, Tatarlar ve Evlâd-i Fâtihân* (İstanbul: İşaret Yayınları, 2008); and Hikmet Çevik, *Tekirdağ Tarihi Araştırmaları: Tekirdağ Yürükleri* (İstanbul: Eko Matbaası, 1971).
14. My hearty thanks to the Tekirdağ Archaeology and Ethnography Museum for showing me the digital photo collection of Greek and Armenian tombstone fragments and allowing me to search the museum depot catalogues during my visit.
15. Özlem Sert Sandfuchs, 'Reconstructing a Town From its Court Records Rodosçuk (1546–1553)', Munich Ludwig-Maximilians University Doctoral Thesis (2008), p. 68.
16. Hacer Ateş, 'Kuzey Marmara Sahilleri ve Ard Alanında Şehirleşmenin Tarihi Süreci: XVI.–XVII. Yüzyıllarda Tekirdağ ve Yöresi', Istanbul University Doctoral Thesis (2009), pp. 159–60.
17. Grigor Daranałts'i, *Zhamanakagrut'iwn Grigor vardapeti Kamakhets'woy kam Daranałts'woy*, Mesrop Nshanean (ed.) (Jerusalem: Tparan Aṙak' At'oṙots' S. Yakobeants', 1915).
18. Grigor Daranałts'i, p. 108.
19. Ibid., p. 320.
20. Ibid., p. 114.
21. Ibid., p. 109.
22. Ibid., p. 110.
23. Ibid., p. 110.
24. Ibid., pp. 110–11.
25. Ibid., p. 111.
26. Ibid., p. 145.
27. Ibid., p. 146.
28. Ibid., pp. 528–30. For Turkish translations of Grigor's descriptions of both the 1609 and 1635 expulsions, see Hrand D. Andreasyan, 'Celâlilerden Kaçan Anadolu Halkının Geri Gönderilmesi', *İsmail Hakkı Uzunçarşılı'ya Armağan* (Ankara: Türk Tarih Kurumu, 1976), pp. 45–53.
29. Grigor Daranałts'i, p. 201.
30. Ibid., pp. 201–2.

31. Ibid., p. 202.
32. Ibid., p. 203.
33. Ibid., p. 204.
34. Ibid.
35. Ibid., p. 192.
36. Ibid., p. 193.
37. Ibid.
38. Grigor Daranaḷtsʻi, pp. 194–201 and Pʻachʻachean, pp. 35–7.
39. Pʻachʻachean, pp. 37–8.
40. *Evliyâ Çelebi Seyahatnâmesi*, 8/349. See also, Çevik, pp. 80–2 and Kalaitzidis, pp. 108–28.
41. A currency denomination, for which 1 *kuruş* was equivalent to 100 *stak*. See note 2, Pʻachʻachean, p. 37.
42. Grigor Daranaḷtsʻi, pp. 141–2.
43. Ibid, pp. lix–lx.
44. RŞS 1553, 73a.
45. See Tom Papademetriou, *Render unto the Sultan: Power, Authority, and the Greek Orthodox Church in the early Ottoman Centuries* (Oxford University Press, 2015).
46. Dror Ze'evi, 'The Use of Ottoman Sharî'a Court Records as a Source for Middle Eastern Social History: A Reappraisal', *Islamic Law and Society* 5.1 (1998): 35–56.
47. For an introduction to Christian and communal courts in the seventeenth-century Ottoman Empire, see Eugenia Kermeli, 'The Right to Choice: Ottoman Ecclesiastical and Communal Justice in Ottoman Greece", in Christine Woodhead (ed.), *The Ottoman World* (London: Routledge, 2012), pp. 347–61.
48. Ronald C. Jennings, *Christians and Muslims in Ottoman Cyprus and the Mediterranean World, 1571–1640* (New York University Press, 1993), p. 166.
49. One consistent exception to this rule is Muslim gypsies. E.g. RŞS 1554, 45a.
50. RŞS 1530.
51. RŞS 1530, 92b.
52. RŞS 1538.
53. RŞS 1538, 49b.
54. RŞS 1539.

55. RŞS 1539, 23a, 71b, 74b, 76b.
56. RŞS 1539, 74b.
57. P'ach'achean, 22–3.
58. RŞS 1540, 11b.
59. RŞS 1541.
60. RŞS 1541, 6a, 7a, 14a.
61. RŞS 1542.
62. RŞS 1542, 3b, 10b, 20a, 32a, 45a, 46a.
63. RŞS 1542, 20a.
64. RŞS 1542, 45a and 46a.
65. RŞS 1542, 32a.
66. RŞS 1543.
67. RŞS 1543, 29b, 30a, 30b, 36b, 45a, 95b, 145b, 149a and 177a.
68. RŞS 1543, 30a.
69. RŞS 1543, 149a.
70. For a similar case of an Armenian being beaten, see also, RŞS 1548, 20a.
71. RŞS 1543, 45a.
72. RŞS 1543, 30b.
73. RŞS 1543, 30a.
74. RŞS 1547.
75. RŞS 1546, 52b, 54a and 93a.
76. RŞS 1547, 1b, 3b, 10a, 10b, 18b, 31b, 32a, 37a, 37b, 41a, 42b, 47b, 48a, 49b and 51a.
77. RŞS 1547–1555.
78. RŞS 1538.
79. RŞS 1545, 55a.
80. RŞS 1545, 85a.
81. RŞS 1546.
82. RŞS 1546, 93a.
83. RŞS 1547, 48a.
84. RŞS 1547, 10b.
85. RŞS 1547, 10a.
86. E.g. RŞS 1545, 9b.
87. See Seta Dadoyan, *The Fatimid Armenians: Cultural and Political Interaction in the Near East* (Leiden: Brill, 1997).
88. E.g. RŞS 1548, 57a and 1554, 20a.
89. E.g. RŞS 1553, 58a and 1554, 58a.

90. E.g. RŞS 1553, 37a and 1553, 55b.
91. E.g. Tijana Krstic, *Contested Conversions to Islam: Narratives of Religious Change in the Early Modern Ottoman Empire* (Stanford University Press, 2011), p. 157.
92. E.g. RŞS 1550, 32a.
93. See Selim Deringil, *Conversion and Apostasy in the Late Ottoman Empire* (Cambridge University Press, 2012), p. 115.
94. RŞS 1551, 59a.
95. Grigor Daranałtsʻi, p. 488.
96. Ibid., p. 462.
97. Ibid., p. 523.
98. RŞS 1547, 37b.
99. RŞS 1550, 37b.
100. See İsmail Hakkı Uzunçarşılı, *Osmanlı Devleti Teşkilâtından Kapukulu Ocakları: Acemi Ocağı ve Yeniçeri Ocağı* II (Ankara: Türk Tarih Kurumu, 1988), pp. 263–7.
101. RŞS 1554, 5a.
102. Grigor Daranałtsʻi, p. 69.
103. Grigor Daranałtsʻi, p. 72.
104. Ibid., p. 606.
105. There were, of course, also many Turkish-speaking Armenians in Anatolia. For example, the Armenian traveller Simēon of Poland notes that the Armenians living in the city centre of Kayseri did not know Armenian, only Turkish or Persian. The Armenian villagers outside the city, however, spoke Armenian. This suggests the link between urban environment and use of the Turkish language. See Simeon of Poland, *Simēon dpri Lehatsʻwoy ułegrutʻiwn*, Ed. Nersēs Akinean (Vienna: Mechitharisten, 1936), p. 326. See also *The Travel Accounts of Simēon of Poland*, George A. Bournoutian (trans.) (Costa Mesa: Mazda Publishers, 2007), p. 272.
106. Eremia Kʻeōmurchean, *Eremya Chelebi Kömürjian's Armeno-Turkish Poem: The Jewish Bride*, Andreas Tietze and Avedis K. Sanjian (trans.) (Wiesbaden: Harrassowitz, 1981), p. 9.
107. See Mehmet Zeki Pakalın, *Osmanlı Tarih Deyimleri ve Terimleri Sözlüğü* II (İstanbul: Milli Eğitim Basımevi, 1951), pp. 236–7.
108. RŞS 1547, 49b and 1554, 69b.
109. RŞS 1545, 82b; 1551, 51a; and 1553, 56b.
110. RŞS 1543, 30a.

111. See Miriam Eliav-Feldon, *Renaissance Impostors and Proofs of Identity* (New York: Palgrave Macmillan, 2012).
112. RŞS 1549, 55a.
113. RŞS 1551, 59a.
114. RŞS 1548, 47b.
115. RŞS 1548, 11a; and 1555, 36a, 47b, and 48a.
116. RŞS 1544, 65a.
117. RŞS 1545, 69a.
118. RŞS 1553, 81a.
119. RŞS 1554, 69b.
120. RŞS 1554, 68b.
121. RŞS 1542, 32a; 1544, 59a; and 1545, 55a.
122. RŞS 1545, 85a; 1550, 23a; and 1553, 60a.
123. RŞS 1548, 20b.
124. RŞS 1548, 11a.
125. RŞS 1555, 9a. See also RŞS 1552, 39b.
126. RŞS 1547, 47b.
127. RŞS 1555, 80b.
128. E.g., RŞS 1547, 6a.
129. E.g., RŞS 1544, 54a.
130. RŞS 1548, 23b.
131. RŞS 1549, 61b.
132. RŞS 1549, 91b.
133. RŞS 1554, 117b.
134. RŞS 1547, 50a.
135. RŞS 1550, 26b.
136. RŞS 1550, 40b.
137. RŞS 1555, 11a.
138. RŞS 1550, 87b.
139. RŞS 1548, 55a.
140. Additional examples include RŞS 1549, 23b; 1550, 34b; and 1554, 73a.
141. RŞS 1543, 45a.
142. RŞS 1547, 47b.
143. For more on the *ispence* see Halil İnalcik, 'İspence,' *İslam Ansiklopedisi*, Vol. 23 (İstanbul: Türkiye Diyanet Vakfı, 2001), p. 177. The precedent for providing exemption to Christian clergy goes back to the days of early Ottoman conquests. For an example of a fifteenth-century *berat* granting tax-exemption to a Greek

metropolitan, see *Kânûnnâme-i Sultânî Ber Müceb-i 'Örf-i 'Osmânî*, Robert Anhegger and Halil İnalcik (eds) (Ankara: Türk Tarih Kurumu Basımevi, 2000), p. 66.

144. RŞS 1548, 57a.
145. Grigor Daranaltsʻi, pp. 201–2.
146. RŞS 1549, 98a.
147. E.g., RŞS 1549, 91b.
148. RŞS 1555, 73a.
149. E.g., RŞS 1553, 37a. For information about Rodosto's numerous pious foundations, see Mehmet Serez, *Tekirdağ ve Çevresi Vakfıyeleri* (Tekirdağ Valiliği Yayınıdır, 1993).
150. RŞS 1553, 54a.
151. The '*yave harâcı*' was a special category of tax 'on those who had strayed'. For other examples, see Bruce Masters, *The Origins of Western Economic Dominance in the Middle East: Mercantilism and the Islamic Economy in Aleppo, 1600–1750* (New York University Press: 1988), p. 85.
152. RŞS 1555, 74a.
153. RŞS 1555, 73a.
154. E.g., RŞS 1552, 8a and 8b.
155. RŞS 1549, 94a.
156. For a critical study of the Kayseri court records from this time period, see Ronald C. Jennings, 'Zimmis (non-Muslims) in Early 17th Century Ottoman Judicial Records: The Sharia Court of Anatolian Kayseri', *Studies on Ottoman Social History in the Sixteenth and Seventeenth Centuries: Women, Zimmis and Sharia Courts in Kayseri, Cyprus and Trabzon* (Istanbul: Isis Press, 1999), pp. 347–412.
157. RŞS 1549, 61b.
158. RŞS 1553, 38b.
159. RŞS 1553, 60a.
160. RŞS 1555, 80b.
161. RŞS 1552, 13b.
162. Grigor Daranaltsʻi, p. 520.
163. See Grigor Daranaltsʻi, p. lxi.
164. RŞS 1570, 66a.
165. RŞS 1570.
166. E.g. RŞS 1570, 63a.
167. RŞS 1570, 30b.

168. RŞS 1576.
169. RŞS 1576, 7b.
170. Extensive property transactions involving Armenians seems to be a common feature of notebooks from the 1620s and 1630s, as further evidenced by perusal of RŞS 1583 for the years 1044–6 (1634–7). E.g. RŞS 1583, 11a, 17b, among others.
171. RŞS 1576, 28a.
172. RŞS 1576, 39b.
173. E.g., RŞS 1577, 73b.
174. RŞS 1576, 41b.
175. For further information about the *'avârız*, see Halil Sahillioğlu, "Avârız', *İslam Ansiklopedisi* 4 (Ankara: Türkiye Diyanet Vakfı, 1991), pp. 108–9.
176. RŞS 1576, 42a.
177. RŞS 1576, 43a.
178. RŞS 1577, 40b.
179. RŞS 1579, 43b.
180. Grigor Daranałts'i, pp. 194–201 and P'ach'achean, pp. 35–7.
181. RŞS 1578, 42b.
182. RŞS 1579, 55a.
183. Çevik, *Tekirdağ Tarihi Araştırmaları*, p. 80.
184. Reşat Kasaba, *A Moveable Empire: Ottoman Nomads, Migrants, and Refugees* (University of Washington Press, 2011).
185. See Halil İnalcik, *The Survey of Istanbul, 1455: The Text, English Translation, Analysis of the Text, Documents* (Istanbul: Türkiye İş Bankası Kültür Yayınları, 2010), p. 248.
186. Halil İnalcik, 'The Policy of Mehmed II Toward the Greek Population of Istanbul and the Byzantine Buildings of the City', *Dumbarton Oaks Papers* 23/24 (1969/1970), p. 238.
187. İnalcik, *The Survey of Istanbul, 1455*, p. 449.
188. Grigor Daranałts'i, p. 135.
189. Halil İnalcik, 'İstanbul', *İslâm Ansiklopedisi*, Vol. 23 (İstanbul: Türkiye Diyanet Vakfı, 2001),p. 233.
190. Vardges Mik'ayelyan, *Hay gałt'ashkharhi patmut'yun (mijnadarits' minch'ev 1920 t'vakanĕ)*, Vol. II (Yerevan: HH GAA "Gitut'yun" Hratarakch'ut'yun, 2003), p. 66.
191. Cem Behar, *Osmanlı İmparatorluğu'nun ve Türkiye'nin Nüfusu: 1500-1927* (Ankara: T. C. Başbakanlık Devlet İstatistik Enstitüsü, 1996), p. 74.

192. *Simēon dpri Lehats'woy ułegrut'iwn*, p. 8. See also *The Travel Accounts of Simēon of Poland*, p. 33.
193. Mik'ayelyan, *Hay gałt'ashkharhi patmut'yun (mijnadarits' minch'ev 1920 t'vakanĕ)*, Vol. II, pp. 69–70.
194. See Daniel Goffman, *Izmir and the Levantine World, 1550–1650* (University of Washington Press, 1990).
195. Mübahat S. Kütükoğlu, 'İzmir', *İslam Ansiklopedisi*, Vol. 23 (İstanbul: Türkiye Diyanet Vakfı, 2001), p. 519.
196. *Simēon dpri Lehats'woy ułegrut'iwn*, pp. 37–8, and *The Travel Accounts of Simēon of Poland*, p. 61.
197. See Kütükoğlu, 'İzmir', 520.
198. Hrach'ya Achaṙyan, *Hay gałt'akanut'yan patmut'yun* (Yerevan: Hrach'ya Achaṙyan Anvan Hamalsaran, 2002), pp. 550–1.
199. Sebouh David Aslanian, *From the Indian Ocean to the Mediterranean: The Global Trade Networks of Armenian Merchants from New Julfa* (Berkeley: University of California Press, 2011), p. 69.
200. Achaṙyan, *Hay gałt'akanut'yan patmut'yun*, p. 550.
201. Aslanian, *From the Indian Ocean to the Mediterranean*, p. 69.
202. See, for example, Bruce Masters, *Christians and Jews in the Ottoman Arab World: The Roots of Sectarianism* (Cambridge University Press, 2001), pp. 71–80, and Goffman, pp. 77–92.
203. *Simēon dpri Lehats'woy ułegrut'iwn*, pp. 40–1. See also *The Travel Accounts of Simēon of Poland*, p. 64.
204. See *The Travel Accounts of Simēon of Poland*, p. 5.
205. P'ach'achean, p. 23, footnote 1.
206. RŞS 1549, 98a.
207. RŞS 1576, 42a.
208. Hacer Ateş, 'Kuzey Marmara Sahilleri ve Ard Alanında Şehirleşmenin Tarihi Süreci: XVI.–XVII. Yüzyıllarda Tekirdağ ve Yöresi', p. 160.
209. Sandfuchs, 'Reconstructing a Town From its Court Records Rodosçuk (1546–1553)', p. 28.
210. Hacer Ateş, 'Kuzey Marmara Sahilleri ve Ard Alanında Şehirleşmenin Tarihi Süreci: XVI.–XVII. Yüzyıllarda Tekirdağ ve Yöresi', p. 164.
211. Mustafa Murat Öntuğ, 'Balıkesir'deki Ermeni Kilisesi ve Mektep Açma Faaliyetleri', *Osmanlı Tarihi Araştırma ve Uygulama Merkezi Dergisi* 19 (2006): 343–64.

212. Minas G. Gasapean, *Hayerĕ Nikomidioy gawaṙin mēj* (Partizak: Azatamart, 1913), pp. 102–3.
213. P. Charanis, *The Armenians in the Byzantine Empire* (Venda Nova: Imprensa, 1963), p. 57.
214. Mik'ayelyan, *Hay gaḷt'ashkharhi patmut'yun (mijnadarits' minch'ev 1920 t'vakanĕ)*, Vol. II, p. 68.
215. Oktay Özel, 'Population Changes in Ottoman Anatolia during the 16th and 17th Centuries: The "Demographic Crisis" Reconsidered', *International Journal of Middle East Studies* 36.2 (2004): 191.
216. In addition to these seven manuscripts with precise copying dates, three manuscripts – M 3074, M 4441 and 5123 – are included in the catalogue's index for Istanbul and attributed to the fifteenth or sixteenth centuries. Upon closer investigation, however, it becomes evident that the portion of M 5123 that was copied in Istanbul took place long after the manuscript's initial creation by another scribe in 1636. As for M 3074 and M 4441, they neither have precise copy-dates nor does there appear to be any solid evidence linking these manuscripts to Istanbul. I am grateful to Garnik A. Harutyunyan, a senior researcher at the Mashtots' Institute of Ancient Manuscripts in Yerevan, for consulting with unpublished catalogue data concerning these manuscripts.
217. See *Ts'uts'ak dzeṙagrats' Mashtots'i anvan Matenadarani I* (Yerevan, 1965); *Ts'uts'ak dzeṙagrats' Mashtots'i anvan Matenadarani II* (Yerevan, 1970); and *Ts'uts'ak dzeṙagrats' Mashtots'i anvan Matenadarani III* (Yerevan, 2007).
218. *Simēon dpri Lehats'woy uḷegrut'iwn*, p. 207. See also *The Travel Accounts of Simēon of Poland*, p. 184.
219. Amirdovlat' of Amassia (1420–96) was an Armenian medical writer active at the court of Mehmed II. While he did complete important works in Middle Armenian in late fifteenth-century Istanbul, he was neither a 'home-born' Istanbul-Armenian author (being from Amassia), nor did he establish a literary tradition that would continue to thrive in Istanbul after his lifetime as Eremia K'eōmurchean would do two centuries later. For more about Amirdovlat' of Amassia, see S.A. Vardanyan, *Amirdovlat Amassiatsi: A Fifteenth-Century Armenian Natural Historian and Physician*, Michael Yoshpa (trans.) (Delmar: Caravan Books, 1999).
220. Edmond Schütz has observed a comparable acceleration in manuscript production in the Crimea during the same time period. See Edmond Schütz, 'An Armeno-Kıpchak Document of 1640 from Lvov and its Background in

Armenia and in the Diaspora', in György Kara (ed.), *Between the Danube and the Caucasus: Oriental Sources on the History of the Peoples of Central and South-Eastern Europe,*(Budapest: Akadémiai Kiadó, 1987), p. 256.

221. Kevork Bardakjian, 'The Rise of the Armenian Patriarchate of Constantinople', *Christians and Jews in the Ottoman Empire: The Functioning of Plural Society,* Vol. I (New York: Holmes and Meier, 1982), p. 97. Bardakjian's work is highly influenced by a series of articles on Istanbul patriarchal history by Hayk Pērpērean, most prominently, Hayk Pērpērean, 'K. Polsoy hay patriark'ut'ean himnarkut'iwnĕ', *Handēs Amsōreay* 7–9 (1964): 338–450.

222. Bardakjian, pp. 94–5.

223. Martiros Łrimets'i, *Martiros Łrimets'i: Usumnasirut'yun ew bnagrer*, A. A. Martirosyan (ed.) (Yerevan: Haykakan SSṘ GA Hratarakch'ut'yun, 1958), p. 151.

224. Nersēs Akinean, 'Taḷ Ararats'ots'', *Handēs Amsōreay* (1937): 334–5.

225. Grigor Daranaḷts'i, p. 476, emphasis added.

226. Ibid., p. 202, emphasis added.

227. Eremia K'ēōmurchean, *Eremia K'ēōmurchean patmut'iwn hamaṙōt DCH tariots' ōsmanean t'agaworats'n*, Zh. M. Avetisyan (ed.) (Yerevan: Haykakan SSṘ GA Hratarakch'ut'yun, 1982), pp. 10–12.

PART II
INTEGRATION AND RENAISSANCE

4

Grigor Daranaltsʻi and the Crisis of Leadership and Infrastructure in the Early Seventeenth-century Western Armenian Diaspora

The second part of this book focuses on the lives and works of two Kemah-Armenian authors, Grigor Daranaltsʻi and Eremia Kʻeōmurchean. They were both unusual men who served as distinguished leaders in their communities: in no way can they be seen as 'typical' of their times and society. But analysis of their lives and writings provides a glimpse into contemporary social changes, and I argue that their biographies can serve as the basis for building a periodisation of Ottoman-Armenian history in the seventeenth century. When first-generation refugees arrived in Istanbul, Western Anatolia and Thrace, they faced a crisis of leadership and infrastructure, and churchmen like Grigor Daranaltsʻi applied themselves to community and infrastructure building. It was only in the second half of the seventeenth century that Western Armenian intellectual and literary life reached its maturity primarily through the literary and intellectual efforts of one man, Eremia Kʻeōmurchean. Analysis of these two authors serves as a means of investigating Armenian settlement and cultural life in the aftermath of the mass migrations.

Grigor Daranaltsʻi and his chronicle – the topic of this chapter – have already been mentioned in this book. In Chapter Two, his chronicle was an important source for describing Kemah and the 'Valley of Monasteries' during the time of the Celali Revolts; in Chapter Three, it was used to construct an account of Armenians' first settlement in Rodosto. Grigor's chronicle is known to Armenian historians, some of whom have used its first part as a repository of data about early seventeenth-century Armenian history in the Ottoman Empire,[1] but these scholars have not considered the chronicle holistically as an artifact of seventeenth-century Ottoman-Armenian cultural and social life.

Here I will remedy this by providing an account of Grigor's life and considering his chronicle in its entirety as a literary work and political testament. The Armenians who fled westwards from the Celalis arrived in a different cultural sphere without extensive Armenian cultural or religious infrastructure outside of Istanbul and with intense political and religious divisions within their own community. Grigor was a pastor, fundraiser and infrastructure builder for the newly arrived Armenians, and his chronicle is the political testament of the leader of an Armenian faction which was written to satisfy the utilitarian needs of a community displaced by migration and divided by internal conflict.

After considering Grigor's biography, this chapter will focus on the second part of his chronicle – which has been neglected both in the first chapters of this book and by Armenian historians in general – using it as a window into the early seventeenth-century disjuncture in Ottoman-Armenian ecclesiastical life. By recounting some of Grigor's stories from this period, we will see how the increased mobility of the seventeenth century – including the movement of refugees, economic globalisation and the spread of Catholic missionaries in Ottoman lands – catalysed changes in Armenian communal life that Grigor interpreted in a highly negative light.[2] In the face of these challenges, Grigor used his chronicle to construct an intellectual bridge between life in the 'Old World' of Anatolia before the Celali Revolts and the unsettling 'New World' in Western Anatolia, Istanbul and its environs after the Great Armenian Flight. He used this contrast didactically, to provide Armenians in his community with a vision of how religious life should and should not function, and perhaps also to bolster his own standing in the community through his link to the 'Old World'. Finally, the focus of this chapter will shift to a description of Grigor's role in infrastructure building, showing, in particular, how Greek churches became the object of intercommunal conflict.

The Life of Grigor Daranałts'i

Grigor's chronicle was first published in 1915 by an Armenian churchman named Mesrop Nshanean, who prefaced his volume with the following short summary of Grigor's life work:

The author of the *Chronicle*, Grigor the *vardapet* Kamakhets'i or Daranalts'i, nicknamed 'Buk'', was a churchman of the first half of the seventeenth century whose fervour and activeness strikes the eye. He made numerous journeys, was involved in the conflicts of contemporary patriarchs of Constantinople and played some role in them, he led the first return of refugees expelled from Constantinople by the power of the state, he renovated and had built monasteries and churches, in Rodosto he pastored with a leadership position, as likewise [he pastored] the refugee Armenians newly-established in the vicinities of Nikomedia [Izmit] and Bursa. Finally, in the dark time period for the national literature in which he lived, he was a lover of books and literature, collecting around him students of letters, copying a multitude of books, and producing one or two works of his own.[3]

Nshanean here presents the main categories of Grigor's achievements: the traveller, the politician, the leader of refugees, the church-builder, the pastor and the teacher and author. The Armenians of Grigor's own times characterised him with a short nickname, 'Buk'', which means 'snowstorm' or 'tribulation'.[4] Nshanean does not venture to consider the significance of this nickname here, a question to which I will return later.

Grigor was born in Kemah around the year 1576, and his father died when he was still a boy. The orphaned Grigor settled in the monasteries of Mount Sepuh, apparently moving among them.[5] His time in the monasteries was unhappy, as he recollects in this passage:

> If we were to write about our misery from the time of birth – about growing up as an orphan and being abandoned, forlorn, and unprotected among monks, not [having] a teacher and not an adviser – if we were to write [everything] one by one, it would be considered unbelievable to many and tedious for listeners.[6]

Elsewhere, he laments that

> We were so miserable, wandering around unbridled. No one was caring to say to me, 'where have you gone', or 'from where are you coming'. Today, still more, our monasteries from Erzurum until here [Rodosto] are houses of women and Kurds. The canonical hours are not fixed, nor the mass, nor

the hierarchy, nor the monks, nor the singing of the Psalms. As the Great Nerses said, 'The holy places will become the dwellings of the ungodly'. Being amidst such misfortunes, we did not know our [own] deficiency and disorderly habits . . .[7]

Perhaps it was in those unhappy days of his childhood that Grigor developed his distaste for monastic irregularity, thus planting the seeds of his later vigorous campaigns for religious order in Western Anatolia.

The year 1590, however, was a turning point in Grigor's life, when he met his first spiritual guide and role model, the ascetic Paron. Paron was an unusual saviour figure. Later in his life Grigor wrote a short biography of Paron, describing how he came to be an ascetic in the Valley of Monasteries:

There was a man named Paron from the village of St. Tiknay of the province of Khordzunkʻ [in the modern-day Bitlis region]. He left his country together with his household and parents, and they came and settled in the Province of Churches in the capital city, Erzincan. He married according to the rules of the worldly order, but after two and a half months his wife died. Again he took a wife for a second time, and she also died after two and a half months, such that the days of his two wives was a time of five months. He was very heart-wrenched and wavered with inconsolable grief, to the point of not knowing how to get out of the situation. Because of excessive sadness, he departed, and in secret from his parents he went far westwards to the capital city Constantinople, not knowing himself why he went. Like [someone] drunk from wine he did not know where he was going. In that way he went. And going he reached until the monastery of Tokat, which is named after St Anne, the parent of the Holy Mother of God. With travelling friends, they passed the night at an inn. And by the providence of the solicitudes of God, St Anne appeared in a vision in the form of his aunt. With many entreating and menacing words, she instructed him that 'The swift death of your wives [happened] by the solicitudes of God. The behest of the Lord wills that you renounce the world and that you entirely throw off that which is of the world. Turn from the path on which you're going, as it is not the will of the Lord for you to go on that pernicious journey'.[8]

Inspired by this dream, Paron renounced the world and took up the life of an ascetic. After some travelling, he returned to the Valley of Monasteries. Grigor writes:

> Again he came to Erzincan and from there he came to Mount Sepuh, to the catacombs of the Holy Illuminator. He stayed there for a short time at the monastery of monks, and from there he descended to the Cave of Mane. He remained there for many days. [Paron] built all its rough rocky benches, making them with great stones and earth. And from there he descended to a valley in solitude, and he found suitable places, little cells on the face of a grotto, in which many hermits before had resided. Now they call it the rock of Shik, calling it by the name of the first inhabitants. He stayed there with great asceticism alone for many years. And many came from the world. They joined him, and they learned his habits . . .⁹

Paron was not a *vardapet* or priest, but a charismatic ascetic who gathered around him a group of loyal followers living together in his grotto of natural caves (see Figure 4.1). Grigor likens Paron to the famous Anthony the Great of the Age of Constantine, who remained the principal model of

Figure 4.1 Hermit caves near Kemah (centre left).

the heroic hermit from Late Antiquity through all ages of Eastern Christian history.[10] On one occasion during the Celali Revolts, Paron had such powers of persuasion that he even succeeded in convincing a bandit to desist from robbery and looting.[11] According to Grigor, Paron wielded broad influence despite – or perhaps because of – his position outside of formal hierarchies, like the famous 'holy man' of Late Antiquity:[12] '. . . [Paron] was an adviser to all, great and small. The dwellers of the monasteries of Sepuh, both bishops and cenobite priests, they were coming and requesting counsel from him, and he was teaching everyone with his God-given graces'.[13]

Much of Paron's biography derives from Late Antique hagiographical tropes, but his story is nonetheless important because it provides insight into the religious landscape of Ottoman Anatolia. Islamic religious authority in Ottoman Anatolia was polycentric, being shared and contested by a diversity of *medrese*-trained jurists and teachers alongside various charismatic mystical leaders. Similarly, the landscape of Armenian religious life was sprinkled with untrained mystical authorities alongside ordained priests and well-educated *vardapets*. At a critical juncture of youthful crisis Grigor made recourse to an alternative authority for care and guidance, the charismatic ascetic Paron. Although Paron lacked a formal education himself, ironically it was he who provided Grigor with his early education. Grigor explains in his chronicle that Paron only gained a basic religious education as an adult: 'Later [Paron] learned scripture and the Psalms, which he had not at all learned in childhood. He learned them later in adulthood, at age thirty'.[14]

With regards to his own education, Grigor describes how he began to study with Paron's encouragement:

> And I, lowest of all, Grigor, servant of the word, I was a child and very ignorant and lacking [any] overseer of advisers. With good advice [Paron] brought us to our senses and exhorted us with many entreating and vehement means, and he convinced us to follow the service of the Scripture.[15]

Elsewhere he writes, 'The Ascetic Paron, who was named a father for us, he exhorted us in the study of the Holy Scripture . . .'[16] It seems that Grigor regularly went back and forth to the grotto from the monasteries. Grigor writes that '. . . I was frequently commuting to and fro to [Paron] on account of much warm affection which we had for him, and he for us . . .'[17]

CRISIS OF LEADERSHIP AND INFRASTRUCTURE | 153

Grigor quickly advanced in learning, and the time came when he had to part from the mentor of his youth. Grigor resided in the Valley of Monasteries until 1597, when he gained the rank of priest.[18] In order to become a learned *vardapet*, however, it became necessary for Grigor to attach himself to another teacher for more formal training.

The opportunity arose when Grigor met the *vardapet* Srapion in the village of Alpʻochʻi, and Srapion invited Grigor to become his student in a monastery near the city of Bayburt. Thus, at approximately the age of twenty, Grigor left his home region for the first time in his life, travelling on foot to Bayburt. It would be his first modest journey in a life of great travels across the breadth of the Ottoman Empire. No doubt the first sight that struck Grigor upon his arrival in Bayburt was its medieval castle, which dominates the city's skyline to this day (see Figure 4.2).

Grigor does not provide extensive details about the content of his education in Bayburt, but we do know that he made acquaintance with many other Armenian churchmen there who would reappear later in his life, such

Figure 4.2 Bayburt.

as *Vardapet* Yakob, who would later become the first Armenian priest in Rodosto.[19] It was during this period of his life, however, that conditions began to deteriorate in Eastern Anatolia. Thus, in 1600 he fled eastward from the instability, first to Kars and, from 1600–3, he continued his education at Saḷmosavankʻ, near Ējmiatsin.[20]

After three years in the South Caucasus – or the 'Land of Ararat' as he called it – Grigor finally returned to Bayburt to complete his education with *Vardapet* Srapion. He relates that

> On 28 May 1052 (1603), on the day of Pentecost, the coming of the Holy Spirit with fiery tongues on the assembly of the apostles, by the will of God we received the *vardapet*'s staff of authority, of which we are not worthy, in the city of Bayburt at the Archangel Church, from my professor Srapion.[21]

It had been Grigor's intention to return to Saḷmosavankʻ after receiving his credentials from Srapion, but he was prevented from doing so by the incursions of Shah Abbas and the Safavid army.[22] Thus, Grigor only narrowly missed intersecting with the momentous Persian campaign that would lead to the displacement of Julfa's Armenian community and its reestablishment at New Julfa in Isfahan. Instead, he remained in Bayburt, where conditions continued to deteriorate because of the Celalis.

Grigor recounts in detail how the political instability of his time impacted his own life at the Vahanshēn Monastery, located in a village near Bayburt (see Figure 4.3). He writes that after a major Celali victory against Ottoman forces,

> ... the bearer of bad news came [saying], 'Laraḷash [a Celali leader] with all his forces is charging and coming to Bayburt'. Some believed it; others didn't. We saw that men on the plain were migrating with all their possessions. They came and passed, going to the mountains and cedar forests. And then we, with the nearby villages, with all our possessions [and] with the *vardapet* and with the monks of the Vahanshēn Monastery, we ran to the mountains and to the wooded thicket of the Kankeli Valley. We stayed there for some days, and we heard that [the Celalis] had filled the country like a multitude of locusts or like torrents of water. Thus, like all-consuming locusts, they were emptying the whole land of food, and like floods they were destroying whatever fruits of labor still remained in cisterns and store-

CRISIS OF LEADERSHIP AND INFRASTRUCTURE | 155

Figure 4.3 Vahanshēn (Vahşen/Çatıksu) Village, Bayburt Province.

rooms. They were eating [that produce] and scattering the left-overs on the streets, [so that it became] mixed with mud, and they were casting fire on the buildings. They couldn't do anything to the city, however, on account of the stronghold of the fortress, but [the residents] gave them four thousand *kuruş*, so that they would not torch the city and all their buildings on the exterior.[23]

In short, after a rout for the Ottoman troops, the Celalis reigned supreme, and Grigor and the Armenian monks literally had to head for the hills in flight. At the end of 1604 Grigor departed for Trabzon, where he remained until Easter 1605. He then travelled by ship to the Crimea, where he encountered many Armenian refugees from Kemah.[24] Soon afterwards he crossed over to Istanbul, and he recounts that the Ottoman capital was also filled with his countrymen:

And when we came from Kefe to Istanbul, [the people of] all the lands of the Armenians from Tʻēodupōlis [Erzurum] to here, many came with me, which was in the year 1054 (1605), while others had come two years prior. Many also came afterward and scattered to Anatolia and Rumelia, to all the cities until Belgrad, the land of Moldavia, and to Poland.[25]

Here Grigor describes the successive waves of migration that characterised the Great Flight.

Soon after Grigor's first arrival in Istanbul in 1605, he was taken in by the priests of the St Nicholas Church at Edirnekapı (see Figure 4.4).[26] Thus began his relationship with that church and its community, one that would last more than twenty years. The first Armenian printing press in the Ottoman Empire had been established in this church in 1567.[27] In 1626 it would be converted into a mosque and currently it is in use as the Kefevi Mosque. Grigor recounts how the church was filled with his family members and acquaintances from Kemah in 1605:

> And there was found our brother Markos and our father's brother's son, Grigor the elder, and Yamuchay Grigor and other relatives. And all of our villagers were there in one place near the church, and they came to see [me] and to catch up, as for a long time we had not seen each other. And we rejoiced very much at seeing one another.
>
> And after a few days there was also our little sister, named Zardar. She also came with her children to catch up and to see [us], as we had not seen [her] since childhood. And many other beloved and friendly people from Erzincan and Bayburt came joyfully to see [us] when they heard [we were there].[28]

This was not only an opportunity for Grigor to get reacquainted with his blood relatives: the greatest joy was to reunite with his mentor Paron, who was in Istanbul on his return from a pilgrimage to Rome and Spain:

> ... Paron, the chief of present-day ascetics, came and found [me]. With four or five students he had come from the land of the Franks ... as he had gone on pilgrimage to St Peter and Paul and to St James. In those days when he came, we found one another and rejoiced with great merriment.
>
> To see them was more delightful for us than everyone [else], because he had been the reason for our becoming a *vardapet*. When we were on Mount Sepuh in the service of the catacombs of the Illuminator, like a father he

Figure 4.4 Kefevi Mosque, Istanbul (formerly St Nicholas Church).

was moved to compassion for us, and frequently he was advising [us] with encouraging words, as we were a child and foolish . . .'[29]

Paron's travels spanned seas and empires, and soon after this reunion, Grigor would join him on his first trip beyond Anatolia, Istanbul and the Black Sea region.

It was probably in the summer of 1605 that Paron and Grigor embarked for Egypt.[30] It is possible to follow Grigor's travels because in Egypt he began copying a Bible. Grigor travelled with this Bible and recorded several years of his travels in multiple colophons written throughout the text. Grigor wrote in one of these that 'Now it's been written, this holy book, which is called inspired Scripture, which began to be written in November of the year 1605 . . . in the land of Egypt and in Jerusalem . . .'[31]

In spring 1606 Grigor arrived in Jerusalem.[32] According to his biography of Paron, Paron stayed in Jerusalem for seven years – until his death[33] – while Grigor remained there for about a year, returning to Istanbul in spring 1607. Soon after returning he made an initial visit to Rodosto, his future bishopric.

Grigor's arrival there and the scandal concerning Naḷash Ḷazar have already been described in Chapter Two. According to Grigor, Ḷazar was enraged at not being granted precedence over the other Armenian priests of Rodosto and slandered the Armenians before an Ottoman judge, thus causing the mass eviction of Armenians from Rodosto. We saw above that this version of events has been cast into doubt by my discovery of a *sicil* banning Armenians from living in Muslim neighbourhoods because of suspicions of thievery, as this may have been the actual justification for the eviction. It is impossible to know exactly what transpired between Grigor and Ḷazar, but Grigor relates in his chronicle how he returned from Rodosto to Istanbul to find him. Grigor tried to organise a church trial against Ḷazar, but he did not show up. Grigor claims that in response to this great impudence, he and his student Siměon gave Ḷazar a vigilante beating.[34] This would be the first – but not the last – episode in which Grigor took pleasure in describing how he used physical violence against an opponent, beating him with his churchman's staff.

In this instance, however, Grigor could not take such drastic measures without negative repercussions, as Ḷazar was a client of the Armenian Patriarch of Constantinople. Ḷazar ran to complain to the patriarch, Grigor of Kayseri, about this act of violence. In punishment, the patriarch confiscated Grigor Daranaḷtsʻi's staff,[35] which had been conferred upon him by Srapion as a sign of his rank of *vardapet*.

The narrative of events offered so far in Grigor's chronicle is inadequate to explain Grigor's conflict with Ḷazar and his patron, the Armenian Patriarch of Constantinople, Grigor of Kayseri. Instead of taking Grigor's stories at face value, we must remember that the arrival of Armenian refugees from Eastern Anatolia prompted political tension between the small Istanbul-Armenian community, which had already been present before the Celalis and the deluge of refugees that arrived as a result of chaos in the East. This tension led to political factionalisation and the emergence of two rival Armenian camps. Grigor Daranaḷtsʻi became the leader of the refugee faction, while the Patriarch of Constantinople, Grigor of Kayseri, as well as various patriarchal deputies (*vekîl*) alternated in representing the interests of the small Istanbul-Armenian elite. Grigor's tales only make sense if we recognise the context of political infighting between Grigor and his refugees, on the one hand, and the local Istanbul elite, represented by the patriarchate, on the other hand. It is impossible to say with certainty if Grigor's tales about Lazar are true, fabricated, or something in between. It can, however, be said with certainty that Lazar was a client of Grigor's political enemies, and it was for this reason that the priests of Rodosto rejected him.

Grigor Daranalts'i was humiliated when the patriarch took his staff, but he was the leader of a powerful faction that would not tolerate this snub. Under pressure from the populace, Grigor Daranalts'i and Grigor of Kayseri met again, and the latter was forced to make a superficial peace with the refugees' leader and to return Daranalts'i's staff.[36] It was only the beginning, however, of a period (1607–9) of intermittent conflict between these two churchmen. Almost immediately after their forced reconciliation, conflict erupted again over financial issues. When Daranalts'i's student Siměon died suddenly, representatives of the patriarchate demanded that his possessions be confiscated and that Grigor pay money in order to be able to bury him. Grigor was indignant at this request, saying to the patriarch's representative that 'Satan has applied [and] cast the disease of avarice on you'.[37]

In fact, the financial dispute that erupted between the Armenian Patriarchate of Istanbul and the refugee clergy was of a deeper and more serious nature than Grigor Daranalts'i suggests in his chronicle. The Armenian Patriarchate was often strapped for cash as a result of tax payments it owed to the Ottoman state, and thus it tried to apply pressure on refugee priests to help collect money to apply to the tax obligations. The refugee priests were, however, unable or unwilling to pay. In his chronicle, Grigor Daranalts'i described the sad situation as follows:

> After so many infringements and oppressions [the problems in the East], [the patriarch] began to write a number for the priests, to demand tax-collection from them. From some, ten red [coins]; from others, a ten-*kuruş* piece; and from the very poor, a five-*kuruş* piece. Thus, [he was] requesting tax-collection in three ways. And a cry of woe and lamentation fell among the newly-arrived emigrant priests, who had just come [to Istanbul], poor, naked, and very indigent, having been afflicted and pillaged. Both the priests and the [common] folks were just barely able to procure [their] daily [piece of] bread, some [only] with great effort.[38]

The refugees' first act of self-defence against the Armenian Patriarchate of Istanbul was to have Grigor Daranalts'i – not the patriarch – officially designated as their leader by the Ottoman state. They achieved this with the assistance of a servant at the Ottoman court who was a Muslim emigrant from Kemah.[39]

But the appointment of Grigor as the formal leader of the Armenian refugees in Istanbul did not stop the conflicts between the refugees and the Armenian Patriarchate. Not long afterwards Grigor Daranalts'i appeared in an Islamic court to argue a case against the deputies of the patriarchate. Daranalts'i narrates how he convinced the judge to sympathise with the emigré priests and to order that they be allowed to enter Istanbul's Armenian churches without hindrance. In a comment indicating the value of Ottoman Turkish documents for Armenians in the Ottoman Empire, Grigor boasts that

> [The judge] in this way made a writ of [his] decision – that is to say, a *sicil* – and leaving we went each to his place. After a few days we were able to take a copy (*suret*) of the writ (*sicil*). Behold, we still have it with us in reserve from that time, which was the year 1057 (1608), until today, which now is the year 1083 (1634) and [the reign of] Murad IV.[40]

Grigor cherished his Ottoman Turkish *sicil* gained in litigation against other Armenian churchmen for more than a quarter century, just as many churches and monasteries throughout the Middle East preserve Ottoman Turkish documentation delineating their properties and prerogatives to this very day.

It was not long before Grigor appeared in court again. He recounts how the Armenian Patriarchate again tried to collect taxes from the impoverished immigrant priests, leading some priests to threaten that they would convert to Islam. After an argument about taxation, Grigor recounts an incident in which

> A pitiful priest went out, and he shouted loudly so that the Armenians who were around might hear: 'Listen up! Listen up! I'm going to take the hand of my wife and children, and I'll have the town-crier proclaim, "Behold, I'm becoming a Turk [converting to Islam] with my whole family, out of the power of the Patriarch of the Armenians!"'[41]

Seeking to avert such desperate acts, the two factions sought arbitration from an Ottoman official. Grigor's partisan account of the affair depicts the Ottoman judge in a heroic light because he made judgement in the refugees' favour. Thus after recounting the story, Grigor prays for the Ottoman judge:

> Because of God, [the judge] made the right judgement and he delivered us from injustice. May the Lord God pay the just judge his wages of compensation, as He knows how to measure and to recompense. And after this, they [the patriarch's party] didn't ever approach us.[42]

The struggles between Grigor, leader of the refugees, and the Armenian Patriarchate continued until 1609. Finally, in that year, geographical spheres of influence were delineated, and Grigor Daranalts'i was granted Rodosto as a bishopric. Grigor's stay in Rodosto was, however, to be very brief.

In 1609, the year that Grigor became bishop in Rodosto, the Ottoman grand vizier Kuyucu Murad Paşa returned from a major campaign against the Celalis. Though the positive benefits of the campaign would prove to be short lasting Grigor considered them to have been a great success. In a chapter purporting to describe – with some hyperbole – 'how the Celalis were entirely erased and were destroyed without a trace', Grigor writes that

> In 1058 (1609) Murad Paşa – the commander, general, grand vizier, and capable [man] – strengthened by God, left with an immense [mass of] troops and went over the rebel Celalis whose multitude had ruined all the land of Asia until the shores of the ocean . . .[43]

Subsequently Grigor adds that

> Such a multitude of Celalis . . . he destroyed entirely in one year. He exterminated them and removed them from the land. The king – on account of terrible fear – could not attack anyone, [so] Murad Paşa, being strengthened by God, completely erased them, like Gideon with three hundred men [destroyed] the Midianites. He destroyed the [supporters of] Murad Han and our Shirin Beg on the plain of Khakhtik', which is called Bayburt, in the Suner Village, and he was filling up wells, which he had dug in front of all the villages, for the Celalis and for all the wicked, of whom those remaining in the land were complaining. He killed them, and he threw them in the

well and there were two or three men in [each] place: spread out they were arranged in order (*istif*), as eyewitnesses recounted. And we, four years later passed by that road. It was in the days of winter, [and] we saw the wells as large as a very big house. One or two had fallen, so they covered the opening with wood and soil. And in this way the impious were removed from the land, and they diminished like vapor diminishes. They did not see the glory of God.[44]

As noted earlier, Murad Paşa's Turkish epithet, 'Kuyucu', means 'well-digger' in Turkish, in reference to the mass graves here described. Though Murad was famed for his violence, Grigor describes him as a hero who was 'strengthened by God', as Grigor deemed the Celalis eminently deserving of massacre.

Convinced that the Celali problem had been solved – and eager to gain more tax revenue from Anatolian provinces – the Ottoman state ordered refugees from Istanbul to return to Anatolia.[45] Grigor was placed at the head of the Armenian caravan's camp and he led them on a forced march eastwards, after which he returned to his home town of Kemah.[46]

Grigor's activities in Rodosto before the march eastwards can be glimpsed in an Ottoman Turkish document (see Figure 4.5) drafted on 8 *Muharrem* 1018 (13 April 1609). It describes how 'the Armenian named Father Krikor son of Krekores' came to the court to sell his share in a piece of property, a house in one of Rodosto's 'infidel neighbourhoods'.[47] Grigor is, of course, a common Armenian name, and normally it would be impossible to prove that this document relates to Grigor Daranalts'i. But in his colophons Grigor Daranalts'i frequently prayed 'for my corporeal parents, for my father Grigorēs'.[48] Thus, it is all but certain that this document summarises his visit to the Rodosto Islamic court to make preparations for an imminent departure. Apparently he planned to settle in Kemah for good and not to return to Rodosto, thus choosing to sell his property.

Grigor reached Kemah in 1609, more than a decade after he had left home to study in Bayburt. While conditions upon his arrival had become calmer thanks to the anti-Celali campaigns of Grand Vizier Kuyucu Murad Paşa the situation did not remain stable for long. Grigor recounts that in Kemah 'we restored many ruined churches and monasteries', which had presumably been damaged by the Celalis.[49] For the first months of his stay conditions

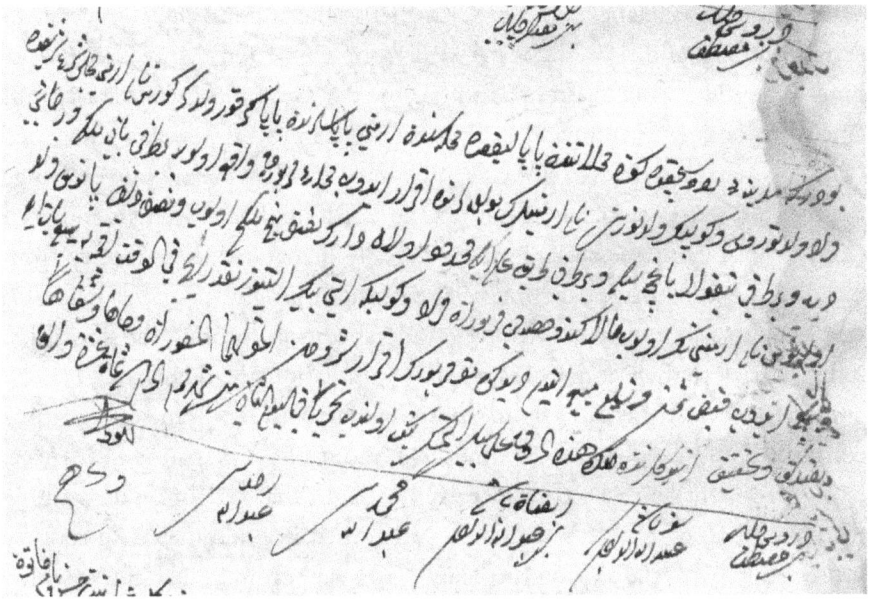

Figure 4.5 *Sicil* from 1609 documenting Grigor Daranałts'i's visit to court (RŞS 1553, 58a). Credit: Thanks to Mustafa Birol Ülker and ISAM for permission to reproduce this image.

were improved by a benevolent Ottoman *paşa* named Hasan, who was 'pro-Armenian (*hayasēr*)'.[50] But thereafter another general took his place and he and his troops began to harass the population and to make unjust appropriations, especially from the new arrivals Grigor had led from Istanbul. Grigor states that '. . . they began to implement their old habits, which they had done during the rebellion, and the land was filled with moans and cries on account of the tyranny of the unjust tormenters'.[51]

In addition to harassment at the hands of Ottoman authorities and Celalis, the Armenians of Kemah also faced another problem common to the entire region: ongoing famine. Grigor says that '. . . there was famine and nothing that could go by the name of wheat, but the only food was millet . . .' Even the millet had to be hauled in from Erzincan, leaving those who could not make the trip in desperate straits. Grigor went himself to Erzincan to gather millet and he reports that conditions there were just as bad, lamenting that 'there was such dearth in the land . . .' As a result, some people 'left and fled naked to Istanbul . . . many fled, not only of the newcomers, but also the old [residents]'.[52]

Grigor tells specific stories of Armenians who were tortured in order to extract money, and how they later fled from the region. Moreover, Grigor himself faced harassment from bandits. One day Grigor learned that a bandit chief was looking for him and he immediately ran for his life. He convinced two Ottoman Janissaries to smuggle him out of the Kemah region in exchange for four *kuruş*. They brought him to the border between Kemah and Akn (Kemaliye), but there the Janissaries allegedly demanded extra money from him.[53] After this unpleasant financial extortion, Grigor gradually made his way back to Istanbul, and thus his grand expedition to bring the Armenian refugees back to their homeland ended in humiliation and flight.

The Great Armenian Flight from Kemah to Istanbul and its environs continued, and Grigor had the dubious honour of participating in it twice. It was probably on this second occasion of flight that Grigor rescued a holy relic from one of Kemah's churches – identified in one nineteenth-century source as the Monastery of the King[54] – a nail from Jesus' cross, which would be brought to Rodosto for safe keeping and preserved there for the next three centuries. The nail became Rodosto's most sacred relic, an object of veneration for visitors that would remain there until the 1920s, when Rodosto Armenians took it to Bulgaria. It is currently in the possession of the Armenian church in Plovdiv.

Grigor arrived in Istanbul in spring 1612, where he was swiftly pulled back into the vortex of intra-Armenian ecclesiastical dispute. After some wrangling, the opponents of Patriarch Grigor of Kayseri ultimately gained the ascendancy in Istanbul. Grigor of Kayseri lost his patriarchal throne and returned to Kayseri in April or May of 1612.[55] Grigor of Kayseri's three main opponents then proceeded to divide ecclesiastical authority over most Ottoman territories among themselves in exchange for a financial payment to the Ottoman court. In this deal and subsequent ones we see how ecclesiastical leadership and taxation were intertwined, as authority was distributed both according to geography and taxation status.[56]

For the next three years Grigor was occupied with his ministry to refugees. Many of the anecdotes Grigor tells about this time in his life appear in the second part of his chronicle and they are best addressed in subsequent discussion of his chronicle's plan and purpose. It suffices to say that Grigor was frequently travelling between Izmit, Istanbul, Rodosto and Iznik, serving communities of refugee Armenians who were establishing new lives, villages and churches in the Marmara Sea region around Istanbul.

In 1616 Grigor withdrew from the patriarchal politics of Istanbul that had preoccupied him intermittently since 1607 when he embarked on his second trip to the Holy Land. At the beginning of the seventeenth century the Celali Revolts had hindered the flow of both pilgrims and donations to Jerusalem, thus causing the accumulation of debts. Upon his second visit to Jerusalem, Grigor rejoiced to discover that these financial problems had been solved and that the governance of the patriarchate was in good order. In contrast to this cause for rejoicing, Grigor was confronted with the sad news of his mentor Paron's passing.[57]

Grigor remained in Jerusalem for two Easters, in 1616 and 1617. He spent his time copying manuscripts, including continued labour over the Bible that he had begun on his first trip to the Holy Land more than a decade earlier. He departed from Jerusalem at the end of 1617 via Cyprus, where he remained for one year. His home in Cyprus was the St Makar Monastery (see Figure 4.6),

Figure 4.6 St Makar Monastery, Cyprus.

which was a way station for Ottoman Armenian pilgrims travelling between Istanbul and the Holy Land throughout the early modern period. Finally, at the beginning of 1619, Grigor returned to his see of Rodosto, where he would remain for seven years.[58]

Information about Grigor's activities and the life of the Armenian community in Rodosto during these years is scattered and sporadic, but we know that Grigor continued to minister to Armenian immigrant communities in Rodosto, Izmit, Iznik and Istanbul during this period. In 1625 Grigor left on a third pilgrimage to Jerusalem. Afterwards, he decided to return by land – arriving in Aleppo in 1627[59] – from where he originally planned to continue to his homeland of Kemah. He was forced, however, to change his mind because of continuing instability. Grigor records that

> After two Easters we endeavoured to go by land to Aleppo and from there to visit our homeland (*sıla*), to our country [Kemah], which we had wanted [to do] for a long time, but from fear [and] terror of lawless devourers we were not able to go . . .
>
> We arrived with great exertion in Aleppo, and from our city [Kemah] two renowned men had come. They gave the sorrowful news (*haber*) that 'Our land is in the midst of famine and captivity more than from the first Celalis, especially in this year. Cavalry have spread like locusts, especially the wolf-toothed Tatars, whose smoke [goes] until the sky and the flashing of their swords undulates like lightning and shines wherever you go. We are fleeing. There is fear and terror from three sides, from the cavalry of the Persians and of Abaza and of the [Ottoman] king. If you had been there, you'd have already fled. Now you want to go among the bloodthirsty, where the ground and water bleed?'[60]

This passage demonstrates that instability, famine and violence continued in the region of Kemah for several decades. The entire seventeenth century was a time of demographic flux and institutional instability for Armenians, and it seems that regular patterns only re-emerged in the eighteenth century, when local power bases in the Ottoman provinces established a new order. The Great Armenian Flight was a phenomenon that spanned the seventeenth century, with ebbs and flows of intensity.

Grigor returned to Istanbul in 1628. Thereafter, his activities during the last fifteen years of life likely conformed to the previous patterns of political manoeuvering in Istanbul and ministry to the refugees in various settlements of the Marmara Sea region. The only major event in Grigor's life that is known for certain after 1629 is his own passing in 1643 at the age of sixty-eight. His tombstone, which remained intact until the early twentieth century, eulogised him in this way:

> This tomb is the [place] of repose of Grigor of Kemah,
> the senior *vardapet*. He grew old, filled with days.
> In September of the year 1092 (1643) he passed away.
> By his hand the nail of the redeeming Cross
> was brought to this place, a source of cleansing healing.
> [Our] former shepherd, noble of rank,
> with good humour he shepherded his flock of migrated newcomers.[61]

Grigor was buried 'in a corner of the left-side of the courtyard of the Holy Redeemer Church',[62] which housed the nail relic he had rescued from Kemah. Rodosto Armenians remembered Grigor until the twentieth century and would gather at his grave annually to celebrate the man who, according to the engraving on his tombstone, had 'shepherded his flock of migrated newcomers'.[63]

Grigor's life can be divided into five main stages: his youthful years in Kemah from 1576 to 1597, his student years in Bayburt and at Salmosavankʻ under the direction of Srapion (1597–1604), the period of his flight to Istanbul and his first pilgrimage to Jerusalem with Paron (1604–7), his politically active years as the leader of the Armenian refugees in Rodosto and Istanbul and during the forced deportation back to Kemah (1607–16), and his later years of quiet preaching and writing (1616–43) based primarily in Rodosto, punctuated intermittently with further travels to Jerusalem and occasional political activities in Istanbul. Throughout his life Grigor was an active priest, book copyist and teacher of students. It was only later in his life that Grigor started to compose his *Chronicle*, his sole large-scale literary endeavour. It is primarily thanks to this work that knowledge of his life and career has been preserved.

Grigor Daranałts'i's *Chronicle*

Grigor's *Chronicle* survives in one autograph manuscript copy, currently located in the St James Manuscript Library of the Armenian Patriarchate of Jerusalem (J 1069). Grigor began its composition in 1634 and completed it in 1640,[64] writing intermittently from the time he was about fifty-eight years old until he was sixty-four. Pages of a draft of Grigor's chronicle seem to have been used as a source by the Istanbul-Armenian historian Ch'amch'ean in the eighteenth century, but it is clear that Ch'amch'ean did not have access to the full original manuscript.[65] The original seems to have languished unread in Rodosto for almost two centuries until finally being transferred to Jerusalem at an unknown date, probably at the beginning of the nineteenth century. Thus, Grigor's complete work was not accessible to a broad readership until Mesrop Nshanean published it in Jerusalem in 1915.

Grigor's chronicle – like many other major works written in Armenian in the seventeenth century – crossed the lines of several genres, modulating between passages of chronology, history, autobiography and hagiography. The chronicle has two main parts. The first part begins with a chronology. Grigor notes the arrival of the Turks in Anatolia in the eleventh century, and then comments on major events in medieval history, of both regional and local importance. For example, he mentions the activities of Saladin in the twelfth century and the Fall of Constantinople in 1453. He also records local natural disasters, such as earthquakes that took place in Erzincan in 1166 and 1236,[66] and he offers a more detailed chronology of developments in the sixteenth-century Ottoman Empire.[67]

Just as the chronicle's theme modulates between genres, so its register of language varies. Grigor usually wrote in the standard Classical Armenian of the churchmen of his day, but he sometimes incorporated colloquial elements from the spoken language, like the verbal particle *ku* (կու). His use of Armeno-Turkish was very limited, and the noted Armenologist Hayk Pērpērean has characterised Grigor's use of Turkish terminology as follows:

> The greatest part of the Turkish words employed by Daranałts'i . . . are either legal words, or words used in state documents which he employed exactly, with the intention of depicting the contents of the document authentically

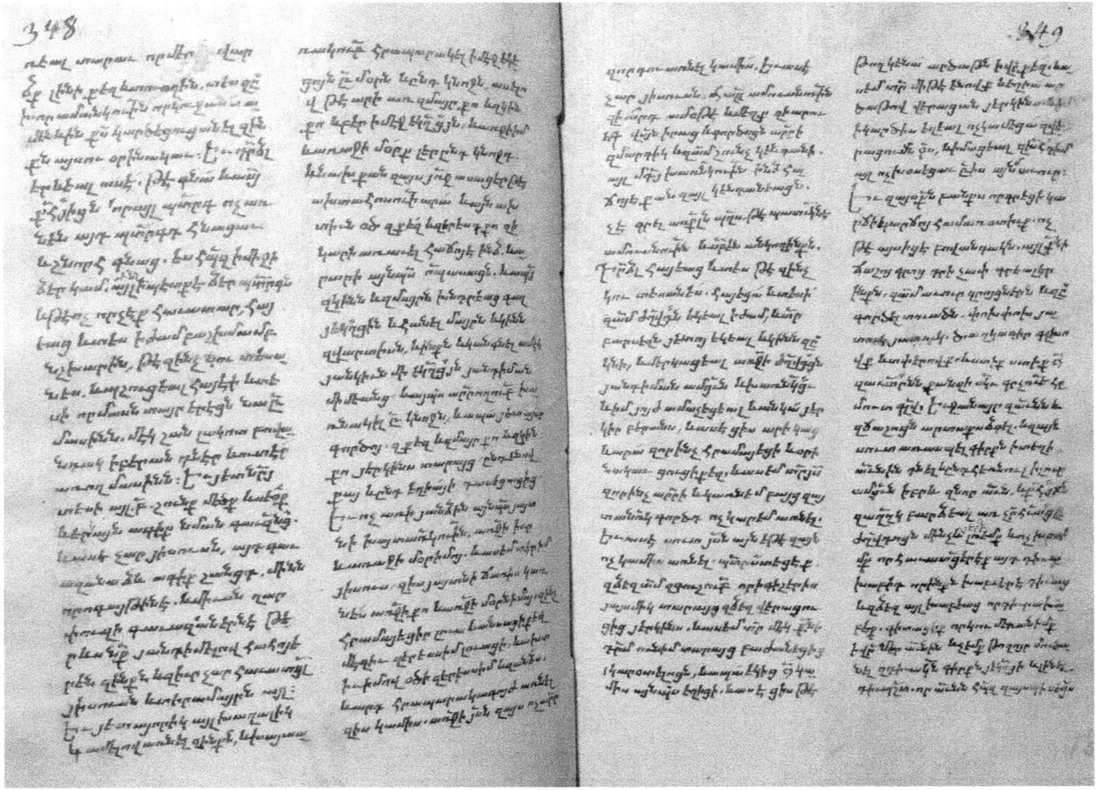

Figure 4.7 Pages of autograph copy of Grigor Daranałts'i's *Chronicle* (J 1069, 180b–181a). Thanks to the Apostolic Armenian Patriarch of Jerusalem Nourhan Manougian for permission to reproduce this image.

as far as he was able. Alternatively, they were uttered by Turkish-speaking individuals and with a concern for authenticity they were not translated into Armenian.[68]

Grigor let the dialects and terminology of his environment enter his chronicle in certain particular contexts.

Grigor's prefatory chronology – which resembles a broad diversity of similar Armenian short chronicles in genre – continues for only about ten pages of Nshanean's printed text. Thereafter Grigor transitions from the genre of chronology based on other historical works to his own original narrative, marking the change with an explicit note.[69] He begins his original narrative by describing the Celali Revolts and the breakdown of order in Anatolia, which he blames on the Ottoman Sultan Mehmed III (r. 1595–1603). His choice of starting point for the original portion of his history is critically important for understanding the structure of his chronicle as a whole. Grigor conceived of it as a description of the history of the Celalis, their destruction of Eastern Anatolian society and the establishment of new Armenian settlements and social life in Western Anatolia, Istanbul and Thrace. Grigor's own biography enters and departs from this broad narrative. By beginning with a passage on the alleged incompetence and negligence of Sultan Mehmed III, however, he sets the stage for a work on a major historical transformation, not an autobiography.

The second part of Grigor's chronicle has largely been neglected by scholarship. Here Grigor shifts his focus to ecclesiastical history, engaging in lengthy descriptions of Armenian holy men, beginning with an account of church affairs in Ējmiatsin, Sis (see Figure 4.8) and Jerusalem, the major ecclesiastical centres of his time. The Catholicosate of Ējmiatsin had been re-established in the fifteenth century. In the Middle Ages, the Catholicosate at Sis – near modern-day Adana – had arisen as the centre of Armenian ecclesiastical life and continued to be an important centre of Armenian church life even after the re-emergence of Ējmiatsin, when the two became competing centres of authority. Grigor also describes the debt crisis in Jerusalem that had been caused by the disruption of pilgrimage routes by the Celalis. Finally, following a general introduction to the states of affairs in the Armenian Church's three holiest sees – Ējmiatsin, Sis and Jerusalem – Grigor proceeds to his main

Figure 4.8 Ruins of the fortress above Sis (modern-day Kozan, Adana).

theme in the chronicle's second part: the lives of contemporary holy men. Grigor makes this transition with a discourse entitled, 'About the *vardapets* of the time we have heard: Who they were, and who they are, now in the present and in the past'.[70] Grigor's subsequent long discussion of the holy men of his time varies in tone, modulating from praiseful hagiography to outright condemnation.

Vardapets *and scribes of Greater Armenia in Grigor Daranalts'i's* Chronicle

Grigor sought to record the lives and achievements of Armenian holy men in his chapters entitled 'The *vardapets* of Mesopotamia: Who were they in our time',[71] 'The *vardapets* of the eastern Ostan provinces and of Mokkʻ (Moxoene) and Baḷesh (Bitlis), from our times until the present',[72] and 'Other *vardapets* of our province, both old and new, some of whom we heard and saw'.[73] The geographical focus of his laudatory biographies is noteworthy, as he aims to record the lives of distinguished holy men of Greater Armenia, focusing on the provinces of Ostan (in modern-day Armenia), Van, Bitlis, Erzincan and Kemah: all territories that were ravaged at the turn of the seventeenth century. Grigor focuses on *vardapets* who were alive during his youth or shortly before, and he notes that he personally knew many of these priests and ascetics. Grigor aims to provide a picture of functioning Armenian religious life in the ancient Armenian heartland just before the Celali Revolts and Great Armenian Flight.

Grigor profiles holy men who had acquired fame in Armenian religious circles and, since Grigor was a man of broad travels with a wide social circle, it seems that he sought to record their stories for students and fellow priests in Rodosto who were not similiarly men of the world of seasoned age. Grigor explicitly notes that he had been urged to write one biography at the insistence of a bishop. At the end of his biography of *Vardapet* Yakob, he concludes with an apology:

> I ask your pardon on account of writing out of order, as I had forgotten him [Yakob] in the course of writing. When Daniel our bishop saw [the lacuna], it was evident to him and with very threatening words [he asked,] 'You remember every *vardapet*, [but] why don't we see him?' On account of which I was obliged to write this passage later, as he [Yakob] is written with all justice in the book of life. Amen. Our Father.[74]

Clearly there was a demand for Grigor's biographies of holy men among the priests of Rodosto, who were reading Grigor's text as he wrote it and could become annoyed in the event of a lacuna.

An example of a laudatory biography in Grigor's chronicle is his description of the life of a *vardapet* named Maḷakʻia from Bayburt. Grigor records that

> In Bayburt near to our time there was an ascetic *vardapet* named Maḷakʻia, and [he was] a dexterous scribe in every art, ornamented with a perfect and virtuous way of life, in the St. Stepʻanos Monastery, which is in a village called by the name Vahanashēn. He lived for a long time a peaceful life in silence in that same monastery, and he never wanted to go to out of the monastery on account of his being a fast writer and concerned with art. He filled with books all the land of Khakhtikʻ. With common books: with Psalters, with Gospels, with hymnals, with lectionaries, with hagiography, with diviniely-inspired prophetic books and other instructive writings. He used to copy all these in night vigils and with restless wakefulness. He was never sleeping on a bed, but in order to take a little energy he used to lay his head on a couch, and he used to sleep for an hour or two while seated. [Then] once more he would awaken quickly, and again he was working on writing, like Grigor Tatʻewatsʻi and Barseḷ Kesaratsʻi [Basil of Caesarea] . . .[75]

According to Grigor, one *vardapet* named Yovhannēs from Bitlis attained such a degree of holiness that when 'Kurds' tried to pillage his tomb, God directly intervened to prevent and execute them. Grigor writes that

> [Yovhannēs] was from the country of Baḷēsh [Bitlis] . . . and he was very meek and humble in heart and [he dressed] in sordid clothes. He was wandering on foot like Nersēs the Walker, and [he was someone] with good works and a holy way of a life, a lover of virtue, compassionate, and clement. [He was] a carer for and consoler of the afflicted . . .[76]

In a later chapter Grigor relates the supernatural events that took place at Yovhannēs' grave:

> The day of his end arrived, and he was transported to God and buried in his monastery. After his death, the lord of the place seized the head of the monastery to request [Yovhannēs's] things. They showed his woollen and haircloth clothes, his mended cloak, his hood, and several of his books, saying 'These are all of his things and possessions'. [The lord] did not believe

them, saying 'Give me his treasure, otherwise I'll send a man to take him from the grave and throw him out'. They said that 'We don't know any other means or remedy: do as you will'. The lord (*âmir*) sent three Kurds, and they went to the cemetery of the *vardapet*. They stood on his grave, and when they began to strike once with an axe, [then] the grave shook and thundered, so that they were terrified by the terrible thunder. They fell and died. When the lord heard, again he sent three Kurds, and they also died in the same way. Again he sent three Kurds, and like those [others], they died in the place. After nine souls died, then the lord believed the facts of what had taken place.[77]

In this passage Grigor begins to construct Yovhannēs's hagiography, depicting his grave as being protected by supernatural forces because of his great piety.

In such biographies Grigor records the lives of *vardapets* from ancient Armenian cities – Bayburt, Diyarbekir and Bitlis – who lived during or 'near to [Grigor's] time', mostly in the generation just before the chaos of the Celali Revolts. Thus he provides an account of religious life in Armenia before the great Celali destruction, and in several instances – as in the biography of Malakʻia – Grigor is eager to note the *vardapets*' scholarly endeavours and scribal productions, as he seems to have deemed their intellectual capacities to have been generally superior to those of the 'short-witted and shallow'[78] men of more recent times. Without doubt, there is an element of nostalgia in Grigor's retelling and also, perhaps, an effort by Grigor to reinforce his own standing through connection to great men of the past.

Grigor's stories about the holy men of the East cannot be described in solely panegyric terms: he also recounts the tales of drunken friars,[79] debauched monks[80] and devil-possessed students gone wrong.[81] Grigor's memories were darkened by his own horrible childhood experiences in the monasteries of Mount Sepuh. Nonetheless, Grigor's accounts of holy life in Greater Armenia in the time of his youth and in the previous generation appear vibrant, standing in stark contrast to his depiction of religious life in contemporary Western Anatolia. When Grigor shifts his focus westward, his descriptions of men of achievement transform into a litany of complaints about uneducated frauds, sinning merchants, heretics and Catholics. In these stories, we see how the increased mobility of the seventeenth century – including the movement of refugees, economic globalisation and the spread of Catholic missionaries in Ottoman lands – catalysed changes in Armenian communal life which Grigor interpreted in a highly negative light.

Refugees, merchants and missionaries in Grigor Daranaḷtsʻi's Chronicle

While Grigor recounts stories about the holy men of Eastern Anatolia in his youth with some nostalgia, his accounts of religious life in Western Anatolia after the Great Armenian Flight have a completely different tone. Much of the second part of Grigor's chronicle consists of lengthy diatribes attacking fake priests, heretics, sinners and contemporary clerics of note, including some of the patriarchs of Constantinople who reigned during Grigor's lifetime. In a chapter from the second part of his chronicle entitled 'concerning laymen practicing false-eldership and false-priesthood',[82] Grigor depicts a crisis of Armenian religious leadership which was caused by the mass migrations of peasants from Eastern Anatolia to Western Anatolia because of the Celali Revolts. He writes that

> ... no one could discern the cenobite priest [from the] lay elder, the lay reader and the deacon without rank [from the] priest. Many of the lay readers and ranking deacons and fornicator priests were doing the work of priests for a long time.[83]

In short, Grigor argues that the anonymity of refugees who had fled from Eastern Anatolia led to a breakdown in mechanisms of communal regulation of religious authority.

An example of one of the 'fake priests' described by Grigor is a certain Abraham. Grigor relates that

> A certain layman named Abraham, knowing well all the learning of childhood, the Psalms and hymns, for thirty years was doing the work of a priest around Nikomedia – which they call Ḷochayēl (*Kocaeli*) – in the villages of the Armenians, even though he was a layman and did not have a single degree [of rank].[84]

Grigor learned about Abraham's background from an Armenian who had fled from Eastern Anatolia along with him during the early seventeenth-century mass migrations. The fellow villager described Abraham's transformation to a life of fraud as originating from a ploy to beg for food on the flight from Divriği, near Sivas, to the region around modern-day Kocaeli:

> . . . a woman died on the road, and because he knew the readings, they called him deacon. When we came near to Tokat, he went to beg for bread from the Armenians. When he came from begging, I called him by the name deacon and chorister, according to [our] frequent custom, but he did not want to be called by his usual name. He said to me, 'Don't call me deacon and chorister, but call my name priest and reverend, because while begging I said that I am a priest, and they gave abundant gifts and accepted [me] with honor.' On account of our needs and necessities I called him priest and reverend on the road until this place [near Izmit]. And when we came to this side, he separated [from us] and went to unknown places. From that time he was serving as a priest. From then until now is near to thirty years.[85]

Finally – after thirty years – the story became known to Abraham's new community and Grigor recounts how 'they drove him out of the village like useless excrement'.[86]

Another 'fake priest' that Grigor describes in the second part of his chronicle was Sahak of Erzincan.

> A certain deacon named Sahak from Erzincan is now a priest in Istanbul in Topkapı over our Armenians and the son-in-law of our priest Bardułimēos. In this year, which is 1084 (1635), in the month of May the expulsion (*sürgün*) was ordered by the king [i.e., the Ottoman sultan].[87] Sahak went to Erzincan, and Bardułimēos, to Jerusalem. This priest Sahak, in the time of his elder deaconship, which was in the year 1067 (1618), went to Ankara. Having confidence in the gracefulness of his learning and lovely voice and on the rank of elder deaconship, he said by the testimony of his mouth and the perfection of his education that he [is a] priest. On many days he offered the mass and performed the Lenten services. When he came to Istanbul, they ordained him as a priest without examination until the coming of K'ot' Karapet *vardapet* of Erzincan, [who] knew [that] such [were] actions of illegality and condemned him very much. [Sahak] assumed responsibility for his act of illegality and he confessed. [Karapet] placed on him the heaviest penitence.[88]

As a result of such frequent acts of fraud, Grigor lamented:

> ... now men readily listen to and believe lies and swindlers and false words and lying men and false histories and easy-preaching and seducers more than the just and the true and the preachers of truth on the slender and narrow path, as the Lord said: 'Few are those who go on it'.[89]

In addition to his tales of fake priests, Grigor also offers several narratives about men who he deemed to be heretics. While the 'fake priests' described above usurped religious authority without challenging orthodoxy, Grigor's heretics openly preached unorthodox teachings. Grigor encountered one such man near Iznik, where he spent seven months endeavouring to establish an Armenian monastery.[90] There he met Yovhannēs, an Armenian from a village near Malatia who had moved to Western Anatolia at the time of the Great Armenian Flight. Grigor explained that '[Yovhannēs] was a drunk, slothful, and lazy man. He [was] the son of a rich man, and he was idle and drunken and moved by lasciviousness. His father drove him from the house. Now he's committing fraud'.[91]

In particular Yovhannēs had convinced both Muslim and Armenian villagers that he had powerful mystical experiences.[92] He was claiming to the Armenians: 'I've seen St John the Baptist and the Mother of God near to God. I saw the father [Grigor the] Illuminator in hell, and I requested from God, and I freed [him] and took him from hell'.[93]

Likewise, he claimed to the Muslims: 'I've seen your prophet [*peygamber*]'.[94] According to Grigor, villagers near Nicaea were enthralled by his stories, and in particular 'many women were gathering around him'.[95] Grigor narrates that his response to Yovhannēs was swift, harsh and severe: '. . . I took a cudgel, and I struck [Yovhannēs] many times. They were barely able to take him from my hands, and [so] I drove him off from the village'.[96] This is but one story among several in which Grigor depicts himself as reimposing ecclesiastical order through physical violence.

Grigor describes another tale of heresy in greater detail. Unlike the lascivious conman Yovhannēs, this heretic is depicted as having been a well-intentioned man who lacked the discipline and proper guidance to live the ascetic life. Grigor explains that

> At the beginning of our [Armenian] year 1079 (1630) there was a devil-possessed man in the city of Silisray. He had studied all the learning of a child and a little bit of scribeship, and by trade he was also a silver-worker and a sculptor, such that they said 'there is no one like him in this land'. At first he lived for a time in the country of Moldova. When his wife died there, he took a second wife, and he regretted it. He repented with fasts, and he departed for a solitary place in the forest, living as an ascetic, [even though] he was uneducated and untrained on the path of asceticism.[97]

Grigor suggests that the man's lack of training left him unprepared for the ascetic life and thus defenseless against dark influences. In particular, he began to be visited by two satanic apparitions, which assumed the form of Jesus Christ and the Virgin Mary, called 'Fake Jesus' and 'Fake Mother of God' in Grigor's chronicle. Upon their first visit to the hapless man, they announced that

> We have come to advise you and to be of assistance to you and to give you grace and wisdom and to make you admirable on the earth. Now, take parchment and write that which we say and show to you, signs and the greatest arts and words of observance. That which we say to you, write it down and recite it often in church.[98]

Under this false inspiration, the beguiled ascetic began to write and to compose. He went to town and told his mother and wife about the revelation, and they believed him with great enthusiasm. So too did his fellow townsmen, with the exception of the priests.

Over time the ascetic's relationship with 'fake Jesus' and the 'fake Mother of God' became more sadistic. While initially the demons incited the ascetic to preach their new gospel, in time their commands took a sexual nature. Jesus commanded the ascetic to 'Rise up, take your mother and your wife and bring [them] into the church, and before me and before your mother, be with your wife'.[99] In response to the poor man's protests, 'Evil Jesus' retorts by asking, 'How could lawful (*helâl*) marriage be a shame and sin? On account of those things and matters I made humans and every living being male and female. But human intercourse is pleasing to me, more than that of the other animals'.[100]

Parts of this convoluted story were censored from the 1915 publication of Grigor's chronicle, but it remains intact in the original manuscript in Jerusalem and was recently published separately in an Armenian scholarly journal.

While the crazed ascetic was initially tolerated and, in fact, encouraged by his community, his heresy eventually reached a point that required the intervention of the local Armenian clergy. According to Grigor,

> [The ascetic] tried to throw out the Gospel and the missal and to put in place of the Gospel this false book of fable and to read it for the hearing of all as a new Gospel. But the priests raised a cry at the people of evil faith, [saying]: 'Until when will we be silent and not speak? You believe this devil-deceived [man] who was deceived by demons, and he has also deceived you, so that you [too] are devil-deceived. Know that we will die over our Gospel and we will not allow that demonic book to enter the church and [for us all] to become devil-worshipers'.[101]

At this point the priests gain outside assistance. By coincidence, Grigor's brother Markos arrives on the scene making collections for the Armenians of Jerusalem. He reprimands the ascetic and his followers and he works to pull the man back to orthodoxy through patient teaching. The ascetic repents in shame and his mother procures all of his writings – which he had written over the course of seven years in nine notebooks – and gives them to Markos.[102] It was from Markos that Grigor later learned the details of this incident. Unlike the story of Yovhannēs, Grigor concludes the account with a sympathetic tone for the hapless ascetic: whereas Yovhannēs had been cunning and opportunistic, this ascetic had been well intentioned but utterly mad, and he arrived in the end at full repentance.

The stories recounted up until now all took place in the aftermath of mass migrations from Eastern Anatolia to Western Anatolia, and Grigor suggests that they were possible because of a breakdown of communal regulation of religious norms in the context of a refugee crisis and a lack of sufficient ecclesiastical infrastructure for Armenians in western parts of the Ottoman Empire. The mobility of Armenians in the Ottoman Empire was not only increased by migrations in the seventeenth century. The early seventeenth century was also the time when the famed New Julfan merchants established their global networks of trade in the aftermath of Shah Abbas's forced population transfer from Julfa to Isfahan.[103] Likewise, Jesuits and Capuchins began arriving in Istanbul at the end of the sixteenth century,[104] and their influence on Ottoman Armenian religious life increased drastically over the course of the seventeenth century. Timothy Brook has decribed the seventeenth century as the 'dawn of the global world', a time in which people, goods and ideas gained a level of mobility unseen in world history beforehand.[105] Grigor found the changes catalysed by this heightened mobility – caused by mass migration, transcontinental trade networks and 'global Catholicism' – to be a threat to religious life as he knew it.

In addition to his diatribes on the disorderly religious life among the Celali refugees, Grigor offers extended discourses on the sin and avarice of the Julfa merchants, whose trade empire spanned Eurasia, including nodes in Aleppo and Izmir.[106] Grigor had a clear disdain for them. He had grown up in an agricultural society and, for most of his adult life in Thrace and around Istanbul, he had ministered mostly to farmers, labourers and craftsmen. The values and culture of the Julfans' hyper-mobile merchant class repulsed him, and Grigor offers both general condemnation of the Julfan merchants and anecdotes about specific unpleasant interactions with them. For example, on a general note, Grigor decries how

> ... they have abandoned the worship of God and become servants of Mammon, blinded by the disease of avarice. They all are trying to become rich, and they are [rich] more than measure, just as the Lord laments in the holy Gospel: 'Woe upon you wealthy [ones], for you have received your consolation' (Luke 6: 24), and 'You cannot serve God and Mammon' (Luke 16: 13), and with many other examples he reproaches the wealthy. With blind eyes they do not consider the holy Gospel. They leave their wives, sons, and daughters forlorn and destitute and in straits. [Meanwhile they are] dispersed and scattered, spreading over all the face of the world like locusts or snow, until inner India, Ethiopia, Egypt, all of the land of the Franks, Constantinople, all of the land of the Thracians and Goths, [and that] which is of the Poles, the Russians, the Muscovites, and the Verkanans, and in all the land of the Turks, Kurds, Chaldeans, and of all the Persians and in the east, until China (*Chʻin ew Matchʻin*), Tʻōn, Tonquin, England,

and in all the land of the Tatars and Abhazians until the extremity of the unknown lands. Like dust they are strewn and scattered on account of the disease of avarice and the accumulation of surpluses of treasure . . .[107]

Elsewhere Grigor adds that '. . . they are all vagabonds [and] uniformly arrogant, haughty, conceited, uncompassionate, unpitying, implacable, [and] dishonourable. They never honour anyone except Jerusalemites and Ējmiatsinites, on account of their vanity'.[108]

Grigor also describes an incident in which he personally confronted Julfans. According to Grigor's account, the confrontation took place in a village near Iznik, part of Grigor's regular tour of ministry to new Armenian settlements established by Celali refugees. In this passage, Grigor punishes some Julfans for allegedly acting like boars in his church. According to Grigor,

> Even if [the Julfans] sleep in a house of prayer, they do not get up at the time of prayer in order to pray with the people, as we [beheld] in a village of Nicaea, which they call Soloz. We lodged at a house of prayer. Three of them came, evil and vacuous [?]. They lodged with us and slept, and when it was the time of prayer, I did not wake them up immediately, [saying] they have been working. We said the daily Psalms and the appropriate daily hymns and prayers until I reached [the hymn] 'Glory to the Most High'. We were standing above their heads. [They were] not deep in sleep, but having awoken in secret they gazed [at us]: on account of much imperfection of faith, they did not want to remember God. When I began 'Glory to the Most High' [and] they did not get up, my heart became very troubled in my chest. I became angry, and I beat them with my staff [for] their iniquity. I tortured them in accordance with their affront. They arose, and with belt unfastened, head uncovered, barefooted, and naked they fled outside . . .[109]

Here we see yet another violent anecdote in which Grigor proudly describes the weaponisation of his clerical staff for the re-imposition of orthopraxy. Grigor's hostility to the Julfa merchants stands in contrast to the attitude of the Kadızadelis – Muslim moral critics of the seventeenth-century Ottoman Empire – who tended to be in alliance with Istanbul's merchants.[110]

The second part of Grigor's chronicle also includes multiple condemnations of ranking Armenian churchmen, particularly the patriarchs of

Constantinople who served during his lifetime. Already mentioned was Grigor's conflict with the patriarch Grigor of Kayseri. Another Armenian Patriarch of Constantinople to whom Grigor devotes a biography in his chronicle is Yovhannēs Khul. While his contempt for Grigor of Kayseri arose out of the latter's policies towards the Anatolian refugees in Istanbul, he depicts his disdain for Khul as arising from Khul's sympathies to Rome. Grigor offers the following discourse on Khul in his chronicle's second part:

> Khul Yovhannēs *vardapet* . . . was deceived by some [with Catholic sympathies] . . . With enticements they took him away from Istanbul, where he had enjoyed a reign with the name patriarch for twenty two years, though he was wicked, defective, weak-skinned, careless, and brutish. 'He was on the same level as animals, and he did not understand his [position of] honour,' [in the words of] the prophet. Another prophet said, 'Whoever the Lord wishes to destroy, first He bewitches him, so that He might destroy him by a foolish work.' . . . in this way it was for [Yovhannēs] . . . for twenty years with afflictions he was in narrow prisons on account of debtors. It was still two years more [before] he was relieved from all the debts. Many venerable sources were taken – stores of gold and silver – on account of his destruction. Some evil [men] duped him, especially our apostate (*aktarma*),[111] Paḷtasar, who was the translator (*tercüman*) of the Franks . . . Duping him, he sent him off praising the Pope. [He said], 'If you go, he will honour you much and bestow countless treasure [on you]. He will send you here [to Istanbul] with the greatest gifts if you accept all their religion and go according to their desire . . .'[112]

Later Grigor proceeds to narrate that

> Khul went to Rome – to the Pope – via Poland. Wherever he went, by deceit they took venerable gifts from [his] hands and little remained. When he reached the Pope, he was received. [The Pope] granted [him] the monastery of the Armenians, and he ordered the daily preparation of food and the granting of a stipend for expenditure [for Khul].[113]

When Khul died, Grigor lamented that 'We did not know by which faith and by what laws he had confessed, or [which] rites he had taken'.[114]

In the above passages, Grigor contemptuously suggests Khul's pro-Catholic sympathies – or potential conversion – arose out of pecuniary interest. Grigor likewise criticised another patriarch, Zak'aria, as having been debt-ridden, leading to his inability to hold the patriarchal throne.[115] It seems certain that Grigor's contempt for the institution of the patriarchate had structural causes that transcended his personal relationships with these three men, given that taxation and debts ultimately lay at the heart of his complaints against all three patriarchs, Grigor of Kayseri, Khul and Zak'aria. It is not coincidental that similar passages against avarice exist in Greek ecclesiastical histories of the early modern period. For example, the sixteenth-century Greek *Patriarchal History of Constantinople* contains lengthy complaints about the way in which competing factions for the patriarchal throne bribed their way to power, prompting the necessity for constant taxation and fund-raising. The author describes how this problem plagued patriarchal politics for about a century, and he narrates stories about intense competition to gain the patriarchal throne and concomitant bribery in great detail.[116] The research of Tom Papademetriou provides rich contextualisation for this early modern patriarchal history, as he describes how the Orthodox patriarchs played a critical role in the Ottoman taxation of non-Muslims.[117] Grigor's chronicle implies that the Armenian Patriarchate of Constantinople had a similar relationship with the Ottoman state, and that Armenian patriarchs were also forced to engage in constant taxation and fund-raising to pay off the state and to stay on the patriarchal throne.

Thus there was a structural reason for Grigor's constant conflicts with the Armenian patriarchs. Mobility was a force that could exacerbate this constant tension, as the refugee crisis led to particularly fierce struggles between our chronicler and Grigor of Kayseri, while 'global Catholicism' and the spread of Catholic sympathies among Ottoman Armenians added bitterness to his relationship with Patriarch Yovhannēs Khul, who allegedly travelled to Rome and accepted gifts from the pope. Khul was not the only Catholic sympathiser that Grigor condemns. In fact, he chose to end his chronicle with a lengthy condemnation of the Catholic missionary Paolo Piromalli, implying subtly that his greatest fears for the future of his community lay with the Catholics.

Paolo Piromalli was an Italian Dominican friar who learned Armenian and travelled to the Caucasus to serve as a Catholic missionary.[118] In his chronicle, Grigor provides a fascinating glimpse into the controversy

Piromalli's missionary work caused among Armenians upon his arrival in the Ottoman capital from Ējmiatsin:

> When he departed, two caught up with him, and a letter came to Istanbul, to Galata in the year 1085 (1636). We were present at that time here in the Church of the Mother of God. That evil [man] was convincing all of the priests of Galata and the credulous people, especially our sons Khochay Tawitʻ and Kirakos of Julfa, saying that 'For three years I lived in Ējmiatsin and I became an Armenian. I am a student of Pʻilippos and I have taken the authority of a *vardapet* to preach.' They put him at the head of a class, and he began to preach in the Armenian language on the history of the Illuminator so that firstly he might convince [them] of his sincerity by it. Word got out in the city; some stormed [after him], going after [his] renown. We listened to his words, and they surprised us. The priests of two churches, St. Sargis and St. Nikoḷayos, were moved to agitation. They went to Zakʻaria, who was patriarch in name, and said to him, 'Did you grant the authority to instruct the Armenian people to that fraud?' Zakʻaria denied it, [saying], 'I don't know him, but the Julfans accepted him, Khochay Tawitʻ and his student Kirakos'.[119]

Grigor describes how they sent a delegation to investigate the theological views of Piromalli and his coterie:

> First [they were] to ask of our faith and our laws and of the true confessions of religion and of [their] loving acceptance and pledging [themselves] to all of our religion and [their] rejection of all of the Chalcedonian heresies, and especially the new-fangled heresy of the Frankish fraud. We ordered that they ask so many firm precepts from him. And taking [a letter] they went, [and] they gave the letter to the priests. The priests did not have the courage to take the letter to him together for fear of some chief [members] of the populace, on account of much warm love [which they had] for him. Lord Ḷazar took courage [and] went without the letter to greet the former [Paul] with his lips and not with his heart. He began to inquire as we had commanded. [Paul] deceptively tried to conceal, saying that 'They are signs of dispute: lay off!' [Ḷazar] said that 'I've been sent from the *vardapets* and the multitude of priests for the sake of this examination. How can I "lay off"?

First say the "We believe" of Nicaea [the Nicaean Creed], which is always said in church.' [Paul] spoke until 'But those who say', but from there he did not want to say more . . .'[120]

Piromalli was unwilling to articulate the anathema of the Armenian version of the Nicaean Creed and, as such, he exposed himself as a Catholic.[121] This prompted strife between Piromalli's sympathisers and his detractors. Grigor was among the latter, and he concludes his chronicle with condemnation of those who could be led astray by such a man and with lament about the state of Armenian ecclesiastical life in Poland, where a Uniate Armenian bishopric was established in 1630. Piromalli proceeded to travel there after leaving Istanbul.[122]

As this passage shows, the clash between Armenian clerics and Catholic missionaries had reached the streets of Istanbul by the 1630s. There had been Armenian Catholics long before this time, in the medieval kingdom of Cilician Armenia, and among the so-called 'Unitor Brothers' of Nakhchivan.[123] But by early modern Ottoman times, the kingdom of Cilicia had become old history and Catholic life in late sixteenth-century Istanbul was primarily limited to European merchants, slaves and prisoners.[124] Grigor's chronicle shows that Catholic missionaries were beginning to make inroads among the Armenians of the Ottoman Empire by the early seventeenth century, in the aftermath of the Great Armenian Flight. Some Armenians were influenced by their personal travels to Rome, where the pope had an Armenian translator and examiner named Łazar of Tokat who would test the faith of visiting Armenian merchants and pilgrims, threatening harassment for those who refused to accept Roman Catholicism.[125] Others, like Khul, developed Catholic sympathies under the influence of Catholics in Istanbul. In the later seventeenth century the growing prosperity of the Armenians in Istanbul, the rise of the *amiras* merchant class with trade ties to Europe,[126] and educational links between Armenians and Jesuit and Capuchin teachers led to a higher rate of conversion, such that by 1700 there were reportedly 8,000 Armenian Catholics in Istanbul, many more than the foreign French and Italian Catholics.[127] These Armenian Catholics operated without official sanction until 1830, when Sultan Mahmud II recognised a separate Armenian Catholic Community.[128]

The second half of Grigor's chronicle is a valuable window into a period of disjuncture in Armenian history, when Armenians moved en masse from

Greater Armenia to Western Anatolia, Istanbul and Thrace. Grigor felt threatened by violations of religious norms that took place amidst migration, by the ways of life of transcontinental merchants and by the ideas and sectarian discord brought by European Catholic missionaries. The first half of Grigor's chronicle provides a narrative which brings Armenians from their 'Old World' in Eastern Anatolia to their 'New World' in Western Anatolia, Istanbul and Thrace, serving as an intellectual bridge across a moment of historical disjuncture comparable to ones crafted by Greeks, such as Laonikos Chalkokondyles,[129] after 1453. The second half of Grigor's chronicle, on the other hand, was his intellectual response to threats that existed in that 'New World', threats created by the increased movement of peoples, goods and ideas at the 'dawn of the global world'[130] in the seventeenth century.

Through these stories Grigor created a didactic work that presented readers and listeners with a vivid – and perhaps exaggerated – picture of what their religious life should and should not look like. Grigor's chronicle should be seen as a political testament aimed at providing a vision of the historical transformations of the time, Grigor's role in them, and a warning about proper religious boundaries in a period of new kinds of destabilising mass mobility.

Grigor's Role in Armenian Infrastructure Building

Grigor's responses to these threats were not limited to storytelling. On the contrary, Grigor was primarily a man of action. Unlike the renowned seventeenth-century Armenian polymath Eremia Kʻeōmurchean – who was Ottoman Istanbul's first great Armenian author – Grigor should be remembered less as an intellectual and more as a politican, fundraiser, preacher and infrastructure-builder.

Grigor's descriptions of his infrastructure building projects are scattered throughout his chronicle; they do not form discrete sections like his discussions of the churchmen described above. Yet if we follow Grigor's comments about his movements, we see that he was engaged in ministry and construction projects for refugee communities in various localities in Istanbul and its environs.

On two occasions Grigor sought to participate in the construction of monasteries. Unlike Eastern Anatolia – which to this day is still littered with the ruins of ancient Armenian monasteries – Western Anatolia and Thrace (outside of Istanbul) at the beginning of the seventeenth century mostly lacked contexts for organised Armenian ascetic life. On one occasion Grigor describes how he tried and failed to build a monastery above a village near Iznik, where he met the above-mentioned Yovhannēs:

> At that time we wanted to dwell there in order to build a monastery, and we stayed there for seven months and built a cell above the village. I wanted to build a monastery for cenobites in a suitable place. For two reasons this was impeded: Firstly, a long-lasting and heavy sickness fell upon me; secondly, I didn't have any friend or a seeker of solitude.[131]

On this attempt, Grigor's monastery building efforts were impeded, but he played a role in another much more successful project. Later, in the nineteenth and twentieth centuries, the Armenian community of Izmit was best known in the Armenian world because of the Armash Monastery. Grigor refers to this monastery as his own 'handiwork' in one passage about a visit there.[132] But whereas Grigor seems to have been the undisputed author of the above-mentioned failure, there is competition for the claim to fame as the founder of the very successful Armash Monastery. The monastery was founded in 1611, and both colophons[133] and a local Armenian history concur in stating that its founder was a certain bishop Tʻadēos.[134] It seems that Grigor's role in the construction of the monastery was limited to fundraising efforts,[135] and he may have downplayed Tʻadēos's critical role in his chronicle out of personal feelings. About Tʻadēos he writes,

> An unbeliever named Tʻadēos, made bishop by a fornicator who had abandoned the priesthood, was staying in the newly-built Armash Monastery. He did not have concern for the laws, did not have fear or dread of God, nor shame of man, did not know of fasting, nor of refrain from wine-drinking. He was never repentant of his sins and was hopelessly committing every evil, hating good and loving evil, and he died in this way, unrepentant.[136]

Whatever Grigor's role had been in establishing the monastery, it seems that after Tʻadēos' passing, the Armash Monastery became one of Grigor's regular haunts in the early 1620s.[137]

Grigor's role in the acquisition of a Greek church in Rodosto has already been discussed. In that instance, Armenians obtained help from the Ottoman state to acquire the Orthodox St Yovhannēs Church for themselves from the Greeks, the same year as they had lost their first Armenian church in Rodosto. That is not the only story in Grigor's chronicle that relates how the destruction of an Armenian church by Muslims led to a counterstrike against the Greeks. Likewise, in 1626, the St Nicholas Church at Edirnekapı[138] in Istanbul was converted into a mosque, and this prompted the local Armenians there to begin searching for another place of worship. They ultimately settled upon a Greek Orthodox Church, the Holy Archangel, in the nearby neighbourhood of Balat. Grigor narrates that

> The unfortunate afflicted priests and people were abandoned and churchless. For a whole year like vagrants they wandered, like lost sheep, and there was no one who visited them and gathered the dispersed into one. And they, in agreement among themselves, found an idle church named the Archangel inside the Gate of Balat by a half-mile distance in a dark place among the Jews. They endeavored to take it from the Romans.[139]

Of course, the Greeks found this solution to be unacceptable and they resisted. As usual in episodes of Greek–Armenian conflict, the Ottoman state eventually had to arbitrate. Grigor triumphantly describes how the Armenians gained victory in the dispute via bribery:

> Exhorting one another, [the Armenians] gathered much money and silver. They bribed the vizier and all the grandees of the palace, and all the Romans were moved to wage war and to fight with the Armenians, [so that] the Armenians not be allowed to take the church. Through the holy prayers of the Illuminator and through the omnipotent power of God the Armenians defeated them and all their supporters. Recep Pasha gave an order to the Armenians, and then three sergeants (*çavuş*) came and opened the church and gave passage into the hands of our Armenians. Among them there was much rejoicing.[140]

Very soon after the Armenians' triumph by bribery over their Greek opponents a fire broke out and the church burnt down. Grigor played a critical role in keeping the church in Armenian hands by rapidly rebuilding it and negotiating with Ottoman authorities to maintain it as an Armenian site of worship, despite opposition from local Greeks and Muslims in Balat.[141]

The examples described in this section are but a few glimpses into a broader process of Armenian infrastructure-building and acquisition that took place in the aftermath of the Great Armenian Flight.

Conclusion

In sum, Grigor spent his life as a travelling preacher and leader of refugee communities. He was greatly disturbed by the collapse of traditional modes of communal regulation which took place in the aftermath of mass migration and by new forms of early modern mobility – including the rise of global merchant networks and 'global Catholicism' – signs of which he encountered in his travelling ministries. Grigor sought to combat this breakdown of order through active political leadership – often in competition with the old Istanbul-Armenian elite – and by helping to build new infrastructure for refugee communities in Rodosto, Istanbul and the general Marmara Sea region.

He also combated it intellectually, through the composition of his chronicle, a multi-faceted polemic. Therein he constructs a vivid world of heroic priests and ascetics in Greater Armenia whose world disintegrated in the time of the Celalis, and he crafts a counter-narrative of chaos in Western Anatolia in the aftermath of migration, chaos which he believed should be fought against tooth and nail, sometimes with preaching and church-building, at other times with violence. Through this dichotomy between a more pious 'Old Word' in Eastern Anatolia before the Celali Revolts and a dangerous 'New World' in Western Anatolia in the aftermath of mass migration, Grigor creates a historical bridge between the world in which he grew up – Kemah – and the world in which he spent his final years – among refugees in the western parts of the Ottoman Empire. In the construction of this bridge, he resembles Greek authors of the fifteenth and sixteenth centuries who engaged in a comparable intellectual project, explaining the end of Byzantine Rule in Constantinople and the rise of the new Ottoman order.

In his chronicle, Grigor depicts himself as a hero, opposing Grigor of Kayseri's unjust treatment of the refugees along with many other threats to the weak 'newcomers' in Istanbul and Western Anatolia. Grigor was a fiery figure who took pleasure in recounting his own willingness – perhaps exaggerated – to make recourse to violence to defend orthodoxy and orthopraxy, and it was no doubt this cold and vicious streak that earned Grigor the nickname 'snowstorm' – or 'Buk'' – among contemporary Armenians.

Grigor Daranałts'i was a first-generation immigrant and refugee, and his chronicle is the work of a man who personally made the journey between two cultural spheres: the 'Valley of Monasteries' on the one hand, and coastal port cities of the Ottoman Empire – Istanbul and Rodosto – on the other. Grigor was a literate man, but his sole major work was a utilitarian polemic written by the veteran of long political infighting. It is comparable to the memoirs of modern politicians who aim to establish their legacies and to provide warnings and advice to younger generations. Let us now skip a generation and consider the literary works of the grandson of a Kemah-Armenian refugee, born a few years before Grigor's passing, in order to gain a glimpse into how the fabric of Armenian cultural and intellectual life transformed over time in its new environment. Grigor's generation was too concerned with crisis management, infrastructure-building and the pragmatic struggles of life as emigrants to produce a great polymath and intellect. Rather, it would be the generation of their grandchildren who would lay the foundation of intellectual and literary life in the Western Armenian Diaspora, building upon the physical infrastructure that had been constructed in Grigor's time.

Notes

1. Hrand D. Andreasyan, 'Bir Ermeni Kaynağına Göre Celâlî İsyanları', *Tarih Dergisi* 17–18 (1962–3): 27–42; Yakob Siruni, *Polis ew ir derě* I (Beruit: Y.Ch. Siruni, 1965); and M. K. Zulalyan, *Jalalineri sharzhumě ew hay zhołovrdi vichakě ōsmanyan kaysrut'yan mej (XVI–XVII darer)* (Yerevan: Haykakan SSH GA Hratarakch'ut'yun, 1966).
2. I'm grateful to Sebouh Aslanian for encouraging me to think about early modern mobility beyond the category of mass migration. Changing forms of mobility will be a theme of his forthcoming book, *Global Early Modernity and Mobility: Port Cities and Printers in the Armenian Diaspora, 1512–1800*.
3. Grigor Daranałts'i, *Zhamanakagrut'iwn Grigor vardapeti Kamakhets'woy kam Daranałts'woy*, Mesrop Nshanean (ed.) (Jerusalem: Tparan Aṙak'. At'oṙots' S. Yokobeants', 1915), p. ix.

4. Matthias Bedrossian, *New Dictionary Armenian-English* (Eugene: Wipf & Stock, 2009), p. 107.
5. Grigor Daranałts'i, pp. ix–x.
6. Ibid., pp. 22–3.
7. Ibid., pp. 73–4.
8. Ibid, 591–592.
9. Ibid, 593–594.
10. Ibid., p. 594.
11. Ibid., pp. 596–7.
12. See Peter Brown, 'The Rise and Function of the Holy Man in Late Antiquity', *The Journal of Roman Studies* 61 (1971): 80–101.
13. Grigor Daranałts'i, p. 595.
14. Ibid., p. 596.
15. Ibid., p. 595.
16. Ibid., p. 342.
17. Ibid., pp. 75–6.
18. Ibid., p. xi.
19. Ibid., p. xiii.
20. Ibid., p. xiv.
21. Ibid., p. 40.
22. Ibid., p. xviii.
23. Ibid., pp. 41–2.
24. Grigor Daranałts'i, pp. xxi–xxii.
25. Ibid., p. 69.
26. Pars Tuğlacı, *İstanbul Ermeni Kiliseleri* (İstanbul: Pars Tuğlacı, 1991), pp. 89–91.
27. Teotig, *Baskı ve Harf: Ermeni Matbaacılık Tarihi*, Sirvart Malhasyan and Arlet İncidüzen (trans.) (İstanbul: Birzamanlar Yayıncılık, 2012), pp. 73–4.
28. Grigor Daranałts'i, pp. 70–1.
29. Ibid., pp. 72–3.
30. Ibid., pp. xxiv–xxv.
31. Ibid., p. 610.
32. Ibid., p. xxv.
33. Ibid., p. 598.
34. Ibid., p. 116.
35. Ibid., p. 118.

36. Ibid., p. xxxi.
37. Ibid., p. 123.
38. Ibid., p. 127.
39. Ibid., p. 128.
40. Ibid., p. 135.
41. Ibid., p. 137.
42. Ibid, 141.
43. Ibid, 142.
44. Ibid., p. 144.
45. For a summary and reference to the Ottoman Turkish documentation about this effort to send refugees back to Eastern Anatolia, see İsmail Hakkı Uzunçarşılı, *Osmanlı Tarihi* III.I (Ankara: Türk Tarih Kurumu, 1951), p. 113.
46. See Hrand D. Andreasyan, 'Celâlilerden Kaçan Anadolu Halkının Geri Gönderilmesi', *İsmail Hakkı Uzunçarşılı'ya Armağan* (Ankara: Türk Tarih Kurumu, 1976), pp. 45–53.
47. RŞS 1553, 58a.
48. Vazgen Hakobyan, *17 dari hayeren dzeṙagreri hishatakaranner* II (Yerevan: Haykakan SSṘ Gitut'yunneri Akademiayi Hratarakch'ut'yun: 1978), p. 53.
49. Grigor Daranalts'i, p. 155.
50. Ibid..
51. Ibid., p. 158.
52. Ibid., pp. 159–60.
53. Ibid., pp. 162–3.
54. Garegin Sruandzteants', *Erker* II (Yerevan: Haykakan SSH GA Hratarakch'ut'yun, 1982), p. 353.
55. A. Alpoyachean, *Grigor Kesarats'i patriark' ew ir zhamanakĕ* (Jerusalem: Tparan Srbots' Yakobeants', 1936), p. 121.
56. See also M. Rahn, *Die Entstehung des Armenischen Patriarchats von Konstantinopel* (Hamburg: Verlag, 2002), pp. 85–9; and Kevork Bardakjian, 'The Rise of the Armenian Patriarchate of Constantinople', *Christians and Jews in the Ottoman Empire: The Functioning of a Plural Society*, Vol. I (New York: Holmes and Meier, 1982), p. 93.
57. Grigor Daranalts'i, pp. xliii–xliv.
58. Ibid., pp. xliiiv–xlvi.
59. Ibid., p. 224.

60. Ibid., pp. 184–5.
61. Ibid., p. lviii.
62. Sargis G. P'ach'achean, *Yushamatean: Ṙotost'ots'i hayerun: 1606–1922* (Beirut: Tonikean, 1971), p. 174.
63. Grigor Daranałts'i, p. lxi.
64. Ibid., p. lxiv.
65. A. A. Ut'uzyan, 'Grigor Daranałts'in M. Ch'amch'yani patmut'yan ałbyur', *Lraber Hasarakakan Gitut'yunneri* (1975/2), pp. 81–9.
66. Grigor Daranałts'i, pp. 4–5.
67. Ibid., p. 6.
68. HaykPērpērean,"Alii Dashnagir'-ĕ Grigor Daranałts'ii 'Zhamanakagrut'ean' mēj', *Sion* (November, 1951), p. 330.
69. Grigor Daranałts'i, p. 13.
70. Ibid., p. 338.
71. Ibid., p. 349.
72. Ibid., p. 371.
73. Ibid., p. 398.
74. Ibid., p. 336.
75. Ibid., pp. 407–8.
76. Ibid., p. 378.
77. Ibid., pp. 388–9.
78. Ibid., p. 350.
79. Ibid., p. 349.
80. Ibid., pp. 353–4.
81. Ibid., p. 372.
82. Ibid., p. 473.
83. Ibid., p. 477.
84. Ibid., p. 477.
85. Ibid., pp. 477–8.
86. Ibid., p. 478.
87. See Hrand D. Andreasyan, 'Celâlilerden Kaçan Anadolu Halkının Geri Gönderilmesi', *İsmail Hakkı Uzunçarşılı'ya Armağan* (Ankara: Türk Tarih Kurumu, 1976), pp. 45–53.
88. Grigor Daranałts'i, p. 480.
89. Ibid., p. 490.
90. Ibid., p. 442.
91. Ibid., p. 444.

92. For an interesting comparison, see Phokion P. Kotzageorgis, '"Messiahs" and Neomartyrs in Ottoman Thessaly: Some Thoughts on Two Entries in a Mühimme Defteri', *Archivum Ottomanicum* 23 (2005/06), pp. 219–31.
93. Grigor Daranałts'i, p. 444.
94. Ibid.
95. Ibid., p. 443.
96. Ibid., pp. 443–4.
97. Ibid., p. 436.
98. Ibid., p. 438.
99. Henry Shapiro, 'Grigor Daranałts'u zhamanakagrut'yan orosh khndirneri shurj', *Ējmiatsin* (February 2016), p. 66.
100. Shapiro, 'Grigor Daranałts'u zhamanakagrut'yan orosh khndirneri shurj', p. 67.
101. Grigor Daranałts'i, p. 440.
102. Ibid., p. 442.
103. See Sebouh David Aslanian, *From the Indian Ocean to the Mediterranean: The Global Trade Networks of Armenian Merchants from New Julfa* (Berkeley, 2011).
104. Charles A. Frazee, *Catholics and Sultans: The Church and the Ottoman Empire: 1453–1923* (Cambridge University Press, 1983), pp. 73–4.
105. See Timothy Brook, *Vermeer's Hat: The Seventeenth Century and the Dawn of the Global World* (New York, 2008).
106. Aslanian, *From the Indian Ocean to the Mediterranean*, pp. 66–70.
107. Grigor Daranałts'i, pp. 457–8. See also Aslanian, *From the Indian Ocean to the Mediterranean*, p. 121.
108. Ibid., p. 465.
109. Ibid.
110. For a rich exploration of this theme, see Marinos Sariyannis, 'The Kadızadeli Movement as a Social and Political Phenomenon: The Rise of a "Mercantile Ethic"?' *Political Initiatives from the Bottom-Up in the Ottoman Empire (Halcyon Days in Crete VII)*, Antonis Anastasopoulos (ed.) (Rethymno: 2012), pp. 263–89.
111. Armenians who embraced Catholicism were usually called '*aktarma*' in the seventeenth-century Armenian texts, a Turkish term deriving from a verb meaning 'transfer', or 'turn over'.
112. Grigor Daranałts'i, p. 384.
113. Ibid., p. 386.

114. Ibid., p. 387.
115. Ibid., pp. 365–6.
116. *Historia Politica et Patriarchica Constantinopoleos*, Corpus Scriptorum Historiae, Immanuel Bekkerus (ed.) (Bonn: Impensis, 1849).
117. Tom Papademetriou, *Render unto the Sultan: Power, Authority, and the Greek Orthodox Church in the early Ottoman Centuries* (Oxford University Press, 2015).
118. For more about Paolo Piromalli, see D. Haft, 'Paolo Piromalli', in David Thomas and John A. Chesworth (eds), *Christian-Muslim Relations. A Bibliographical History* 10 (Leiden: Brill, 2017), pp. 582–7. I am grateful to Dr Paolo Lucca of the University of Venice for suggesting this reference.
119. Grigor Daranałts'i, pp. 585–6.
120. Ibid., pp. 586–7.
121. For an explanation of the theology of this orthodoxy test see Anna Ohanjanyan, 'Creedal Controversies among Armenians in the Seventeenth-Century Ottoman Empire Eremia Č'ēlēpi K'ēōmiwrčean's Polemical Writing against Suk'ias Prusac'i', *Journal for the Society of Armenian Studies* 27 (2020): 39–40.
122. Grigor Daranałts'i, p. 588
123. Frazee, pp. 46–7.
124. Ibid., p. 72.
125. Grigor Daranałts'i, pp. 381–2.
126. See Hagop L. Barsoumian, *The Armenian Amiras of the Ottoman Empire* (Yerevan: American University of Armenia, 2006).
127. Frazee, p. 178.
128. Kemal Beydilli, *II. Mahmud Devri'nde Katolik Ermeni Cemâati ve Kilisesi'nin Tanınması (1830)* (Cambridge, MA: Department of Near Eastern Languages and Civilizations, Harvard University, 1995).
129. See *Laonikos Chalkokondyles: The Histories*, 2 vols, Anthony Kaldellis (trans.) (Cambridge, MA: Harvard University Press Dumbarton Oaks Medieval Library, 2014).
130. See Brook, *Vermeer's Hat*.
131. Grigor Daranałts'i, p. 442.
132. Ibid., p. 361.
133. Ibid., p. xlvii.
134. Minas G. Gasapean, *Hayerĕ Nikomidioy gawaṙin mēj* (Istanbul: Azatamart, 1913), p. 106.
135. Grigor Daranałts'i, p. 423.

136. Ibid., p. 478.
137. Ibid., p. xlvii.
138. Pars Tuğlacı, *İstanbul Ermeni Kiliseleri* (İstanbul: Pars Tuğlacı, 1991), pp. 89–91.
139. Grigor Daranaḷtsʻi, pp. 186–7.
140. Ibid., p. 187.
141. An unpublished alternative account of this incident can be found in M 9704, 1a–10b.

5

Eremia Kʻeōmurchean and the Foundation of the Western Armenian Intellectual Tradition in Ottoman Istanbul

In 1550 – before the Great Armenian Flight – Istanbul was not an important centre of Armenian intellectual, cultural or ecclesiastical life. The city had never produced a significant native-born Armenian author or thinker; it did not have an Armenian printing press; and it was not a centre of Armenian manuscript production. The Armenian Patriarchate of Istanbul was an institution of limited regional influence, which was dwarfed in prestige by the traditional Armenian religious centres at Ējmiatsin and Sis. Moreover, Armenians in Istanbul did not have prose traditions in vernacular languages.

By the end of the seventeenth century the landscape had fundamentally changed, as Istanbul had become a major Armenian cultural and demographic centre. Bolstered by the arrival of the Armenian refugees, the Armenian Patriarchate in Istanbul gradually rose from regional obscurity to become an influential ecclesiastical see in the seventeenth century, expanding to official jurisdiction over territories from Rumeli to Tokat by 1695.[1] In the same period, Istanbul became a major centre of Armenian manuscript copying and the site of experimentations with book printing. Most importantly, seventeenth-century Istanbul produced its first great Armenian author and intellect, Eremia Kʻeōmurchean, establishing its tradition in Armenian letters and scholarship composed in both classical and vernacular languages. For this reason, I propose in this chapter that the life and work of Eremia Kʻeōmurchean constitute the most logical point of origin for charting a distinct intellectual and cultural tradition in the Western Armenian Diaspora centred around Istanbul, which would come in time to pride itself on its rich Armenian literary life. Eremia was such a significant figure in the second half of the seventeenth century that a study of his life and work can serve as the basis for considering intellectual and cultural developments in the Western Armenia Diaspora in general during his lifetime.

The life and works of Eremia have been studied by multiple scholars, mostly in Western and Eastern Armenian language studies, and by some Turkologists interested in his Armeno-Turkish corpus. These authors include Nersēs Akinean,[2] Vahram Y. Tʻorgomean,[3] Mesrop Nshanean,[4] Hasmik Sahakyan,[5] Zhozef Avetisyan,[6] Gevorg Bampukʻchean,[7] Edmond Schütz,[8] Andreas Tietze, Avedis K. Sanjian[9] and, most recently, Gayane Ayvazyan.[10] In this chapter, I will first rely on this Armenian-language secondary literature and Eremia's corpus to provide a broad picture of his life and works. Moreover, I offer an interpretation of Eremia's overarching intellectual projects that situates him as a product of cultural changes that had been set in motion by the Great Armenian Flight. I suggest that Eremia's intellectual achievements were fourfold. Firstly, Eremia – the grandson of emigrés from Kemah – revived the medieval Armenian literary traditions of Eastern Anatolia that had declined in the sixteenth century to meet contemporary needs in Istanbul. Secondly, he was the first Armenian author to write extended works on Ottoman history based on primary-source research in Ottoman Turkish. Thirdly, Eremia was part of a wave of early modern Armenian authors who pioneered genres of first-person narratives and travel literature comparable to contemporaneous works being produced by other communities in the Ottoman Empire and the Islamic world, as well as in Europe. Finally, Eremia also translated numerous works from Armenian into Armeno-Turkish.

In sum, Eremia represents a meeting between the traditions of Armenian learning of Kemah, of Ottoman Istanbul, and of the broader Mediterranean Basin. He wrote at the nexus of Armenian, Islamic and early modern intellectual traditions, and he was an epitome of the hybrid cultural interaction that would come to define the Western Armenian Diaspora. This chapter will describe Eremia's contributions to Armenian letters and add to research on him by providing many samples of his work translated into English and through analysis of unpublished manuscripts, all interpreted within a framework that emphasises the importance of the Great Flight for shaping Eremia's historical context. I will leave consideration of his Armeno-Turkish corpus to the next chapter, as those works have a special significance in the history of Turkish literature in the Ottoman Empire that warrants separate treatment.

The Life of Eremia Kʻeōmurchean

Eremia's biography is largely known to scholars through his own works, especially his diary, poems and letters. For example, Eremia relates his genealogy in a poetic lamentation composed for his father, Martiros, wherein he writes that

> By stock he [Martiros] was from great lineage, from nobility.
> Firstly, from the East, from the family of his ancestors, they came to the West.
> To Daranalikʻ [Kemah], dwelling in a settlement called Khocha.
> There [they lived] from generation to generation, family and descendants, [each] in their time.
> Later from the Celalis, from the suffering of their tribulations, [Martiros's] father departed from there,
> he came to these regions, to Gallipoli, seeing the birth of a boy [Martiros].
> Parting from [there], [they came to] a new [place of] repose, a new dwelling [i.e., Istanbul].[11]

While the verse's beginning is rather opaque, it explicitly states that Eremia's grandfather was a native of the Kemah region who fled because of the Celali Revolts. Eremia's father was born in Gallipoli in the midst of their flight, but the family eventually continued its migration to Istanbul, where Eremia was later born.

In confirmation of the above verse, elsewhere it is written that 'Eremia of Byzantium, whose ancestors were easterners, [they were] deprived of their homeland called Daranalikʻ',[12] and in a colophon of 1640 a scribe wrote that Eremia's father Martiros was 'from the land of Kemah from the village Apushtay . . .'[13] Of the Celalis, Eremia remarks in one of his unpublished histories that

> . . . in the time of Yavuz Ali Paşa [Ottoman Grand Vizier, 1603–1604], the Celalis of Anatolia appeared. Our grandfathers fled from them and they would narrate [about them] to us in the time of our childhood . . . Concerning these things I have written a book filled with their history.[14]

This book is unknown to modern scholars and thus it seems that one of Eremia's lost works focused on the history of the Celali Revolts. In any case, the facts of Eremia's links to Kemah and his grandfather's flight from there because of the Celalis are uncontestable.

Although Eremia himself did not spend time in Kemah, he conceived of it as his ancestral land. It was his paternal homeland, or *'memleket'* to use the modern Turkish colloquial expression. This connection is demonstrated by one of his epithets. While Eremia usually used the family name 'K'eōmurchean' he also signed his works with other appellations, such as 'Eremia the scribe', 'Eremia of Byzantium' and Eremia 'Daranalts'i',[15] an explicit reference to his ancestral homeland's Classical Armenian province name. The origin of the surname K'eōmurchean is debated, but it has been proposed that it derives from the name of the village Kömür, situated in the province of Daranalik' very close to the above-mentioned villages (Khocha and Apushtay).[16] It has also been proposed that it was artisanal in origin,[17] or perhaps connected with a neighbourhood of seventeenth-century Istanbul called the 'Kömürcü Odalar', or 'coal-venders' cells'.[18] The present author considers the first explanation most likely.

Eremia K'eōmurchean was born in Istanbul on 13 May 1637.[19] His father Martiros was a priest at the St Sargis Armenian Church (no longer extant), and a man of influence. Though we know from Grigor Daranalts'i that relations between the Istanbul-Armenians and refugees were initially fraught with tension, by the time of Martiros's adulthood the refugees who had arrived in Istanbul at the turn of the century had become integrated into the Istanbul-Armenian community's ecclesiastical, economic and civic life. Martiros married rich, to the niece of *Mahtesi* Ambakum,[20] and he was granted various clerical honours. For example, when the Catholicos of Ējmiatsin visited Istanbul in 1652, he made Martiros his 'deputy (*vekîl*) and archpriest', an honour which mostly entailed responsibility for Ējmiatsin's treasury in Istanbul.[21]

Like his brother-in-law Martiros K'eōmurchean, *Mahtesi* Ambakum was a refugee whose family hailed from Akn (Kemaliye) (see Figure 5.1), a region directly southwest of neighbouring Kemah.[22] Ambakum had become rich by supplying bread and flour to the Ottoman imperial army and he supervised a large bread-baking operation. Thus he established himself as an early example

Figure 5.1 Akn (Kemaliye).

of an Akn Armenian who succeeded in business in Ottoman Istanbul, one of many to come, as in the eighteenth century Akn Armenians played a noted role in Ottoman finance.[23] Ambakum officially adopted his grandnephew Eremia,[24] and it was through his adopted guardian that Eremia gained experience working as a baker in Ambakum's shops. It was also thanks to Ambakum that Eremia had the opportunity to travel great distances within the Ottoman Empire while still a twelve-year old boy, when they departed together on a pilgrimage to Jerusalem.[25]

It is unlikely that Eremia ever met Grigor Daranalts'i, as the latter passed away in Rodosto when Eremia was about six years old, but Eremia met Grigor's brother, Markos, before embarking on his pilgrimage. Markos had been a refugee from the Celalis in his youth, but he was rescued from servitude by Grigor and later became a servant of the Holy Sepulchre of Jerusalem.[26] In his diary entry for 1649, Eremia writes that

> Our mother's uncle was called *Mahtesi* Ambakum. He made a vow to go to Jerusalem, and he was preparing beforehand provisions for the journey.

From fear of the Franks, for many years pilgrimage ships were not going on the Mediterranean Sea. He prepared to go by land, with the *surrē* of the Turks [the yearly procession of sultanic gifts for Mecca] by the Damascus Road. [But] by the influence of the Holy Spirit, a great ship was found, which was from the island called *Mis*, which was departing for Egypt. And there was a messenger (*sâ'i*) from Jerusalem, a man [named] Markos, the brother of *Vardapet* 'Buk'' Grigor. He was acquainted with the ship captain and spoke with him. [People] from all the churches, who had a desire to go to holy Jerusalem, joined with us. And when they saw that there was a ship, our friends increased in number up to 90, both man and woman . . .[27]

Thanks to Markos's intercession, Eremia, Ambakum and Ambakum's wife were able to depart for Jerusalem by ship on 5 August 1649.[28] Eremia would see Markos again several times in his youth, both at his home and church, and thus he was a recurrent though minor character in his life and diary.[29]

Eremia's pilgrimage to Jerusalem was a turning point in his youth, as it exposed him to the breadth of the Ottoman Empire and inspired his earliest literary efforts. The oldest portions of Eremia's first literary work – his diary – describe his pilgrimage in detail. While Eremia's diary begins with an account of the deposition of the Ottoman Sultan Ibrahim I in 1648, Gayane Ayvazyan has shown that that passage was a later interjection.[30] The authentic diary begins with the year 1649 and his voyage to Jerusalem, and thus the work begins as travel literature.

This pilgrimage to Jerusalem was to be the second for Ambakum, and Eremia records that he had decided to embark on a trip to the Holy Land again at the invitation of the Armenian Catholicos of Ējmiatsin, P'ilippos, who also planned to make the journey from Ējmiatsin to meet Ambakum in Jerusalem. Eremia provides details about their voyage. For instance, he notes that the ship set anchor in Rodosto after leaving Istanbul and that the passengers disembarked there. He writes that

> . . . [in Rodosto] we worshiped at the Holy King [Church], where [is kept] the nail of the plank which Pilate put above the head of our redeemer, Jesus Christ, [which said] 'this is the king of the Jews'. It is in the hands of the Armenian priests, hidden in the sacristy.[31]

This was the sacred relic that Grigor Daranałts'i had brought from Kemah, and the Church of the King – which was also called the Holy Redeemer – was where Grigor had been buried about six years beforehand in 1643.

Out of fear of pirates Eremia's ship did not take the usual route via Cyprus but travelled to the Holy Land by hugging the Western Anatolian coast, avoiding the high sea as much as possible.[32] The ship captain's great caution did not prevent the pilgrims from having one close call, when they encountered a 'Frankish' ship on 22 August 1649. Upon seeing the foreign ship, the sailors opened full sail and, in terror, both the sailors and passengers joined together in rowing to evade the 'Franks' with speed. They succeeded in escaping and Eremia writes that 'God visited [us], [and] we withdrew from them [the Franks] on Wednesday evening at the second hour of night . . .'[33]

Ambakum, his wife and the young Eremia finally arrived in the city of Jerusalem after three weeks of travelling, on 28 August 1649. Ambakum must have been disappointed when the Catholicos tarried in his travels and failed to arrive in Jerusalem on time for their meeting.[34] Eremia provides a brief summary in his diary of his visits to the essential holy sites, including the Monastery of St James, the Church of the Holy Sepulchre, the Monastery of St Sabbas and other sites.[35] His diary descriptions are surprisingly undetailed and superficial, given his demonstrated capacity for expansion and detail on other themes in the same work, but he would make up for this lacuna in a book on the subject written many years later.

In sum, Eremia spent approximately ten months on his pilgrimage, including eight months in Jerusalem and two months travelling.[36] He returned to Istanbul alone with Ambakum's wife, and on their return trip their ship embarked on the high seas and took the traditional route via Cyprus,[37] just as Grigor Daranałts'i had done in prior years. Ambakum, on the contrary, chose to return overland and to make an additional pilgrimage to Kemah and the 'Province of Churches'.[38] This fact implies that by the mid-seventeenth century the monasteries of Daranalik' had recovered from the traumas of the beginning of the century and had renewed operation. They continued to attract Armenian pilgrims until 1915.

After his pilgrimage, the next major episode about which Eremia elaborates in his diary is the visit of the Catholicos P'ilippos to Istanbul from Ējmiatsin in 1652. The Armenian Patriarch of Constantinople at the time,

Eḷiazar of Antep, led a procession to meet and to escort him to the St George Church of Samatya and the fifteen-year-old Eremia also participated.³⁹ The patriarch's visit was of political significance to the Istanbul-Armenian community because it seems to have caused a power shift among the factions of Armenian clergy.

Though the refugee crisis of the early seventeenth century had ended by Eremia's adolescent years, political factionalism continued within the Armenian community. According to Mesrop Nshanean – the learned editor of Eremia's diary – Catholicos Pʻilippos 'worked to put an end to the distinction of insider and outsider between the native and refugee [Armenians] of the capital'.⁴⁰ To understand this statement, it is important to note that by the mid-seventeenth century those who had been refugees at the beginning of the century, like the Kʻeōmurcheans and Ambakum's family, had become integrated into Istanbul urban life, just as the deported (*sürgün*) populations of the fifteenth century had become by Grigor's lifetime. But refugees continued to arrive in Istanbul throughout the century and they continued to destabilise power balances within the Armenian community. In a recent article entitled 'Armenians in Urban Order and Disorder of Seventeenth-Century Istanbul' Polina Ivanova argues that these factional struggles '[represented] a conflict between two different kinds of legitimisation', the ecclesiastical authority of Ējmiatsin, on the one hand, and 'popular support' on the other hand. She notes that 'power based on popular support was a precarious and contingent one'.⁴¹ It was also one that was related to continued migrations into Istanbul. It is likely that the wild demographic fluctuations taking place in seventeenth-century Rodosto, where the Armenian population peaked at mid-century, were also taking place in Istanbul during Eremia's adolescent years and that they had a continuing impact on church politics. The irony of infighting between different generations of migrants was best articulated by the Ottoman judge who had chided the airs of superiority of the 'local' Istanbul Armenians of the beginning of the century by asking, 'Infidels (*kâfir*), are *you* not exiles (*sürgün*) brought from Karaman by Sultan Mehmed?'⁴²

It is clear that with the arrival of the Catholicos and his partisans from Ējmiatsin the Armenian Patriarch of Constantinople Eḷiazar of Antep felt that his position had been weakened. He resigned from his post in September 1652 and travelled to the Holy Mother of God Monastery in Diyarbekir.⁴³ After a brief interlude, the Catholicos appointed one of his own followers, Yovhannēs Muḷnetsʻi (Muḷni being a village in modern-day Armenia), who ascended to the patriarchal throne of Constantinople.[44] According to Maḷakʻia Ōrmanean – one of the most authoritative authors on Armenian church history – the new patriarch was chosen because he was unemployed at the time and because he was an unknown 'no-name'.[45] This was a temporary victory for the influence of Ējmiatsin, but it only set the stage for future conflict.

Catholicos Pʻilippos spent about ten months in Istanbul. Eremia often visited with the Catholicos, who had warm relations with both Ambakum and the Kʻeōmurcheans. In addition to the new Armenian Patriarch of Constantinople, he also granted a staff of authority to several new *vardapets*, and he ordained a bishop. Finally, he departed from Istanbul in late April 1653. His departure occasioned another opportunity for the young Eremia to travel, as the patriarch spent about a month in Bursa and the Kʻeōmurcheans visited him there.[46]

Before continuing with his narrative of Istanbul-Armenian church politics, Eremia's diary next provides a personal interlude. Eremia married on Monday 22 May 1654 at the age of seventeen in a large ceremony involving most of Istanbul's ranking Armenian clergy.[47] Eremia provides little information about his wife or her family in his works, and it seems likely that his marriage was not as financially and politically important in his life as his father Martiros's had been. In 1690, thirty-four years after their marriage, Eremia and his wife were still wed, and together they would have four children, three boys and one girl.[48]

Until the time of his marriage, Eremia had been only an observer of ecclesiastical affairs in Istanbul, but thereafter he would assume a formal role as a secretary and adviser to the Armenian Patriarchate.[49] All of his formal positions were those of a layman. In 1649 he became a *dpir*, the lowest church rank, but Eremia rejected subsequent advancement within the church hierarchy despite encouragement.[50] This decision has attracted attention, as some scholars have attributed it to anti-clerical sentiment.[51] It seems noteworthy to this author, however, that by 1649 Eremia had already begun his first literary efforts and become a client of his wealthy uncle Ambakum. He had independent means, and it seems to me that Eremia probably preferred to spend his time reading and writing than being obliged to perform church services.

In that choice, he was not unlike other great Ottoman authors of the seventeenth century, like Kâtip Çelebi and Evliya Çelebi, who had opportunities to lead intellectual lives of leisure rather than having to pursue full-time vocations.

The time of Eremia's formal transition to manhood and active involvement in political affairs coincided almost exactly with the rise of heightened tensions within the Istanbul-Armenian church and community. Eḷiazar of Antep returned to Istanbul on 15 December 1654, only a few months after Eremia's marriage. He was very close to the Kʻeōmurcheans and to Ambakum, who were his friends and allies. In general, his arrival was well received and he visited all six of Istanbul's Armenian Churches – St Sargis, the Holy Mother of God, St George, the Holy Illuminator, St Nicholas and the Holy Archangel – to preach and to perform the liturgy.[52] But church politics is politics nonetheless, and from the time of his arrival the potential for conflict arose between Eḷiazar's faction and that of Yovhannēs Muḷnetsʻi, the Armenian Patriarch of Constantinople who had been appointed by the Catholicos from Ējmiatsin.

The spark that lit the flame of conflict between Istanbul's two main Armenian factions sprung forth when news arrived in Istanbul on 30 May 1655 that the Catholicos had died a few weeks prior in Ējmiatsin.[53] With his death Patriarch Yovhannēs lost a pillar of support and legitimation and Eḷiazar proceeded to challenge him. Yovhannēs' position was weakened by the fact that he had only been appointed for a one-year term.[54] The partisans of both men began corresponding with Ējmiatsin in order to win support for their side, and Yovhannēs' side even resorted to forging a fake letter from the new Catholicos.[55] Ējmiatsin chose not to take sides in the conflict, thus forcing both factions to resort to unusual measures. Accusations of sorcery were made, and Yovhannēs's camp even spread the rumour that Eḷiazar had converted to Islam ('Turkified') as a child.[56] The details of the ugliness are not important here, except to say that Eḷiazar sought for increased independence from Ējmiatsin in opposition to Yovhannēs, while the Catholicos at Ējmiatsin deemed himself too far away to intervene effectively.

In almost all episodes of the conflict, Eremia was a strong supporter of Eḷiazar. Throughout their lives of friendship and collaboration, Eremia really only opposed Eḷiazar once, almost a decade later in 1664.[57] On that occasion, Eḷiazar gained the support of the Ottoman state for forming an indepedent position as Catholicos for all Armenians in the Ottoman Empire.[58] Eremia deemed this to be an excessively bold move within the internal Armenian politics of the time, but the power grab was an intimation of things to come, as the Armenian Patriarchate of Constantinople would eventually gain independence from Ējmiatsin in the eighteenth century.[59]

On 23 November 1658 an important turning point occurred in Eremia's life because Ambakum died that day.[60] Ambakum had been both a financial and political patron of great influence in the Istanbul-Armenian community, and it is possibly his patronage that influenced Eremia's decision not to join the clergy. It seems that Eremia was always in need of reliable patronage, and he soon found another ally of comparable wealth and means, Apro Çelebi, a merchant and man of political influence in Istanbul.[61] Apro had already been Eremia's godfather, but after Ambakum's death their cooperation intensified. Apro commissioned Eremia to oversee important projects for the Armenian community, like the rebuilding of the St Nicholas Church which had burned in a fire,[62] and he also financially supported Eremia in the establishment of Istanbul's second Armenian printing press, an essential role given that the press ran at a financial loss.[63] Though he funded the project, Apro did not live to see its establishment, as he died before the press entered operation in 1677.[64] The day of Apro's death in 1676 was tragic for Eremia, just as Ambakum's had been.[65] It is clear that Eremia initially needed patronage to produce his works and maintain his influence in civic and church affairs, and in his life, first Ambakum and then Apro played this role with affection and constant support.

I have already mentioned Eremia's childhood travels to Jerusalem and Bursa, but his participation in church affairs and politics led him to other parts of the Ottoman Empire as well later in life. Eremia had several audiences with Grand Viziers of the Ottoman court in his lifetime. For instance, a meeting with the Grand Vizier Köprülü Mehmed Paşa drew him to Edirne in 1660.[66] He also travelled much further from home in 1664 when he journeyed to Aleppo to dissuade Eḷiazar from his bid for an independent catholicosate.[67] Much later in his life in May 1685 he made a pilgrimage to Ējmiatsin. He went to visit his son Grigoris, who was a young *vardapet* studying at the renowned Hovhannavankʻ, and he travelled with his other son Malakʻia. Eremia was unable to see Grigoris, who had himself decided to visit Istanbul and was absent when his family arrived. He visited Hovhannavankʻ and Saḷmosavankʻ (where Grigor Daranaḷtsʻi spent time in his youth) during his time in Ējmiatsin, and he also edited some Armeno-Turkish letters and translated an Armenian hagiography collection into Armeno-Turkish while he was there. Eremia returned to Istanbul via Trabzon and the Crimea.[68]

The nature of the sources for Eremia's biography changes across the course of his lifetime. Scholars are best informed about his early years, because the earliest entries of his diary are detailed and filled with information about his personal movements and activities, his family and his family's influential friends. Gayane Ayvazyan notes, however, that as Eremia grew older the nature of his diary changed with him. From 1649 until 1659 Eremia was diligent about keeping very detailed and frequent entries. Thereafter, however, he kept journal entries more intermittently and selectively. After 1659 there was a tendency for him to prefer descriptions of social and political importance over the details of his personal life.[69] Finally, he abandoned the project altogether when he was twenty-five years old, and there are no more entries after 1662.

To fill in the data for his later life, scholars have relied primarily on two sources: colophons and the diary of Minas Amdetsʻi. Minas – who would rise to be the Armenian Patriarch of Jerusalem – kept a journal of his life from 1680 to 1704.[70] During those years he travelled extensively, spending time in Jerusalem, Istanbul, Tokat and Ējmiatsin. He often ran into Eremia and his family and he would mention them in his journal. For example, he was in Ējmiatsin at the same time as Eremia and he commented on Eremia's movements in the region.[71] He was in Istanbul when Martiros Kʻeōmurchean died and he noted this in his diary as well.[72] Without doubt, the change of source bases across Eremia's lifespan influences our knowledge and mental picture of his life.

Eremia had two brothers, Gevorg and Komitas, both of whom became priests. The former died naturally in 1700,[73] while the latter – who became famed for his Catholic leanings – was executed in Istanbul in 1707 in the midst of religious tensions between Apostolic and Catholic Armenians.[74] It has already been mentioned that Eremia's eldest son Grigoris was a priest and *vardapet* who had studied far from home at the renowned Hovhannavankʻ, near Ējmiatsin and modern-day Yerevan, Armenia. He then became a priest at the Church of the Archangel in Balat, Istanbul, where he died young in a fire in 1692. Eremia's only daughter, Soḷomē, also died young in 1690. By that time Eremia had also already lost his youngest son, Hovsepʻ, who had died at the age of fourteen sometime in the first half of the 1680s. Eremia would die later, on 15 July 1695, and thus he witnessed the deaths of three of his four children. His second youngest son Maḷakʻia the scribe was the only one of his children to survive him.[75]

In his later years, after his return from Ējmiatsin, it seems that Eremia withdrew entirely from public and political life and lived in isolation. Both Gayane Ayvazyan and Mesrop Nshanean suggest that it was the loss of his children that pushed Eremia into seclusion. Ayvazyan writes that '. . . after the death of his children, it is as if Eremia Kʻeōmurchean turned away from life. In his final years he lived solitarily and tried to drive away his sorrow in creative investigations'.[76] According to Nshanean,

> On his return from Holy Ējmiatsin (1686), Eremia, seeing the disordered national-ecclesiastical affairs, lived from then on an isolated life. His advanced years and the early deaths of two children – a girl Soḷomē and his son Grigoris *vardapet* – one after the other . . . completely overwhelmed him, and he remained far from social life.[77]

According to Akinean, from that time forward Eremia only 'lived among his books'.[78]

Certainly, it is unlikely that Eremia's withdrawal was occasioned by the 'disordered national-ecclesiastical affairs' as they had been 'disordered' throughout his life. Ayvazyan is probably closer to the truth in suggesting that Eremia's withdrawal and focus on work was a subliminal response to the death of his children. I would speak more broadly, however, as some process of sublimation must have impelled him throughout his life, not only at the end: from the time he began writing his diary at the age of twelve until his death Eremia single-handedly produced a flowering of Armenian literary production the likes of which had not been seen in centuries.

Eremia's Education and Literary Corpus

Before entering into a detailed analysis of individual works by Eremia, a note should be made about his education, intellectual influences and literary corpus as a whole. In his youth, Eremia was the student of a priest and associate of his father's at the St Sargis Church, a certain Yovhannes.[79] It is clear, however, that his intellectual influences must have been much broader. Throughout his youth Eremia was frequently in the company of some of the most learned Armenians of the seventeenth century, and it is likely that his education progressed via informal mechanisms. As a young man, his most important intellectual influences were Eḷiazar of Antep, mentioned above, and Martiros of Crimea, who was the author of a previously mentioned history in verse of the Crimea and a former student of a Celali refugee from Tokat. Both of these priests served tenures as the Armenian patriarch of Constantinople, and later in his life Eremia alludes to their great literary influence on him in one of his letters.[80]

Almost all biographical accounts of Eremia make mention of his multilingualism. In Armenian secondary literature it is frequently reported that, in addition to Armenian and Turkish, Eremia knew Greek, Persian, Arabic and Hebrew,[81] as well as 'Latin and European languages'.[82] These claims derive in part from the testimony of the eighteenth-century Armenian historian Mikʻayel Chʻamchʻean, who made passing reference to Eremia's abilities in Latin and Greek.[83] Chʻamchʻean, however, was not Eremia's contemporary, and these claims seem to be based in large part on local Istanbul-Armenian lore emphasising Eremia's great learnedness. While it is likely that Eremia learned some Greek on the streets of Istanbul[84] and that he may have learned the basics of Arabic and Persian for the sake of his Ottoman Turkish, the sure facts about Eremia's linguistic capacities concern his Armenian and Turkish.

Eremia could both read and write in Classical Armenian and, like Grigor Daranaḷtsʻi, he sometimes wrote in a mixture of Classical Armenian and a western vernacular. Eremia also wrote Armeno-Turkish, mostly at a colloquial level. Although his written Turkish was usually not high Ottoman prose, he was capable of modulating his level of composition, and he could certainly read works in high Ottoman Turkish. While Eremia undoubtedly learned to speak Turkish as a child on the streets of Istanbul, he did not learn literary Ottoman Turkish until he was eighteen. He explicitly mentions in his diary that he finished learning the 'Turkish' alphabet on 15 April 1656.[85] It must have been at this time that he began working to read Ottoman literary texts, probably with the aid of a tutor. As we will see below, these efforts bore fruit in his historical works on Ottoman history.

Eremia's literary corpus was diverse.[86] He wrote primarily about three themes – history, religion and geography – and he also prepared translations. Eremia wrote numerous letters and poems, many of which have been compiled and published by Nersēs Akinean, Mesrop Nshanean and Hasmik Sahakyan. Among his histories are diverse works on Ottoman history both in prose and in verse. Some of them cover the empire's entire history from its foundation until Eremia's lifetime in the seventeenth century, while others focus only on Eremia's own lifetime. Eremia also wrote historical works on more specified contemporary themes, such as the Ottoman conquest of Crete and the Istanbul fire of 1660.

On religious themes, Eremia wrote sermons and polemical works against other religious communities, like 'the Greeks' and 'the Jews', as well as defences of his own Armenian Apostolic Church. One of his printed works was a text on the holy sites of Jerusalem, and he also wrote a catechismal manual entitled *Questions and Answers*. Unfortunately, his geographical treatises have been lost, but his mistitled *Istanbul History* is both extant and published and it constitutes more of a topographical walking tour of Istanbul à la Evliya Çelebi than a true history, though like Evliya he discusses history in the course of his tour. His translations from Armenian into Turkish – the topic of the next chapter – include an Armenian history, a life of Alexander the Great, a translation of Armenian hagiography and translations of biblical tracts.

If we compare Eremia's corpus with one of the greatest Ottoman Muslim intellectuals of the seventeenth century – Kâtip Çelebi – we see thematic similarity. Some of their works overlap exactly in genre, such as their biographies of the Ottoman sultans, Eremia's written in Armenian and Kâtip Çelebi's written in Arabic. Looking at his corpus as a whole, it is clear that when writing in Armenian, Eremia was occupied simultaneously by three grand projects: engagement with the intellectual life of seventeenth-century Istanbul through research on Ottoman history, the development of early modern Armenian literature focused on the individual and place, and the revival of the medieval Armenian intellectual tradition. In order to untangle these scholarly identities, let us turn to a more detailed analysis of works that exemplify these overlapping intellectual projects. Overall, I argue that in each of these spheres, Eremia sought to meet the intellectual needs of a population that experienced cultural rift in the aftermath of mass migrations.

Writing Ottoman History in Armenian

Grand narratives

Eremia was the first Armenian author to write major works focused on Ottoman history. These works are noteworthy because of the palpable influence of Islamicate primary sources in Ottoman Turkish and perhaps also Arabic. Eremia's history writing represents an integration of Armenian and Ottoman Turkish perspectives, mixed in different ways according to the topic and audience of individual works. Eremia's works on Ottoman history include both general histories of the empire and some topical histories on contemporary themes. In this section, attention will be paid to his general histories of the Ottoman Empire, including *Concise History of 400 Years of Ottoman Kings*, *Concise History of the Ottoman Kings*, *Chronological History* and *Historical Notes of His Own Times, Until 1682*.[87]

Some insight into Eremia's *Chronological History* and *Historical Notes of His Own Times, Until 1682* – which have not been studied directly by modern scholarship – can be gleaned from research by Mesrop Nshanean. Nshanean notes that parts of the famed eighteenth-century Istanbul-Armenian Ch'amch'ean's *Armenian History* relied on Eremia's *Chronological History*.[88] Nshanean compared Eremia's diary with those sections of Ch'amch'ean's history to find that they were almost identical, suggesting that the diary was Eremia's source for much of his *Chronological History*, and that Eremia converted passages of his diary to a standard annalistic form.[89] While Nshanean did not study Eremia's *Historical Notes of His Own Times, Until 1682*, it seems likely that Eremia probably used his own diary as a primary source 'scrapbook' for all of his historical writings about the years 1648–62.

Explanation of Eremia's *Concise History of 400 Years of Ottoman Kings* and *Concise History of the Ottoman Kings* need not be so speculative. The latter work remains unpublished, but several manuscript copies are extant and one of them is housed in the Matenadaran in Yerevan (M 1786), an eighteenth-century manuscript compilation. The compilation is a fascinating amalgam prepared by a Safavid Armenian named Step'anos Dashtets'i. The compilation's first section is a history of the kings of the three great early modern Islamic empires: the Ottomans, Mughals and Safavids. The longest of the three sections concerns the Ottomans,[90] followed by a king list for the Mughals[91] and an account of the Safavid kings.[92] In this work Stepʻanos was not always a very ambitious original author, as he copied extensively from Eremia in his section on Ottoman history, while his sections on the Mughals and Safavids are much briefer. It seems that his Ottoman history section was a direct copy of Eremia's work. This supposition is supported by occasional instances of first-person speech in Eremia's text, which Stepʻannos qualifies with statements like 'this was written by Eremia Çelebi in this way'[93] in order to make it clear that readers understood 'I' to be the author Eremia, not the compiler Stepʻanos.

Accepting, then, that Stepʻannos' Ottoman history is largely an accurate copy of Eremia's *Concise History of the Ottoman Kings*, how then do we assess and describe the work? Comparatively speaking, it closely resembles other seventeenth-century works in Greek and Arabic, namely the anonymous Greek *Chronicle of Turkish Sultans*,[94] and Kâtip Çelebi's Arabic *Digest of Histories* (*Fezleketü't-tevârîh*, separate from his Ottoman Turkish *Digest*).[95] Of course, biography is a genre with roots going back at least to Plutarch in Greek and with a millennium of history in Arabic as well by Eremia's lifetime. The fact that Muslims, Greeks and Armenians were all writing biographies should not be surprising, as there was demand for biographies of the Ottoman sultans written in simple and readable Arabic, Greek and Armenian in the mid-seventeenth century. The above-mentioned texts were written in registers accessible to anyone with a basic education in these three languages.

Eremia's book of biographies is very systematic in its presentation, beginning with a methodological introduction. Eremia writes that he first seeks to explain genealogy, recording 'who is whose son', before proceeding to note how many sons each sultan had. He would explain the sultan's martial achievements and conquests, then state how long he lived. Next, Eremia would list the sultan's viziers and *şeyhü'l-İslams* (grand *mufti*), before concluding with a summary of the sultan's charitable endowments.[96] Eremia also includes a short historical introduction to the work, wherein he describes pre-Ottoman Anatolia and Sultan Osman's commission to rule, granted by the Seljuk Sultan Aladdin through dispensation of symbols of sovereignty and command.[97] Of course, this connection between Osman and the Seljuks is a largely fictitious tale that appears in several Ottoman-Turkish chronicles, most notably Neşri, and which was also repeated by the pro-Ottoman Greek historian Chalkokondyles.[98] Thus, via Eremia this pro-Ottoman propaganda entered the Armenian historiographical tradition almost two hundred years after it had begun circulating in Turkish and Greek.

Signs of Ottoman Turkish linguistic influence permeate Eremia's biographies. In the course of one biography Eremia referred to Christians as '*gâvur*', a derogatory term used by Muslims for non-Muslims. In apparent shame at this, Stepʻanos interjected within the text, noting that 'the author is Kʻēōmurji oḷli (*oğlu*) Eremiay Chʻēlēpi of Istanbul, who translated the history from the Ottoman language to the Armenian language'.[99] This interjection shows that Stepʻanos sought to copy Eremia's text faithfully – as he could have just deleted the term in his version – while also assuring readers that the choice of derogatory language was not his own, but rather that it derived from an Ottoman primary source that Eremia had translated. This comment suggests that Eremia's book of biographies was an adaptation based directly on an original in Ottoman Turkish or Arabic.[100] Among extant works in Ottoman Turkish and Arabic, Kâtip Çelebi's Arabic *Digest of Histories*[101] most closely resembles Eremia's history in its biographical format.

Let us analyse one of Ermeia's biographies and see how it compares with the corresponding biography in Kâtip Çelebi's *Digest of Histories*. Here is a complete translation of his biography of Sultan Ahmed I (1603–17):

> Sultan Ahmed ibn Muhammad Han: When he sat on the throne, he delighted the Janissaries and the cavalrymen (*sipâhî*) with [their] salaries. He transferred some people from [their] posts, and he sent Chḷalizade (Cağaloğlu) Sinan Paşa to the East. He made the vizier Ali Paşa the commander (*serdar*), and he sent him to the West, which he subjugated and brought to submission. In his time clever viziers (*vüzera*) – with the assistance of God – destroyed and annihilated all of the Celalis, especially Murad Paşa, called Ḷu[y]iwchi or Ḷĕyĕchi (*Kuyucu*), was a victorious opponent of the Celalis, as is explained in the sequence of the History of the Celalis [presumably a lost work of Eremia's]. Very terrible [things] appeared in Persia. Shah Abbas grew strong, and he took back all the lands which Sultan Murad, the grandfather of Sultan Ahmed, had taken. He built as a pious

endowment (*hayrât*), a new mosque in the Hippodrome (*At Meydanı*) with six slender (*nazik*) and beautiful minarets, [the mosque was] glorious more than all [other] mosques. The banishment (*sürgün*) of the Armenians [was] at this time by Nasuh Paşa, and the banishment of dogs [?] also. *Dolmabahçe* was filled [garden made from filled '*dolma*' coastal land]. Princes (*şehzade*), 5: Bayezid, Mustafa, Kâzım, Selim, Muhammad. Clerics (*mufti*): Ebülmeyâmin Mustafa Efendi, Sun'ullah Efendi, Mustafa Efendi, Hocazade Muhammad Efendi, Es'ad Efendi. Viziers: He made his vizier Yavuz Ali Paşa: he died on the Belgrade Campaign (*sefer*). Lala Muhammad Paşa: Returning from Estergon, he died. Derviş Muhammad Paşa next he killed. Then Murad Paşa for five years. He passed to Anatolia and totally destroyed Kalenderoğlu and other Celalis like him, and with great effort he annihilated all of them. He died in Diyarbekir [Amid]. Then Nasuh Paşa, who performed the banishment (*sürgün*), then Kara Muhammad Paşa, who went to Yerevan. Then Halil Paşa, who was captain (*kapudan*), and he was by race Armenian and from Zeytun. Three sons of his became king: Osman, Murad, and Ibrahim. Let me relate to you their deeds next.[102]

Comparison of this biography with Kâtip Çelebi's version reveals parallels and divergences. The most striking point of similarity is the biographical format, and the fact that both authors append their biographies with similar lists of officials and princes.[103] Kâtip Çelebi's biography of Ahmed I is much longer and more detailed, particularly with regards to the histories of the grand viziers. Although Eremia covers much of the same content, he also adds mention of the 'exile of the Armenians' and other observations of interest to Armenians that were not present in the Arabic biography. Eremia's version was definitely not a direct translation of Kâtip Çelebi. If Eremia did 'translate', it must have been from another work unknown to this author, or his work may have been a compilation based on a variety of primary sources. In any case, the influence of Islamicate sources is palpable on Eremia's biographies and there is no doubt that Eremia relied on some Arabic or Ottoman Turkish text, either directly or with the help of a learned friend.

Even if Eremia did rely on Kâtip Çelebi as one of his sources, his work was nonetheless not entirely derivative, as he provides such biographies for all the Ottoman sultans from Osman I to Sultan Mustafa II (1695–1703),[104] who was reigning in the year of his death, long after the passing of Kâtip Çelebi in 1657. Step'annos also took the liberty of adding a shorter entry for Sultan Ahmed III (1703–30).[105] In the Yerevan manuscript, the prose biographies are appended with a series of genealogical charts for the Ottoman sultans (see Figure 5.2).[106] It is likely that these charts were an addition made by Step'annos, as he seems to have had a liking for such tables and includes a similar one in his section on the Mughal sultans, showing how the Mughal dynasty was related to Timur.[107]

While it does not rank as a general history of the Ottoman Empire, a poem about the Ottoman sultans is appended to Eremia's book of biographies in Step'annos Dashtets'i's compilation, and it is also considered to be part of Eremia's corpus.[108] The poem covers two manuscript pages, and it provides a single couplet for each sultan. It begins as follows:

> The first was brave Osman, a man expert at arms and martial.
> He conquered lands, lords, and princes, and he looted villages and towns.
> His son was called Orhan, and he seized all of Nicomedia.
> He put his throne in Bursa, and it was called Bursa-*cihan*.

Not all of the entries are filled with praises. Some are more matter-of-fact and sombre:

> [Murad I]'s son was Bayezid Han, who they nicknamed thunderbolt (*yıldırım*).
> He fought a war with Tamerlane, and thus he entered a dungeon (*zindan*).

In some of the verses, Eremia becomes downright critical. Of Sultan Mehmed III (1595–1603), for example, he writes,

> [Murad III]'s son was Mehmed Han, he was unsuccessful and worthless.
> His lands were inundated by Celalis, they put it under [them].[109]

This poem is not literature of the highest order, nor does it provide any in-depth commentary on Ottoman history comparable to Eremia's other works. Given its mixture of Turkish epithets and vocabulary with Armenian verse, it must have been written for Ottoman-Armenian subjects already familiar with basic Turkish vocabulary and Ottoman history. I would propose that

WESTERN ARMENIAN INTELLECTUAL TRADITION | 217

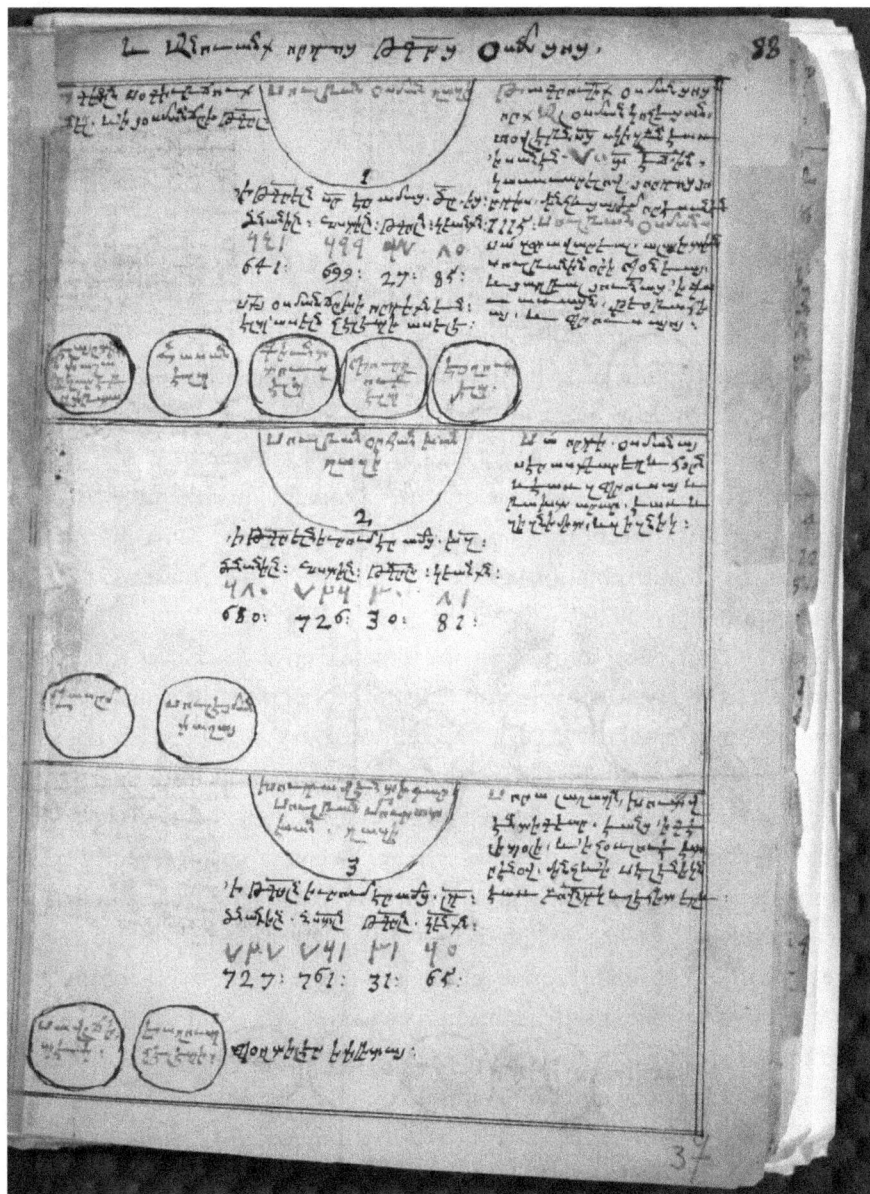

Figure 5.2 Genealogical chart for Sultans Osman, Orhan and Murad, prepared in the eighteenth century by Step'anos Dashtets'i (M 1786, 37a). Thanks to the Director of the Mesrop Mashtots Institute of Ancient Manuscripts (Matenadaran) Vahan Ter-Ghevondyan for granting permission to reproduce this image.

the poem's purpose was probably pedagogical and mnemonic, for helping young Armenians memorise the names, order and basic achievements of the Ottoman sultans, just as British schoolchildren memorise the names and order of their kings through verse.

Of Eremia's general histories of the Ottoman Empire, the most original is his *Concise History of 400 Years of Ottoman Kings*, a complete history of the empire in Armenian verse from its foundation to the time of the work's composition in the 1670s. This work was transcribed and published in 1982 by Zhozef M. Avetisyan, along with a rich scholarly introduction. It survives in only one copy, currently housed at the Matenadaran in Yerevan, and it is one of the most important histories both of Eremia's corpus and of early modern Armenian literature in general. The work's source base is hybrid, as it was written under the influence of both Ottoman Turkish and Armenian historiographical traditions. To fully understand the amalgam, both Avetisyan's rich introduction and the primary text itself deserve detailed consideration.

In his introduction to the *Concise History* Avetisyan achieves three main contributions to research on Eremia. Firstly, he describes the work's origins, showing from colophons that Eremia composed the work between the years 1675 and 1678, and that the autograph copy – which is now lost – was written at the request of the Catholicos of Ējmiatsin at the time, Yakob Julayets'i.[110] Moreover, colophons show that the eighteenth-century copy currently extant in Yerevan was prepared in Gallipoli for a latter-day Catholicos of Ējmiatsin, Abraham of Crete.[111] These requests show that there was a demand for knowledge about the Ottoman Empire among the clergy at Ējmiatsin throughout the late seventeenth and early eighteenth centuries. Abraham of Crete – who lived during the time of the famed Persian military commander Nader Shah (1688–1747) and met him on several occasions – wrote an original history about his own times,[112] and it may have been that he sought Eremia's work for the sake of his own historical research. It was thanks to Abraham of Crete's order that a copy of the history arrived at Ējmiatsin and thus survived intact for inclusion in the Matenadaran's collection.[113]

Avetisyan also provides a basic description of the work's scope and structure. The *Concise History* was written before Eremia's book of biographies and it includes descriptions of the reigns of only nineteen sultans, from

Osman I (1299–1326) to Mehmed IV (1648–87). The work is divided into four parts, and it is written in verse. Avetisyan explains the poetic structure as follows:

> The *Concise History of 400 Years of Ottoman Kings* is a work in verse, consisting of 1,811 bipartite stanzas. Every single line consists chiefly of 16 syllables (there are lines with fewer syllables), and it is divided into two hemistichs with fixed segmentation. The stanza is thus a totality of two rhyming lines. The way that they are rhymed with one another is parallel hemistichs, the second and the fourth, although, stanzas are also encountered where the first, second and fourth hemistichs are rhymed, or the second, third and fourth. The whole [work] has a single rhythmic [pattern] . . .[114]

For the poem's four parts, Eremia employed different calendrical systems in alternation. For the first part, consisting of the reigns of Osman I until the accession of Selim I (1512–20), he employed the Islamic *hijri* calendar; from Selim I until the accesion of Mehmed III (1595–1603), he employed the Armenian calendrical system; then from Mehmed III until the accession of Mehmed IV (1648–87) he again employed the Islamic calendar; and finally for the last portion covering the reign of Mehmed IV until the date of completion of the work in 1678, he again used the Armenian calendar.[115] Avetisyan suggests that there was a tendency for Eremia to employ the Islamic calendar in sections based on Ottoman Turkish primary sources, while he preferred the Armenian calendar in sections based on Armenian primary sources. This tendency was by no means absolute.[116] In addition to the four-part division within the poem, there is also a division into two parts separating history that took place before Eremia's lifetime and latter parts of the poem, for which oral history, Eremia's memory and his own works on contemporary history would have served as source material.[117]

In addition to these basic descriptions, Avetisyan's critical contribution to the study of Eremia lies in his analysis of the *Concise History*'s primary source material. Avetisyan is a Turkologist, and he systematically attempted to correlate Eremia's Armenian poem with its Ottoman Turkish primary source base. Through side-by-side comparison, he demonstrated close correlation – and sometimes even word-for-word correspondence – between passages on early Ottoman history in Eremia's *Concise History* and the Ottoman Turkish

Histories of the Lineage of Osman (*Tevârîh-i Âl-i Osman*) of Lütfi Paşa (1488–1563?).[118] For Ottoman history between 1595 and 1648 Avetisyan also found close correspondence between passages in Eremia's history and Kâtip Çelebi's Ottoman Turkish *Digest* (*Fezleke*).[119] At some points Eremia even abandoned translation into Armenian and quoted the original Ottoman Turkish text of the *Digest* with the Armenian alphabet, in Armeno-Turkish. Similarly, he adapted and altered a poem by the brother of Sultan Bayezid II (1481–1512), Cem Sultan, for inclusion in the *Concise History* in Armeno-Turkish.[120] Avetisyan shows that Eremia also relied on a diversity of Armenian authors, and he suggests that Eremia may have consulted additional Ottoman Turkish and Arabic materials – beyond those analysed in detail – such as the histories of Kemalpaşazâde (d. 1534) and Müneccimbaşı Ahmed Dede (d. 1702). These suggestions were not decisively demonstrated, however, and it is clear that further work is needed on the *Concise History*'s Islamic source materials.[121] What Avetisyan did show definitively, however, was that Eremia did research in Ottoman Turkish for his *Concise History* and that passages based on Ottoman Turkish sources perpetuate the tone and character of their source material in the Armenian work.

Let us now provide translations of three passages from Eremia's *Concise History* so as to convey its character and style directly. The following passage occurs in the *Concise History*'s section on Sultan Mehmed III (1595–1603):

> And the above-mentioned Celalis
> came forth in many places and became numerous:
> around Amid (Diyarbekir), Kayseri,
> Cilicia, Beria (Aleppo), and so on.
> Malatia and Urfa,
> and they spread overland:
> Sebastia (Sivas), Eudokia (Tokat),
> Galatia, Konya, and so on.
> Erzincan and Kemah,
> until the City (Istanbul) they spread:
> Izmir, Lycia,
> Manisa, reaching to the sea-coast.

Joining them were robbers and thieves,
Medes and Arabs following them . . .
[two lines missing from original manuscript]

The lords ran to them from their households (*ocak*),
so that they might not be killed by them,
they left behind houses and estates,
leaving women and children exposed.
Many Armenians did this [as well],
and not only did they leave their homes,
they were disavowing their holy faith,
hastening to shed innocent blood.
A vulgar mob, bands of barbarians,
whoever saw them would shudder,
they were taking women and children captive,
and leading them around with them.
Churches and monasteries,
they trampled; their estates they plundered,
they carelessly put many to the sword,
burning the dwellings of many with fire.[122]

The latter part of this section clearly derives from Armenian primary sources, like those presented in Chapter Two, as evidenced by a direct concern for the fate of Armenians that is absent from the Ottoman Turkish primary source material.

The following discussion of the Celali Revolts is taken from the *Concise History*'s section on Sultan Ahmed I (1603–17):

In 1017 (1608–9)
a commander (*serdar*) went up to Aleppo,
There was news about the Celalis,
that again they had united.
Canpolatoğlu with his [men]
committed villainy in Karaman,
with Kalenderoğlu they set out,
going out from the land of Karaman.

> They plundered Elbistan
> when plundering the tents of the Turkmen,
> they heard of the arrival of the commander (*serdar*),
> when they had reached Göksu.

After the arrival of the Ottoman 'commander (*serdar*) of Egypt (*Mısır*)', battle ensues:

> For many days there was combat,
> and the war intensified,
> the royal [troops] were victorious
> and they pillaged the encampment.
> The Celalis turned back,
> whom the *paşa* had reached,
> and the Tatar Han was appointed (*tayin*),
> he captured and killed them.
> Until Persia they fled,
> when they entered Yerevan,
> they said to Emir Güne Han,
> 'We submit ourselves to your *Shah*'.[123]

In this section, it is likely that Eremia's source material is Ottoman Turkish, as implied by his use of the Islamic calendar for dating. Gone are all references to the suffering Armenians. Instead, Eremia here discusses the Celalis in the manner of Muslim Ottoman chroniclers, describing them solely as opponents of the Ottoman state. The anecdote of the Celali flight to Safavid Persia is, of course, present in Ottoman Turkish sources, and Avetisyan points readers to compare the tract with Kâtip Çelebi's Ottoman Turkish *Digest*.[124]

Let us provide an example of a passage in the *Concise History* referring to events that took place in Eremia's lifetime. For the latter part of the *Concise History* Eremia's source base would have been his own memory, oral transmission and his own works about contemporary Ottoman history. Mediterranean piracy, the Ottoman wars in Crete and Istanbul's periodic fires were persistent interests of Eremia's addressed in multiple works, and Eremia discusses all three of these themes side-by-side in one passage of the *Concise History*. Concerning them Eremia writes,

> In 1054 (1644)[125]
> Sümbül Ağa, an honoured [man],
> the *kızlar ağası,* head of the eunuchs,
> wealthy and corpulent,
> He took an order from the king,
> he was to go to Egypt.
> The Maltese found him on the sea,
> apprehending the ship of the Turks.
> The Ethiopian [i.e., Sümbül Ağa] and others with him,
> died from the Maltese cannon (*top*) . . .

As a result of the attack, the Ottoman sultan sends a fleet. Eremia writes,

> In 1055 (1645)
> at the end of the spring
> when with great merriment
> [the Ottoman fleet] reached near to the island of Ch'ukha,
> Captain Yusuf Paşa
> took out there an imperial edict (*hatt-ı şerîf*)
> they opened the counsels of the king
> which they read to everyone:
> 'To the *paşas*, captains,
> and commanders: collecting [our] strength,
> we must go to Crete
> and endeavour to take it, by God.'
> They listened together,
> prayed (*dua*) and said '*amen*'.
> And they sailed to Crete
> blockading it for fifty four days.
> They beat and stabbed,
> they butchered, and corpses fell,
> inside the Franks grew weary,
> willing to give the city.
> At the place of the charge (*yürüyüş*) of the Turks,
> the lord of the city planted a flag (*bayrak*)
> Three ships with their acquisitions

they left and departed.
And others, remaining as subjects (*re'âyâ*)
entered under their rule.
When the news came to Istanbul,
a great triumph-procession (*donanma*) took place.
In 1055 (1645)
they arrived at the Rhethymno fortress
as they besieged Chania,
plundering the diocese and territory, they ruled it.
They strived for Candia,
where the general was residing,
they waged unceasing war with him
from two sides they were routed.
And Istanbul was burning,
in [the neighbourhood] they name Kumkapı
there are churches which burned,
four of the Greeks and one of the Armenians.
Civan vizier wished to build,
from the king he took a decree (*hatt*)
they built four proper [churches],
those days were blessed for us.[126]

In this passage, the sections on the Maltese pirates and the beginning of the war in Crete are, of course, thematically connected, while the mention of the fire in Kumkapı is appended at the end before Eremia moves on to relate the events of the next *hijri* year. In this passage – and most of the latter parts of the *Concise History* – there is no obvious written primary source. Rather, Eremia recounts the history of his own lifetime freely and with emphasis on his own interests.

In the preceding examples, we have seen the diverse textures of the *Concise History*, which nimbly changed according to the source base. How do we assess the work as a whole? In her writings on the chronicle, Gayane Ayvazyan notes that Eremia conspicuously avoided discussion of the Istanbul Armenian community's history: in no way can the *Concise History* be considered an 'ethnic' history.[127] With regards to his competing tendencies for depicting history from an 'Ottoman' or 'Armenian' point of view, she refers to the 'split-personality' of a man with one historical homeland – where he was not born and did not live – and his actual lived environment, thus contrasting the places of Kemah and Istanbul in Eremia's imagination.[128] I would be more reluctant to psychoanalyse Eremia, noting that he was similar to Ottoman Muslim intellectuals of the seventeenth century – such as Hezarfen Hüseyin[129] and Kâtip Çelebi – who used both Muslim and Christian sources and had visions of history that could reconcile the sources' points of contrast. But as Ayvazyan also emphasised, there is no confusion about the driving force of the *Concise History*'s narrative. Like the seventeenth-century Ottoman Turkish sources described in Chapter Two, the Ottoman state was at the narrative centre of Eremia's text from start to finish, with only passing mention of the Armenians. In many ways, Eremia wrote more in the tradition of any number of Ottoman Turkish histories in verse than anything that had yet appeared in Armenian. Eremia was consciously importing the Ottoman Turkish historical tradition – with its focus on the state, panegyric tone and even calendrical system – into the Armenian literary tradition.

Topical histories

Eremia wrote various histories on more specific themes but unfortunately an unknown number of them are lost. No trace exists of his above-mentioned history of the Celali Revolts, beyond brief mention in his biographies of the Ottoman sultans. Eremia makes reference to a treatise on Tamerlane – likely inspired by T'ovma Metsop'ets'i's fifteenth-century work[130] – but its whereabouts are similarly unknown.[131] He also wrote treatises on the famous Ottoman Battle of Peç, a lost work on the Bosporus and a history about the seizure of a church in Macedonia from the Greeks.[132] Here I focus on three of his topical histories, namely his history of the Ottoman conquest of Crete, his work on the Istanbul fire of 1660 and a tribute to his patron, Apro Çelebi.

Eremia's history of the conquest of Crete was originally entitled *History on the Taking of the Island Crete*, and it survives in a manuscript located in the Armenian section of the French National Library in Paris (P 338).[133] In recent years Ottoman historians have carefully studied the transition to Ottoman rule in Crete using Greek, Italian and Ottoman Turkish sources.[134] Eremia's text provides us with a view of the war as understood by elite Armenians living in the imperial capital, informing us as much about their complex view of the Ottoman state as of the details of affairs on the ground in Crete. Moreover, Eremia was a very well connected man and he undoubtedly had an eyewitness informant about the war. Below we will learn the informant's identity from a separate work.

Eremia's *History on the Taking of the Island Crete* begins with a one-page table of contents or, as Eremia explicitly headed the page, 'This is what is written in this book'. The narrative begins in earnest with a description of 'the reason for the war' and the Ottoman forces' initial acquisitions on the island. It presents a substantial discourse on the Grand Vizier Köprülü Mehmed Paşa (1656–61) and his son, Köprülü Fazıl Ahmed Paşa (1661–76). Köprülü Mehmed was, of course, the founder of the distinguished Köprülü dynasty of Ottoman grand viziers, and it is noteworthy that Eremia describes his tenure as grand vizier as 'propitious', in spite of the fact that Eremia's general tone regarding the war in Crete was far more negative. Eremia proceeds to describe Fazıl Ahmed's final assault on Crete and the fall of Candia in 1669. He offers a lament on the 'disaster' for the residents of the island, and he notes with horror that the Ottomans seized an Armenian church in Candia, St Karapet Church.[135]

Let us turn to a single passage, so as to get a sense of Eremia's prose and narrative style. For the sake of comparison, I present Eremia's description of the war's origins – the same incidents described above in the *Concise History* – to demonstrate how Eremia re-worked the same material in new formats:

> ... in the time of the kingship of Sultan Ibrahim in the Armenian year 1093 (1644), the king removed the great head of the eunuchs from the royal palace – his Ethiopian – and he dispatched him to Egypt, so that having gone he might reside there, spending [the rest of his] life in peace [and] free.[136] He sailed by sea. He encountered the Frankish Maltese, and they took him prisoner with all his possessions and those who were with him. When the king heard the news of this, immediately he took his stablemaster (*rikâbdar*), named Hüseyin, and he appointed him captain (*kapudan*), giving him ships with troops. He sent him on the sea-ocean to go to the island of Malta to wage war with its residents and to release those taken captive by them, or to take revenge on their actions. While [the captain] was going on the sea near

to Crete, they were incited by the author of all evil [Satan]. Unexpectedly sounding the trumpet, they struck the city of Chania, and they filled it with all the troops from the ships. Having taken it, they ruled it along with all the provinces of the residents of the country. In that year after [some] days there was a great fire in Istanbul, and the death of Grigor, the bishop of Jerusalem.[137]

There are striking divergences between this passage and its corresponding section of the *Concise History*, quoted above. Firstly, the *Concise History* situates the event chronologically using the Islamic calendar, while this passage relies on the Armenian year. Similarly, the *Concise History* employs many more Turkish words: *bayrak, donanma, top, hatt-ı şerif* and others, while in the prose passage Eremia tends to prefer Armenian vocabulary, limiting the use of Ottoman Turkish vocabulary to formal titles, such as *rikâbdar*. Whereas the *Concise History* had a patriotic tinge, mentioning the Ottoman troops' prayers and triumphal procession, in this passage the whole assault on Crete is seen as the work of Satan, or 'the author of all evil'. The passages really only correspond in the basic story and in the appending of reference to the Istanbul fire to both passages.

Overall, the general tone of Eremia's treatise on Crete stands in stark contrast to his general histories of the Ottoman Empire. Whereas in the general histories Eremia sometimes conveys a tone of pro-Ottoman panegyric and describes Ottoman victories as triumphs of valour, here Eremia's Christian identity is more prominent, and he conveys sadness for the local Christian population of Crete as they fall under Ottoman rule. In particular, Eremia grieves about the capture of the Armenian St Karapet Church in Candia, showing that he could not always take pleasure in Ottoman martial victories. Eremia had multiple literary identities: he could consciously alternate between emphasising his Armenian Christian identity or his Ottoman imperial subjecthood, depending on the work, its target audience and its patron.

The next topical history under discussion is Eremia's *History of the Fire of Constantinople*, which describes the conflagration of 1660. In this work too, Eremia's interest in churches and their fates is prominent. Unlike in his work on Crete, however, the outcome is fortunate. Whereas in Crete the St Karapet Church was captured, in the course of the fire of 1660, the

Holy Mother of God Church of Kumkapı was miraculously saved from sure destruction.

Eremia explains the plan of the work as follows:

> This has been written in verse, of which the arguments, distributed into six chapters, are given in a list. This is needed to make reading easier, and for the readers not to be bored. 1) The first chapter is about the origin of the fire and how the sight was terrible. 2) The second chapter narrates in verse the lamentation and the shock of the inhabitants of the city. 3) The third chapter describes those who fled with their goods and explains one by one with their names the places and how they burnt. 4) The fourth chapter says something about those who stayed on the spot and about the refuge of those who fled with anguish. 5) The fifth chapter speaks about the very real mystery of the miracle of God for the deliverance of the Church of the Holy Mother, and about other churches. 6) The sixth chapter recounts how the fire advanced from one point to the other, and reveals what happened around the gates. The conclusion summarises again the damages.[138]

Eremia's *History of the Fire of Constantinople* alternates between poetry and prose. Here is an example of Eremia's prose, in which he exults over the fate of the Holy Mother of God Church in Kumkapı:

> ... and people of all faiths went far and wide to proclaim the marvellous wonder and miracle of the church, which took place in the middle of the indescribable scourge endured by the city of Constantine, and it was all the more astonishing for those who belonged to another faith and the unbelievers, on account of which they praised and thanked God the all-powerful. And all of the proprietors came to the threshold of [the church's] gate: they worshipped, they expressed their gratitude, and they gave blessings to God from the depth of their hearts. And they kissed the right hand of the *vardapet*, praying for him. And they took their belongings and they went joyfully, as though they had received them as gifts from the Holy Mother. And this was the fire that passed through Kumkapı and burnt the newly built church of the Greeks, which they had built at the same time as our church of the Holy Mother...[139]

He also provides a poem of praise, exclaiming that

> Open-winged derivatives from the fiery stock, came to you from the air
> they formed a veil around you like a baldaquin;
> they drove off the elemental fire.
> This is what the Ancients proclaimed: the miraculous and wonderful work,
> Here is the fire spread all over; they did not succeed in staining you.[140]

In this poem Eremia likens the church to the burning bush of the Hebrew Testament, saved from destruction by the miraculous intervention of God. Of course, Eremia's anti-Greek bias is palpable throughout, given that their churches received no such divine protection despite their proximity. In addition to this detailed history of the fire of 1660 Eremia also wrote a chronicle of multiple fires which broke out in Istanbul between 1569 and 1694.[141]

Finally, mention should be made of another one of Eremia's topical histories, a work about Eremia's patron, Apro Çelebi, written in 1672. Unfortunately, the poem is unpublished and inaccessible, but the noted Armenologist Nersēs Akinean had the opportunity to peruse it in 1930 while it was in a private collection in Germany and he took notes of its content. Therein we find important clues about the motivation for Eremia's interest in both the Ottoman war in Crete and the Istanbul fires. Eremia records that

> In the time of Sultan Ibrahim they took Crete. The *paşa* Deli Hüseyin went there as captain. Abraham [Apro] Çelebi went there with him for commerce. He was eyewitness to the destruction in the land, the killing and captivity of Christians, the breaking of holy places and their being sold.[142]

Thus, we learn the identity of Eremia's informant about the Ottoman campaign in Crete: Eremia's writings on the war in Crete must have been based on the oral report of his patron Apro Çelebi, who was present there at the side of the captain of the Ottoman fleet. Elsewhere in the list of the poem's contents Eremia writes that 'The Holy St Nikoḷayos and St Sargis churches of the Armenians burned down . . . The Church of St Nikoḷayos was built with the property of [Apro] Çelebi'.[143] Thus, yet another of Eremia's literary interests was surely dictated by Apro's activities. It is likely that a good number of Eremia's literary works and scholarly interests were conceived in dialogue with his wealthy and influential patron, who was closely connected to high officials of the Ottoman state.

Eremia's Narrations of Self and Place

In addition to his trailblazing work on Ottoman history, Eremia also contributed to Armenian literary history with works on his own life, travels and place in the world. In these works we see Eremia addressing themes of interest to early modern authors across cultures – Armenian, Islamic and European – and treating them in ways that were new in the Armenian literary tradition.

This section will primarily focus on Eremia's diary and topographical works. The diary was Eremia's first literary endeavour and survives in a single autograph copy located at the St James Manuscript Library of the Armenian Patriarchate of Jerusalem (J 1893). Eremia's diary is an example of a Near Eastern 'first-person narrative' or 'ego-document' which, though not satisfying the literary definition of 'memoir', represents a shift in literary interest towards personal experience which spanned various literary traditions in the Ottoman Empire.[144]

Eremia's diary contains entries for the years 1648–62. It should first be noted that he gave the work a different title and that modern scholars designated it his 'diary'. Eremia originally entitled the work *Chronicle and History*,[145] though really all three titles are necessary to convey the nature of the work as it constitutes an amalgam of genres. For the most part, the text is indeed a diary, including daily entries about Eremia's movements and activities. But, as noted above, over time Eremia's literary emphasis changed and he turned his focus from himself to politics and church affairs, conveyed chronologically.[146] Moreover, there are some passages of the diary in which Eremia abandons his annalistic style and enters into expanded historical prose. And it must be emphasised that the work began as a travelogue.

Eremia's diary formally begins with the year 1648, but his entry for this year has been shown by Gayane Ayvazyan to be a later interjection. Whereas the entries for 1649 and henceforth are real diary entries, the single entry for 1648 is a polished historical narrative on one topic: the execution of the Ottoman Sultan Ibrahim (r. 1640–8). It seems clear that an older and more mature Eremia, when looking over his old diary entries, thought it necessary to add the passage, given its political importance and temporal proximity to his diary's starting point, taking place only a year before he actually began his youthful diary. Thus he adapted it from a separate colophon.[147] Eremia sometimes left whole pages blank, apparently to allow for such later additions.[148]

Skipping over this later addition, let us assess the early entries in Eremia's diary. In those entries it was not uncommon for Eremia to document his own physical movements, to list his companions and even to mention the weather. Eremia very often mentioned religious feasts along with calendar dates. An example of one of Eremia's more mundane entries is this passage from his diary entry for the year 1652:

> Friday (April 23) was in commemoration of St George, who the foreigners [i.e. Muslims] call *Hıdırellez*. We went with our [friends] to Ortaköy in vow to St George, and from there, to Beşiktaş. With us was Vardan and Zardar and their Petros, and there we stayed. And on the new Sunday (25 April) we came home in the evening, and it was raining very softly.[149]

As was common for Eremia, this passage about his mundane comings and goings preceded description of a more important event for his community, a fire at his father's St Sargis Church.

Interspersed with such personal descriptions, Eremia often noted changes of officials in the Ottoman state. In one of his more dramatic records of a change of grand vizier, for instance, Eremia writes that

> On Thursday the 10th [of March 1653], the king called in the vizier. In his palace he had him strangled to death and thrown outside. He committed the injustice on the advice of the eunuchs and the inner elites, because they wanted to make [a vizier] of the household of the king. And they put [as] vizier Çerkez Derviş Mehmed Paşa.

> On Wednesday (23 March) [Ambakum] reined in the bread ovens. He beat several workers and their bread-sellers, as in several places they had decreased [the output] of bread.[150]

In one entry, the strangling of the grand vizier; in the next, troubles at Ambakum's bread ovens. Such juxtapositions from entry to entry are characteristic of Eremia's diary.

Eremia also describes historical events taking place in the Ottoman Empire outside Istanbul, and for such references he sometimes used written sources in addition to his own experience. For example, he refers to a historical source – presumably in Ottoman Turkish – in connection to the mid-seventeenth-century 'Celali' rebel Hasan.[151] As noted, Eremia was greatly interested in the Ottoman campaigns in Crete. Already in his diary entry for 1659 we see him complaining of the Ottomans' activities there. He writes that

> ... we were at the gate of the vizier. The vizier had [them] bring Deli Hüseyin Paşa, who for fourteen years had been keeping the island of Crete. He had taken many towns from the Frankish Christians, destroyed churches, pillaged the country, and driven off captives. All the moveable property of the churches they had taken for sale; all the troops and also their elites had some of the movables. And there he built a mosque and appointed an *imam*, increasing the [number] of Turks.[152]

Eremia learned this information about the Crete campaign via word of mouth 'at the gate of the vizier', and throughout his corpus he often refers to eyewitness testimony. In his diary, he sometimes even records news that he heard from Istanbul's official town heralds and criers.[153]

While Eremia's diary is undoubtedly diverse in the information it provides about Ottoman history and daily life in Istanbul, Eremia was nonetheless disproportionately preoccupied with the Armenian ecclesiastical politics of his day. Much of this testimony was summarised above in connection with his biography, as he was deeply involved in the political affairs of the Armenian patriarchate in Istanbul as an ally of Eḷiazar. It is in passages about church affairs and high clergy – like Eḷiazar, P'ilippos and later Martiros of Crimea – that Eremia writes with the greatest detail and passion in his diary. For example, one of his diary's passages concerns the arrival of Catholicos P'ilippos from Ējmiatsin. Eremia writes that

> And today *Vardapet* Eḷiazar went with six boats, with the lords of the city, to receive Catholicos P'ilippos. He put in his place [as patriarchal deputy] my family member, named Lord Martiros [Eremia's father]. From the time when the *vardapet* [Eḷiazar] came here, from that day they have been

acquainted with one another and he has not grown distant from him, but he always attended to him early.

On this Saturday June 19 [1652], the *vardapet* came. And on the 20th, on Sunday, a feast of the church, they had them open the Davutpaşa Gate in the night, and they brought the catholicos. When he approached the St George Arch, over the baths, then *Vardapet* Eḷiazar went forth from the church to meet him. And I too, humblest and lowest of all, was by my grandfather, lodging [at the home of] *Maḷtesi* Yaḷup; having heard of his coming, we were going forth to meet him. We heard the cry. The *vardapet* went out to meet [him] with incense and candles, with robed scribes and deacons, with bells and cymbals, with priests and countless pilgrims. And the *vardapet* was going in front with unlit wax candles in his two hands. He was hitting against the crowd to go forward, so that they might not press upon the catholicos, as they were on both sides on the pass of the road up to the gate of the church. They were lingering about, falling one on top of the other, so that they might kiss the right hand of the catholicos or perhaps only see him. But [Eḷiazar] was not allowing it, he was going before and beating everyone [back] with the [large] candlestick, until he pushed into the church, and [thus] no one was able to kiss or see him . . .[154]

The teenaged Eremia continued to describe the procession with similar detail, such that one could almost hear the clamour and smell the incense.

If we compare Eremia's diary with other contemporary works we see that he was not alone in taking up this mixture of diary, history and travelogue. Among seventeenth-century Armenian authors, we see that Minas Amdets'i wrote a similar chronological diary, and Zak'aria Agulets'i's journal was simultaneously a diary, travelogue and history written by an Armenian merchant.[155] While there were Armenian authors who discussed their own lives in colophons and chronicles for centruies before Eremia, Minas and Zak'aria, the format of these seventeenth-century diaries was new within the Armenian literary tradition,[156] implying a heightened interest in the individual and mobility. This was likely catalysed by the mass migrations of the seventeenth century, namely the Great Armenian Flight and the deportations of Shah Abbas. Moreover, the acceleration of international trade led to a change in patronage and consumption patterns. Zak'aria was himself a merchant, while Eremia was supported by the wealthy merchants Ambakum and Apro Çelebi.

Among Eremia's most important geographical works, several are lost. Already mentioned is his lost work on the Bosporus, and he also wrote a general geographical treatise which has not survived. We know from Mik'ayel Ch'amch'ean that the latter described the geography of Persia, India, Anatolia and Armenia, and that it was written at the request of a European ambassador.[157] Just as Step'anos would compile a history of the three great early modern Islamic empires – Ottoman, Safavid and Mughal – in the eighteenth century, this reference from Ch'amch'ean shows that Eremia had also conceived of a tripartite division of the Islamic world and that he served as a conduit for conveying information about the Islamic empires to a curious European audience. This work further shows the degree to which Eremia's range of literary activities overlapped with that of contemporary Muslims in Istanbul, most notably Kâtip Çelebi, whose geography has survived and remains one of the classics of Ottoman Turkish letters.[158]

Thankfully, two of his topographical works have survived. The first to be considered is a map that Eremia designed at the request of an Italian in 1691.[159] The map depicts Armenian monasteries and holy places and it has been published in an Italian edition.[160] Therein, Eremia shows the rough relative locations and names of Armenian churches, with a focus on the historical Armenian heartland of Eastern Anatolia,[161] but also including Cilicia,[162] Georgia,[163] Jerusalem,[164] Istanbul,[165] the Marmara region[166] and even a corner-note for New Julfa.[167]

Eremia's map includes Kemah and Mount Sepuh, T'ordan and the Avag Vank'.[168] Eremia also includes Tekirdağ on his map of the Marmara region, referring to it as a 'sometime bishopric',[169] as it had been one during Grigor's lifetime, and also marking the nail relic discussed in Chapter Two as a site of pilgrimage.[170] In the map's notes Eremia's interest in the history of the Islamic Empires is also on display, as he includes king lists for both the Safavid and the Ottoman dynasties written in the Arabic alphabet.[171] Overall, the map shows the seventeenth-century spread of the Armenian world outside Greater Armenia and Cilicia, both westwards with the formation of the Western Armenian Diaspora and eastwards after the forced migrations of Shah Abbas.

Eremia also wrote a mis-titled *History of Istanbul* in verse. In reality, the work is not a history or a chronology. Rather, it resembles Evliya Çelebi's *Seyahatnâme* in its themes and structures, differing primarily in scope: whereas Evliya provides a guide of the entire Ottoman Empire, Eremia offers a poetic tour of Istanbul. Eremia's *History of Istanbul* was published in Armenian in 1913 by Vahram T'orgomean and its Modern Turkish translation was published in 1956 by Hrant D. Andreasyan.[172] Thanks to the efforts of Andreasyan, the *History of Istanbul* is one of the only early modern Armenian primary sources that is known to Ottoman historians.

Eremia's *History of Istanbul* has never been translated into English, however, so in order to get a sense of the nature of this topographical work, I present its preamble and description of Yedikule, the first major site on Eremia's Istanbul tour:

> Let this be a copy of my word
> which will give an answer to the learned,
> in memory of an urgent request,
> I offer it to my lord Vardan.
> Oh lord, my great *vardapet*,
> respects and greetings to you!
> I will take you [first] to the south,
> we are going to have a stroll in the country.
> Then let's turn to Bithynia,
> and contemplate (*seyran*) the sea.
> From here let's go to the north,
> before us comes Byzantium.
> You know that he built it,
> a certain king Vizantis long ago,
> he called it Vizantia,
> staying here as an independent sovereign.
> [Then] comes great Constantine,
> he surrounded it [with a wall] and called it after his own name.
> Let's look left at this [part] of the city:
> on the west is the Yedikule Fortress.
> Let's not leave the boat,

but on the course of the sea shore,
thanks to our attentive and skillful observation,
we'll go eastward happily.
Those who see this, they mock me:
'Why do you do this?'
'You explain to us things we [already] know.'
We don't have a reply for such fools.
On our right lies Byzantium,
on our left side is its wall,
we mean, Yedikule Fortress,
which holy Constantine built.
In ancient times,
they were filling it with barley and wheat,
keeping it in a granary (*ambar*) in the winter,
being enough for the population.
Having built private [sections] one by one,
now they put *paşas* in prison [there],
[as well as] viziers and the Tatar Han,
and it's [also] where they killed Sultan Osman.
The master generals of the Franks,
they are here for imprisonment, when they seize them.[173]

As this short passage shows, Eremia's *History of Istanbul* is not a history: it's a boat tour of Istanbul's sites, beginning from Yedikule. In the course of the work, Eremia personifies the city and gives it human traits.[174] Eremia's tour is not devoid of history; for example, he mentions the Greek colony that was present on the city's site before Constantine, as well as Constantine's renaming of the city and construction of its famous walls. Eremia makes multiple such digressions on history throughout the work, but the driving force of the narrative is the tour, not history.

The *History of Istanbul* offers a vivid picture of the the topography and social life of seventeenth-century Istanbul which cannot be given justice here, as it is worthy of a separate book. Nonetheless, I would like to present one more passage – about St Grigor the Illuminator Church in Tophane (see Figure 5.3), the oldest Armenian church in Istanbul – in order to highlight

Figure 5.3 St Grigor the Illuminator Church in Tophane, Istanbul (modern structure).

this work's importance for understanding Istanbul's architectural history. Sometimes Eremia's verses preserve unique historical information about Istanbul's Armenian churches:

> Let the boat stop at Tophane,
> now let's enter Galata,
> let's make a pilgrimage to the Illuminator Church,
> the Armenians' place of consolation.
> [People from] Kefe built it,
> merchants (*bazirgân*) of Ani in former [times].
> Some of the [Kefe natives] passed to Poland,
> [others] in Istanbul [became] called locals.
> In 885 (1436),
> in [the time] of Greek rule, [it was built].
> You can see a tomb in the bulwark,
> it [is] Grigor of Kayseri's.

In 1084 (1635),
at the death of the master, the burial took place,
being requested by a certain Şahin Çelebi
from Bayram Paşa.[175]

Here, we learn that the oldest Armenian church in Istanbul was built by Armenian merchants from the Crimea. Moreover, this Grigor of Kayseri was the grand opponent of Grigor Daranałts'i discussed in Chapter Four. Like Daranałts'i, he was buried in the grounds of his church. The *History of Istanbul* is filled with such rich information about many of Istanbul's seventeenth-century sites. Armenians in the eighteenth and nineteenth centuries would write comparable tours of Istanbul and the Bosporus.[176]

Eremia did not only experiment with literary form and theme but also with new technology. As has already been noted, the first Armenian books printed in Istanbul were a product of the printing press of a certain Abgar T'okhat'ets'i, who made history with the printing of an Armenian 'Small Grammar' in 1567. Abgar had imported the science of printing from Venice, where he had been active as a publisher only one year prior.[177] His initiative in Istanbul would be short-lived, however, and Armenian printing activity would cease for a century until it was revived in the last quarter of the seventeenth century by Eremia K'eōmurchean.

Eremia's printing press was also a short-lived project, and it would only produce two books. Those were a version of Nersēs Shnorhali's *Jesus Son*, printed in 1677,[178] and an original work on the *Places Relating to Our Lord*, published in 1678.[179] The former work was a commonly read part of the educational curriculum for young Armenians, although Eremia did not actually print the entire medieval primary source. Instead, he printed some excerpts, complemented by his own riddles and verses.[180] The second book was a guide to the holy places of Jerusalem, which would have been of interest both to pilgrims and to devout Armenians who could not make the pilgrimage but wanted to read about the Holy Land.[181] Many similar works exist in both Armenian and Greek.

What motivated Eremia to establish this printing press? In an article on the topic, Gayane Ayvazyan argues that the cost and labour involved in printing in the mid-seventeenth century implies that the establishment of a press cannot be explained by a love of books alone. Rather, the foundation of a printing press had political significance. Ayvazyan notes that Eremia was ordered to establish the press by Eḷiazar of Antep – who had obtained a grant from the Ottoman state to establish a counter-patriarchate for Ottoman Armenians in 1665 – and she argues that the printing press was intended as a political tool for this faction of Ottoman-Armenian ecclesiastical and communal politics.[182] For Eremia this was a frightful venture, and he even composed a verse imploring Eḷiazar's ally and Eremia's own patron, Apro Çelebi, not to support the project, writing:

> Çelebi I implore you,
> It is a great request, which I supplicate:
> On your mind you have something, I think,
> I mean, the printing of books.
> Take this from your mind, oh eminent one,
> as it is not suitable, but rather an improper work,
> it is not agreeable for you,
> as that fruit is not fecund.[183]

Eremia's objections were overridden, nonetheless, and he was forced to found the printing press, despite his fear of entering the crossfire of intracommunal political conflict.

Why, then, was the press disbanded so soon, after so much exertion and effort? Ayvazyan notes a change in the political winds. In 1679 the Catholicos of Ējmiatsin, Hakob Juḷayetsʻi, arrived in Istanbul, and he died there in 1680. This event changed Eḷiazar's political fortunes and he himself would become Catholicos of Ējmiatsin in 1681. With his rise it seems that he lost interest in the Istanbul printing press and Eremia disbanded it.[184] Politics aside, Eremia's second printed book, on the Holy Land, must have had a personal significance for him. At long last, twenty years after his childhood pilgrimage to Jerusalem, Eremia finally offered his description of the *Places Relating to Our Lord* that had been so conspicuously scant in his childhood diary.

Reviving Medieval Genres for Contemporary Use

In the works described above, Eremia narrated Ottoman history, his own life and the space of the Ottoman Empire in ways that were innovative in the Armenian literary tradition and in tune with his times in early modern Istanbul. Eremia was also deeply versed and rooted in the medieval Armenian literary tradition and he produced many works that revived medieval genres and themes for contemporary use in seventeenth-century Istanbul. As already seen, Eremia wrote in both poetry and prose, and he could modulate his literary identity, alternating between emphasising his Armenian and Christian identity at times – such as in his work on Crete – or his Ottoman identity at other times – as was the case in his *Concise History*. Another facet of his literary personality is seen in his polemical and pedagogical writings, both genres with roots going far back in the Armenian literary tradition.

Eremia's polemical writings are best understood in the context of research on 'confessionalisation' in the Ottoman Empire, a body of research which argues that 'confession-building' processes known to European historians of the early modern period were actually a pan-Eurasian phenomenon. By 'confession-building' scholars refer to a process by which religious norms were established and reinforced by social disciplining, reigning in broader diversities of practice that had been more common in prior eras, all related to an expansion of state-building in the early modern period. Armenians of Eremia's time lived in a period of profound religious tension in the Ottoman Empire, characterised – in the words of Tijana Krstic – by the 'confessionalisation initiatives of various sociopolitical groups jockeying for power in the seventeenth century'.[185] Among Sunni Muslims, the so-called *Kadızadeli* movement was well known for its efforts to enforce strict religious norms, protesting a range of activities from Sufi mystical practices to smoking tobacco.[186] With regards to the Armenians, missionary activity had already brought some segments of the Ottoman-Armenian community under Roman Catholic spiritual and intellectual influence by Eremia's lifetime, thus commencing what would become a bloody denominational competition by the turn of the eighteenth century.[187] Accounts of Sabbatai Zevi show how the Jewish community endured a period of severe internal conflict, and this was also a time of tense and vocal inter-communal competition between the Greeks and Armenians. Greek-Armenian tension – over the holy places of Jerusalem, for instance[188] – was a major theme of seventeenth-century Armenian literature and histories.

The first generation of Armenian refugees had arrived in this environment of religious tension. But whereas the first half of the seventeenth century was a period of crisis management and infrastructure building, it is only at the end of the seventeenth century that we see Armenian writers shifting focus to a process of intellectual 'confession-building'. Eremia spearheaded those efforts.

Eremia's confessional works are currently scattered around the Armenian libraries of Venice, Yerevan and Jerusalem, unpublished and in manuscript form. One example is Eremia's *History of the Neomartyrs* of 1686.[189] 'Neomartyrology' was a genre of Greek and Armenian devotional writing which provided stories about people executed by the Ottoman state for their faith. They were generally apostates from Islam – Christians who had converted to Islam and later decided to revert back to their original religion – and their stories were apparently aimed at discouraging Orthodox Christians from conversion to Islam or, perhaps, Catholicism.[190]

Eremia also wrote various polemical discourses against Greeks and Jews,[191] and in defence of the Armenian Church. One of his polemical discourses that is worthy of special note is his *Apology of the Armenian Church*, a copy of which is housed in the Armenian Patriarchate of Jerusalem (J 533). This manuscript is noteworthy for its use of colloquial Armenian. While Eremia usually wrote in Classical Armenian, there are multiple instances in this apology where he uses verbs conjugated with a colloquial particle *ku* (կու), just as Grigor Daranałts'i sometimes did in his chronicle.[192] Eremia's use of colloquial Armenian for composing religious manuals is reminiscent of Sunni 'catechisms' studied by Derin Terzioğlu. These were written in lower registers of Ottoman Turkish aimed at providing linguistically clear guidelines of orthodoxy for less educated Muslims.[193] In the same time period we see the rise of 'the common language' in Greek texts on religion, a semi-standardised demoticising style that differed from regional dialects.[194] Clearly, Eremia's choice of theme and language were part of a much broader trend that transcended religion and community. In this manuscript Eremia provides a vigorous defence of the Apostolic Armenian Church in the context of competition with Catholics.

Eremia also wrote a catechismal text entitled *Concise Questions and Answers*.[195] Whereas Eremia's diary and Ottoman historical works showcase the 'early modern' Eremia, who was a pioneer in changes taking place within the Armenian literary tradition in the seventeenth century, the *Concise Questions and Answers* provides us a glimpse of the 'medievalist' Eremia, who was reviving ancient literary forms for contemporary usage. The genre of 'Question and Answer' goes all the way back to the fifth century CE, the golden age of Classical Armenian literature,[196] and examples also exist from the fourteenth century in Armenian.[197]

Much of Eremia's *Questions and Answers* concerns biblical history. For example, in one line Eremia asks: 'Question: Who took Israel captive?' The answer provided is, of course, Nebuchadnezzar.[198] But there are also several volleys of question and answer that provide important insight into Eremia and Armenian intellectual history during his lifetime. One of them concerns Eremia's vision of Armenian history and its periodisation:

> Question: How are the dynasties of our Armenians divided?
> Answer: Historically, the dynasties of the Armenians are divided into four sceptres. The first Hayk established in the land our habitation of towns and palaces, from which the clans and clan patriarchs multiplied with the name of Hayk, from whom was Aramshah, famous for valour and warlike, from whose name we are called *Aramean* and *Ērmenian*.[199] The second spectre of kingship [was] of the Arsacid monarchs, of whom Abkar believed in Christ and noble Trdat [as well] by the miracles of St Grigor the Illuminator in the time of Sahak the patriarch. And the third sceptre [was] of the kingship of the Bagratunids, who sat in the city of Ani. And the fourth sceptre, smaller than the Bagratunids, [was] of the Rubenids, who sat in Cilicia.
>
> Question: Of these four, what were the reasons of the overthrow of the above-mentioned dynasties?
> Answer: Alexander the Macedonian terminated the dynasty of Hayk and Aram, the last of whom [was] Vahē. King Vŕam of the Persians destroyed the Arsacids, [and] the last king of the Armenians was Artashēs. Those who held the throne of the Bagratunids were of Muhammad, whose seat was Baghdad, by whom the caliphate was rotted. The last [of the Bagratunids] was Gagik II the philosopher. The sultan of Egypt (*Mısır*) put an end to the Rubenids of Cilicia, the last of whom was Levon.
>
> Question: And afterwards?
> Answer: Until this time nowhere has there been found any part of sovereignty, but all are scattered and dispersed to the edges of the world, [some-

thing] which the prophets in ancient time prophesied concerning Israel and which our Patriarch Nersēs the Great prophesied through curses, that 'your land [will be] torched, your country will be a ruin, foreigners will consume your labour's fruits before your eyes', along with other [such curses].

Question: What is the reason for the curses?
Answer: Read, look and listen to the lamentation of Moses Khorenats'i, who is our sun. By poisoning Trdat,[200] he says our lords cast darkness on the Armenians. And they were disobedient to Nersēs and Sahak the patriarchs, those who martyred some of the sons and grandchildren of the holy Illuminator . . . Read also the Vision of Patriarch Sahak and the word of the Short Yohannēs and the compact of the Illuminator with St P'esros the patriarch.

Question: After the Cilicians and so on, who were the others who brought suffering on this people of ours?
Answer: The Tatar, Shah Abbas, Timur Lane (about the time of the destruction of the Cilicians), the Ottomans and the Celalis, who divided and scattered this people of the Armenians according to [the word of] the prophet: 'Every head in pain and every heart in sorrow, from the feet until the head no health, and those led astray (Isaiah 1: 5–6)', 'for them there shall be no shepherd, according to the words of the Lord (Num. 27: 17)'.[201]

After this passage, Eremia moves on to discussion of the history of ancient Israel, which he clearly saw as a historical parallel to Armenian history in his own times.

From these passages we see that Eremia's conception of Armenian history was based on classical and medieval sources and that he remembered Armenian sovereignty with some nostalgia. For him the loss of Armenian statehood was a 'curse', and the Ottomans and Celalis were both part of a list of scourges, two of 'those who brought suffering on all our peoples'. Did Eremia really believe that the Armenians' loss of sovereignty was a punishment for the poisoning of King Trdat III (250–330) – the first Christian Armenian king – or is this merely a literary flourish? Portents appear in his diary and it seems that he probably did believe in supernatural signs and retributions.

In another passage we see Eremia's concept of the Armenian historical 'canon'. Eremia asks: 'Question: Who are the historians of the Armenians?' His response is a long and comprehensive list, beginning with 'Eusebius from the Greeks', and moving on to the great classical Armenian authors, such as Moses Khorenats'i and Agat'angeḷos. It continues all the way until the seventeenth century with, for instance, explicit reference to Aṙakel of Tabriz. Finally, at the end, Eremia adds himself to the list of great Armenian authors. He even includes a list of his own works, including his 'Concise [History] of the Ottomans' (probably referring to the above-mentioned *Concise History of the Ottoman Kings*) and his lost geographical treatise. Eremia was aware that he was the next link in the development of the Armenian literary tradition and he was not afraid to express this conviction.[202] Though he often signed his works with the adjective 'abject' or 'humble', here we see that Eremia did indeed have a justifiably large ego.

Whereas in the previously mentioned *Apology of the Armenian Church* Eremia writes as an Apostolic Armenian Christian, he wrote his book of *Questions and Answers* for an Armenian Catholic priest. In her research on Eremia's polemical writings, Anna Ohanjanyan identifies a shift in Eremia's attitude towards the Catholics that takes place in 1692, arguing that before that date Eremia was more tolerant of Catholics. In the course of his career, he wrote catechisms for both sides of the Apostolic-Catholic competition, with a stark shift towards the Apostolic camp in his final years.[203]

Another work in which Eremia refashioned a medieval tradition is his Armenian romance about an Albanian Christian youth, a baker named Dimo and a Jewish woman. The poem is based on a medieval Armenian precedent, the tale of 'Hohannēs and Asha', which also addressed the theme of love across denominational lines.[204] But not unlike Leonard Bernstein's retelling of Shakespeare's *Romeo and Juliet* in the setting of twentieth-century New York City in *West Side Story*, Eremia recasts the medieval Armenian tale of inter-confessional love in the context of mid-seventeenth-century Ottoman Istanbul.

According to Hasmik Sahakyan, the poem's editor, Eremia recrafted the story of 'Hohannēs and Asha' with an anti-Ottoman agenda. She writes '. . . for K'eōmurchean and other advanced Western Armenian thinkers of the time, the most important problem was the conflict against the Ottoman tyranny's policy of national persecution, which the Ottoman government drove on its subject peoples . . .'[205] In support of this she notes that the work is a Christian polemic, in so far as it displays a Christian youth who is firm in his faith and is able to convince his bride to convert. Moreover, she quotes the following exclamation, wherein a character says: 'Let's depart from the land of the snake-like Turks'.[206]

While the work is essentially Christian polemic literature, I am reluctant to agree with Sahakyan's claims about its anti-Ottoman nature. Eremia's views about the Ottoman Empire were both conflicted and complex, and they cannot be generalised from one quotation. That is not to deny, however, that such exclamations are informative if considered in a broader context. Another example of an exclamation which casts light on Armenians' conception of history is a striking reference to the Celalis: the Jewish girl's mother, enraged because the Christian Dimo stole away her daughter, exclaims of him that 'You are for me a Tamerlane, a Celali . . .'[207] In his childhood, Eremia would walk the streets of Istanbul with his grandfather, a Celali refugee, and reference to the bandits would undoubtedly still have had an emotional sting for Eremia and Armenians of his generation.

Finally, I will conclude this section by mentioning a poem of Eremia's that very explicitly addressed an event of contemporary importance in Istanbul. One of Eremia's recurring interests was his contemporary, the Jewish messianic leader Sabbatai Zevi[208] and, indeed, Eremia wrote a biographical poem about him which also served as a piece of religious polemic aimed at his own Armenian community. While it is logical that tales about Sabbatai's messianic claims, imprisonment and conversion to Islam would be well known to everyone living in Istanbul at the time, it is noteworthy how much interest Eremia took in Sabbatai's youth and education, which were probably less well known to the general public. Here I translate the poem's first chapter:

> [Let's] expound on a certain Jew named Sabbatai,
> the son [of one] named Laray Ment'ēsh,
> who was the mediator (*miyancı*) and town-crier (*tellâl*) there,
> in the city of Izmir, he beget Sabbatai.
> He grew up there, and he was instructed in the law
> becoming well versed in the books of his people.

He earned a name [for himself] for the resolution of commentaries,
as a successful respondent to questions.
He gathered many students there,
showing fame from signs,
writing the name of God backwards,
teaching his [students] to read that way.
When they read [it], they trembled [and] shuddered,
as if he had healed [them] by sprinkling with waters,
they set up a tribunal for him, calling him rabbi (*haham*),
[they said, 'we've] opened [the tribunal] for you, come speak on the books.'
He went to Jerusalem,
wanting to kindle the same understanding of wisdom,
like a bigwig he demanded honour,
[so that] perhaps he might ensnare the people who were there.
Some were persuaded by him,
little by little word spread [of him],
showing some small knowledge, a bit of false doctrine,
he had them speak of him as if he was a great man.
An old Portuguese man who was found there,
was a physician and learned man, versed in books,
taking with him some notables,
he condemned Sabbatai harshly.
He read a sermon [saying] that he had lost his mind,
he wanted to show him as being unlearned and insignificant,
a child gone astray, insolent and rash,
he wants to lead our people away with him.
Disdaining and putting him to shame,
he wanted to hand him over to the tyrant,
and he warned [Sabbatai] to take flight,
from Jerusalem he was driven off.
Sabbatai was wounded and grieving in the heart,
when he could not be honoured,
he descended to Gaza [where he] he found a certain Nathan,
entering into his counsel, he formed an alliance with him.
Staying many days in one place,

he said to Nathan, [now] you see me,
when I reach the fullness of my greatness,
I will take you as Caesar, honoured equally with me.
Nathan prophesised to the Jews concerning him,
proclaiming him from country to country,
showing the day and time mysteriously,
delivering oracles about Sabbatai.
He wrote about him, that he was chosen,
that he is among you something you have not known,
he has arrived for the salvation of our people,
the Messiah has been revealed in Izmir of Lycia.[209]

What motivated Eremia to write about Sabbatai? As an Armenian religious polemicist, Eremia took keen interest in both Orthodox Christianity and Judaism, in the creeds of his religious opponents (it would have been dangerous for Eremia to write an anti-Islamic work). Moreover he was always interested in current affairs and the recent history of the Ottoman Empire and it seems that here his two interests – in religious polemics and recent history – converged. Eremia's source for information about Sabbatai was at least in part translations from Jewish sources,[210] and it is likely that his poetic version of the story was intended for oral recitation. Thus the poem probably served as a conduit for spreading the Jewish community's account of Sabbatai in Armenian at social gatherings, simultaneously providing entertainment and a concrete rebuttal of a religious upstart disfavoured by all representatives of the status quo, Jewish, Muslim and Christian alike. Eremia probably took such great interest in Sabbatai because he likened the internal divisions within the Jewish community to those within his own between Apostolic and Catholic Armenians, or alternatively, to the struggles for legitimation between Armenian churchmen and holy sees.[211] Thus he thought it necessary to articulate his vehement disapproval of Sabbatai.

In sum, Eremia reshaped a diversity of medieval literary genres – polemical, catechysmal and poetic – to comment on problems confronting Armenians of seventeenth-century Istanbul.

Conclusions: Eremia at the Crossroads of Three Traditions

Eremia lived a rich life of diverse activities. In his youth he baked bread for Ottoman troops at Ambakum's shop, travelled to Jerusalem, wandered the streets of Istanbul with his grandfather and friends, and spent time in the entourages of the Ottoman Empire's most learned Armenian priests. As a man he was a freelance scholar of leisure, serving as a secretary for the Armenian Church without ever becoming a priest, negotiating with multiple Ottoman grand viziers on behalf of the Armenian community and as a client of his patron Apro Çelebi, and acting as an ecclesiastical partisan of Eḷiazar of Antep. In his middle and old age he established a printing press, travelled to Ējmiatsin, prepared books for his children and, finally, upon the death of his daughter and two sons, retreated into seclusion. It seems, however, that the most consistent theme of his life was his love of reading, intellectual discourse and books. His massive productivity can only be explained if we picture him as having spent the majority of his time in his study. Whereas Grigor Daranalts'i had primarily been a politician and bishop who also wrote a chronicle and political testament, Eremia was the reverse: a prolific author and intellectual who occasionally participated in politics.

How do we assess Eremia's intellectual contribution? As we have seen, Eremia's corpus bridged three traditions: the medieval Armenian tradition, the intellectual world of Ottoman Istanbul and a new vein of original early modern Armenian literature paralleling literary developments in both the Islamic world and Western Europe. Eremia the medievalist revived Armenian literary traditions that had waned in the sixteenth century, producing works in old Armenian genres, such as his *Questions and Answers*. The Ottomanist Eremia wrote tomes on Ottoman history which drew on the Islamicate historiographic tradition, using Ottoman Turkish texts as primary sources, as well as a geography of the Islamic world, focusing on the Ottoman Empire, Iran and India. Finally, the early modern Eremia developed writings on self and place – such as his diary and tour of Istanbul – which were innovative in the Armenian literary tradition. In all three cases, Eremia used his erudition and literary talents to address problems facing the descendants of the early seventeenth-century Armenian migrations.

Armenian cultural and social life changed with the move from Greater Armenia and Cilicia to the western parts of the Ottoman Empire, particularly

Ottoman port cities such as Istanbul, Izmir and Rodotso. Eremia did more than any other author to create literature that had utility in the Armenians' new environment, and he represents the starting point of Istanbul's great Armenian literary tradition. Not all of Eremia's works would be directly influential on coming generations, but the mass arrival of Armenians in Istanbul at the beginning of the seventeenth century created a new environment for the production of Armenian literature – an urban context that would shape literary activity in common ways, even when there was not a direct link between individual authors.

There was yet another facet to Eremia's intellectual identity, Eremia the translator from Armenian into Armeno-Turkish. Let us now turn our attention to this aspect of Eremia's contribution to both Armenian and Turkish literature.

Notes

1. Kevork Bardakjian, 'The Rise of the Armenian Patriarchate of Constantinople', *Christians and Jews in the Ottoman Empire: The Functioning of a Plural Society*, Vol. I (New York: Holmes and Meier, 1982), p. 94.
2. Nersēs Akinean, *Eremia Chʻēlēpi Kʻēōmurchean: Keankʻn ew grakan gortsunēutʻiwně* (Vienna: Mkhitʻarean Tparan, 1933).
3. Eremia Kʻēōmurchean, *Eremia Chʻēlēpi Kʻēōmurchean Stampoloy patmutʻiwn*, Vahram Y. Tʻorgomean (ed.) (Vienna: Mkhitʻarean Tparan, 1913).
4. Eremia Kʻēōmurchean, *Ōragrutʻiwn Eremia Chʻēlēpi Kʻēōmurcheani*, Mesrop Nshanean (ed.) (Jerusalem: Tparan Srbotsʻ Yakobeantsʻ, 1939).
5. H. S. Sahakyan, *Eremia Kʻyomurchyan* (Yerevan: Haykakan SSṚ GA Hratarakchʻutʻyun, 1964).
6. Eremia Kʻēōmurchean, *Eremia Kʻēōmurchean patmutʻiwn hamaṙōt DCH tariotsʻ ōsmanean tʻagaworatsʻn*, Zh. M. Avetisyan (ed.) (Yerevan: Haykakan SSH GA Hratarakchʻutʻyun, 1982).
7. Eremia Kʻēōmurchean, *Patmutʻiwn hrakizman Kostondnupolsoy (1660 tarwoy)*, G. Bampukʻchean (ed.) (Istanbul: Sholakatʻ, 1991).
8. E. Shütz, 'Jeremia Çelebi Türkische Werke (Zur Phonetik des Mittelosmanischen)', *Studia Turcica* (1971): 401–30.
9. Eremia Kʻēōmurchean, *Eremya Chelebi Kömürjian's Armeno-Turkish Poem: The Jewish Bride*, Andreas Tietze and Avedis K. Sanjian (trans.) (Wiesbaden: Harrassowitz, 1981).

10. I am grateful to Dr Ayvazyan for many edifying and lively conversations about Eremia in Yerevan. Her articles are all included in the bibliography.
11. Eremia Kʻeōmurchean, *Ōragrutʻiwn*, pp. 623–4. See also Avetisyan, pp. 10–11 and Gayane Ayvazyan, 'Eremia Chʻelepi Kʻyomurchyani kyankʻě', *Patmutʻyun ew Mshakuytʻ* (2014), p. 171.
12. Eremia Kʻeōmurchean, *Eremia Kʻēōmurchean patmutʻiwn hamaṙōt DCH tariotsʻ ōsmanean tʻagaworatsʻn*, p. 11.
13. Ibid.
14. M 1786, 22a. See also Gayane Ayvazyan, 'Ōsmanyan Kaysrutʻyan patmutʻyuně Eremia Chʻelepi Kʻyomurchyani patmutʻyunnerum', unpublished article, pp. 4–5.
15. Eremia Kʻeōmurchean, *Eremia Kʻēōmurchean patmutʻiwn hamaṙōt DCH tariotsʻ ōsmanean tʻagaworatsʻn*, p. 11.
16. Ibid., p. 12.
17. Ayvazyan, 'Eremia Chʻelepi Kʻyomurchyani kyankʻě', p. 172.
18. Eremia Kʻeōmurchean, *Eremia Kʻēōmurchean patmutʻiwn hamaṙōt DCH tariotsʻ ōsmanean tʻagaworatsʻn*, p. 13.
19. Ayvazyan, p. 171.
20. The title 'Mahtesi' derives from the Arabic word '*makdisî*' and was used to indicate people who had made the pilgrimage to Jerusalem, like the Turkish term '*hacı*'. For more information about Ambakum, see Garegin Sruandzteantsʻ, *Tʻoros Aḷbar* II (Istanbul: G. Baḷtatlean, 1884), pp. 398–410.
21. Ayvazyan, p. 172.
22. Ayvazyan, 'Eremia Chʻelepi Kʻyomurchyani kyankʻě', p. 173.
23. See Ali Yaycıoğlu, 'Perdenin Arkasındakiler Osmanlı İmparatorluğunda Sarraflar ve Finans Ağları Üzerine bir Deneme', in Nil Tekgül (ed.), *Festschrift in Honor of Özer Ergenç I* (Cambridge, MA: Department of Near Eastern Languages and Civilizations Harvard University, 2019).
24. Sahakyan, *Eremia Kʻyomurchyan*, p. 10.
25. Ibid., p. 11 and Ayvazyan, 'Eremia Chʻelepi Kʻyomurchyani kyankʻě', p. 173.
26. Grigor Daranaḷtsʻi, p. 606.
27. Eremia Kʻeōmurchean, *Ōragrutʻiwn*, p. 7.
28. Ibid., p. 8.
29. Ibid., pp. 43, 76, 85.
30. Gayane Ayvazyan, 'Eremia Chʻelepi Kʻyomurchyani 'Ōragrutʻyun' erki mi anhayt skzbnaḷbyuri masin', *Hayagitutʻyan Hartsʻer* 1.7 (2016): 51–60.
31. Eremia Kʻeōmurchean, *Ōragrutʻiwn*, pp. 8–9.

32. For a discussion of piracy on the Mediterranean in the seventeenth century, see Molly Greene, *Catholic Pirates and Greek Merchants: A Maritime History of the Early Modern Mediterranean* (Princeton University Press, 2013).
33. Eremia Kʻeōmurchean, *Ōragrutʻiwn*, p. 10.
34. Ibid., pp. xx–xxi.
35. Ibid., pp. xxi–xxii, 11.
36. Ibid., p. xxi.
37. Ibid., p. 15.
38. Ibid., p. 310.
39. Ibid., pp. xxii–xxiii, 29–30.
40. Ibid., p. xxiv.
41. Polina Ivanova, 'Armenians in Urban Order and Disorder of Seventeenth-Century Istanbul', *Journal of the Ottoman and Turkish Studies Association* 4.2 (2017): 259.
42. Grigor Daranaḷtsʻi, p. 135.
43. Eremia Kʻeōmurchean, *Ōragrutʻiwn*, p. 31.
44. Ibid., pp. xxiii–xxiv, 31–33. See also Maḷakʻia Ōrmanean, *Azgapatum* II (Ējmiatsin: Mayr Atʻoṙ S. Ējmiatsin, 2001), pp. 2877–8.
45. Ōrmanean, *Azgapatum* II, p. 2878.
46. Eremia Kʻeōmurchean, *Ōragrutʻiwn*, pp. xxiv–xxviii, 36–41.
47. Ibid., pp. xxviii, 53.
48. Ibid., p. xxx.
49. Ayvazyan, 'Eremia Chʻelepi Kʻyomurchyani kyankʻě', p. 178.
50. Ibid., p. 176.
51. Sahakyan, *Eremia Kʻyomurchyan*, p. 12.
52. Eremia Kʻeōmurchean, *Ōragrutʻiwn*, pp. xxxi–xxxii, 59–64.
53. Ibid., pp. iiiv, 75.
54. Ibid., p. iiiv.
55. Ibid., pp. iiivii–iiiviii.
56. Ibid., p. lvii.
57. Ibid., p. lv-lvi.
58. For a rich account and interpretation of this incident, see H. S. Anasyan, *XVII dari azatagrakan sharzhumnern Arevmtyan Hayastanum* (Yerevan: Haykakan SSṘ GA Hratarakchʻutʻyun, 1961), pp. 241–72.
59. Ayvazyan, 'Eremia Chʻelepi Kʻyomurchyani kyankʻě', p. 182; and Bardakjian, pp. 94–5.
60. Eremia Kʻeōmurchean, *Ōragrutʻiwn*, pp. lii, 307.

61. Sahakyan, *Eremia K'yomurchyan*, pp. 12–13. For more about Apro's lineage and biography see Y. K'iwrtean, 'Aproy Chelepi, 1620–167?', *Bazmavēp* 9 (1925): 258–61; and 'Aproy Chelepi, 1620–167?' *Bazmavēp* 10 (1926): 37–42.
62. Ayvazyan, 'Eremia Ch'elepi K'yomurchyani kyank'ĕ', pp. 179–80.
63. Eremia K'eōmurchean, *Ōragrut'iwn*, p. lvii.
64. Eremia K'eōmurchean, *Eremia K'ēōmurchean patmut'iwn hamaṙōt DCH tariots' ōsmanean t'agaworats'n*, p. 16.
65. Ayvazyan, 'Eremia Ch'elepi K'yomurchyani kyank'ĕ', p. 181.
66. Eremia K'eōmurchean, *Ōragrut'iwn*, pp. liv–lv, 347.
67. Ibid., p. lvi.
68. Ibid., pp. lx–lxiv.
69. Gayane Ayvazyan, 'Eremia K'omurchyani 'Ōragrut'yun' erkĕ', *Hayots' Patmut'yan Harts'er* 15 (2014): 103–4.
70. For a summary of the diary's contents, see Eremia K'eōmurchean, *Ōragrut'iwn*, pp. ciiiv–cxliv.
71. Eremia K'eōmurchean, *Ōragrut'iwn*, p. lxiii.
72. Ibid., p. lxviii.
73. Eremia K'eōmurchean, *Eremia K'ēōmurchean patmut'iwn hamaṙōt DCH tariots' ōsmanean t'agaworats'n*, p. 13.
74. H. Riondel, *Une page tragique de l'histoire religieuse du Levant* (Paris: Gabriel Beauchesne, 1929).
75. Ayvazyan, 'Eremia Ch'elepi K'yomurchyani kyank'ĕ', p. 175.
76. Ayvazyan, 'Eremia Ch'elepi K'yomurchyani kyank'ĕ', p. 185.
77. Eremia K'eōmurchean, *Ōragrut'iwn*, p. lxv.
78. Akinean, p. 57.
79. Eremia K'eōmurchean, *Ōragrut'iwn*, p. xvii.
80. Ibid., pp. xvii–xviii.
81. Eremia K'eōmurchean, *Eremia K'ēōmurchean patmut'iwn hamaṙōt DCH tariots' ōsmanean t'agaworats'n*, p. 14.
82. Sahakyan, *Eremia K'yomurchyan*, p. 14.
83. *Mik'ayel Ch'amch'yants' hayots' patmut'yun (skzbits' minch'ev 1784 t'vakanĕ)*, III (Yerevan: Erevani Hamalsarani Hratarakch'ut'yun, 1984), p. 723.
84. For comments on how one of Eremia's work may have been inspired by a Greek original, see Eremia K'eōmurchean, *Eremya Chelebi Kömürjian's Armeno-Turkish Poem: The Jewish Bride*, Andreas Tietze and Avedis K. Sanjian (trans.) (Wiesbaden: Harrassowitz, 1981), pp. 37–46.

85. Eremia Kʻeōmurchean, *Ōragrutʻiwn*, p. 150. See also Ayvazyan, 'Eremia Chʻelepi Kʻyomurchyani kyankʻě', p. 177.
86. For the most updated and comprehensive list of Eremia's extant corpus, see Gayane Ayvazyan, 'Eremia Chʻelepi Kʻyomurchyani dzeṙagrakan zhaṙangutʻyuně', *Banber Matenadarani* 20 (2014): 349–98. See also Sahakyan, *Eremia Kʻyomurchyan*, pp. 167–74.
87. Sahakyan, *Eremia Kʻyomurchyan*, pp. 167–8.
88. See *Mikʻayel Chʻamchʻyantsʻ hayotsʻ patmutʻyun (skzbitsʻ minchʻev 1784 tʻvakaně)*, III, p. 723.
89. Mesrop Nshanean, 'Ōragrutʻiwn Eremia Chʻēlēpi Kʻeōmurcheani', *Shoḷakatʻ* (1913): 48–55. See also Akinean, pp. 90–5 and H. S. Eremean, 'Eremia Chēlēpi taregrakan patmutʻiwn', *Bazmavēp* (1902): 367–9, 473–9.
90. M 1786, pp. 1a–42a.
91. M 1786, pp. 42b–43b. See S. Melikʻ-Bakhshyan, 'Stepʻanos Dashtetsʻi mi zhamanakagrutʻyan masin', *Gitakan Ashkhatutʻyunner* 47 (1955): 117–33.
92. M 1786, pp. 44b–49b. See Ash. Abrahamyan, 'Martiros Di Aṙakʻeli zhamanakagrutʻyuně', *Gitakan Nyutʻeri Zhoḷovatsu* 1 (1941): 93–100.
93. M 1786, p. 22a.
94. See *Chronikon peri tōn Tourkōn Soultanōn*, G. T. Zoras (ed.) (Athens: The Department of Byzantine and Neo-Hellenic Philology of the University of Athens, 1958); and *Byzantium, Europe, and the Early Ottoman Sultans, 1373–1513: An Anonymous Greek Chronicle of the Early Seventeenth Century (Codex Barberinus Graecus 111)*, Marios Philippides (trans.) (New Rochelle: A. D. Caratzas, 1990).
95. Kâtip Çelebi, *Fezleketü akvâli'l-ahyâr fî ilmi't-târîh ve'l-ahbâr (Fezleketü't-tevârîh): târîhu mülûki Âli 'Osmân*, Seyyid Muhammed es-Seyyid (ed.) (Ankara: Türk Tarihi Kurumu, 2009).
96. M 1786, p. 1a.
97. M 1786, p. 1b.
98. Henry R. Shapiro, 'Legitimizing the Ottoman Sultanate in Early Modern Greek', *Journal of Turkish Studies* 42 (2014), p. 294.
99. M 1786, pp. 21b–22a.
100. Ayvazyan, 'Ōsmanyan Kaysrutʻyan patmutʻyuně Eremia Chʻelepi Kʻyomurchyani patmutʻyunnerum', p. 9.
101. For a description of the work in Turkish, see Orhan Şaik Gökyay, 'Kâtip Çelebi: Hayatı, Şahsiyeti, Eserleri', *Kâtip Çelebi: Hayatı ve Eserleri Hakkında İncelemeler* (Ankara: Türk Tarih Kurumu, 1957), pp. 40–3.

102. M 1786, pp. 22b–23a.
103. For Kâtip Çelebi's biography of Ahmed I, see Kâtip Çelebi, *Fezleketü akvâli'l-ahyâr fî ilmi't-târîh ve'l-ahbâr (Fezleketü't-tevârîh)*, p. 361.
104. M 1786, pp. 34b–36b.
105. M 1786, p. 36b.
106. M 1786, pp. 37a–40b.
107. M 1786, p. 43a. See also Melik'-Bakhshyan, 'Step'anos Dashtets'i mi zhamanakagrut'yan masin', pp. 130–1.
108. Sahakyan, *Eremia K'yomurchyan*, p. 167.
109. M 1786, p. 41b.
110. For information about the life and times of Yakob, see Ōrmanean, *Azgapatum* II, pp. 2911–3052. See also Y. K'iwrtean, *Yakob Kat'oḷikos Juḷayets'i* (Antelias: Kat'oḷikosut'ean Hayots' Metsi Tann Kilikioy, 1965).
111. See Ōrmanean, *Azgapatum* II, pp. 3335–70.
112. See Abraham Kretats'i, *Abraham Kretats'i: Patmut'yun*, N. K. Ḷorḷanyan (ed.) (Yerevan: Haykakan SSH GA Hratarakch'ut'yun, 1973); and *Chronicle of Abraham of Crete*, George A. Bournoutian (trans.) (Costa Mesa, Mazda Publishers, 1998).
113. Eremia K'ēōmurchean, *Eremia K'ēōmurchean patmut'iwn hamaṙōt DCH tariots' ōsmanean t'agaworats'n*, pp. 17–22.
114. Ibid., p. 22.
115. Ibid., p. 24.
116. Ibid., p. 27.
117. Ayvazyan, 'Ōsmanyan Kaysrut'yan patmut'yunĕ Eremia Ch'elepi K'yomurchyani patmut'yunnerum', p. 3.
118. Eremia K'ēōmurchean, *Eremia K'ēōmurchean patmut'iwn hamaṙōt DCH tariots' ōsmanean t'agaworats'n*, pp. 30–2. For the original Ottoman Turkish work, see Lütfi Paşa, *Tevârih-i Âli Osman*, Âli Bey (ed.) (İstanbul: Matbaa-yi Âmire, [1341] 1925).
119. Eremia K'ēōmurchean, *Eremia K'ēōmurchean patmut'iwn hamaṙōt DCH tariots' ōsmanean t'agaworats'n*, pp. 34–7. For the original Ottoman Turkish work, see Kâtip Çelebi, *Fezleke-i Kâtip Çelebi* (İstanbul: Ceride-i Havadis Matbaası, [1286] 1869–70).
120. Eremia K'ēōmurchean, *Eremia K'ēōmurchean patmut'iwn hamaṙōt DCH tariots' ōsmanean t'agaworats'n*, pp. 33–4.
121. Ayvazyan, 'Ōsmanyan Kaysrut'yan patmut'yunĕ Eremia Ch'elepi K'yomurchyani patmut'yunnerum', p. 3.

122. Eremia Kʿeōmurchean, *Eremia Kʿēōmurchean patmutʿiwn hamaŕōt DCH tariotsʿ ōsmanean tʿagaworatsʿn*, pp. 162–3.
123. Ibid., pp. 173–4.
124. Ibid., p. 323. Compare with *Fezleke-i Kâtip Çelebi* I, pp. 306–10.
125. Gregorian calendar date chosen according to timing of the event in the *hijri* year.
126. Eremia Kʿeōmurchean, *Eremia Kʿēōmurchean patmutʿiwn hamaŕōt DCH tariotsʿ ōsmanean tʿagaworatsʿn*, pp. 233–5.
127. Ayvazyan, 'Ōsmanyan Kaysrutʿyan patmutʿyunĕ Eremia Chʿelepi Kʿyomurchyani patmutʿyunnerum', p. 12.
128. Ayvazyan, 'Ōsmanyan Kaysrutʿyan patmutʿyunĕ Eremia Chʿelepi Kʿyomurchyani patmutʿyunnerum', p. 1.
129. See Cumhur Bekar, 'A New Perception of Rome, Byzantium and Constantinople in Hezarfen Hüseyin's Universal History', MA Thesis, Boğaziçi University Department of History, 2011.
130. See Tʿovma Metsopʿetsʿi, *Tʿovma Metsopʿetsʿi patmagrutʿyun*, L. Khachʿikean (ed.) (Yerevan: Magaḷatʿ, 1999); and *Tʿovma Metsobetsʿi's History of Tamerlane and his Successors*, Robert Bedrosian (trans.) (New York: Sources of the Armenian Tradition, 1987).
131. Eremia Kʿeōmurchean, *Eremia Kʿēōmurchean patmutʿiwn hamaŕōt DCH tariotsʿ ōsmanean tʿagaworatsʿn*, p. 33.
132. Ayvazyan, 'Eremia Chʿelepi Kʿyomurchyani dzeŕagrakan zhaŕangutʿyunĕ', pp. 352–4.
133. Ibid., p. 355.
134. See Molly Greene, *A Shared World: Christians and Muslims in the Early Modern Mediterranean* (Princeton University Press, 2002).
135. P 338, p. 1a.
136. For an explanation of the career trajectories of Ottoman chief eunuchs in the early modern Ottoman Empire, see Jane Hathaway, *Beshir Agha, Chief Eunuch of the Ottoman Imperial Harem* (London: Oneworld Publications, 2006).
137. P 338, pp. 9b–10a.
138. Eremia Kʿeōmurchean, *Patmutʿiwn hrakizman Kostondnupolsoy (1660 tarwoy)*, G. Bampukʿchean (ed.) (Istanbul: Shoḷakatʿ, 1991), p. 31.
139. Ibid., p. 77.
140. Ibid., p. 76.
141. Hrand D. Andreasyan, 'Eremya Çelebi'nin Yangınlar Tarihi', *Tarih Dergisi* 27 (1973): 59–84.

142. Akinean, pp. 97-8.
143. Ibid., p. 99.
144. See Cemal Kafadar, 'Self and Others: The Diary of a Dervish in Seventeenth Century Istanbul and First-Person Narratives in Ottoman Literature', *Studia Islamica* 69 (1989): 121-50; and Ralph Elger and Yavuz Erköse (eds), *Many Ways of Speaking About the Self, Middle Eastern Ego-Documents in Arabic, Persian and Turkish (14th-20th Century)* (Wiesbaden: Harrassowitz, 2010).
145. Eremia Kʻeōmurchean, *Ōragrutʻiwn*, p. xii.
146. Ayvazyan, 'Eremia Kʻomurchyani 'Ōragrutʻyun' erkě', pp. 103-4.
147. Ayvazyan, 'Eremia Chʻelepi Kʻyomurchyani 'Ōragrutʻyun' erki mi anhayt skzbnaḷbyuri masin', pp. 51-60.
148. Ayvazyan, 'Eremia Kʻomurchyani 'Ōragrutʻyun' erkě', p. 91.
149. Eremia Kʻeōmurchean, *Ōragrutʻiwn*, p. 24.
150. Eremia Kʻeōmurchean, *Ōragrutʻiwn*, p. 36.
151. Ayvazyan, 'Eremia Kʻomurchyani 'Ōragrutʻyun' erkě', p. 105; and Eremia Kʻeōmurchean, *Ōragrutʻiwn*, p. 305. For an Ottoman Turkish account of the rebel Hasan, see also *Evliyâ Çelebi Seyahatnâmesi*, Seyit Ali Kahraman, Yücel Dağlı and Robert Dankoff (eds) (İstanbul: Yapı Kredi Yayınları, 2011), pp. 5/122-9.
152. Eremia Kʻeōmurchean, *Ōragrutʻiwn*, pp. 321-2.
153. Ayvazyan, 'Eremia Kʻomurchyani 'Ōragrutʻyun' erkě', pp. 98-9.
154. Eremia Kʻeōmurchean, *Ōragrutʻiwn*, pp. 29-30.
155. See Zakʻaria Aguletsʻi, *Zakʻaria Aguletsʻu ōragrutʻyuně,*, S. V. Ter-Avetisyan (ed.) (Yerevan: Armfani Hratarakchʻutʻyun, 1938) and *Journal of Zakʻaria of Agulis*, George A. Bournoutian (trans.) (Costa Mesa: Mazda Publishing, 2002).
156. For an excellent account of the history of narratives of self within the Armenian literary tradition, see K. A. Danielyan, *Hay memuarayin grakanutʻyan patmutʻyunits*ʻ (Yerevan: Haykakan SSṘ GA Hratarakchʻutʻyun, 1961).
157. Akinean, pp. 135-6.
158. See Kâtip Çelebi, *Kitâb-ı Cihânnümâ li-Kâtib Çelebi* I (Ankara: Türk Tarih Kurumu, 2009).
159. Yarutʻyun Pztikean, 'Hayastani hin kʻartēs mě XVII dareru vankʻern u srbavayrerě', *Bazmavēp* (2000): 296.
160. Gabriella Uluhogian, *Un' Antica Mappa dell'Armenia: Monasteri e santuari dal I al XVII secolo* (Ravenna: Longo Editore, 2000).

161. Uluhogian, pp. 48–9. Between these two pages can be found a full reproduction of the entire map.
162. Ibid., p. 141.
163. Ibid., p. 66.
164. Ibid., p. 153.
165. Ibid., p. 168.
166. Ibid., p. 171.
167. Ibid., p. 62.
168. Ibid., p. 125.
169. Ibid., p. 172.
170. Ibid.
171. Ibid., pp. 62, 168.
172. Eremya Çelebi Kömürciyan, *İstanbul Tarihi: XVII. Asırda İstanbul*, Hrand D. Andreasyan (trans.) (İstanbul: Eren, 1988).
173. Eremia Kʻeōmurchean, *Eremia Chʻēlēpi Kʻēōmurchean Stampoloy patmutʻiwn*, pp. 4–5.
174. Gayane Ayvazyan, 'The Perception of the City in Topographic Works of Yeremia Chelebi Qyomurtchyan', *Osmanlı İstanbulu III: III. Uluslararası Osmanlı İstanbulu Sempozyumu Bildirileri 25–26 Mayıs 2015, İstanbul 29 Mayıs Üniversitesi*, Feridun Emecen, et al. (eds) (İstanbul Büyükşehir Belediyesi, 2015), p. 216.
175. Eremia Kʻeōmurchean, *Eremia Chʻēlēpi Kʻēōmurchean Stampoloy patmutʻiwn*, p. 74.
176. E.g. Ḷukas Inchichean, *Amaṙanotsʻ Biwzandean* (Venice: S. Lazzaro, 1794). The work has also been translated into Turkish: G. V. İnciciyan, *Boğaziçi Sayfiyeleri* (Istanbul: Eren, 2002).
177. N. A. Oskanyan, Kʻ. A. Korkotyan, et al., *Hay girkʻě 1512–1800 tʻvakannerin* I (Yerevan: Haykakan SSH Kulturayi Ministrutʻyun, 1988), pp. 8–9.
178. Ibid., pp. 78–9.
179. Ibid., p. 81.
180. Gayane Ayvazyan, 'Eremia Chʻelepi Kʻyomurchyani tpagrakan gortsuneutʻyuně', *Ējmiatsin* (2012/8): 50.
181. Eremia Kʻeōmyurchean, *Govabanutʻiwn tnōrinakan teḷeatsʻ yErusaḷēm* (Istanbul: Kʻeōmyurchean, 1678).
182. Ayvazyan, 'Eremia Chʻelepi Kʻyomurchyani tpagrakan gortsuneutʻyuně', pp. 51–2.
183. Eremia Kʻeōmurchean, *Ōragrutʻiwn*, p. 562. See also Ayvazyan, p. 53.

184. Ayvazyan, p. 54.
185. Tijana Krstic, *Contested Conversions to Islam: Narratives of Religious Change in the Early Modern Ottoman Empire* (Stanford University Press, 2011), p. 174.
186. For a classic introduction to the Kadizadelis, see Madeline C. Zilfi, 'The Kadizadelis: Discordant Revivalism in Seventeenth-Century Istanbul', *Journal of Near Eastern Studies* 45/4 (October 1986): 251–69. For a more recent interpretation of the movement, see Marinos Sariyannis, 'The Kadızadeli Movement as a Social and Political Phenomenon: The Rise of a "Mercantile Ethic"?', *Political Initiatives from the Bottom-Up in the Ottoman Empire (Halcyon Days in Crete VII)*, Antonis Anastasopoulos (ed.) (Rethymno: 2012), pp. 263–89.
187. Sebouh Aslanian, Anna Ohanjanyan and Cesare Santus have begun to consider the confessionalisation paradigm in the context of Armenian history. See Sebouh Aslanian, 'The "Great Schism" of 1773: Venice and the Founding of the Armenian Community of Trieste', in *Reflections on Armenian Identity in History and Historiography*, H. Berberian and J. Daryaee (eds) (Irvine: Jordan Center for Persian Studies, 2018); Anna Ohanjanyan 'Gēorg Mxlayim Ołli: An Overlooked Agent of Armenian Apostolic Confession-Building in Ottoman Constantinople'; and Cesare Santus, 'The Şeyhülislam, the Patriarch, and the Ambassador: A Case of Entangled Confessionalization (1692–1703)'. Ohanjanyan and Santus's works are both forthcoming in a volume edited by Tijana Krstic based on proceedings of a conference that took place in June 2018 in Budapest, Hungary.
188. Eremia Kʻeōmurchean, *Ōragrutʻiwn*, pp. xxxiii–lii. See also Oded Peri, *Christianity under Islam in Jerusalem: The Question of the Holy Sites in Early Ottoman Times* (Leiden: Brill, 2001).
189. See Akinean, pp. 95–6, and H. V. Hatsʻuni, 'Kusastankʻ Hayastani mēj', *Bazmavēp* (1923), p. 76.
190. For examples of this genre in Armenian and Greek, respectively, see Hakob Manandyan and Hrachʻya Achaṙyan, *Hayotsʻ nor vkanerě: 1155–1843* (Ējmiatsin: Tparan Mayr Atʻoṙoy S. Ējmiatsin, 1903), and Nikodēmos o Agioreitēs, *Neon martyrologion: ētoi martyria tōn theophanōn martyrōn tōn meta tēn alōsin tēs Kōnstantinoupoleōs kata diaphorous kairous kai topous martyrēsantōn* (Athens: F. Karampini and K. Vafa, 1856). For a discussion of these tales within the discourse of Ottoman historical research, see Krstić, *Contested Conversions to Islam*.
191. Ayvazyan, 'Eremia Chʻelepi Kʻyomurchyani dzeṙagrakan zhaṙangutʻyuně', p. 362.

192. Eremia's use of colloquial verbs can been seen in J 533 on pp. 127, 233 and 239. I'm grateful to Anna Ohanjanyan for pointing out these examples to me.
193. Derin Terzioğlu, 'Where ʿIlm-i Ḥāl Meets Catechism: Islamic Manuals of Religious Instruction in the Ottoman Empire in the Age of Confessionalization', *Past and Present* 220.1 (2013): 79–114.
194. Geoffrey Horrocks, *Greek: A History of the Language and its Speakers* (London: Longman, 1997), pp. 325–8.
195. Sahakyan, *Eremia K'yomurchyan*, p. 167.
196. For information on Armenian books of 'questions and answers' on biblical texts see Michael E. Stone, 'Biblical Text and Armenian Retelling', *Journal of the Society for Armenian Studies* 26 (2017), p. 86.
197. Seta B. Dadoyan, *The Armenians in the Medieval Islamic World: Paradigms of Interaction, Seventh to Fourteenth Centuries,* III (London: Routledge, 2014), pp. 149, 193–215.
198. M 72, pp. 136b–137a.
199. This folk etymology derives from Moses Khorenats'i. See Moses Khorenats'i, *History of the Armenians*, Robert W. Thomson (trans.) (Cambridge, MA: Harvard University Press, 1978), pp. 95–6.
200. See Moses Khorenats'i, pp. 250–3, for the story of King Trdat's murder.
201. M 72, pp. 131a–133a.
202. M 72, pp. 154a–155a. This passage has attracted the attention of Armeniologists, e.g. H. Anasyan, *Haykakan matenagitut'yun* I (Yerevan: Haykakan SSṘ GA Hratarakch'ut'yun, 1959), pp. lii–liii.
203. Anna Ohanjanyan, 'Creedal Controversies among Armenians in the Seventeenth-Century Ottoman Empire Eremia Č'ēlēpi K'ēōmiwrčean's Polemical Writing against Suk'ias Prusac'i', *Journal for the Society of Armenian Studies* 27 (2020): 15–17.
204. Hasmik Sahakyan, 'Eremia Ch'elepi K'yomurchyani mi antip poemĕ', *Banber Matenadarani* 6 (1962): 409. For more about the story of 'Hohannēs and Asha', see Peter Cowe, 'The Politics of Poetics: Islamic Influence on Armenian Verse', in *Redefining Christian Identity: Cultural Interactions in the Middle East Since the Rise of Islam*, H. L. Murre-van den Berg, et al. (eds) (Louvain: Peeters, 2005), pp. 379–403.
205. Sahakyan, 'Eremia Ch'elepi K'yomurchyani mi antip poemĕ', p. 410.
206. Ibid., p. 411.
207. Ibid., p. 412.

208. For literature on Sabbatai Zevi, see Gershom Gerhard Scholem, *Sabbatai Sevi: The Mystical Messiah* (Princeton University Press, 1976); and David J. Halperin, *Sabbatai Zevi: Testimonies to a Fallen Messiah* (Oxford: Littman Library of Jewish Civilization, 2012).
209. Y. Kʻyurtean, 'Nor nyutʻer Eremia Chʻēlēpi Kʻēōmyurcheani masin', *Bazmavēp* (1967), p. 89.
210. According to Aṙakʻel of Tabriz's *History* Eremia translated one of Sabbatai's own texts from a Greek version into Armenian. Aṙakʻel's *History* also makes reference to an Ottoman Turkish translation of one of Sabbatai's writings, and I consider it more likely that Eremia based his rendition of Sabbattai's message on the Turkish version. The poem analysed above would likely have been based on a combination of that Turkish translation and stories about Sabbatai circulating in Istanbul. For discussion of the pertinent passage in Aṙakʻel's history, see Ayvazyan, 'Ōsmanyan Kaysrutʻyan patmutʻyunĕ Eremia Chʻelepi Kʻyomurchyani patmutʻyunnerum', pp. 11–12. For the original reference, see Aṙakʻel Davrizhetsʻi, *Aṙakʻel Davrizhetsʻi girkʻ patmutʻeantsʻ*, L. A. Khanlaryan (ed.) (Yerevan: Haykakan KhSH GA Hratarakchʻutʻyun, 1990), p. 495 and *Aṙakʻel of Tabriz: Book of History*, George A. Bournoutian (trans.) (Costa Mesa: Mazda Publishers, 2010), pp. 555–6. Note that in Bournoutian's translation he translates the term 'Roman language' as 'Latin', when the text more likely refers to a Greek version.
211. The latter point was suggested by Paolo Lucca in 'Šabbetay Ṣewi and the Messianic Temptations of Ottoman Jews in the Seventeenth Century According to Christian Armenian Sources', in C. Adang and S. Schmidtke (eds), *Contacts and Controversies between Muslims, Jews and Christians in the Ottoman Empire and Pre-Modern Iran* (Würzburg: Ergon-Verlag, 2010), pp. 197–206.

6

Eremia K'eōmurchean and the Establishment of an Armeno-Turkish Translation Movement in Ottoman Istanbul

While the previous chapter offered an overview of Eremia K'eōmurchean's biography and the main themes of his writings in Armenian, this chapter considers his diverse corpus in Armeno-Turkish. In the aftermath of the Great Armenian Flight the demand for works in Armeno-Turkish greatly increased. Istanbul, in particular, thrived as a centre for literary production and translation in Armeno-Turkish from the seventeenth century until the twentieth, when the Armenian Genocide and the collapse of the Ottoman Empire obliterated the structural needs for the composition of Turkish literature written in the Armenian alphabet. Eremia expanded the types of translations produced in Armeno-Turkish, recrafting the tradition to suit the needs of readers or, more likely, listeners in seventeenth-century Istanbul. It is not clear if subsequent translators and authors of Armeno-Turkish were directly influenced by Eremia, but he and later authors in Istanbul responded to a common urban milieu. Eremia produced all of his Armeno-Turkish works in manuscript form, but by the 1730s Istanbul had become a centre for printing devotional works in Armeno-Turkish.[1]

Before Eremia, Armeno-Turkish literature in Anatolia was primarily used in poetry. Eremia's most significant contribution to the hybrid language's development was to use Armeno-Turkish as a vehicle for long-form prose translations in the Ottoman capital, Istanbul. This chapter will cast light on both a critical aspect of Eremia's intellectual activity and also on an unrecognised turning point in the development of Armeno-Turkish. This chapter differs from previous overviews of Eremia's Armeno-Turkish corpus[2] in three main ways: it includes new transcriptions and translations; it highlights linguistic differences between Eremia's devotional and secular translations; and it marks Eremia as the starting point of a translation movement based in Istanbul that arose both to meet the needs of Armenians living in the aftermath of the Great Flight and also to satisfy the curiosity of some Muslim intellectuals.

The History of Armeno-Turkish

The deep interaction between Armenian and Turkish cultures in Anatolia began with the Seljuk incursions of the eleventh century. Examples of Armeno-Turkish poetry go back to the Middle Ages, with the oldest concrete sample dating from late thirteenth-century Erzincan.[3] Most Armeno-Turkish writings of the medieval period are poetical, the works of a diversity of troubadour-like minstrels called *gusans*, *ozans* and, later, *aşıks*, whose tradition of poetry spanned the medieval, early modern and modern periods, continuing into the nineteenth century. Academic literature on the *aşıks* delineates them into two groups: those who improvised their songs and performed them musically, called 'poets of the square (*meydân şu'arâsı*)', and those who wrote them down, called 'poets of the pen (*kalem şu'arâsı*)'.[4] Armenia's foremost expert on Armeno-Turkish, Hasmik Step'anyan, argues that the motivation for writing in Turkish was that the demand for such poetry spanned the religious and ethnic groups of the Ottoman Empire: 'Since Turkish was comprehensible to all peoples, it is natural that . . . the *aşıks* performed mainly in Turkish'.[5]

Of the oldest manuscripts with elements in Armeno-Turkish, some were written in a dialect called Armeno-Kıpçak.[6] In the history of the Armeno-Turkish language, there are two main trajectories – one that developed among Armenians in the territories of modern-day Ukraine in the Kıpçak dialect of Turkish,[7] and the Armeno-Turkish of the Ottoman Empire that was written in the Oğuz dialects of Anatolia and Istanbul. This chapter focuses on the Ottoman Armeno-Turkish tradition.

In the late Ottoman Empire there was a linguistic distinction between the Armenians living in Eastern Anatolia and the Caucasus, on the one hand, and those in Western Anatolia and the Balkans, on the other hand, with the former being more likely to speak primarily in Armenian, while the latter were more likely to be Turkish-speaking.[8] This discrepancy was probably a result of the relative isolation of many communities in Eastern Anatolia and the South Caucasus as compared with higher rates of urbanisation in territories that gained their first major Armenian populations after the Great Flight. While new infrastructure, such as the Armash Monastery, was built in Western Anatolia in the seventeenth century and served as incubators of Armenian high culture, the number of people trained in reading Classical Armenian would nevertheless have been scant compared to the number of Turkish-speaking and bilingual Armenians, meaning Armenians speaking Turkish and a colloquial Armenian dialect. The grammatical and lexigraphical differences between Classical Armenian and spoken Armenian dialects would have meant that even for most fluent Armenian-speakers who also knew Turkish, it would have been easier to read in Armeno-Turkish than in Classical Armenian, as Armeno-Turkish was usually written in colloquial Turkish, not high Ottoman.

In the history of medieval Armenian literature, there are some non-poetic works written before the end of the sixteenth century with Armeno-Turkish elements. An example is the medical writings of Amirdovlatʻ of Amassia (1415–96), a physician at the court of Sultan Mehmed II who prepared medical dictionaries that included translations of terms into Armeno-Turkish.[9] It is only at the end of the sixteenth century, however, that both the quantity of manuscripts surviving in Armeno-Turkish and the range of genres represented greatly expands. Hasmik Stepʻanyan notes, for instance, that the composition and translation of spiritual tracts in Armeno-Turkish – such as prayer books and hagiographies – begins in earnest in the sixteenth and seventeenth centuries.[10]

In the eighteenth and nineteenth centuries a great volume of printed books, periodicals and newspapers were printed in Armeno-Turkish for consumption in Istanbul and Anatolia. Many early examples were produced by the printers of the Mkhitʻarean Orders in Venice and Trieste for the Ottoman market.[11] The Abbot Mkhitʻar Sebastatsʻi (1676–1749)[12] is a crucial figure in Armenian cultural and religious history because he founded the Mkhitʻarean Order, based in Venice, which simultaneously sought to preserve and develop Armenian cultural and intellectual life while also accepting the authority of the Vatican. A large part of this dual mission lay in training missionaries for work in the Ottoman Empire and publishing books that would help missionaries and develop Armenian intellectual life. The Mkhit'areans printed a diversity of works in Armeno-Turkish, and Mkhit'ar even personally prepared and published a grammar book of colloquial Armenian (*ashkharhabar*) in the Armeno-Turkish language in 1727 to help Ottoman Armenians learn their ancestral language. In the words of Sebouh Aslanian, Catholics like the Mkhit'areans saw Armeno-Turkish as 'the key means for the conversion of the Ottoman Empire's many Armenians'.[13]

While the study of Armeno-Turkish literature in the Ottoman Empire remains in its infancy in general, printed texts from the eighteenth and nineteenth centuries are more easily accessible than the manuscripts of the medieval and early modern periods and thus they are better known. As a result of this, a major turning point in Armeno-Turkish literature's development has been overlooked. The seventeenth century was a critical bridge between the medieval period – with production largely of poetry – and the eighteenth and nineteenth centuries, when the Armeno-Turkish literary tradition reached its highpoint in terms of volume and variety of works produced, including extensive writings and translations in prose. Eremia K'eōmurchean was a key exponent of that transition.

Eremia's Original Works in Armeno-Turkish

Eremia's original works in Armeno-Turkish ranged from short letters and poems of a personal nature[14] to major compositions for broader consumption. An example of the former category is a short poem that Eremia wrote for his wife upon the death of their daughter, Saḷomē, in 1690. It is a poem of religious consolation in which Eremia tries to assuage his wife's grief. Here is a direct transcription of the poem's first stanzas in Armeno-Turkish – written from the perspective of Saḷomē – followed by its English translation:

1. Nene beni siz ağlaman sızlaman
   Mum, don't cry [and] lament [for] me
2. Ecel geldi emrullahdi siz anlan,
   The hour of death came, it was the will of God, you must understand
3. Soğımenız oldi deyi pek yanman,
   Saying, 'Salome died', don't grieve too much

4. Hemen deyın ki Soğome kurtuldi
   Now, say that Salome was saved.

5. Ben duneaden behaberdım bilırsız,
   I was ignorant of the world, you know
6. Bir ter konçe ondordonde ben heniz,
   A green bud I [was], still fourteen [years old]
7. Geoz ümubda tezce ere verdınız
   In the blink of an eye you quickly ripened
8. Firaklenmen ki elımızden kuş uçti
   Don't grieve from separation, because the bird flew from our hand
9. Hemen deyın ki Soğome kurtuldi.
   Now say that Salome was saved.

10. Bu onulmaz derde gafil sataşdım
    I met this incurable grief unwary
11. Olum hattını bildım his ettım
    I knew and felt the edge of death
12. Sizi anıb geoz yaşımi kan iterdım
    By thinking of you, I would turn my eyes' tears into blood
13. Yanman ki gencecık kızımız oldi
    Don't grieve because our little young daughter died
14. Hemen deyın ki Soğome kurtuldi
    Now say that Salome was saved.[15]

Given Eremia's great learning within the Armenian intellectual, theological and literary tradition, one would think that he would draw upon it when grieving for his daughter. Thus, this poem begs the question: Why would Eremia have chosen to write in vernacular Turkish in his family's moment of grief? There are many Istanbul-Armenians today who – though fluent in Western-Armenian – still instinctively make recourse to Turkish at moments of surprise, joy or grief, using the language of their urban environment more than Armenian in daily life. This may not have been the case for Eremia, who passed most of his life reading, writing and conversing in Armenian with erudite clergy, but it may very well have been the case for his wife, to whom he addressed this lament.[16]

In addition to being a poet, Eremia was also an avid letter-writer. While he generally wrote in Armenian, he sometimes mixed in Armeno-Turkish. For example, in one letter concerning the death of his son he composed a section in Armeno-Turkish:

> Bir zeman salınub alem içre muhteremidi desinler, şimdi kare topraklerde mekean tutmuş deyu madem okusunlar. Dosdlari kare yaslere girub efsus u hayf, yazık evah deyu, acısınler. Bazilerın yeri geniş olduği içun, allar geyinub, kınalanub, başlerine reyhan takınub, horoz tepsınler. Ululerın sozi dır, bu tutun her ocakdan tutecek. Neçe padişah cihangiran alempenahlere oğradi, neçe azizler, nazeniler, khubler, güzeller bu perdeden geçdiler. İskenderden ileri, Okosdosdan usdun, Drtadden dilaver, Suleymanden alim, Üsufden güzel olmayak. *Marminn tarnay i hog yev hokin.*

> Let them say that he was esteemed, when once he loitered in the world. Now that he's taken his place in the black soil, let them grieve. Entering into black mourning, let his friends feel sorrow saying, 'Alas, what a pity', [and], 'Oh, what a shame!' Because some [people]'s situation is carefree, they will dress in red, decorate themselves with henna, wear basil on their heads, and dance. But the word of the great men [is this]: This smoke will fume from every hearth. It [the smoke of death] has visited many world-conquering sultans, 'Refuges of the Universe'. How many saints, graceful ones, good ones, and beauties passed by this curtain! There will be no one further ahead than Alexander, more victorious than Augustus, braver than Trdat, wiser than Solomon, more beautiful than Joseph. '*The body returns to the ground, and the soul . . .*' [final verse in Armenian].[17]

Since the letter begins in Armenian before turning to Turkish, it is clear that the recipient was bilingual, like Eremia himself. It is noteworthy that he paraphrases biblical verse – Ecclesiastes 12: 7 – in Armenian, and he assumes that the recipient will both understand and remember the verse's ending, that 'the soul returns to God'. Also noteworthy is his reference to the sultanic epithet, 'Refuge of the Universe'. We see that in Eremia's less formal works – his poetry and letters – he used Armeno-Turkish creatively and sometimes in combination with Armenian. That is to say, he sometimes abandoned his formal literary identities and allowed the bilinguality of his daily life in Ottoman Istanbul to enter his oeuvre. It seems that Eremia created such mixtures particularly at his life's saddest moments. Despite all his learning and immersion in Armenian books, it may be that Eremia wept in Turkish after all.

Eremia also adapted original compositions in Armenian into Armeno-Turkish versions. The previous chapter includes discussion of Eremia's Armenian retelling of the medieval tale of 'Hohannēs and Asha'. Eremia also created a distinct Armeno-Turkish version of this poem, which was translated and published under the title *The Jewish Bride* by Andreas Tietze and Avedis K. Sanjian.[18] As was the case with his repeated treatments of the Ottoman war in Crete, here again we see Eremia reworking the same theme for different audiences. Eremia not only adapted an old Anatolian tale to the new context of early modern Istanbul but also to the linguistic needs of the descendants of Armenian refugees of the Great Flight.

Eremia used Armeno-Turkish as a creative vehicle for writing letters, short poems and extended compositions such as *The Jewish Bride*. I would argue that Eremia's main contribution to the history of Armeno-Turkish literature in the Ottoman Empire, however, remains mostly unpublished and largely neglected. It is in prose translations of other authors' works into Armeno-Turkish that we see Eremia's most ambitious and extended uses of Armeno-Turkish, the one that most differentiates him from the medieval tradition of Armeno-Turkish poetry.

Eremia's Armeno-Turkish Translations

Before analysing samples of Eremia's translations from Armenian into Armeno-Turkish, some consideration should be made of his method of 'translation'. The Armenian scholar K. A. Melikʻ-Ohanjanyan has highlighted the ambiguity of the concept of 'translation' in the early modern period. With respect to one of Eremia's translation works, he asks,

> ... what must be understood by saying 'he translated'? Translations are literal, when with precision word-for-word or sentence-for-sentence, they translate some original [work] from one language into another language. Translations of a doctrinal or legal/legislative type carry such a nature,

where the most trivial deviation from the original can give rise to misunderstandings and have undesirable consequences. There are also free translations, when the translator does not fetter himself to the arrangement of the words of the original, but works to express the contents [and] the sequence of its composition in his own way, while, of course, not violating the work's structure, its creative construction. But there are also translations, when the translator retains for himself authorial rights. While translating the given work, he works to remake it according to his own conception, making additions and subtractions, subjecting the structure and arrangement of chapters to necessary and seemly changes, and, finally, to localise [and] to nationalise the contents in this or that way. Translations of this last class have already departed from the scope of the translation genre, and they have become transpositions, in which the transposer author makes a significant original work, putting on the work his personal and national (local) stamp. Such transpositions – in the process of development – become 'independent creations'.[19]

As we consider Eremia's Armeno-Turkish corpus we must continually assess how he was 'translating', whether it was literal, 'free', or the creation of new and innovative works based only loosely on the foreign language original.

Keeping this question in mind, I would divide Eremia's Armeno-Turkish works into two broad categories: Christian devotional works and 'secular' translations. By 'secular' I mean merely that they were historical in nature or aimed to entertain, not primarily aimed for use in public or private worship. In these two categories Eremia consciously adopted different translation strategies and it is more often in the translation of sacred texts that he made careful word-for-word translations, which satisfy even our modern criteria for the term.

Eremia's devotional translations

The best example of Eremia's word-for-word translations into Armeno-Turkish are his biblical translations, such as an unpublished translation of the book of John found in the Matenadaran in Yerevan (M 1645). The text is preserved in a manuscript copied in 1735, which shows the Armenian original in a column on the left next to the Turkish translation in a column on the right of each manuscript page. Here is a transliteration and translation of the first four verses, John 1: 1–1: 4:

1: 1. Kitabn [?] ide kelime ve kelime Allahde idi ve Allah idi ok kelime.
The book [*sic*] was the word, and the word was with God, and God was that word.

1: 2. Ol idi kadimde Allahde.
He was with God [in times] of old.

1: 3. Külli şey anun ile mevcud oldi ve ansuz ne bir şey mevcud oldi ne ki olmüşdır.
Everything came to be with him, and without him nothing came to be which came to be.

1: 4. Anınile ide heyat ve ol heat adamlern nuri idi.
With him was life, and that life was the light of men.[20]

It is unclear why Eremia wrote 'book' in place of the well known 'in the beginning' in the Turkish version, while the correct wording is clear in the Armenian version written on the same page. Otherwise, the translation is unambigous and literal, demonstrating that Eremia could and did strive to make word-for-word translations from Armenian into Armeno-Turkish. Another word-for-word devotional translation of Eremia's which survives in a similiar bilingual format is his Armeno-Turkish *Prayers of Nerses, Catholicos of the Armenians*, currently preserved in Yerevan in a seventeenth-century manuscript (M 1644).

It is noteworthy that Eremia's literal biblical translations into Turkish were not the only ones being made in seventeenth-century Istanbul. Better known than Eremia's Armeno-Turkish work is the complete biblical translation from Latin to Ottoman Turkish prepared by the Muslim convert Ali Ufkî, a famed Ottoman composer who was originally born in Poland with the name Albert Bobovius.[21] Here is an Ottoman Turkish transcription and English translation of his version of John 1: 1–1: 4:

1: 1. Evvelde kelime idi ve kelime Rabb'ın yanında idi ve Rabb o kelimedir.
In the beginning was the word, and the word was next to God, and God is that word.

1: 2. O idi ibtidâda Rabb'ın yanında.
   He was next to God in the beginning.
1: 3. Her şey olmuş oldu ondan ve onsuz bir olmuş şey olmuş olmadı.
   Everything came into being from him, and without him, it did not come into being, [that] which came into being.
1: 4. Ondan oldu hayât ve hayât idi adamlerin nûru.
   From him came life, and the life was the light of men.[22]

Ali Ufkî prepared his translation at the request of the Dutch ambassador to Istanbul, Levinus Warner,[23] a noted book collector who amassed a collection of about 900 Oriental manuscripts during his tenure in Istanbul. Currently, this biblical translation is housed in the Leiden University Library Levinus Warner collection, and it was probably commissioned to satisfy Warner's philological curiosity.

Another example of one of Eremia's Armeno-Turkish devotional works is a book of Christian sermons. Eremia drafted the sermons in 1679, and they survive in a single autograph copy found in the Mkhit'arean Monastery Manuscript Library of Vienna (W 408). A colophon in the manusucript explicitly states that Eremia prepared the sermon for his son Grigoris and that it is an abridged translation from an Armenian original. The colophon – which was written in Armenian – reads as follows: 'Testament of the crucifixion of our Lord Jesus Christ, translated into its Turkish epitome (*Türkî muhtasarî*) in 1679 by humble Eremia of Byzantium at the request of his son, master Grigoris'.[24]

Grigoris was born in 1658 and thus he would have been about twenty-one years old at the time he received this manuscript. At that point he would have been a friar (*abełay*) but not yet granted the learned rank of *vardapet*. We know this because, in 1680, Eremia and his father Martiros applied to the Catholicos at Ējmiatsin and requested that he make Grigoris a *vardapet*. The Catholicos rejected the petition, however, because he was too young, saying that 'he is a boy and a new friar'.[25] In the following years Grigoris would be a very mobile student. He spent time at the Armash Monastery near Izmit, which Grigor Daranałts'i had helped to establish at the turn of the century, as well as in Izmir, and finally Ējmiatsin. It is unclear whether or not he brought this book of sermons along with him on his travels.

What purpose would this manuscript have served for the young friar Grigoris? A mere glance at the manuscript's third sermon reveals that the text is a mixture of Armenian and Armeno-Turkish which would have been utterly incomprehensible and unusable for anyone but a bilingual. Here is a transcription and English translation of a passage about the Christ child with Armenian portions in italics, both in the transcription and translation:

> Onay geore Melkon, Kasbar, Bağbasar padaşhler buncay asker ile kymetli peşkeşler ile lanazir niazler ile gelup secde eylediler *zmayrn yev zvortin miadzin paravorein*. Onay geore krk günlug *dacar*e geoturdugi zeman fakir kocaman Simeon alıb kucağıne çoz benım canımı bu natuvan tenımden. *Art artzagea zdzarays ko der ěsd pani kum i khagagutün, loys yaydnetsar hetanosats yev park jogovrtots* nur izhar oldun putperestlere ki sanay iman getirecek dırlar demegile ol sahet *surp Mariam Asdvadzadzin'ın* ayağıne duşub olmesi var dır Simeon *dzeruni*. Onay geore Mısıre gitdigi zeman bir karının evine kondukleri gibi karıdır alıb kucağıne ...
>
> ... the kings Melchior, Caspar and Balthazar, with many soldiers, with valuable gifts, [and] with matchless prayers came and prostrated themselves. *They were honouring the mother and [her] only begotten son.* Accordingly, when [after a] forty day [period] they brought [him] to the *temple*, poor large Simeon embraced [him], saying 'unfasten my soul from this weak body of mine. *Now Lord, release your servant in peace, in accordance with your word. You cast light on the pagans and glory on the people*'. 'You cast light on the pagans, that they might bring faith to you'. At that hour, Simeon *the old man* fell at the feet of *Holy Mary, Mother of God*, and died. Accordingly, when they went to Egypt, since they lodged in the house of an old woman, the woman embraced [Jesus] ...[26]

This passage embellishes the biblical stories of the 'three Magi', the 'Presentation of Jesus at the Temple' and the 'Flight to Egypt' with apocryphal traditions. Of course, the story of the three kings is biblical (Matthew 2: 1–12), but the names are not mentioned in the Bible. Rather, the names Melchior, Caspar and Balthazar come from a much later Greek tradition. The story of Simeon is biblical, appearing in Luke 2: 25–35. Eremia, in fact, quotes the Armenian version of verses Luke 25: 29 and Luke 25: 32, while skipping over the intermediate verses. The ending of this passage – about the woman caretaker in Egypt – is non-biblical, deriving from apocryphal traditions.

As this passage shows, Eremia uses Armenian terminology even when writing Turkish, such as the Armenian words 'temple' and 'old man', as well as the epithets for the Virgin Mary. Moreover, passages from the Bible are often quoted directly from the orginal, sometimes with the Turkish translation next to it. Looking at the sermon as a whole it is clear that most of the text is written in a similar hybrid language, though sometimes Eremia departs from writing in Turkish entirely. For example, he provides a poem of rejoicing written entirely in Armenian.[27]

Overall, this is a work written for use by a bilingual priest who preached to Turkophone Armenians. Those Turkophone Armenians would not have been completely culturally illiterate. They would have had a basic Armenian vocabulary, a knowledge of some verses of scripture and a receptivity to Armenian poems and song. That is to say, they were used to hearing Armenian terms, verses and songs in church, while nonetheless using Turkish as their primary language for communication. This situation is comprehensible to anyone who has been to an American synagogue, where most worshippers would know a fair bit of Hebrew vocabulary, song and prayer, without being able to communicate in Hebrew.

There are other examples of devotional works translated into Armeno-Turkish by Eremia, such as a book of hagiography currently housed in the St James Manuscript Library of the Armenian Patriarchate of Jerusalem (J 1076).[28] Eremia prepared the text in 1685 on his visit to Ējmiatsin, and like the above-mentioned sermons, it was also for his son Grigoris, who had by this time become a *vardapet*.[29] Together these two manuscripts suggest the highly personal nature of Eremia's translation projects, usually aimed at a particular person – like Grigoris – and with a very clear sense of the broader audience or context in which they would be used – such as Grigoris's congregation. Just as Apro Çelebi's interests shaped Eremia's Armenian corpus, Eremia's son's and friends' needs often determined his choices of texts for translation into Armeno-Turkish.

Eremia's 'secular' translations

Eremia's second group of translations are 'secular' – by which I merely mean that their primary purpose was education or entertainment, not devotion. It is likely that Eremia generally translated secular works for a different audience than his devotional works: Muslim intellectuals. This is made clear by three pieces of evidence: censorship of the primary text, 'pure' Ottoman Turkish vocabulary that is not mixed with Armenian words and phrases as in the sermons described above, and even precise identification of one work's target audience.

An example of one of Eremia's 'secular' translations is of a fifteenth-century French romance, the *History of Vienna and Paris*.[30] The history's title refers to the work's main characters, a princess and a knight, named Vienna and Paris. The romance was translated into Armenian by a certain Yovhannes Terznts'i at the end of the sixteenth century,[31] and it was subsequently translated into Armeno-Turkish by Eremia. Later it was published in 1871. The book's description reads as follows:

> Hikeayei Faris ve Vena, teelif olunmuş latin lisanında ve terceme olunmuş hay lisanına, bir ehli mearif zat marifetiyle, Homeros istillahi ile, ve tekrar terceme olunmuş lisani türkiye, mevzun ve mukaffa (*vodavor vociv*) olarak, Eremia Çelebi Kömürceants marifetiyle, ol ki müellif dakhi tesmiye olunmuş dur, okuyan ikhfane, sefabakhş eylence olmak içün.

> The Story of Paris and Vienna, [which was] written in the Latin language and translated into the Armenian language in Homeric style by the skill of a learned man. It was translated again into the Turkish language in verse and rhyme by the skill of Eremia Çelebi Kömürcean – who was named the author – in order to be pleasant entertainment for reading friends.[32]

From this description we learn explicitly that Eremia did not translate from the romance's original version, but rather from the Armenian translation, and that the work was intended to be 'pleasant entertainment'. Eremia's intentions as an author varied widely depending on the work. Often he was a serious historian, poet, pedagogue and polemicist, but he also had his light-hearted side. Here it seems that his intent was to entertain friends at a gathering, or perhaps at the local coffee house.[33]

Melikʻ-Ohanjanyan provides a detailed comparison of Eremia's Armeno-Turkish version with its Armenian original. Firstly, he was able to postulate which Armenian manuscript Eremia used as his source by noting variation in the Armenian manuscript tradition and observing which variation Eremia followed in his translation.[34] Thereafter, he proceeds to consider the degree to which Eremia's Turkish version can really be considered a 'translation'. He answers that it was not a literal translation according to the modern sense of the term, nor even a free translation, but rather an adaptation with significant variation from the original. That is to say, we must consider the Armeno-Turkish text to be a new version.

The differences between the Armenian and Turkish versions begin on the structural level. While the Armenian original had 577 stanzas and 2,308 lines, the Turkish version had 549 stanzas and 2,196 lines, as well as a completely new division system among the chapters.[35] Thus Eremia reorganised the work; but to what end? According to Melikʻ-Ohanjanyan he intervened in two significant ways. Firstly, 'he shortened or edited carefully all that which carried a purely Christian nature and could have left an undesirable impression in the Islamic world'.[36] And secondly, 'he shortened or expounded in brief those sections which the Armenian "translator" had introduced into the French original according to his project of nationalisation and localization'.[37]

That is to say, both the original and its Armenian translation had Christian devotional passages, while the Armenian translation had amendations for an Armenian audience that had not been present in the original. Eremia strove to both de-Christianise and to de-Armenise the work in his Armeno-Turkish version. Thus he created a text that was substantially different from both the original and the intermediary Armenian translation, aimed for consumption in the Islamic world. Since we know that Eremia could compose freely for Armenians without such censorship, his interventions strongly suggest that he translated the *History of Vienna and Paris* for a Muslim audience, in stark contrast to his devotional translations.

If Eremia's audience was indeed Muslim, it begs questions about both the more precise identity of the intended recipient and the process of reading. At this time period in the Ottoman Empire a broad popular reading audience of printed works did not yet exist, so it is probable that the work was not prepared for an anonymous broad audience, but rather for some of Eremia's personal Muslim friends – who are referred to as his 'reading friends'. It is unclear, however, whether or not these imagined Muslim readers learned the Armenian alphabet and read the book themselves or whether or not they had it read to them by an Armenian, perhaps by Eremia himself.

As evidence to support the former possibility, we know that in the nineteenth century some Muslim intellectuals would learn the Armenian alphabet in order to read Armeno-Turkish. An alphabet primer book published in 1892, misleadingly entitled *A Method for Reading Armenian in Four Days for [People] Who Know Ottoman Turkish*,[38] was written in Ottoman Turkish by a Muslim named Ahmed Muhtâr. He explicitly writes that 'this book is for those wanting to read newspapers, illustrated weekly pamphlets, novels, etc. which were written, printed and published in Turkish with Armenian letters'.[39] Muhtâr even wrote a note in Western Armenian asking pardon if any Armenian found a spelling mistake, as he was a 'foreigner',[40] that is, Muslim. Thus we know that Muslim intellectuals were learning the Armenian alphabet in order to follow the vibrant Armeno-Turkish print culture of nineteenth-century Istanbul. On the other hand, this motivation to read printed works did not yet exist in the seventeenth century, as no book had yet been printed in Armeno-Turkish and manuscripts were a rare commodity. Eremia's manuscript would more likely have been read – or perhaps sung – aloud.

Another example of one of Eremia's extended prose translations from Armenian into Armeno-Turkish is his version of Moses Khorenats'i's *History of the Armenians*.[41] In this instance, the audience is not speculative, but rather we know from a separate primary source that Eremia prepared the work for Muslims interested in ancient Armenian history. In the eighteenth century the great Istanbul-Armenian historian Ch'amch'ean wrote that '[Eremia] translated a history compiled from Khorenats'i at the request of learned Turks into their language, [and] with it also concise information on the Bagratunis and the Ṙubenids'.[42] As Ch'amch'ean noted, the work is not solely a translation, as Eremia appends the work with discussion of the Bagratunis and the Ṙubenids, dynasties which ruled in the ninth through eleventh and eleventh through fourteenth centuries CE, respectively, periods outside the scope of Khorenats'i's work. This history is currently housed in the Mkhit'arean Monastery Manuscript Library of Venice (V 411).

Putting aside the sections on the Bagratunis and the Ṙubenids, it is evident that even in the history's first parts the Armeno-Turkish translation does not formally correspond with Khorenats'i's original. For example, Eremia skips the proemium and first chapters of Khorenats'i's history and jumps to the fifth chapter to begin his work with the genealogy of Hayk[43] (see Figure 6.1). Eremia's work really is a compilation or abridgement, not a complete translation.

Let us proceed to a direct transcription and translation of a segment of Eremia's work that does overlap in content with Moses Khorenats'i, in order to see how the translation relates to its original source. Here is a section discussing how Hayk, the eponymous founder of the first Armenian kingdom, refused to be subject to Bēl (Nemrut) and travelled with his family to the Land of Ararat:

> ... ve Nemrut muti olmayub Armaneag evladi doğdukden sonray evladi ve evladi evladi ile 300 nefer ve yanaşme ve kul carie ve kul ve cariesi evladi ile ve emvali ile esgi Bağdad semtından çkub şmal tarafıne gelub Ararad dağı demeg ile Tevratde marufdır ki Nuhın gemisi orade yanaşdi ol deare Nakhçivan dimeg lisani Ermenean ilk menzil tabir olunur. Ol Ararad dağın eteginde ve ovasınde durakler ve mekeanler ebna edub Hayg ve Armaneagın oğli Gatmuse virdi ve Armaneage dakhi konakler yapti ve kendi bir ükseg ovaye dakhi mekean tutub bir kasaba yapıb kendi namında Haygabad kaldi ve birez makhluk ki perakendeden ol semte suluk etmişler idi onlari dakhi musekher eyledi. Nemrut khalifelığınde metin ve sahib kadem işidub Haygın khanadanlığını hased idub adem göndurub ne aceb ol şımel tarafın sovuklığıne suluk idub durak tutdun elbete ol senın sovuk ğurur meşrebını gelub bize ısıtdırasın ve benım memleketımde begendığın yerde teskin olub bize muti olasın didi

> ... and [Hayk] was not obedient to Nemrut. After his son Aramaneak was born, with his son and grandson and with 300 men and hirelings and slaves and concubines and with the children of his slaves and concubines and with [their] property they departed from the neighbourhood of old Baghdad and came to the north, called Mt Ararat, known in the Hebrew Testament as [the place of] Noah's boat. He approached that land called Nakhchivan, which means 'halting place' in the Armenian language. At the foot of Mt

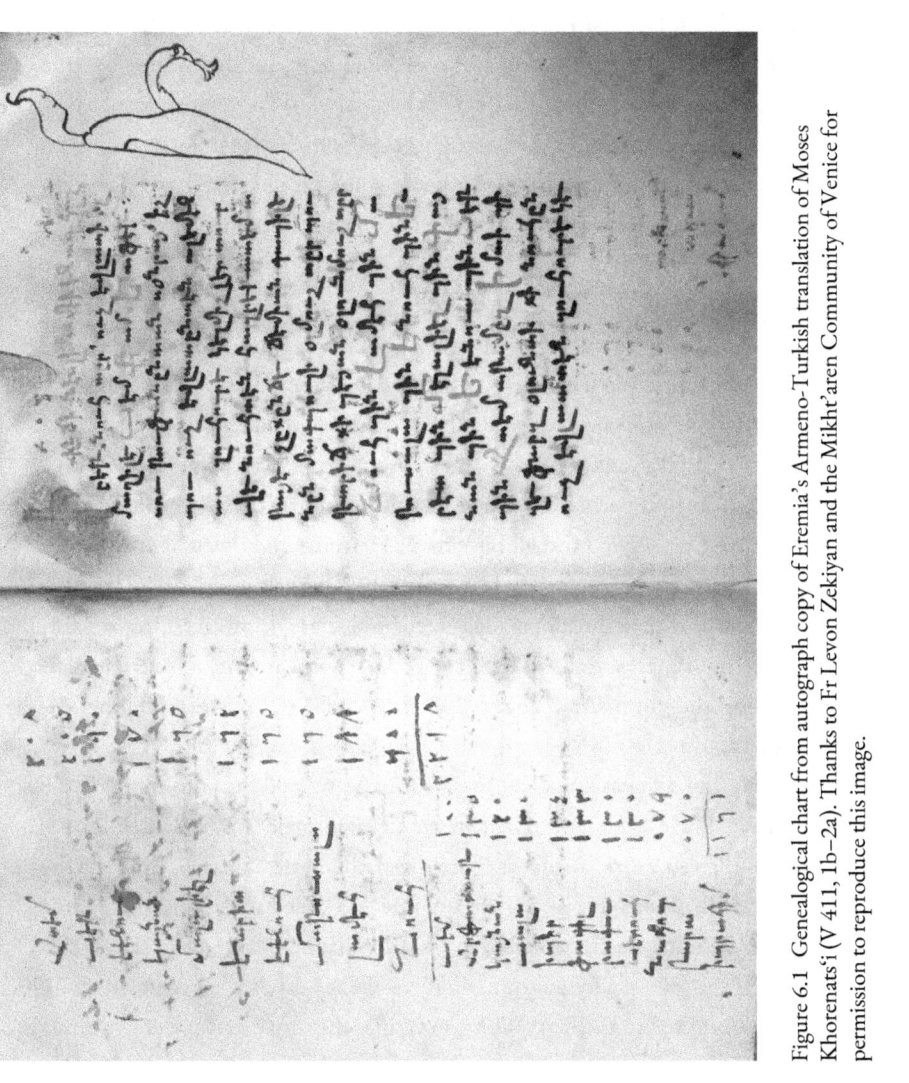

Figure 6.1 Genealogical chart from autograph copy of Eremia's Armeno-Turkish translation of Moses Khorenats'i (V 411, 1b–2a). Thanks to Fr Levon Zekiyan and the Mikht'aren Community of Venice for permission to reproduce this image.

Ararat and in the plain he built stations and abodes, and Hayk gave them to Armaneak's son Cadmos. For Armaneak he also built residences, and he himself settled a high plain and built a town. He called it after his own name, Haykabad. A few creatures who had been scattered in that district became his followers. He subdued them. In the Nemrut caliphate [they] heard [that Hayk was] strong and possessing good luck, and they became envious of Hayk's caliphate. They sent a man [who] said: 'How strange that you subject [yourself] to that northern cold and stay [there]. By all means, let that cold proud temperment of yours come, let us warm it up. Dwell in my country, in any place you like, and become subject to us'.[44]

This passage was based on parts of the tenth and eleventh chapters of Khorenats'i's history, which Robert W. Thomson translated as follows:

> But Hayk refused to submit to [Bēl], and after begetting his son Aramaneak in Babylon he journey [sic] to the land of Ararad, which is in the northern regions, with his sons and daughters and sons' sons, martial men about three hundred in number, and other domestic servants and the outsiders who had joined his service and all his effects. He came and dwelt at the foot of a mountain in a plain where had lingered and dwelt a few of the human race who had been previously scattered. These Hayk subjected to himself, and he built there a residence for the property and gave it in inheritance to Cadmos, the son of Aramaneak. This verifies the old unwritten tales mentioned above.
>
> He himself hastened, he says, with the rest of his entourage to the northwest. He came and dwelt in an elevated plain and called the name of the plateau *Hark'* – that is, here dwelt the fathers of the family of the house of T'orgom. He also built a village and called it after his own name Haykashēn. It is also recorded in this history that on the southern side of this plain at the foot of a long mountain there already dwelt a few men who willingly submitted to the hero. This too verifies the unwritten tales mentioned above...
>
> Continuing his narrative [Mar Abas Catina] says: When the Titan Bēl had confirmed his rule over everyone, he sent to the northern region to Hayk one of his sons with trustworthy men to bring him into obedience so they might live in peace. 'You have made your habitation,' he said, 'in the

icy cold; now warm and melt the freezing cold of your haughty conduct, submit to me and live in tranquillity in my empire wherever you please.'[45]

Comparison of my translation of Eremia's Turkish text with Thomson's direct translation from Khorenats'i reveals that in places Eremia's methodology approaches literal translation. Elsewhere Eremia follows Khorenats'i's wording more loosely, while sometimes he cuts out parts. Moreover, he does not even try to imitate Khorenats'i's high level of Classical Armenian in Ottoman Turkish. The result is indeed an 'abridged' translation, written in a colloquial Turkish that does not resemble the original version in register or length.[46] It is noteworthy that Eremia translates Armenian terminology into Islamicate equivalents. The city Haykashēn becomes Haykabad, with a Persian suffix instead of an Armenian one. Hayk's 'kingship' becomes a 'caliphate', Babylon becomes Baghdad and Hayk's opponent Bēl becomes Nemrut. This choice of vocabulary stands in stark contrast to Eremia's use of Armenian terms for basic words, like 'king' and 'temple', seen above in his Armeno-Turkish sermon. Here we see how he consciously chose different vocabulary depending on whether or not his audience was Christian or Muslim. Eremia also used Khorenats'i as a source for ancient Armenian history in other contexts. One manuscript contains a very brief Armenian history, covering exactly the same span of history as Eremia's Armeno-Turkish work, from Hayk to the Rubenids. Therein, Eremia offers only a single sentence in place of the above-quoted passage: 'Hayk came to the land of Ararat, which was named Hayastan; he it is, who killed Bēl'.[47]

It is possible to precisely identify at least one of those 'learned Muslims' who requested the translation from Eremia. In 1960 a Soviet Armenian scholar named A. N. Ter-Ḷevondyan wrote an article entitled 'Eremia Çelebi as one of the Sources for Müneccimbaşı'. Therein he argues that one of the 'learned Muslims' must have been the noted Ottoman historian Müneccimbaşı Ahmed Dede (1631–1702), as Müneccimbaşı was the first Ottoman intellectual to include a tract on ancient Armenian history in his writings on history. Ter-Ḷevondyan made this suggestion on the basis of indirect evidence, as he did not have access to the unpublished manuscript of Müneccimbaşı's Arabic-language universal chronicle, located at the Süleymaniye Manuscript Library in Istanbul,[48] or to Eremia's Armeno-Turkish translation. Instead he compared an Ottoman Turkish translation of Müneccimbaşı's Arabic work – which has still not been published in its entirety in the original – with one of Eremia's Armenian-language historical works, noting some common idiosyncracies. I have procured all pertinent original texts, and study of Müneccimbaşı's Arabic passage on ancient Armenian history confirms Ter-Ļevondyan's hypothesis that Müneccimbaşı used Eremia as a primary source, as the translation Ter-Ļevondyan used was indeed literal. This collaboration between Eremia and Müneccimbaşı proves that Eremia's Armeno-Turkish translations were sometimes prepared for a Muslim audience. Müneccimbaşı's Arabic history was translated into Ottoman Turkish in the eighteenth century and the Ottoman Turkish version was published in the nineteenth century.[49] Thanks to Eremia, Ottoman Muslim readers had access to stories about ancient Armenian history in multiple languages and formats for centuries. Thus we know that Eremia served as a conduit of information to Europeans about the Islamic world – as was the case with his geographical work – and to Muslim intellectuals in Istanbul about Christian history.[50]

Another example of one of Eremia's Armeno-Turkish translations of a 'secular' nature is his Armeno-Turkish history of Alexander the Great. It was written in prose and is currently housed in the Mkhit'arean Monastery Manuscript Library in Venice (V 473). The text's opening lines strongly imply a Muslim audience:

> Kitab hekeayei cihangir İskender Zuılkarniyn, lisan Ermeneanden lisan Turkçe tercumei est. Elhakir İremia.

> Book of the story of the world conquerer Alexander, the two-horned one. It is a translation from the Armenian language to the Turkish language. Your humble servant, Eremia.[51]

Even in this single sentence, Eremia demonstrates a clear inclination to use Islamic vocabulary and terminology. Eremia uses both Arabic (*Zulkarneyn*) and Persian (*cihangir*) epithets for Alexander and an Arabic statement of humility for himself (*el-hakir*). This usage was not merely superficial, as Eremia clearly knew of the Qu'ranic Alexander, 'the two-horned one',[52] which was a symbol with great significance in Ottoman Turkish discourses on the legitimacy of the sultanate.[53]

After this heading, the translation continues with a passage about the Egyptian sorcerer Nectanebo, whom the Romance claimed was the real father of Alexander, not Philip of Macedon:

> Zira Nihtanibus'i akhir padşah dirler. Anden sonra Mısır'ın saltaneti macusi cadulıgi ile cemian devletden usdun ve ileri olub ta ki terkibler ana munis oldiler. Şoyle ki bunun uzerıne gelen duşmen askeri için tabure yakhod asker çoklugıne yakhod kılıc ve silah mihimatıne mihim ve zahmet çekmez idi. Lakin kendusi pur polad olub khalvete girub legene su doldurub ve bal mumından gemiler ve ademler yapub ademleri gemilere koyub ve ol legende nefeslenub muherik olur idi ol mumden yapılan ademler. Zira Nihtanibus kendu khurmayi asa elınde butleri ve cinleri durme davet idicek legende olan gemiler sude üruyub ündukce ve ademleri tahrik etdıkce imdi ol dem Mısır uzerıne gelen duşmen gemileri ansız gayibden muharebe frtunayi azim ceng zuhur olub ol aralıkde hep gark ve helak olurler idi. İşbu macusi senaati kuveti ile anın saltaneti selamet uzre kalır idi bir zeman.

> They called Nectanebo [Latin spelling] the last king. By means of Zoroastrian witchcraft the Sultanate of Egypt became superior and surpassed all other states, so much so that they became obedient to him. Indeed, when faced with an invading enemy, he was not troubled by battalions or a host of soldiers or of swords and weapon provisions. Rather, he became filled with strength. He would retire to a private place and fill a basin with water. He would make ships and men from wax and put the men on the ships. Then he would breathe on the basin and cause them all to move about, those men made from wax. Nectanebo had a dark wand in his hand, and he would continually invite idols and demons. He would sink the boats in the basin and burn the men. At that very moment, a great storm would suddenly arise out of nowhere, and the enemy ships approaching Egypt would all be sunk and destroyed. With the power of Zoroastrian arts, for some time his authority remained in security.[54]

Eremia's translation was based on Pseudo-Callisthenes' *Historia Alexandri Magni*, for which there was already a long manuscript tradition in Armenian translation by Eremia's lifetime.[55] Leaving aside the content of the story – which would definitely have been of interest to Muslim intellectuals of early modern Istanbul given Alexander's importance for Ottoman political theory – it is clear from the language that Eremia's Alexander translation was likely made for a Muslim audience, like his version of Khorenats'i, as it is lacking in the linguistic and lexicographical hybridity that often characterised Armeno-Turkish works written for Christians. Muslim intellectuals had access to versions of the Alexander Romance in Islamicate languages, but it seems likely that Eremia's 'reading friends' wanted to hear the version of Alexander's life known to Armenians.

Among Eremia's translations, his rendition of the Alexander Romance and of Khorenats'i are of particular importance, because they represent long-form prose work that distinguish his writings in Armeno-Turkish from devotional aids and the medieval tradition of troubadour poetry. Whereas Eremia produced his translations in manuscript form, by the 1730s Istanbul would be a centre for book printing in Armeno-Turkish. Armeno-Turkish prose became a language of choice for anyone seeking to reach a broad audience of Armenian readers in the Ottoman Empire, particularly in Istanbul, in the eighteenth and nineteenth centuries.

Conclusion

In sum, Eremia produced multiple translations from Armenian into Armeno-Turkish prose. His translations can be divided roughly into two groups: his devotional translations, including translations from the Bible, hagiography and sermons; and his secular prose translations, such as his translations of Khorenats'i and the Alexander Romance. The first group sought to provide priests – like Eremia's own son – with aids for preaching and ministry, helping them to shore up Armenian religious identity in a multicultural urban environment. Meanwhile, the second group seems to have been aimed primarily at Muslim intellectuals, like Müneccimbaşı, providing an example of intellectual mutual interraction between Christians and Muslims at the level of high culture. In both instances, Eremia's translation initiative represents a critical moment in the history of Armeno-Turkish literature, because it was Eremia who first began writing extended Armeno-Turkish prose works in Istanbul, in contrast to the Armeno-Turkish poetic tradition of the medieval period. The production of diverse Armeno-Turkish prose works and translations would come to be one of the hallmarks of Western Armenian literary life in the eighteenth and nineteenth centuries.

Eremia's lifetime can be used as an important marker in the cultural history of Armenians in the Ottoman Empire. By the end of Eremia's life in 1695 the Western Armenian Diaspora in the Ottoman Empire had gone far in developing distinct patterns of settlement, cultural production and ecclesiastical governance. The Armenian Patriarchate of Constantinople had risen from being a minor ecclesiastical centre to having authority throughout the empire, thanks in part to the efforts of Eḷiazar of Antep supported by Apro and Eremia, reluctant though he may have been at times. While the Western Armenians' importance in church politics was rising, they were simultaneously engaged in linguistic experimentation, spearheaded by Eremia's development of Armeno-Turkish into a vehicle for extended prose composition. Overall and most importantly, Eremia was the first great Istanbul-Armenian author and intellectual. While many of his works were lost, some of them set precedents for trends that would reappear in the eighteenth century. Whereas at the turn of the century the Western Armenians had been a struggling group of refugees, by century's end they boasted a rich intellectual and literary life, prospering merchants like Ambakum and Apro, an influential ecclesiastical centre and a thriving new local culture that was branching off from its Anatolian roots in the Ottoman Empire's coastal cities.

The flow of refugees from Eastern Anatolia westward would continue throughout the seventeenth century, and it is only in the eighteenth century that the chaotic ecclesiastical and intracommunal politics of the Istanbul-Armenians began to stabilise. By the eighteenth century the infancy of this new Western Armenian Diaspora had come to an end, and its economic, intellectual and demographic clout had taken deep root. That society – like Eremia's corpus – existed at the crossroads of three traditions: those of medieval Armenia, the Islamic Ottoman Empire and the early modern Mediterranean. As the first great Istanbul-Armenian author and intellectual, Eremia began a tradition of Western Armenian letters that would thrive in the Ottoman capital until the empire's end.

Notes

1. See Hasmik Stepanyan, *Ermeni Harfli Türkçe Kitaplar ve Süreli Yayınlar Bibliyografyası (1727–1968)* (Istanbul: Turkuaz Yayınları, 2005), pp. 29–30.
2. For previous overviews of this topic, see E. Shütz, 'Jeremia Çelebi Türkische Werke (Zur Phonetik des Mittelosmanischen)', *Studia Turcica* (1971): 401–30; and Eremia Kʻeōmurchean, *Eremya Chelebi Kömürjian's Armeno-Turkish Poem: The Jewish Bride*, Andreas Tietze and Avedis K. Sanjian (trans.) (Wiesbaden: Harrassowitz, 1981). For a bibliography of some recent studies and transcriptions of Armeno-Turkish literature in the Ottoman Empire see Laurent Mignon, 'A Pilgrim's Progess: Armenian and Kurdish Literatures in Turkish and the Rewriting of Literary History', *Patterns of Prejudice* 48:2 (2014): 182–200.
3. See Rachel Goshgarian, 'Futuwwa in 13th-century Rum and Armenia: Reform Movements and the Managing of Multiple Allegiances in Medieval Anatolian Urban Centers on the Periphery of the Seljuk Sultanate', in A. C. S. Peacock and Sarah Nur Yıldız (eds), *The Seljuks of Anatolia: Court and Society in the Medieval Middle East* (London: I. B. Tauris, 2013), pp. 244–6.
4. Hasmik Stepʻanyan, *Hayataŕ tʻurkʻeren grakanutʻyunĕ* (Yerevan: Erevani Hamalsarani Hratarakchʻutʻyun, 2001), p. 36.
5. Stepʻanyan, *Hayataŕ tʻurkʻeren grakanutʻyunĕ*, p. 40.
6. See Hasmik Stepanyan, *Catalogue of Turkish Materials Written in Armenian Letters of Armenian Manuscripts and Turkish Manuscripts in Armenian Letters: Manuscripts from 'Matenadaran' in Yerevan and Mother See Holy St Echmiadzin* (Yerevan: National Academy of Sciences of Armenia Institute of Oriental Studies, 2008).
7. For an introduction to the Armeno-Kıpçak dialect and its literature, the following bibliography is recommended: Henryk Jankowski, 'Professor Edward Tryjarski', *Rocznik Orientalistyczny*, LVII 2 (2004): 5–17. See also Edroğan Altınkaynak, *Gregoryan Kıpçak Dil Yadigarları* (İstanbul: IQ Kültür Sanat Yayıncılık, 2006).
8. Eremia Kʻeōmurchean, *Eremya Chelebi Kömürjian's Armeno-Turkish Poem: The Jewish Bride*, Andreas Tietze and Avedis K. Sanjian (trans.) (Wiesbaden: Harrassowitz, 1981), p. 9.
9. Stepʻanyan, *Hayataŕ tʻurkʻeren grakanutʻyunĕ*, p. 46.
10. Ibid., pp. 44–5.
11. The diversity and richness of this literary tradition is evident from inspection of

Stepanyan, *Ermeni Harfli Türkçe Kitaplar ve Süreli Yayınlar Bibliyografyası (1727–1968)*.

12. For an English biography of his life, see Minas Nurikhan, *The Life and Times of the Servant of God, Abbot Mechitar, Founder of the Mechitarist Fathers* (Venice: St. Lazarus Island Press, 1915).
13. Sebouh David Aslanian, '"Prepared in the Language of the Hagarites": Abbot Mkhitar's 1727 Armeno-Turkish Grammar of Modern Western Armenian', *Journal of the Society for Armenian Studies* 25 (2016): 76.
14. See Eremia K'eōmurchean, *Ōragrut'iwn*, pp. 516–23, 565–6, 578–86 and 632–4.
15. Eremia K'eōmurchean, *Ōragrut'iwn*, p. 632.
16. Transcriptions of some of Eremia's other Armeno-Turkish poems can be found in Kevork Pamukciyan, *Ermeni Harfli Türkçe Metinler* (İstanbul: Aras, 2002), pp. 232–5.
17. Eremia K'eōmurchean, *Ōragrut'iwn*, 486–7.
18. Eremia K'eōmurchean, *Eremya Chelebi Kömürjian's Armeno-Turkish Poem: The Jewish Bride*.
19. K. A. Melik'-Ōhanjanyan, *Patmutiwn P'arēzi ew Vennayi* (Yerevan: Haykakan SSH Gitut'yunneri Akademiayi Hratarakch'ut'yun, 1966), p. 60.
20. M 1645, 119a.
21. A. Turgut Kut, "Ali Ufkî Bey ve Eserleri Hakkında," *Musiki Mecmuası* 332 (1977): 5.
22. Leiden University Library, Levinus Warner Codex 390, p. 200a.
23. Kut, pp. 14–15.
24. W 408, p. 94a.
25. Eremia K'eōmurchean, *Ōragrut'iwn*, p. xcviii.
26. W 408, pp. 80b–81b.
27. W 408, pp. 88a–88b.
28. For more about Armenian synaxaria, see Jean Mecerian, *Introduction à l'étude des Synaxaires Arméniens* (Bayreuth: Bulletin Arménologique, 1953).
29. Eremia K'eōmurchean, *Ōragrut'iwn*, p. lxiii.
30. Melik'-Ōhanjanyan, p. 37.
31. Melik'-Ōhanjanyan, p. 47.
32. Ibid., p. 58.
33. In his article on the romance of Vienna and Paris, Paola Mildonian refers to Yovhannes Terznts'i's Armenian version as an 'opera', and it seems that some of Eremia's poetic works might have been intended for musical performance. The

musical element of Eremia's corpus stands outside of this author's expertise, but it is being explored by the scholar and musician Mehmed Ali Sanlıkol, who is currently working on a musical rendition of Eremia's *The Jewish Bride*. See Paola Mildonian, 'L'Occidente fantastico. Note sulla tradizione orientale del "Paris e Vienna"', in *Studi medievali e romanzi in memoria di Alberto Limentani*, M. Eusebia (ed.) (Rome: Jouvence, 1990), pp. 101–22.

34. Melikʻ-Ōhanjanyan, p. 59.
35. Ibid., p. 61.
36. Ibid., p. 66.
37. Ibid.
38. Ahmed Muhtâr, '*Osmânlıca Bilenlere Dört Günde Ermenice Okumanın Usûlü* (İstanbul: Berberyan, 1892).
39. Ibid., p. 3.
40. Ibid.
41. Ayvazyan, 'Eremia Chʻelepi Kʻyomurchyani dzeṙagrakan zhaṙangutʻyunĕ', p. 356.
42. Chʻamchʻean III, p. 723.
43. Compare W 411, p. 1b with Khorenatsʻi, p. 74.
44. W 411, pp. 3b–4b.
45. Khorenatsʻi, pp. 85–6.
46. For the passage's Armenian original, see Moses Khorenatsʻi, *Movsēs Khorenatsʻi patmutʻiwn hayotsʻ*, M. Abeḷean and S. Yarutʻunean (eds) (Yerevan: Haykakan KhSH GA Hratarakchʻutʻyun, 1991), pp. 33–4.
47. M 72, pp. 123a–123b.
48. Süleymaniye Manuscript Library Nuruosmaniye 3171, pp. 112a–114b.
49. For the section on Armenian history see Müneccimbaşı Şeyh Ahmed Dede Efendi, *Sahaifü'l-ahbar* I, Ahmed Nedim (trans.) (Istanbul: Matbaa-i Amire, 1285/1868), pp. 652–62.
50. Recent research has highlighted both types of information exchanges. See John-Paul A. Ghobrial, *The Whispers of Cities: Information Flows in Istanbul, London, and Paris in the Age of William Trumbull* (Oxford University Press, 2013), and Cumhur Bekar, 'A New Perception of Rome, Byzantium and Constantinople in Hezarfen Huseyin's Universal History', Boğaziçi University MA Thesis (2011).
51. V 473, p. 1a.
52. Discussion of Alexander (*Zulkarneyn*) appears in verses 18: 83–18: 99 of the Qu'ran.

53. See Tursun Bey, *Târîh-i Ebü'l-Feth*, Mertol Tulum (ed.) (Istanbul: Baha, 1977), p. 3.
54. V 473, 1a–1b.
55. See Y. Tashean, *Usumnasirutʻiwnkʻ stoyn Kalistʻeneay varutsʻ Alekʻsandri* (Vienna: Mkhitʻarean tparan, 1892).

Conclusions: Legacies of the Great Armenian Flight

This book has argued that the Western Armenian Diaspora emerged in the coastal cities of the Ottoman Empire in the aftermath of the Great Armenian Flight. It was composed of diverse communities of Armenians – mostly descendants of the refugees of the seventeenth century – living in Western Anatolia, Istanbul and Thrace, places where there had been scant Armenian populations before the migrations. While the standardised Western Armenian literary language is a product of the nineteenth century, the populations that would embrace it as their modern literary language in Istanbul and Izmir had begun their distinct literary and cultural development long beforehand, in the seventeenth century, after a transfer of the centres of Armenian intellectual life from Eastern Anatolia to the coastal cities of the Ottoman Empire. The move is a story of urbanisation, as villagers and residents of provincial cities transformed Istanbul into the most important Armenian demographic and cultural centre in the world. The Armenians of Istanbul and other centres in the western parts of the Ottoman Empire would demand new kinds of Armenian and Armeno-Turkish literature. The new context created a different literary mood from that of the historic cultural centres of Eastern Anatolia, the South Caucasus and Cilicia, and this would lead to the rise of a literary tradition and translation movement aimed at meeting the needs of refugees and their descendants.

Grigor Daranalts‘i and Eremia K‘eōmurchean were two key architects of the new society that developed after the migrations. The former had been the fervent political leader of the first refugees, while the latter was Ottoman Istanbul's first prominent Armenian intellectual and author. In spite of their contributions to the settlement and intellectual life of the Western Armenian Diaspora, neither Grigor Daranałtsi nor Eremia Kʻeōmurchean are celebrated or remembered as having great significance among Armenians of the world today. Not a single street in Armenia is named after them, nor are their works studied in Armenian schools. Rather than having become Armenian national heroes, they have been relegated to sporadic study by Armenologists, without having entered into the Armenian national consciousness.

Part of the reason for this relates to the subsequent histories of their life works. While Chʻamchʻean seems to have had access to copies of some short draft pages of Grigor's chronicle in the eighteenth century,[1] Grigor's complete autograph copy languished unread in Rodosto for centuries until finally being transferred to Jerusalem, probably at the beginning of the nineteenth century. It was not accessible to a broad audience until Nshanean published it in 1915. Eremia's influence on subsequent generations of Armenian intellectuals was more mixed. After his death, his works were bequeathed to heirs whose lives did not facilitate the safe transmission of texts and, as already noted, some of Eremia's major works were lost.[2] Many others survived, but only in single manuscripts which never gained wide distribution. Many of them remain unpublished to this day in the libraries of Jerusalem, Venice, Vienna and Yerevan.

Nonetheless, other works of Eremia's were read and did become influential. Eremia was read by great eighteenth-century Armenian scholars such as Chʻamchʻean and Inchichean and thus his influence carried on into that century. Eremia's use of Armeno-Turkish as a vehicle for long-form prose works – seen in translations like his Alexander Romance and Khorenatsʻi history – was a precedent that would be repeated extensively.

Although Eremia was undeniably Ottoman Istanbul's first great native-born Armenian author and thinker, he is not celebrated as such by experts on Armenian history and literature. In the nineteenth and twentieth centuries the study of both Eremia and Grigor became merely a narrow domain within the field of Armenology, while neither were granted the status of 'great' Armenian authors, thinkers or political leaders. For example, in his noted *History of Armenian Literature*, Manuk Abełyan does not focus on either in his discussion of the seventeenth and eighteenth centuries. He was probably taking aim at them, however, when he wrote that

> In the period of rebirth [i.e., after the sixteenth century], history-writing, in a true sense, did not exist. Several [men] bearing that name are only artless describers of their time, or, of events which happened a little bit before them ... chiefly descriptions of exploitation and duress brought by foreigners. Those historians, in fact, cannot be a subject of literature, as much as they can serve as a source for research on history.[3]

Indeed, both Grigor's and Eremia's works have been used as sources for seventeenth-century history, but I have argued with a wealth of evidence that their significance is far greater than that of merely 'artless' source material.

How can we account for this contemporary neglect of two of the early modern Ottoman Empire's most important Armenian political leaders and thinkers? While the Western Armenian Diaspora came into being in the seventeenth century, it was not a static phenomenon. It quickly changed and developed. In the eighteenth century the rise of the Mkhit'arean Brotherhood in Venice played a critical role in the subsequent development of Western Armenian cultural life. Their efforts led simultaneously to an increased interest in ancient and medieval Armenian language and culture, while also deepening the cultural influence of Europe, as mediated by the Mkhit'areans through an influx of books and translations from French and Italian. While in the seventeenth century – and even into the eighteenth century – Islamic cultural life deeply influenced Armenian authors like Eremia in the Ottoman Empire, and the famed troubadour Sayat Nova in the Caucasus, in time European cultural influence would become more dominant in the sphere of high culture. When the Western Armenian literary language was finally standardised in the nineteenth century its inventors sought consciously to de-Turkify it: to create a national language which ripped much of the rich Islamicate vocabulary that authors like Grigor and Eremia had employed out of the Armenian language.

In short, Western Armenian cultural life was initially characterised by hybridity and deep engagement with the Muslim intellectual life of Ottoman Istanbul. But in the age of nationalism, authors and linguists sought to reshape the literary tradition and language in another direction, by embracing European genres and influence, while simultaneously creating a cleansed national language that could be conceived of as a 'pure' cultural form. After

1915 Armenian intellectual efforts shifted yet again to preserving memory of an Armenian homeland in what would become modern Turkey. The distinction between an ancient Armenian homeland in Eastern Anatolia and a more recent one in Istanbul, Izmir and Thrace was often lost. Since Armenian centres in Eastern Anatolia revived after the seventeenth century, it was possible to forget the traumas and impact of the seventeenth-century crisis on them, especially when the destruction of the early twentieth century was so much more complete.

In the aftermath of these cultural changes and dispersion caused by the Armenian Genocide, the writings of Grigor and Eremia – with their literary mixtures of Classical language and dialect, Armenian and Turkish – came to look very foreign, and perhaps even backward and 'artless'. While the Armenians of Rodosto had preserved memory of the Great Flight and celebrated Grigor's leadership into the twentieth century, after 1915 survivors of genocide had another mass dispersion to commemorate. As a result, a critical turning point in Armenian and Ottoman history has been overlooked and its literary relics largely ignored.

It has been the goal of this book to reorient the fields of Ottoman and Armenian history to the rise of the Western Armenian Diaspora in the early modern Ottoman Empire: the creative process by which a new Armenian culture formed in Ottoman coastal cities in the aftermath of a mass migration from the ancient and medieval cultural and demographic centres of Eastern Anatolia, the South Caucasus and Cilicia. This book has told the story of how Armenians arrived and became deeply integrated into social and intellectual life in the centre of Ottoman imperial culture, both contributing to it and also being shaped by it. These Armenian migrants changed Istanbul's demographic and cultural landscape, just as better-known migrants had done in previous centuries, namely Christians brought to Istanbul by Mehmed II and the Sephardic Jews. Throughout the eighteenth and nineteenth centuries Ottoman Armenian merchants, financiers (*sarraf*), authors, musicians, translators, printers and bureacrats would play key roles in Ottoman trade, art and and even governance – that is, in most spheres of the empire's economic and cultural life. This book has shown how their cosmopolitan world came into being, opening a vibrant new chapter in the long history of non-Muslims' contributions to Islamic civilisation.

Notes

1. A. A. Ut'uzyan, 'Grigor Daranalts'in M. Ch'amch'yani patmut'yan albyur', *Lraber Hasarakakan Gitut'yunneri* (1975/2): 81–9.
2. Eremia K'eōmurchean, *Eremia K'ēōmurchean patmut'iwn hamaṙōt DCH tariots' ōsmanean t'agaworats'n*, p. 18.
3. Manuk Abeḷyan, *Hayots' grakanut'yan patmut'yun* II, (Yerevan: Haykakan SSṘ Gitut'yunneri Akademiayi Hratarakch'ut'yun, 1946), pp. 441–2.

Bibliography

Ottoman Turkish Archival Sources

Prime Ministerial Archives, Istanbul
Rodosçuk Şer'iyye sicilleri (RŞS)
1530, 1538–55, 1570, 1576–9, 1583

Ottoman Turkish and Arabic Manuscripts

Leiden University Library, Leiden
Levinus Warner Codex 390
Süleymaniye Manuscript Library, Istanbul
Esad Efendi 2236
Nuruosmaniye 3171

Armenian and Armeno-Turkish Manuscripts

French National Library (Bibliothèque nationale de France), Paris (P)
Armenian Collection Manuscript 338
Mesrop Mashtots' Institute of Ancient Manuscripts (Matenadaran), Yerevan (M)
72, 1644, 1645, 1786, 1903, 2292, 9704
Mkhit'arean Monastery Manuscript Library, Venice (V)
411, 473
Mkhit'arean Monastery Manuscript Library, Vienna (W)
408
St James Manuscript Library of the Armenian Patriarchate, Jerusalem (J)
533, 988, 1069, 1076

Ottoman Turkish and Arabic Primary Sources (Printed)

'Abdülkâdir (Kadrî) Efendi, *Topçular Kâtibi 'Abdülkâdir (Kadrî) Efendi Tarihi (Metin ve Tahlîl)* I and II, ed. Ziya Yılmazer. Ankara: Türk Tarih Kurumu, 2003.

Anonim Tevârîh-i Âl-i Osman, ed. Nihat Azamat. İstanbul: Marmara Üniversitesi Yayınları, 1992.

Evliyâ Çelebi, *Evliyâ Çelebi Seyahatnâmesi* I and II, ed. Seyit Ali Kahraman, Yücel Dağlı and Robert Dankoff. İstanbul: Yapı Kredi Yayınları, 2011.

Evliyâ Çelebi, *An Ottoman Traveler: Selections from the Book of Travels of Evliya Çelebi*. London: Eland, 2010.

Islami, Agron, '1579 Numaralı Rodoscuk (Tekfurdağı) Şer'iyye Sicilinin Transkripsiyonu ve Değerlendirilmesi'. Sakarya University MA Thesis, 2010.

Kâtip Çelebi, *Fezleke-i Kâtip Çelebi* I. İstanbul: Ceride-i Havadis Matbaası, [1286] 1869–70.

Kâtip Çelebi, *Fezleke [Osmanlı Tarihi (1000–1065/1591–1655)*, Vols I–II, ed. Zeynep Aycibin. İstanbul: Çamlıca, 2016.

Kâtip Çelebi, *Kitâb-ı Cihânnümâ li-Kâtib Çelebi I*. Ankara: Türk Tarih Kurumu, 2009.

Kâtip Çelebi, *Târih-i Kostantiniyye ve Kayâsire*, ed. İbrahim Solak. Konya: Gençlik Kitabevi Yayınevi, 2009.

Kâtip Çelebi, *Fezleketü akvâli'l-ahyâr fî ilmi't-târîh ve'l-ahbâr (Fezleketü't-tevârîh): târîhu mülûki Âli 'Osmân*, ed. Seyyid Muhammed es-Seyyid. Ankara: Türk Tarihi Kurumu, 2009.

Koçi Bey, *Koçi Bey Risaleleri*, ed. Seda Çakmakçıoğlu. İstanbul: Kabalcı Yayınevi, 2007.

Lütfi Paşa, *Tevârih-i Âli Osman*, ed. Âli Bey. İstanbul: Matbaa-yi Âmire, [1341] 1925.

Muhtâr, Ahmed, *Osmanlıca Bilenlere Dört Günde Ermenice Okumanın Usûlü*. İstanbul: Berberyan, 1892.

Müneccimbaşı Ahmed Dede, *Sahaifü'l-ahbar* I–III, trans. Ahmed Nedim. Istanbul: Matbaa-i Amire, [1285] 1868.

Mustafa Ali, *Künhü'l-Ahbâr: Fatih Sultan Mehmed Devri, 1451–1481*. Ankara: Türk Tarihi Kurumu Basımevi, 2003.

Naili, Pertev, *Köroğlu Destanı*. İstanbul: Evkaf Matbaası, 1931.

Oruç Beğ, *Oruç Beğ Tarihi*, ed. Necdet Öztürk. İstanbul: Çamlıca, 2008.

Sâfî, Mustafa, *Zübdetü't-Tevârîh'i*, ed. İbrahim Hakkı Çuhadar. Ankara: Türk Tarih Kurumu, 2003.

Şahin, Mehmet, *Kuyucu Murad Paşa'nın Celali seferi mühimmesi (1607)*. İstanbul University MA Thesis, 2002.
Schütz, Edmond (ed.), *An Armeno-Kipchak Chronicle on the Polish-Turkish Wars in 1620–1621*. Budapest: Akademiai Kiado, 1968.
Selânikî Mustafa Efendi, *Tarih-i Selânikî* I–II, ed. Mehmet İpşirli. Ankara: Türk Tarih Kurumu, 1999.
Şems-ed-dîn Receb-üs Sıvâsî, *Hidâyet Yıldızı: Şems-ed-dîn-i Sıvâsî Hazretlerinin Menkıbeleri*. İstanbul: Seçil Ofset, 2000.
Tursun Bey, *Târîh-i Ebü'l-Feth*, ed. Mertol Tulum. Istanbul: Baha, 1977.
Vartan Paşa, *Akabi Hikyayesi: İlk Türkçe Roman, 1851*, ed. Andreas Tietze. İstanbul: Eren, 1991.

Armenian Primary Sources (Printed)

Abraham Kretatsʻi, *Abraham Kretatsʻi patmutʻyun*, ed. N. K. Ḷorḷanyan. Yerevan: Haykakan SSH GA Hratarakchʻutʻyun, 1973.
Abraham Kretatsʻi, *Chronicle of Abraham of Crete*, trans. George A. Bournoutian. Costa Mesa: Mazda Publishers, 1998.
Agatʻangeḷos, *History of the Armenians*, trans. R. W. Thomson. Albany, NY: State University of New York Press, 1976.
Akinean, Nersēs, 'Taḷ Araratsʻotsʻ', *Handēs Amsōreay* (1937): 328–38.
Alishan, Ḷ. (ed.), *Hayapatum*. Venice: S. Ḷazar, 1901.
Aṙakʻel Davrizhetsʻi, *Aṙakʻel Davrizhetsʻi girkʻ patmutʻeantsʻ*, ed. L. A. Khanlaryan. Yerevan: Haykakan Khah GA Hratarakchʻutʻyun, 1990.
Aṙakʻel Davrizhetsʻi, *Aṙakʻel of Tabriz: Book of History*, trans. George A. Bournoutian. Costa Mesa: Mazda Publishers, 2010.
Chʻamchʻyantsʻ, Mikʻayel, *Mikʻayel Chʻamchʻyantsʻ hayotsʻ patmutʻyun (skzbitsʻ minchʻev 1784 tʻvakanĕ)*, Vols I–III. Yerevan: Erevani Hamalsarani Hratarakchʻutʻyun, 1984–5.
Eremia Kʻeōmurchean, *Govabanutʻiwn tnōrinakan teḷeatsʻ yErusaḷēm*. Istanbul: Kʻeōmyurchean, 1678.
Eremia Kʻeōmurchean, *Eremia Chʻēlēpi Kʻeōmurchean Stampoloy patmutʻiwn*, ed. Vahram Y. Tʻorgomean. Vienna: Mkhitʻarean Tparan, 1913.
Eremia Kʻeōmurchean, 'Eremia Chʻēlēpioy gandz ew oḷb i veray Yakob Katʻoḷikosi', ed. Mesrop Nshanean. *Handēs Amsōreay* (1933): 589–95.
Eremia Kʻeōmurchean, *Ōragrutʻiwn Eremia Chʻēlēpi Kʻeōmurcheani*, ed. Mesrop Nshanean. Jerusalem: Tparan Srbotsʻ Yakobeantsʻ, 1939.
Eremia Kʻeōmurchean, 'Eremia Chʻelepi Kʻyomurchyani mi antip poemĕ', ed. H. S. Sahakyan. *Banber Matenadarani* 6 (1962): 409–27.

Eremia Kʻeōmurchean, *Eremya Chelebi Kömürjian's Armeno-Turkish Poem 'The Jewish bride'*, trans. Andreas Tietze and Avedis K. Sanjian. Wiesbaden: Harrassowitz, 1981.

Eremia Kʻeōmurchean, *Eremia Kʻēōmurchean patmutʻiwn hamaṙōt DCH tariotsʻ ōsmanean tʻagaworatsʻn*, ed. Zh. M. Avetisyan. Yerevan: Haykakan SSṘ GA Hratarakchʻutʻyun, 1982.

Eremia Kʻeōmurchean, *İstanbul Tarihi: XVII. Asırda İstanbul*, trans. Hrand D. Andreasyan. Istanbul: Eren, 1988.

Eremia Kʻeōmurchean, *Patmutʻiwn hrakizman Kostondnupolsoy (1660 tarwoy)*, ed. G. Bampukʻchean. Istanbul: Sholakatʻ, 1991.

Grigor Daranaltsʻi, *Zhamanakagrutʻiwn Grigor vardapeti Kamakhetsʻwoy kam Daranaltsʻwoy*, ed. Mesrop Nshanean. Jerusalem: Tparan Aṙakʻelakan Atʻoṙoy S. Yakobeantsʻ, 1915.

Hakobyan, Tʻ. Kh., Melikʻ-Bakhshyan, S.T. and H. Kh. Barselyan (eds), *Hayastani ew harakitsʻ shrjanneri telanunneri baṙaran* II and IV. Yerevan: Yerevani Hamalsarani Hratarakchʻutʻyun, 1988/1998.

Hakobyan, V. A., *Manr zhamanakagrutʻyunner XIII–XVIII darer*. I and II. Yerevan: Haykakan SSṘ Gitutʻyunneri Akademiayi Hratarakchʻutʻyun, 1951/1956.

Hakobyan, V. A., *17 dari hayeren dzeṙagreri hishatakaranner I–III*. Yerevan: Haykakan SSṘ Gitutʻyunneri Akademiayi Hratarakchʻutʻyun: 1974/1978/1984.

Inchichean, Lukas, *Amaṙanotsʻ Biwzandean*. Venice: S. Lazzaro, 1794.

Inchichean, Lukas, *Boğaziçi Sayfiyeleri*. Istanbul: Eren, 2002.

Manandyan, Hakob, and Hrachʻya Achaṙyan. *Hayotsʻ nor vkaneṙě: 1155–1843*. Ējmiatsin: Tparan Mayr Atʻoṙoy S. Ējmiatsin, 1903.

Martiros Lrimetsʻi, *Martiros Lrimetsʻi: Usumnasirutʻyun ew bnagrer*, ed. A. A. Martirosyan. Yerevan: Haykakan SSṘ GA Hratarakchʻutʻyun, 1958.

Matthew Uṙhayetsʻi, *The Chronicle of Matthew of Edessa*, trans. Ara Edmond Dostourian. Lanham, MD: University Press of America, 1993.

Mkrtchʻyan, Manik, *Hay mijnadaryan pandkhtutʻyan taler (XV–XVIII darer)*. Yerevan: Haykakan SSH GA Hratarakchʻutʻyun, 1979.

Moses Korenatsʻi, *History of the Armenians*, trans. Robert W. Thomson. Cambridge, MA: Harvard University Press, 1978.

Moses Korenatsʻi, *Movsēs Khorenatsʻi patmutʻiwn hayotsʻ*, ed. M. Abelean and S. Yarutʻunean. Yerevan: Haykakan KhSH GA Hratarakchʻutʻyun, 1991.

Nerses Mokatsʻi, *Banasteltsutʻyunner*, ed. A. G. Dolukhanyan. Yerevan: Haykakan SSH GA Hratarakchʻutʻyun, 1975.

Ōrmanean, Malakʻia, *Azgapatum* I–IV. Ējmiatsin: Mayr Atʻoṙ S. Ējmiatsin, 2001–2.

Pʻawstos Buzandatsʻi, *The Epic Histories Attributed to Pʻawstos Buzand (Buzandaran patmutʻiwnkʻ)*, trans. Nina G. Garsonian. Cambridge, MA: Harvard University Press, 1989.

Sahakyan, Hasmik (ed.), *Hay ashulner (XVII–XVIII darer)*. Yerevan: Haykakan SSṚ GA Hratarakchʻutʻyun, 1961.

Sevan, Sevda, *Ṙodosto, Ṙodosto . . .*, trans. Margarit Tʻerzyan. Yerevan: Sovetakan Groḷ, 1989.

Shnorhali, Nerses, *Yisus ordi*. Yerevan: Apolon Hratarakchʻutʻyun, 1991.

Simēon Lehatsʻi, *Simēon dpri Lehatsʻwoy ulegrutʻiwn*, ed. Nersēs Akinean. Vienna: Mechitharisten, 1936.

Simēon Lehatsʻi, *The Travel Accounts of Simēon of Poland*, trans. George A. Bournoutian. Costa Mesa: Mazda Publishers, 2007.

Sruandzteantsʻ, Garegin, *Tʻoros Aḷbar*, Vol. II. Istanbul: G. Baḷtatlean, 1884.

Sruandzteantsʻ, Garegin, *Erker* I–II. Yerevan: Haykakan SSH GA Hratarakchʻutʻyun, 1982.

Tʻovma Metsopʻetsʻi, *Tʻovma Metsobetsʻiʻs History of Tamerlane and his Successors*, trans. Robert Bedrosian. New York: Sources of the Armenian Tradition, 1987.

Tʻovma Metsopʻetsʻi, *Tʻovma Metsopʻetsʻi patmagrutʻyun*, ed. L. Khachʻikean. Yerevan: Magaḷatʻ, 1999.

Vardan Areweltsʻi, *Ashkharhatsʻoytsʻ Vardanay vardapeti*, ed. Hayk Pērpērean. Paris: Arakʻs, 1960.

Yakob Karnetsʻi, *Erzeroum ou Topographie de la Haute Armenie: Texte Armenien de Hakovb Karnetsi (XVII Siècle)*, ed. K. Kostaneants and M. Frederic Macler. Paris: Imprimerie Nationale, 1919.

Yovhannēs Kamenatsʻi, *Patmutʻyun paterazmin Khotʻinu*, ed. H. Asasyan. Yerevan: Haykakan SSṚ GA Hratarakchʻutʻyun, 1964.

Zakʻaria Aguletsʻi, *Zakʻaria Aguletsʻu ōragrutʻyunĕ*, ed. S. V. Ter-Avetisyan. Yerevan: Armfani Hratarakchʻutʻyun, 1938.

Zakʻaria Aguletsʻi, *Journal of Zakʻaria of Agulis*, trans. George A. Bournoutian. Costa Mesa: Mazda Publishers, 2003.

Zakʻaria Kʻanakʻeṙtsʻi, *The Chronicle of Deacon Zakʻaria of Kʻanakʻeṙ*, trans. George A. Bournoutian. Costa Mesa: Mazda Publishers, 2004.

Zakʻaria Kʻanakʻeṙtsʻi, *Patmutʻiwn: Kondak surb ukhtin Yohannu Vanitsʻ*, ed. Armen Virabyan. Yerevan: Heḷinakayin Hratarakutʻyun, 2015.

Greek Primary Sources (Printed)

Bekkerus, Immanuel (ed.), *Historia Politica et Patriarchica Constantinopoleos, Corpus Scriptorum Historiae* 28. Bonn: Impensis, 1849.

Chalkokondyles, Laonikos, *Historiarum Demonstrationes*, ed. E. Darko. Budapest: Hungarian Academy of Letters, 1922.

Chalkokondyles, Laonikos, *A Translation and Commentary of the 'Demonstration of Histories' (Books I–III)*, trans. Nicolaos Nicoloudis. Athens: St. D. Basilopoulos, 1996.

Chalkokondyles, Laonikos, *Laonikos Chalkokondyles: The Histories* (2 vols), trans. Anthony Kaldellis. Cambridge, MA: Harvard University Press Dumbarton Oaks Medieval Library, 2014.

Crusius, Martin, *Turcograecia*. Basel: Leonardum Ostenium, 1584.

Dositheos of Jerusalem, *Historia peri tōn en Hierosolymois Patriarcheusantōn*. Bucharest, 1715.

Kritovoulos, *History of Mehmed the Conqueror*, trans. Charles T. Rigg. Princeton: Princeton University Press, 1954.

Kritovoulos, *Critobuli Imbriotae Historiae*, ed. Diether Roderich Reinsch. Berlin: W. de Gruyter, 1983.

Kritovoulos, *Kritoboulou tou Imbriou Historia: Eisagōgē-Metaphasē-Scholia*, ed. Diether Roderich Reinsch and Foteini Kolovou. Athens: Kanaki, 2005.

Kritovoulos, *Kritovulos Tarihi: 1451–1467*, trans. Ari Çokona. Istanbul: Heyamola Yayınları, 2012.

Nikodēmos o Agioreitēs, *Neon marturologion: ētoi marturia tōn theophanōn marturōn tōn meta tēn alōsin tēs Kōnstantinoupoleōs kata diaphorous kairous kai topous marturēsantōn*. Athens: F. Karampini and K. Vafa, 1856.

Papasynadinos, *Conseils et Memoires de Synadinos, Pretre de Serres en Macedoine (XVIIe Siècle)*, ed. Paolo Odorico. Paris: Pierre Belon, 1996.

Philippides, Marios (trans.), *Emperors, Patriarchs, and Sultans of Constaninople, 1373–1513: An Anonymous Greek Chronicle of the Sixteenth Century*. Brookline, NY: Hellenic College Press, 1990.

Philippides, Marios (trans.). *Byzantium, Europe, and the Early Ottoman Sultans, 1373–1513: An Anonymous Greek Chronicle of the Seventeenth Century (Codex Barberinus Graecus 111)*. New Rochelle, NY: A. D. Caratzas, 1990.

Zoras, G. T. (ed.). *Chronikon Peri tōn Tourkōn Soultanōn*. Athens: The Department of Byzantine and Neo-Hellenic Philology of the University of Athens, 1958.

Turkish Secondary Literature

Akdağ, Mustafa, *Türk Halkının Dirlik ve Düzenlik Kavgası: Celâlî İsyanları*. Istanbul: Yapı Kredi, 2009.

Altınkaynak, Edroğan, *Gregoryan Kıpçak Dil Yadigarları*. Istanbul: IQ Kültür Sanat Yayıncılık, 2006.

Andreasyan, Hrand D., 'Bir Ermeni Kaynağına Göre Celâlî İsyanları', *Tarih Dergisi* 17–18 (1962-3): 27–42.

Andreasyan, Hrand D., 'Abaza Mehmed Paşa', *Tarih Dergisi* 13 (1967): 131–42.

Andreasyan, Hrand D., 'Eremya Çelebi'nin Yangınlar Tarihi', *Tarih Dergisi* 27 (1973): 59–84.

Andreasyan, Hrand D., 'Celâlilerden Kaçan Anadolu Halkının Geri Gönderilmesi', *İsmail Hakkı Uzunçarşılı'ya Armağan*. Ankara: Türk Tarih Kurumu, 1976.

Arslantaş, Nuh and Yaron Ben-Naeh (eds), *Anonim Bir İbranice Kroniğe Göre 1622–1624 Yıllarında Osmanlı Devleti ve İstanbul*. Ankara: Türk Tarih Kurumu, 2014.

Ateş, Hacer, 'Kuzey Marmara Sahilleri ve Ard Alanında Şehirleşmenin Tarihi Süreci: XVI.–XVII. Yüzyıllarda Tekirdağ ve Yöresi'. Istanbul University Doctoral Thesis, 2009.

Ateş, Hacer, 'Tekirdağ', *İslâm Ansiklopedisi*, Vol. 40. Istanbul: Türkiye Diyanet Vakfı, 2011.

Aykut, Nezihi, 'Dilâver Paşa', *İslâm Ansiklopedisi*, Vol. 9. Ankara: Türkiye Diyanet Vakfı, 1994: p. 297.

Bardakjian, Kevork, *Modern Ermeni Edebiyatı*. Istanbul: Aras, 2013.

Behar, Cem, *Osmanlı İmparatorluğu'nun ve Türkiye'nin Nüfusu: 1500-1927*. Ankara: T. C. Başbakanlık Devlet İstatistik Enstitüsü, 1996.

Beydilli, Kemal, *II. Mahmud Devri'nde Katolik Ermeni Cemâati ve Kilisesi'nin Tanınması (1830)*. Cambridge, MA: Department of Near Eastern Languages and Civilizations, Harvard University, 1995.

Çevik, Hikmet, *Tekirdağ Tarihi Araştırmaları*. Istanbul: Ahmet Sait Basımevi, 1949.

Çevik, Hikmet, *Tekirdağ Tarihi Araştırmaları: Tekirdağ Yürükleri*. Istanbul: Eko Matbaası, 1971.

Faroqhi, Suraiya, 'İstanbul'un İaşesi ve Tekirdağ-Rodoscuk Limanı (16.–17. yüzyıllar)', *ODTÜ Gelişme Dergisi Özel Sayısı*, (1979–80): 139–54.

Gökbilgin, Tayyib M., *Rumeli'de Yürükler, Tatarlar ve Evlâd-i Fâtihân*. Istanbul: İşaret Yayınları, 2008.

Gökyay, Orhan Şaik, 'Düstûrü'l-amel', *İslâm Ansiklopedisi*, Vol. 10. Istanbul: Türkiye Diyanet Vakfı, 1994, pp. 50–1.
Gökyay, Orhan Şaik (ed.), *Kâtip Çelebi: Hayatı ve Eserleri Hakkında İncelemeler*. Ankara: Türk Tarih Kurumu, 1957.
Göyünç, Nejat, 'Hâne', *İslâm Ansiklopedisi*, Vol. 15. Istanbul: Türkiye Diyanet Vakfı, 1997, 552–3.
Gündoğdu, Hamza, Ahmet Ali Bayhan, Ali Murat Aktemur, Sibel Tiğci and Muhammet Arslan, *Kültür Varlıkları ile Kemah*. Ankara: Kariyer Matbaacılık, 2009.
İlgürel, Mücteba, 'Abaza Paşa', *İslâm Ansiklopedisi*, Vol. 1. Ankara: Türkiye Diyanet Vakfı, 1988, 11–12.
İnalcık, Halil and Robert Anhegger, *Kânûnnâme-i Sultânî Ber Müceb-i 'Örf-i 'Osmânî*. Ankara: Türk Tarih Kurumu Basımevi, 2000.
İnalcık, Halil, 'İspence', *İslam Ansiklopedisi*, Vol. 23. Istanbul: Türkiye Diyanet Vakfı, 2001, p. 177.
İnalcık, Halil, 'İstanbul', *İslam Ansiklopedisi*, Vol. 23. Istanbul: Türkiye Diyanet Vakfı, 2001, pp. 220–39.
İnan, Kenan, 'Sade Nesirden Süslü Nesire: Fatih'in Tarihçisi Tursun Bey ve Tarih Yazma Tarzı', *Osmanlı/Bilim*, Vol. III (1999): 293–300.
Kevorkian, Raymond H. and Paul B. Paboudjian, *1915 Öncesinde Osmanlı İmparatorluğu'nda Ermeniler*. Istanbul: Aras, 2012.
Köker, Osman (ed.), *100 Yıl Önce Türkiye'de Ermeniler*, Vol. I. Istanbul: Birzamanlar Yayıncılık, 2008.
Kut, Turgut A., 'Ali Ufkî Bey ve Eserleri Hakkında', *Musiki Mecmuası* 332 (1977): 5–19.
Kütükoğlu, Mübahat, 'İzmir', *İslam Ansiklopedisi*, Vol. 23. Istanbul: İSAM, 2001, 515–24.
Levend, Agah Sırrı, *Türk Edebiyatında Şehrengizler ve Şehrenizlerde İstanbul*. Istanbul: Baha, 1957.
Miroğlu, İsmet, *16. Yüzyılda Bayburt Sancağı*. Istanbul: Bayburt Kültür ve Yardımlaşma Derneği, 1975.
Miroğlu, İsmet, *Kemah Sancağı ve Erzincan Kazası (1520–1566)*. Ankara: Türk Tarih Kurumu Basımevi, 1990.
Öztürk, Necdet and Murat Yıldız, *İmparatorluk Tarihinin Kalemli Muhafızları: Osmanlı Tarihçileri, Ahmedî'den Ahmed Refik'e*. Istanbul: Bilge Kültür Sanat, 2013.
Pakalin, Mehmet Zeki, *Osmanlı Tarih Deyimleri ve Terimleri Sözlüğü* I–II. Istanbul: Milli Eğitim Basımevi, 1951.

Pamaukciyan, Kevork, *Ermeni Harfli Türkçe Metinler*. Istanbul: Aras, 2002.
Pul, Ayşe, 'Kuyucu Murad Paşa'nın Anadolu'da Celâlilerle Mücadelesine Dair bir Osmanlı Kaynağı', *Uluslararası Sosyal Araştırmalar Dergisi* 5.20 (2012): 206–12.
Sahillioğlu, Halil, "Avârız', *İslam Ansiklopedisi*, Vol. 4. Ankara: Türkiye Diyanet Vakfı, 1991, 108–9.
Şahin, İlhan, 'Kemah', *İslam Ansiklopedisi*, Vol. 25. Ankara: Türkiye Diyanet Vakfı, 2002, 219–20.
Serez, Mehmet, *Tekirdağ ve Çevresi Vakfiyeleri*. Tekirdağ Valiliği Yayınıdır, 1993.
Shapiro, Henry R., '17. Yüzyıl Osmanlı-Ermeni Sosyal ve Entelektüel Tarihine Aralanan Yeni bir Pencere: Ermenice Elyazması Kolofonlar', *Toplumsal Tarih* 265 (January 2016): 41–3.
Teotig, *Baskı ve Harf: Ermeni Matbaacılık Tarihi*, trans. Sirvart Malhasyan and Arlet İncidüzen. Istanbul: Birzamanlar Yayıncılık, 2012.
Tuğlacı, Pars, *İstanbul Ermeni Kiliseleri*. Istanbul: Pars Tuğlacı, 1991.
Tveritinova, Anna S., *Türkiye'de Kara Yazıcı-Deli Hasan İsyanı (1593–1603)*, ed. Ali Haydar Avcı. Ankara: Barış, 2012.
Uluçay, M. Çağatay, *Sancaktan Saraya Seçme Yazılar*. Istanbul: Yapı Kredi Yayınları, 2012.
Uzunçarşılı, İsmail Hakkı, *Osmanlı Devleti'nin Merkez ve Bahriye Teşkilâtı*. Istanbul: Türk Tarih Kurumu, 1948.
Uzunçarşılı, İsmail Hakkı, *Osmanlı Tarihi*, Vol. III.I. Ankara: Türk Tarih Kurumu, 1951.
Uzunçarşılı, İsmail Hakkı, *Osmanlı Devleti Teşkilâtından Kapukulu Ocakları: Acemi Ocağı ve Yeniçeri Ocağı* I–II. Ankara: Türk Tarih Kurumu, 1988.
Yaycıoğlu, Ali, 'Perdenin Arkasındakiler Osmanlı İmparatorluğunda Sarraflar ve Finans Ağları Üzerine bir Deneme', *Festschrift in Honor of Özer Ergenç* I, ed. Nil Tekgül. Cambridge, MA: Department of Near Eastern Languages and Civilizations Harvard University, 2019.
Yurtoğlu, Bilal (ed.), *Katip Çelebi'nin Yunan, Roma ve Hristiyan Tarihi Hakkındaki Risalesi*. Ankara: Atatürk Kültür Merkezi Yayını, 2012.

Armenian Secondary Literature

Abeḷyan, Manuk, *Hayotsʻ grakanutʻyan patmutʻyun*, Vol. II. Yerevan: Haykakan SSṘ Gitutʻyunneri Akademiayi Hratarakchʻutʻyun, 1946.
Abrahamyan, Ashot, 'Martiros Di Aṙakʻeli zhamanakagrutʻyunĕ', *Gitakan Nyutʻeri Zhoḷovatsu* 1 (1941): 93–100.

Achaṙyan, Hrachʻya, *Hayerēn armatakan baṙaran*. Yerevan: Yeravani Hamalsarani Hratarakchʻutʻyun, 1926.
Achaṙyan, Hrachʻya, *Hay gaḷtʻakanutʻyan patmutʻyun*. Yerevan: Hrachʻya Achaṙyan Anvan Hamalsaran, 2002.
Achaṙyan, Hrachʻya, *Polsahay angir banahyusutʻyun*. Yerevan: EPH Hratarakchʻutʻyun, 2009.
Achaṙyan, Hrachʻya, *Hayotsʻ lezvi patmutʻyun* II. Yerevan: EPH Hratarakchʻutʻyun, 2013.
Akinean, Nersēs, *Eremia Chʻēlēpi Kʻēōmurchean: Keankʻn ew grakan gortsunēutʻiwnĕ*. Vienna: Mkhitʻarean Tparan, 1933.
Akinean, Nersēs, *Baḷeshi dprotsʻē 1500-1704: Npast mĕ hayotsʻ ekeḷetsʻwoy patmutʻean ew matenavn grutʻean*. Vienna: Mkhitʻarean Tparan, 1952.
Alpoyachean, A., *Grigor Kesaratsʻi patriarkʻ ew ir zhamanakĕ*. Jerusalem: Tparan Srbotsʻ Yakobeantsʻ, 1936.
Amatuni, Karapet, *Minas vrd. Amdetsʻi patriarkʻ Yerusaḷēmi (1630-1704 noymb 24)*. Vienna: Mkhitʻarean Tparan, 1984.
Anasyan, H. S., *Haykakan matenagitutʻyun*, Vol. I. Yerevan: Haykakan SSṘ GA Hratarakchʻutʻyun, 1959.
Anasyan, H. S., *XVII dari azatagrakan sharzhumnern Arevmtyan Hayastanum*. Yerevan: Haykakan SSṘ GA Hratarakchʻutʻyun, 1961.
Anasyan, H. S., *Manr erker*. Los Angeles: Armenian American International College, 1987.
Asatur, Hrant, *Kostandnupolsoy hayerĕ ew irentsʻ patriarkʻnerĕ*. Istanbul: Patriarkʻutʻiwn Hayotsʻ, 2011.
Avetisyan, Zhozef, *Eremia Kʻyomurchyani patmagrakan ashkhatutʻyunnerĕ orpes aḷbyur ōsmanyan kaysrutʻyan ew arewmtahayutʻyan patmutʻyan (17-rd dari 3-rd kʻaṙord)*. Yerevan: Azgayin Akademia, 2016.
Ayvazyan, Gayane, 'Eremia Chʻelepi Kʻyomurchyani 'Ōragrutʻyun' erki mi anhayt skzbnaḷbyuri masin' Erki Mi Anhayt Skzbnaḷbyuri Masin', *Hayagitutʻyan Hartsʻer* 1.7 (2016): 51–60.
Ayvazyan, Gayane, 'Eremia Chʻelepi Kʻyomurchyani tpagrakan gortsuneutʻyunĕ', *Ējmiatsin* (2012/8): 48–54.
Ayvazyan, Gayane, 'Eremia Chʻelepi Kʻyomurchyani dzeṙagrakan zhaṙangutʻyunĕ', *Banber Matenadarani* 20 (2014): 349–98.
Ayvazyan, Gayane, 'Eremia Chʻelepi Kʻyomurchyani kyankʻĕ', *Patmutʻyun ew Mshakuyt* (2014): 170–86.
Ayvazyan, Gayane, 'Eremia Kʻomurchyani 'Ōragrutʻyun' erkĕ', *Hayotsʻ Patmutʻyan Hartsʻer* 15 (2014): 89–108.

Ayvazyan, Gayane, 'Ōsmanyan Kaysrut'yan patmut'yunĕ Eremia Ch'elepi K'yomurchyani patmut'yunnerum', Unpublished Article, 1–12.

Bogharean, Norayr, *Grand Catalogue of the St. James Manuscripts*, Vols III–IV. Jerusalem: Armenian Convent Printing Press, 1968/1969.

Danielyan, K. A., *Hay memuarayin grakanut'yan patmut'yunits'*. Yerevan: Haykakan SSṘ GA Hratarakch'ut'yun, 1961.

Erem[ean], S., 'Eremia Chēlēpi taregrakan patmut'iwn', *Bazmavēp* (1902): 367–9, 473–9.

Gasapean, Minas G., *Hayerĕ Nikomidioy gawaṙin mēj*. Istanbul: Azatamart, 1913.

Hats'uni, H. V., 'Kusastank' Hayastani mēj', *Bazmavēp* (1923): 72–8.

Jahukyan, G. B., *Hay barbaṙagitut'yan neratsut'yun (vichakagrakan barbaṙagitut'yun)*. Yerevan: Haykakan SSH GA Hratarakch'ut'yun, 1972.

Khaṙatyan, Albert, *Kostandnupolsi hay gaḷt'ojakhĕ (XV–XVII darer)*. Yerevan: Yerevani Hamalsarani Hratarakch'ut'yun, 2007.

K'iwrtean, Y., 'Aproy Chelepi, 1620–167?', *Bazmavēp* 9 (1925): 258–61.

K'iwrtean, Y., 'Aproy Chelepi, 1620–167?', *Bazmavēp* 10 (1926): 37–42.

K'iwrtean, Y., *Yakob Kat'oḷikos Juḷayets'i*. Antelias: Kat'oḷikosut'ean Hayots' Metsi Tann Kilikioy, 1965.

K'iwrtean, Y., 'Nor nyut'er Eremia Ch'ēlēpi K'ēōmyurcheani masin', *Bazmavēp* (1966): 175–82.

K'iwrtean, Y., 'Nor nyut'er Eremia Ch'ēlēpi K'ēōmyurcheani masin', *Bazmavēp* (1967): 88–94.

Ḷaribyan, A., *Hay barbaṙagitut'yun: Hnchyunabanut'yun ev dzevabanut'yun*. Yerevan: Haykakan SSṘ Petakan Heṙaka Mankavarzhakan Institut, 1953.

Ḷazaryan, S. Ḷ., *Hayots' lezvi hamaṙot patmut'yun*. Yerevan: Erevani Hamalsarani Hratarakch'ut'yun, 1981.

Mayr ts'uts'ak hayerēn dzeṙagrats': Mashtots'i anuan Matenadarani, Vols I–IX. Yerevan: Nairi, 1984–2017.

Melik'-Bakhshyan, S., 'Step'anos Dashtets'i mi zhamanakagrut'yan masin', *Gitakan Ashkhatut'yunner* 47 (1955): 117–33.

Melik'-Ōhanjanyan, K. A., *Patmutiwn P'arēzi ew Vennayi*. Yerevan: Haykakan SSH Gitut'yunneri Akademiayi Hratarakch'ut'yun, 1966.

Mik'ayelyan, Vardges, *Hay gaḷt'ashkharhi patmut'yun (mijnadarits' minch'ev 1920 t'vakanĕ)* I–III. Yerevan: HH GAA 'Gitut'yun' Hratarakch'ut'yun, 2003.

Nshanean, Mesrop, 'Ōragrut'iwn Eremia Ch'ēlēpi K'ēōmurcheani', *Shoḷakat'* (1913): 47–65.

O.K. [signed only with initials], 'Tsanōt'ut'iwnk' inch' zvaruts' Eremeay Ch'ēlēpioy eranelwoyn Komitasay yeḷbōrē iwrmē', *Bazmavēp* (1926): 197–8.

Ōrmanean, Maḷakʻia, *Azgapatum*, Vols I–IV. Ējmiatsin: Mayr Atʻoṙ S. Ējmiatsin, 2001–2.
Oshakan, Y., 'Matenagrutʻean hamar: Eremia Chʻēlēpi A.', *Sion* (1939): 331–8.
Oshakan, Y., 'Matenagrutʻean hamar: Eremia Chʻēlēpi B.', *Sion* (1939): 367–9.
Oshakan, Y., 'Matenagrutʻean hamar: Eremia Chʻēlēpi G.', *Sion* (1940): 30–5.
Oshakan, Y., 'Matenagrutʻean hamar: Eremia Chʻēlēpi', *Sion* (1940): 71–4.
Oshakan, Y., 'Matenagrutʻean hamar: Eremia Chʻēlēpi', *Sion* (1940): 103–9.
Oshakan, Y., 'Matenagrutʻean hamar: Eremia Chʻēlēpi', *Sion* (1940): 142–5.
Oshakan, Y., 'Matenagrutʻean hamar: Eremia Chʻēlēpi', *Sion* (1940): 194–8.
Oskanyan, N. A., Kʻ. A. Korkotyan, A. M. Savalyan and Ṙ .A. Ishkhanyan, *Hay girkʻĕ 1512–1800 tʻvakannerin*, Vol. I. Yerevan: Haykakan SSH Kulturayi Ministrutʻyun, 1988.
Oskean, Hamazasp, *Bardzr Haykʻi vankʻerĕ*. Vienna: Mkhitʻarean Tparan, 1951.
Pʻachʻachean, Sargis G., *Yushamatean: Ṙotostʻotsʻi hayerun: 1606–1922*. Beirut: Tonikean, 1971.
Pērpērean, Hayk, 'Grigor Daranaḷtsʻii dzhuarimatsʻ mēk hatuatsin masin', *Sion* (September 1951): 273–4.
Pērpērean, Hayk, 'Alii Dashnagirʼ-ĕ Grigor Daranaḷtsʻii ʻZhamanakagrutʻeanʼ mēj', *Sion* (November 1951): 302–4 and 330–1.
Pērpērean, Hayk, 'K. Polsoy hay patriarkʻutʻean himnarkutʻiwnĕ', *Handēs Amsōreay* 7–9 (1964): 338–450.
Pztikean, Yarutʻyun, 'Hayastani hin kʻartēs mĕ XVII dareru vankʻern u srbavayrerĕ', *Bazmavēp* (2000): 296–300.
Sahakyan, H. S., *Eremia Kʻyomurchyan*. Yerevan: Haykakan SSṘ GA Hratarakchʻutʻyun, 1964.
Shapiro, Henry, 'Grigor Daranaḷtsʻu zhamanakagrutʻyan orosh khndirneri shurj', *Ējmiatsin* (February 2016): 57–68.
Siruni, Y. Ch., *Polis ew ir derĕ* I. Beruit: Y.Ch. Siruni, 1965.
Stepʻanyan, Hasmik, *Hayataṙ tʻurkʻeren grakanutʻyunĕ*. Yerevan: Erevani Hamalsarani Hratarakchʻutʻyun, 2001.
Stepʻanyan, Hasmik, *Catalogue of Turkish Materials Written in Armenian Letters of Armenian Manuscripts and Turkish Manuscripts in Armenian Letters:. Manuscripts from 'Matenadaran' in Yerevan and Mother See Holy St. Echmiadzin*. Yerevan: National Academy of Sciences of Armenia Institute of Oriental Studies, 2008.
Tashean, Y., *Usumnasirutʻiwnkʻ stoyn Kalistʻeneay varutsʻ Alekʻsandri*. Vienna: Mkhitʻarean tparan, 1892.

Ter-Levondyan, A. N., 'Eremia Chʻelepin orpes Munajjim Bashii albyurnerits' mekě', *Haykakan SSṘ Gitutʻyunneri Akademiayi Telekagir* 7–8 (1960): 143–51.

Tsʻutsʻak dzeṙagratsʻ Mashtotsʻi anvan Matenadarani I-III. Yerevan: Haykakan SSṘ Gitutʻyunneri Akademiayi Hratarakchʻyutʻyun, 1965, 1970, 2007.

Utʻuzyan, A. A., 'Grigor Daranalts'in M. Chʻamchʻyani patmutʻyan albyur', *Lraber Hasarakakan Gitutʻyunneri* (1975/2): 81–9.

Zulalyan, M. K., *Jalalineri sharzhumě ew hay zholovrdi vichakě ōsmanyan kaysrutʻyan mej (XVI–XVII darer)*. Yerevan: Haykakan SSH GA Hratarakchʻutʻyun, 1966.

Greek Secondary Literature

Kalaitzidis, Nikiforos, *I eparchia Raidestou apo tin alosi tis Konstantinoupoleos eos ti Mikrasiatiki Katastrofi (1453–1922)*. Thessaloniki: Mygdonia, 2007.

Western Secondary Literature

Aslanian, Sebouh David, *From the Indian Ocean to the Mediterranean: The Global Trade Networks of Armenian Merchants from New Julfa*. Berkeley: University of California Press, 2011.

Aslanian, Sebouh David, 'Port Cities and Printers: Reflections on Early Modern Global Armenian Print Culture', *Book History* 17 (2014): 51–93.

Aslanian, Sebouh David, 'The Marble of Armenian History: Or Armenian History as World History', *Études arméniennes contemporaines*, 4 (2014): 129–42.

Aslanian, Sebouh David, '"Prepared in the Language of the Hagarites": Abbot Mkhitar's 1727 Armeno-Turkish Grammar of Modern Western Armenian', *Journal of the Society for Armenian Studies* 25 (2016): 78–9.

Aslanian, Sebouh David, 'From Autonomous to Interactive Histories: World History's Challenge to Armenian Studies', in K. Babayan and M. Pifer (eds), *An Armenian Mediterranean: Words and Worlds in Motion*. New York: Palgrave Macmillan, 2018.

Aslanian, Sebouh David, 'The "Great Schism" of 1773: Venice and the Founding of the Armenian Community of Trieste', in H. Berberian and J. Daryaee (eds), *Reflections on Armenian Identity in History and Historiography*. Irvine, CA: Jordan Center for Persian Studies, 2018.

Aslanian, Sebouh David, *Global Early Modernity and Mobility: Port Cities and Printers in the Armenian Diaspora, 1512–1800*, forthcoming.

Awde, Nicholas (ed.), *Armenian Perspectives*. Richmond: Curzon, 1997.

Ayvazyan, Gayane, 'The Perception of the City in Topographic Works of Yeremia

Chelebi Qyomurtchyan', *Osmanlı İstanbulu III: III. Uluslararası Osmanlı İstanbulu Sempozyumu Bildirileri 25–26 Mayıs 2015, İstanbul 29 Mayıs Üniversitesi*, ed. Feridun Emecen, et al. Istanbul Büyükşehir Belediyesi, 2015, pp. 211–17.

Baer, Marc David, 'The Great Fire of 1660 and the Islamization of Christian and Jewish Space in Istanbul', *International Journal of Middle East Studies* 36. 2 (2004): 159–81.

Baer, Marc David, *Honored by the Glory of Islam: Conversion and Conquest in Ottoman Europe*. Oxford: Oxford University Press, 2011.

Baibourtyan, Vahan, *International Trade and the Armenian Merchants in the Seventeenth Century*. New Delhi: Sterling, 2004.

Bardakjian, Kevork, 'The Rise of the Armenian Patriarchate of Constantinople', *Christians and Jews in the Ottoman Empire: The Functioning of Plural Society*, Vol. I. New York: Holmes and Meier, 1982, pp. 89–100.

Barkan, Ömer Lütfi, 'The Price Revolution of the Sixteenth Century: A Turning Point in the Economic History of the Near East', *International Journal of Middle Eastern Studies* 6 (1975): 3–28.

Barkey, Karen, *Bandits and Bureaucrats: The Ottoman Route to State Centralization*. Ithaca: Cornell University Press, 1994.

Barsoumian, Hagop L., *The Armenian Amiras of the Ottoman Empire*. Yerevan: American University of Armenia, 2006.

Bedrossian, Matthias, *New Dictionary Armenian-English*. Eugene, OR: Wipf & Stock, 2009.

Bekar, Cumhur, 'A New Perception of Rome, Byzantium and Constantinople in Hezarfen Huseyin's Universal History', Boğaziçi University MA Thesis, 2011.

Ben-Naeh, Yaron, *Jews in the Realm of the Sultans: Ottoman Jewish Society in the Seventeenth Century*. Tübingen: Mohr Siebeck, 2008.

Bournoutian, George A., *A History of the Armenian People, Volume I: Pre-History to 1500 A.D.* Costa Mesa: Mazda Publishers, 1993.

Brady, Thomas A., Heiko A. Oberman and James D. Tracy (eds). *Handbook of European History, 1400–1600: Late Middle Ages, Renaissance, and Reformation*. Leiden: Brill, 1994.

Brook, Timothy, *Vermeer's Hat: The Seventeenth Century and the Dawn of the Global World*. New York: Bloomsbury Press, 2008.

Brown, Peter, 'The Rise and Function of the Holy Man in Late Antiquity', *The Journal of Roman Studies* 61 (1971): 80–101.

Calzolari, Valentina (ed.), *Armenian Philology in the Modern Era: From Manuscript to Digital*. Leiden: Brill, 2014.

Carlson, Thomas A., *Christianity in Fifteenth-Century Iraq*. Cambridge: Cambridge University Press, 2018.

Charanis, P., *The Armenians in the Byzantine Empire*. Venda Nova: Imprensa, 1963.

Cook, M. A., *Population Pressure in Rural Anatolia: 1450-1600*. London: Oxford University Press, 1972.

Cowe, Peter, 'The Armenian Oikoumene in the Sixteenth Century: Dark Age or Era of Transition?' in K. Babayan and M. Pifer (eds), *An Armenian Mediterranean: Words and Worlds in Motion*. New York: Palgrave Macmillan, 2018.

Dadoyan, Seta B., *The Fatimid Armenians: Cultural and Political Interaction in the Near East*. Leiden: Brill, 1997.

Dadoyan, Seta B., *The Armenians in the Medieval Islamic World: Paradigms of Interaction, Seventh to Fourteenth Centuries*, Vols I–III. London: Routledge, 2011–14.

Dankoff, Robert, *An Ottoman Mentality: The World of Evliya Çelebi*. Leiden: Brill, 2004.

Darling, Linda T., *A History of Social Justice and Political Power in the Middle East: The Circle of Justice from Mesopotamia to Globalization*. London: Routledge, 2013.

Davis, Natalie Zemon, *Trickster Travels: A Sixteenth-Century Muslim Between Worlds*. New York: Hill and Wang, 2006.

Deringil, Selim, *Conversion and Apostasy in the Late Ottoman Empire*. Cambridge: Cambridge University Press, 2012.

Elger, Ralph and Yavuz Köse (eds), *Many Ways of Speaking about the Self: Middle Eastern Ego-Documents in Arabic, Persian, and Turkish (14th–20th Century)*. Wiesbaden: Harrassowitz Verlag, 2010.

Eliav-Feldon, Miriam, *Renaissance Impostors and Proofs of Identity*. New York: Palgrave Macmillan, 2012.

Faroqhi, Suraiya, *Coping with the State: Political Conflict and Crime in the Ottoman Empire, 1550–1720*. Istanbul: Isis Press, 1995.

Finkel, Caroline, *The Administration of Warfare: The Ottoman Military Campaigns in Hungary, 1593–1606*. Vienna: VWGÖ, 1988.

Finkel, Caroline, *Osman's Dream: The Story of the Ottoman Empire, 1300–1923*. New York: Basic Books, 2005.

Fleischer, Cornell, *Bureaucrat and Intellectual in the Ottoman Empire: the Historian Mustafa Ali (1541–1600)*. Princeton: Princeton University Press, 1986.

Frazee, Charles, *Catholics and Sultans: The Church and the Ottoman Empire: 1453–1923*. Cambridge: Cambridge University Press, 1983.

Ghobrial, John-Paul A., *The Whispers of Cities: Information Flows in Istanbul, London, and Paris in the Age of William Trumbull*. Oxford: Oxford University Press, 2013.

Göçek, Fatma Müge, *East Encounters West: France and the Ottoman Empire in the Eighteenth Century*. Oxford: Oxford University Press, 1987.

Goffman, Daniel, *Izmir and the Levantine World, 1550–1650*. Seattle: University of Washington Press, 1990.

Goshgarian, Rachel, 'Futuwwa in 13th-century Rum and Armenia: Reform Movements and the Managing of Multiple Allegiances in Medieval Anatolian Urban Centers on the Periphery of the Seljuk Sultanate' in A. C. S. Peacock and S. N. Yıldız (eds), *The Seljuks of Anatolia: Court and Society in the Medieval Middle East*. London: I. B. Tauris, 2013.

Greene, Molly, *A Shared World: Christians and Muslims in the Early Modern Mediterranean*. Princeton: Princeton University Press, 2002.

Greene, Molly, *Catholic Pirates and Greek Merchants: A Maritime History of the Early Modern Mediterranean*. Princeton: Princeton University Press, 2013.

Grigoryan, Gohar, 'Two Armenian Manuscripts in Switzerland (with an annotated translation of a newly-found abridgement of the Commentary of Canon Tables attributed to Stepʻanos Siwnecʻi)', *Le Muséon* 133 (2020): 87–139.

Griswold, William J., *The Great Anatolian Rebellion, 1000–1020/1591–1611*. Berlin: K. Schwarz Verlag, 1983.

Gutas, Dimitri, *Greek Thought, Arabic Culture: The Graeco-Arabic Translation Movement in Baghdad and Early ʻAbbasaid Society (2nd–4th/5th–10th c.)*. London: Routledge, 1998.

Halperin, David J., *Sabbatai Zevi: Testimonies to a Fallen Messiah*. Oxford: Littman Library of Jewish Civilization, 2012.

Hathaway, Jane, *Beshir Agha, Chief Eunuch of the Ottoman Imperial Harem*. London: Oneworld Publications, 2006.

Horrocks, Geoffrey, *Greek: A History of the Language and its Speakers*. London: Longman, 1997.

Hovannisian, Richard G. (ed.), *The Armenian People From Ancient to Modern Times*, Vol. I. London: Palgrave Macmillan, 1997.

Hovannisian, Richard G. (ed.), *Armenian Baghesh/Bitlis and Taron/Mush*. Costa Mesa: Mazda Publishers, 2001.

İnalcik, Halil, 'The Policy of Mehmed II Toward the Greek Population of Istanbul and the Byzantine Buildings of the City', *Dumbarton Oaks Papers* 23/24 (1969/1970): 229–49.

İnalcik, Halil, 'Military and Fiscal Transformation in the Ottoman Empire, 1600–1700', *Archivum Ottomanicum* 6 (1980): 283–337.

İnalcik, Halil, *The Survey of Istanbul, 1455: The Text, English Translation, Analysis of the Text, Documents*. Istanbul: Türkiye İş Bankası Kültür Yayınları, 2010.

Ivanova, Polina, 'Armenians in Urban Order and Disorder of Seventeenth-Century Istanbul', *Journal of the Ottoman and Turkish Studies Association* 4.2 (2017): 239–60.

Jacob, Margaret C., *Strangers Nowhere in the World: The Rise of Cosmopolitanism in Early Modern Europe*. Philadelphia: University of Pennsylvania Press, 2006.

Jankowski, Henryk, 'Professor Edward Tryjarski', *Rocznik Orientalistyczny*, LVII 2 (2004): 5–17.

Jennings, Ronald C., *Christians and Muslims in Ottoman Cyprus and the Mediterranean World, 1571–1640*. New York: New York University Press, 1993.

Jennings, Ronald C., *Studies on Ottoman Social History in the Sixteenth and Seventeenth Centuries: Women, Zimmis and Sharia Courts in Kayseri, Cyprus and Trabzon*. Istanbul: Isis Press, 1999.

Kafadar, Cemal, 'Self and Others: The Diary of a Dervish in Seventeenth Century Istanbul and First-Person Narratives in Ottoman Literature', *Studia Islamica* 69 (1989): 121–50.

Kara, György (ed.), *Between the Danube and the Caucasus: Oriental Sources on the History of the Peoples of Central and South-Eastern Europe*. Budapest: Akademiai Kiado, 1987.

Karateke, Hakan and Hatice Aynur (eds), *Evliya Çelebi Seyahatnamesi'nin Yazılı Kaynakları*. Ankara: Türk Tarih Kurumu, 2012.

Kasaba, Reşat, *A Moveable Empire: Ottoman Nomads, Migrants, and Refugees*. Seattle: University of Washington Press, 2011.

Kermeli, Eugenia, 'The Right to Choice: Ottoman Ecclesiastical and Communal Justice in Ottoman Greece', in C. Woodhead (ed.), *The Ottoman World*. London: Routledge, 2012, pp. 347–61.

Khachikyan, Levon, 'Mongols in Transcaucasia', *Journal of World History* (1958): 98–125.

Krikorian, Haig Aram, *The Lives and Times of the Armenian Patriarchs of Jerusalem: Chronological Succession of Tenures*. Sherman Oaks, CA: H. A. Krikorian, 2009.

Krstic, Tijana, 'Illuminated by the Light of Islam and the Glory of the Ottoman Sultanate: Self-Narratives of Conversion to Islam in the Age of Confessionalization', *Comparative Studies in Society and History* 51.1 (2009): 35–63

Krstic, Tijana, *Contested Conversions to Islam: Narratives of Religious Change in the Early Modern Ottoman Empire*. Stanford: Stanford University Press, 2011.

Kunt, Metin I., *The Sultan's Servants: The Transformation of Ottoman Provincial Government, 1550–1650*. New York: Columbia Univeristy Press, 1983.

Lint, Theo von, 'Kostandin of Erznka: An Armenian Religious Poet of the XIII–XIVth Century', Dissertation of University of Leiden, 1996.

Lucca, Paolo, 'Šabbetay Şewi and the Messianic Temptations of Ottoman Jews in the Seventeenth Century According to Christian Armenian Sources', in C. Adang and S. Schmidtke (eds), *Contacts and Controversies between Muslims, Jews and Christians in the Ottoman Empire and Pre-Modern Iran*. Würzburg: Ergon-Verlag, 2010.

McCabe, Ina Baghdiantz, *The Shah's Silk for Europe's Silver: The Eurasian Trade of the Julfa Armenians in Safavid Iran and India, 1530–1750*. Atlanta: University of Pennsylvania Armenian Texts Series, 1999.

Masters, Bruce, *The Origins of Western Economic Dominance in the Middle East: Mercantilism and the Islamic Economy in Aleppo, 1600–1750*. New York: New York University Press, 1988.

Masters, Bruce, *Christians and Jews in the Ottoman Arab World: The Roots of Sectarianism*. Cambridge: Cambridge University Press, 2001.

Matthee, Rudolph, *The Politics of Trade in Safavid Iran: Silk for Silver, 1600–1730*. Cambridge: Cambridge University Press, 1999.

Mecerian, Jean, *Introduction à l'étude des Synaxaires Arméniens*. Bayreuth: Bulletin Arménologique, 1953.

Melville, Charles (ed.), *Pembroke Papers: Persian and Islamic Studies in Honour of P.W. Avery*. Cambridge: University of Cambridge Centre for Middle Eastern Studies, 1990.

Meninski, Franciscus a Mesgnien, *Thesaurus Linguarum Orientalium Turcicae-Arabicae-Persicae* I-III. Istanbul: Simurg, 2000.

Mignon, Laurent, 'A Pilgrim's Progess: Armenian and Kurdish Literatures in Turkish and the Rewriting of Literary History', *Patterns of Prejudice* 48:2 (2014): 182–200.

Mildonian, Paola, 'L'Occidente fantastico. Note sulla tradizione orientale del "Paris e

Vienna"', in M. Eusebia (ed.), *Studi medievali e romanzi in memoria di Alberto Limentani*. Rome: Jouvence, 1990.

Murphey, Rhoads, 'Population Movements and Labor Mobility in Balkan Contexts: A Glance at Post-1600 Ottoman Social Realities', in M. Delilbaşı and Ö.Ergenç (eds), *Southeast Europe in History: The Past, the Present, and the Problems of Balkanology*. Ankara: Ankara University Press, 1999.

Murre-van den Berg, H. L. (ed.), *Redefining Christian Identity: Cultural Interaction in the Middle East Since the Rise of Islam*. Louvain: Peeters, 2005.

Nichanian, Marc, *Âges et usages de la langue arménienne*. Paris: Éditions Entente, 1989.

Nirenberg, David, *Communities of Violence: Persecution of Minorities in the Middle Ages*. Princeton: Princeton University Press, 1996.

Ohanjanyan, Anna, 'Creedal Controversies among Armenians in the Seventeenth-Century Ottoman Empire Eremia Č'ēlēpi K'ēōmiwrčean's Polemical Writing against Suk'ias Prusac'i', *Journal for the Society of Armenian Studies* 27 (2020): 7–69.

Ohanjanyan, Anna, 'Gēorg Mxlayim Ołli: An Overlooked Agent of Armenian Apostolic Confession-Building in Ottoman Constantinople', in T. Kristic (ed.) forthcoming based on proceedings of conference which took place in June 2018 in Budapest, Hungary.

Oppenheim, A. Leo, *Ancient Mesopotamia: Portrait of a Dead Civilization*. Chicago: University of Chicago Press, 1977.

Ortaylı, İlber, 'Rodosto (extension en Marmara de la Via Egnatia) au XVIe siècle', *The Via Egnatia under Ottoman Rule: 1380–1699*. Rethymnon: University of Crete Press, 1996, pp. 193–202.

Oxford Dictionary of Byzantium, Vols I–III, ed. A. P. Kazhdan. Oxford: Oxford University Press, 1991.

Özel, Oktay, 'Population Changes in Ottoman Anatolia during the 16th and 17th Centuries: The Demographic Crisis Reconsidered', *International Journal of Middle East Studies* 36.2 (2004): 183–205.

Özel, Oktay, *The Collapse of Rural Order in Ottoman Anatolia: Amasya 1576–1643*. Leiden: Brill, 2016.

Papademetriou, Tom, *Render unto the Sultan: Power, Authority, and the Greek Orthodox Church in the early Ottoman Centuries*. Oxford: Oxford University Press, 2015.

Parker, Geoffrey, *Global Crisis: War, Climate Change, and Catastrophe in the Seventeenth Century*. New Haven, CT: Yale University Press, 2013.

Peirce, Leslie P., *The Imperial Harem: Women and Sovereignty in the Ottoman Empire*. New York: Oxford University Press, 1993.
Peirce, Leslie P., *Morality Tales: Law and Gender in the Ottoman Court of Aintab*. Berkeley: University of California Press, 2003.
Peri, Oded, *Christianity under Islam in Jerusalem: The Question of the Holy Sites in Early Ottoman Times*. Leiden: Brill, 2001.
Pfeifer, Helen, 'To Gather Together: Cultural Encounters in Sixteenth-Century Ottoman Literary Salons", Princeton University Doctoral Thesis, 2014.
Piterberg, Gabriel, *An Ottoman Tragedy: History and Historiography at Play*. Berkeley: University of California Press, 2003.
Pohl, Walter and Helmut Reimitz (eds), *The Construction of Ethnic Communities, 300–800*. Leiden: Brill, 1998.
Pohl, Walter and Mathias Mehofer (eds), *Archeology of Identity*. Vienna: Austrian Research Academy, 2010
Rahn, M., *Die Entstehung des armenischen Patriarchats von Konstantinopel*. Hamburg: Verlag, 2002.
Riedlmayer, András J., 'Ottoman Copybooks of Correspondence and Miscellanies as a Source for Political and Cultural History', *Acta Orientalia Academiae Scientiarum Hungaricae*, 61.1/2 (2008): 201–14.
Riondel, H., *Une page tragique de l'histoire religieuse du Levant*. Paris: Gabriel Beauchesne, 1929.
Russell, James R., *Zoroastrianism in Armenia*. Cambridge, MA: Harvard University Department of Near Eastern Languages and Civilization, 1987.
Samuelian, Thomas J. and Michael E. Stone (eds), *Medieval Armenian Culture: Proceedings of the Third Dr. H. Markarian Conference on Armenian Culture*. Philadelphia: University of Pennsylvania Press, 1982.
Sandfuchs, Özlem Sert, 'Reconstructing a Town From its Court Records Rodosçuk (1546–1553)", Munich Ludwig-Maximilians University Doctoral Thesis, 2008.
Sanjian, Avedis K., *Colophons of Armenian Manuscripts, 1301–1480: A Source for Middle Eastern History*. Cambridge, MA: Harvard University Press, 1969.
Santus, Cesare, 'The Şeyhülislam, the Patriarch, and the Ambassador: A Case of Entangled Confessionalization (1692–1703)', in T. Kristic (ed.) forthcoming based on proceedings of conference which took place in June 2018 in Budapest, Hungary.
Sariyannis, Marinos, 'The Kadızadeli Movement as a Social and Political Phenomenon: The Rise of a "Mercantile Ethic"?', in A. Anastasopoulos (ed.),

Political Initiatives from the Bottom-Up in the Ottoman Empire (Halcyon Days in Crete VII). Rethymnon: 2012.
Scholem, Gershom Gerhard, *Sabbatai Sevi: The Mystical Messiah*. Princeton: Princeton University Press, 1976.
Schütz, Edmond, 'Jeremia Çelebi Türkische Werke (Zur Phonetik des Mittelosmanischen)', *Studia Turcica* (1971): 401–30.
Schütz, Edmond, 'An Armeno-Kıpchak Document of 1640 from Lvov and its Background in Armenia and in the Diaspora', in György Kara (ed.), *Between the Danube and the Caucasus: Oriental Sources on the History of the Peoples of Central and South-Eastern Europe*. Budapest: Akademiai Kiado, 1987.
Shapiro, Henry R., 'Legitimizing the Ottoman Sultanate in Early Modern Greek', *Journal of Turkish Studies* 42 (2014): 285–316.
Shapiro, Henry R., 'The Great Armenian Flight: Migration and Cultural Change in the Seventeenth-Century Ottoman Empire', *Journal of Early Modern History* 23 (2019): 67–89.
Shapiro, Henry R., 'Grigor Daranalts'i: An Armenian Chronicler of Early Modern Mass Mobility', forthcoming in volume edited by Tijana Kristic.
Sinclair, T. A., *Eastern Turkey: An Architectural and Archaeological Survey* II. London: Pindar Press, 1989.
Sinclair, T. A., 'The Use of the Colophons and Minor Chronicles in the Writing of Armenian and Turkish History', *Journal for the Society of Armenian Studies* 10 (1998): 45–53.
Singer, Amy, *Palestinian Peasants and Ottoman Officials: Rural Administration around Sixteenth-Century Jerusalem*. Cambridge: Cambridge University Press, 1995.
Stone, Michael E., 'Biblical Text and Armenian Retelling', *Journal of the Society for Armenian Studies* 26 (2017): 82–7.
Terzioğlu, Derin, 'Where 'İlm-i Ḥāl Meets Catechism: Islamic Manuals of Religious Instruction in the Ottoman Empire in the Age of Confessionalization', *Past Present* 220.1 (2013): 79–114.
Tezcan, Baki, *The Second Ottoman Empire: Political and Social Transformations in the Early Modern World*. Cambridge: Cambridge University Press, 2012.
Thierry, Michel, 'L'église martyriale triconque de Vasli (Haute Arménie)', *Revue des Études Arméniennes* 25 (1994–5): 255–69.
Thierry, Michel, 'Données archéologiques sur les principautes arméniennes de Cappadoce orientale au XIe siècle', *Revue des Études Arméniennes* 26 (1996–7): 119–72.

Thomas, David and John A. Chesworth (eds), *Christian-Muslim Relations. A Bibliographical History*. Vol. 10. Leiden: Brill, 2017.

Thomson, R. W., *A Bibliography of Classical Armenian Literature to 1500 A.D.* Turnhout: Brepols, 1995.

Uluhogian, Gabriella, *Un' Antica Mappa Dell'Armenia: Monasteri e santuari dal I al XVII secolo*. Ravenna: Longo Editore, 2000.

Vacca, Alison, *Non-Muslim Provinces under Early Islam: Islamic Rule and Iranian Legitimacy in Armenia and Caucasian Albania*. Cambridge: Cambridge University Press, 2017.

Vardanyan, S. A., *Amirdovlat Amassiatsi: A Fifteenth-Century Armenian Natural Historian and Physician*, trans. M. Yoshpa. Delmar: Caravan Books, 1999.

Verneuil, Henri, *Mayrig*, trans. E. A. Bayizian. New York: St Vartan Press, 2006.

White, Sam, *The Climate of Rebellion in The Early Modern Ottoman Empire*. Cambridge: Cambridge University Press, 2011.

Woodhead, Christine (ed.), *The Ottoman World*. London: Routledge, 2012.

Yerasimos, Stephane, *Legendes d'Empire: La Fondation de Constantinople et de Sainte-Sophie dans les Traditions Turques*. Paris: Institut Français d'Études Anatoliennes d'Istanbul, 1990.

Ze'evi, Dror, 'The Use of Ottoman Sharî'a Court Records as a Source for Middle Eastern Social History: A Reappraisal', *Islamic Law and Society* 5.1 (1998): 35–56.

Zilfi, Madeline C., 'The Kadizadelis: Discordant Revivalism in Seventeenth-Century Istanbul', *Journal of Near Eastern Studies* 45/4 (October 1986): 251–69.

Index

Note: page numbers in **bold** refer to figures

Abbas, Shah of Persia, 15, 47, 48, 51, 54, 62, 67, 154, 233, 234
Abelyan, Manuk, 289–90
Abgar T'okhat'ets'i, 238
Abraham of Crete, 218
'Abdülkâdir Topçular Kâtibi Efendi, 41, 42–3, 44
Achaṙyan, Hrach'ya, 17, 126
Agat'angeḷos, 31, 32–3
Ahmed I, 214–15
Akdağ, Mustafa, 9, 30
Akinean, Nersēs, 198, 211, 229
Akn (Kemaliye), 164, 200, 201, **201**
Alexander the Great, 280–2
Ali Ufkî, 269–70
alphabet, Armenian, 5, 19, 38, 275
Amasya region, 11, 43–4, 112
Ambakum, *Mahtesi*, 200–2, 203, 206, 207, 250n
Amirdovlat' of Amassia, 143n, 263
Anasean, Y. S., 11–12
Anatolia, map, **2**
Andreasyan, Hrant D., 235

Ani (fortress), 31, 33, 39
Ankara, 46
Anthony the Great, 151–2
Apro Çelebi, 207, 225, 229–30, 239, 248, 272
Aṙak'el of Tabriz, 15, 48–50, 67
Archangel Church, Rodosto, 92, 122, 123
Armash Monastery, Izmit, 187, 263, 270
Armenian Genocide, 8, 22, 261, 291
  Armenian views on the causes of the Celali Revolts, 60–4
Armenian Patriarchate of Constantinople/Istanbul, 131, 157–61, 163, 164, 182–3, 189, 197, 203–5, 206–7, 232, 237–8, 283
Armenian Patriarchate of Jerusalem, 46–7, 70
Armeno-Turkish *see* translation movement, Armeno-Turkish
Arsacid treasury, 31
aşıks, 262
Aslanian, Sebouh, 18, 54, 264

Ateş, Hacer, 86, 127
Attic Greek, 16
Avag Monastery, 34–6, **36**, 38–9, 234
Avetisyan, Zhozef, 198, 218–20
Ayvazyan, Gayane, 198, 208, 209, 224–5, 230, 238–9
Azaria Sasnets'i, 51–3, 60–2, 64–5

Baer, Marc David, 20–1
Balıkesir, 128
Bampuk'chean, Gevorg, 198
Bardakjian, Kevork, 131
Bayburt, 153–5, **153**, 155, 174
Bible, 271–2
  book of John, translation of by Eremia, 268–9
  Ali Ufkî's translations, 269–70
biographies, 213–16
Bitlis, 16, 130, 172, 173, 174
Brook, Timothy, 180
Bursa, 46

calendars, 219
cannibalism, 50, 53–5, 54, 57
catechismal texts, 241–4
Catholicism, 6, 21, 22, 170, 180, 182–5, 189, 208, 240, 264
Catholicos of Ējmiastin, 170, 200, 202, 203–5, 206, 218, 232–3, 239, 270
Caves of Manē, 31, 32, 33–4
Celali Revolts, 9–12, 15, 19, 22, 29–30, 40, 41, 126, 152, 170, 175, 199–200, 221–2
  in Armenian literary sources, 44–59
  Armenian views on the causes of, 60–4

colophons and short chronicles, 50–7
  in Kemah and the Valley of the Monasteries, 70–2
  Ottoman sources on, 41–4, 72–3
  poetry and verse, 57–9, 60–2
  travelogues and major chronicles, 45–50
Chalkokondyles, Laonikos, 186
Ch'amch'ean, Mik'ayel, 168, 210, 212, 234, 275, 289
chronicles, 30, 31–3, 39–43, 41, 84
  major chronicles, 45–50
  short chronicles, 44, 55–7
  see also Daranałts'i, Grigor
churches
  in court records, 122–3
  destruction of, 92
  Istanbul, 207, 227–8, 236–8, **237**
  Rodosto, 88, 92, 122–3, 124, 167, 188
Cilicia, 5, 6–7, **7**, 8, 234
clergy, 88–9, 114, 125; *see also* Daranałts'i, Grigor
climate change, 10
colophons, 29, 34, 35, 36, 44, 50–5, 162, 187, 199, 208, 218, 231, 270
  testimonies of the Great Armenian Flight, 65–6
confessionalisation, 240–1
Constantinople *see* Istanbul
court records, 19–20, 83, 85, 86, 93, 119–24, 128, 133
  Armenian converts to Islam, 101–5
  Armenians' arrival in Rodosto, according to Islamic court records 1595–1611, 94–119
  Celalis, 111–13

Cyprus, 94–5
debt disputes, 101–2
demographic information in court records, 121–2
distinctions between Christian communities, 95
divorce, 103, 111
dress regulations, 105–7
of economic activities, 119–20
first Kemah Armenians at the Rodosto court, 96–101
occupations and housing of Armenians, 110–11
sartorial violations, 105–7, 119
surety documents and eviction notices for Armenian refugees, 107–10, **109**
taxation, 113–18, 120–1, 123–4
thefts, 99–101
women, 103, 104, 108, 112, 120
zimmi, 95, 120
Crete, 225–7, 229, 232
Cyprus, 94–5, 165–6, **165**

Dadoyan, Seta, 6, 7, 8, 11
Daranałikʻ, 31, 32–3, 39
demographic change, 124–9
Diyarbekir, 130, 174

Eastern Anatolia
 at the turn of the seventeenth centuries, 41–4
 war, rebellion, scarcity and cannibalism in Armenian literary sources, 44–59
Ējmiatsin, 15, 16, 48, 49, 170, 197, 207–8, 270

Eḷiazar of Antep, 203–4, 206–7, 210, 232–3, 239, 248, 283
Eremia Kʻeōmurchean, 3, 14, 20, 21, 131, 132, 186, 205
 Apology of the Armenian Church, 241, 244
 and the Armeno-Turkish translation movement, 261–87
 biographies, 213–16
 book of John, translation of, 268–9
 brothers, 208
 calendars, 219
 catechismal texts, 241–4
 children, 208–9, 264–6, 270–1, 272
 Christian identity, 227
 Chronological History and Historical Notes of His Own Times, Until 1682, 212
 Concise History of 400 Years of Ottoman Kings, 212–13, 218–25, 227, 240
 Concise History of the Ottoman Kings, 212, 213–14, 244
 Concise Questions and Answers, 211, 241–4, 248
 death, 209
 devotional translations, 268–72
 diary, 3, 199, 201–2, 203–4, 205, 208, 210, 212, 230–4
 and ecclesiastical politics, 232–3
 education and literary corpus, 209–12
 and the foundation of Western Armenian intellectual tradition, 197–260
 geographical works, 234
 history of Alexander the Great (translation), 280–2

Eremia K'eōmurchea (*cont.*)
  History of Istanbul, 211, 235–8
  History of the Armenians
    (translation), 275–80, **277**, 282
  History of the Neomartyrs, 241
  History of Vienna and Paris
    (translation), 273–5
  History on the Taking of the Island
    Crete, 225–7
  Jerusalem pilgrimage, 201–3
  The Jewish Bride, 267
  letter-writing, 265–6
  life of, 199–209
  living in isolation, 209
  marriage, 205
  method of translation, 267–8
  multilingualism, 210
  origin of name, 200
  original works in Armeno-Turkish, 264–7
  patronage, need of, 207
  Places Relating to Our Lord, 238, 239
  poetry and verse, 199, 216, 218, 219–24, 229, 235–6, 237–8, 239, 244–7, 264–5, 267
  polemical writings and confessionalisation, 240–1
  Prayers of Nerses, Catholicos of the Armenians, 269
  printing press, 238–9
  reviving medieval genres for contemporary use, 239–47
  'secular' translations, 273–82
  self and place narratives, 230–9
  sermons, 270–2
  topical histories, 225–30
  translations, 267–82
  travels, 207–8
  writing Ottoman history in Armenian, 212–30
Erzincan, 20, 38, 70, 72, 130, 133, 163, 172, 176
Erzurum, 29, 39, 40, 55, 56, 57
Euphrates, River, 29
Evilya Çelebi, 39, 40, 41, 43–4, 84–5, 92, 206, 211, 235

famine, 48, 50, 52, 53, 54–5, 56–7, 65, 163

Gasapean, Minas, 128
gazavatnâme (war epic), 43, 44
Georgia, 65, 85, 234
grabar (Classical Armenian), 16, 17, 18
Great Armenian Flight *see* migration
Greater Armenia, 6–7, **7**
Greek-Armenian animosity, 90–1, 94–5, 188–9, 240
Grigor Daranałts'i, 14, 15, 19, 20–1, 44, 47–8, 60, 118–19, 124, 125, 147–96, 200, 201, 203, 248, 270
  Armenians' arrival in Rodosto, account of, 87–94
  bishop of Rodosto, 161, 166
  on causes of the Celali Revolts, 62–4
  on the Celali Revolts in Kemah, 70–1, 73–4
  Chronicle, 87–94, 168–86, **169**, 241, 289
  conception of geography, 131–2
  condemnations of ranking churchmen in the *Chronicle*, 181–3
  conflict with Patriarchs of

Constantinople, 157–61, 163, 182–3
conversion narratives, 104–5
and the crisis of leadership and infrastructure, 147–96
in Cyprus, 165–6, **165**
death and epitaph, 167
education, 152–3
on evictions, 108–10
on fake priests, 175–7
flight from Celali Revolts, 155–6
formal leader of Armenian refugees, 160
on the Great Armenian Flight, 65, 66–7
on heretics, 177–9
and infrastructure building, 186–9
in Jerusalem, 157, 165
in Kemah, 162–4
language and terminology in the *Chronicle*, 168, 170
life of, 148–67
ministry to refugees, 164–5, 166
on monasteries of his childhood, 149–50
and Paron, 150–3, 156–7, 165
refugees, merchants and missionaries in the *Chronicle*, 175–86
on taxation, 115, 117
travels, 157–8
at Vahanshēn Monastery, Brayburt, 153–5
vardapets and scribes of Greater Armenia in the *Chronicle*, 172–5
and violence, 158, 181, 190
Grigor of Kayseri, 158–9, 164, 182, 183, 189, 237–8

Grigor the Illuminator, 5, 31, 32–3, 71, 72, 177
Grigor the Illuminator Monastery, 33–4, **34,** 71, 72, 75n
Grigoris (son of Eremia), 207–8, 209, 270–1, 272
Grigoryan, Gohar, 66

Hasan, Deli, 47, 51–3
heresy, 177–9
hermit caves, **151**
Herodotus, 83
Herzig, Edmund M., 54
history writing, 12–16, 39–42
    gazavatnâme (war epic), 43, 44
    see also Kʻeōmurchean, Eremia
Holy Archangel Church, Balat, 188
Holy Mother of God Church, Istanbul, 227–8
Holy Mother of God Monastery, Diyarbekir, 204
Holy Redeemer Church, Rodosto, 123, 124, 167, 202–3
Hovannavankʻ Monastery, 49–50
Hovhannēs Holov, 18
Hüseyin, Hazarfen, 225

Inalcık, Halil, 10, 124–5
Inchichean, Lukas, 289
infrastructure, 186–9
Islam, 21
    conversions to, 101–5, 118, 119
    religious authority, 152
Istanbul, 3, 4, 8–9, 13, 14, 18, 22, 67, 155–6, 190, 212–30, 249, 288, 291
    Armeno-Turkish translation movement, 261–87

Instanbul (*cont.*)
  as a centre for Armenian manuscript copying, 129–32, 197
  demographic change, 124–6, 204
  Eremia's Armenian writing on Ottoman history, 212–30
  fire of 1660, 227–9
  forced migration from, 89
  History of the Fire of Constantinople, 227–9
  life of Eremia, 199–209
  religious conflict, 206–7, 208
  St Grigor the Illuminator Church, Tophane, 236–8, **237**
  Western Armenian intellectual tradition, foundation of, 197–260
Ivanova, Polina, 204
Izmir, 126–7, 128–9, 180, 249, 270, 288, 291
Izmit, 4, 128, 187

Jennings, Ronald, 94
Jerusalem, 170, 201–3, 234

Karapet of Bitlis, 131
Karasu, River, 29
Kars, 40
Kâtip Çelebi, 7, 206, 211, 225, 234
  Cihânnümâ, 40
  Digest, 41–2, 213, 214, 215–16
Kayseri, 45–6, 116–17
Kefe, 14, 15, 69–70
Kefevi Mosque, Istanbul (formerly St Nicholas Church, Edirnekapı), 156, **157**
Kemah, 19–20, **28**, 29–82, **30**, 100, 133, 162–3, 166, 172, 198, 234

  Celali Revolts in Kemah, 70–2
  Eastern Anatolia at the turn of the seventeenth century, 41–4
  Great Armenian Flight, testimonies of, 64–70
  hermit caves, **151**
  and its environs, 30–41
  origins of the name, 30–1
Konstandin Erznkats'i, 38
Köprülü Mehmed Paşa, 226
Kouymijian, Dickran, 13–14
Krstic, Tijana, 20–1, 240
Kunt, Metin, 61–2
Kuyucu Murad Paşa, 41, 43, 44, 72, 161, 161–2, 162

language, 6, 8, 290
  Armeno-Turkish, 19
  dialectic diversity, 17–18
  grabar (Classical Armenian), 16–17, 18, 19, 39
  linguistic transformations in early modern Armenian, 16–19
  Middle Armenian, 16–17, 18
  multilingualism, 210
  Turkish, 17
  Western Armenian, 18–19
  see also translation movement, Armeno-Turkish
Lazar, Nalash, 88–9, 158
Lazaryan, S. L., 17–18
Lüfti Paşa, 220

manuscript production, 12–16, 197
  and the cultural impact of the Great Armenian Flight, 129–32
Manushkut, 45

Markos (brother of Daranałts'i), 106–7, 156, 179, 201–2
marriage, 90–1, 103, 111
Martiros Łrimets'i, 15, 69–70, 131, 210, 232
Mehmed II, 22, 125, 131, 291
Mehmed III, 41, 62–3, 170, 216, 220–1
Melik'-Ohanjanyan, K. A., 267–8, 274
merchants, 179–81, 233–4
Mesrop Mashtots', 5
Mesrop Mashtots' Institute of Ancient Manuscripts (Matenadaran), 129–30
Middle Armenian, 16–17, 18
migration, 3–4, 5, 6, 7–8, 12, 19, 22, 155–6, 175, 179–80, 185–6
   Armenian communal leadership, 92–3
   Armenian converts to Islam, 101–5, 118, 119
   Armenian sartorial violations, 105–7, 119
   Armenians' arrival in Rodosto, according to Daranałts'i, 87–94
   Armenians' arrival in Rodosto, according to Islamic court records 1595–1611, 94–119
   Celalis, 111–13
   court records of 1620–2 and 1627–32, 119–24
   demographic change, evidence for, 124–9
   demographic information in court records, 121–2
   economic activities of Armenians, 119–20
   first Armenian neighbourhood in Rodosto, 122
   first Kemah Armenians at the Rodosto court, 96–101
   Great Armenian Flight, 3–4, 8, 12, 14, 19, 30, 42, 86, 166, 198, 233
   Greek-Armenian animosity, 90–1, 94–5, 188–9, 240
   legacies of the Great Armenian Flight, 288–92
   manuscript production and the cultural impact of the Great Armenian Flight, 129–32
   occupations and housing of Armenians, 110–11
   to Rodosto, 83–144
   Rodosto at the turn of the seventeenth century, 83–7
   surety documents and eviction notices for Armenian refugees, 107–10, **109**
   and taxation, 113–18, 120–1, 123–4, 127–8, 129
   testimonies of, 64–70, 73
   treatment by state officials, 91–2, 98–9
Minas Amdets'i, 14–15, 208, 233
Miroğlu, İsmet, 38
Mkhit'areans, 22, 263–4, 290
Mkhit'ar Sebastats'i, 263–4
monasteries, 33–8, **34**, **36**, **37**, 38–9, 149–50, 186–7, 203, 234
   and the Celali Revolts, 70–2
   and torture, 49–50
Monastery of the King, 36–8, **37**, 164
Mount Sepuh, 31, 32, 33–4, 38, 39, 70–1, 149, 234

Moses Khorenats'i, 31–2
　History of the Armenians, 275–80, 277, 282
Muhtâr, Ahmed, 275
Müneccimbaşı Ahmed Dede, 39–40, 279–80
Murad IV, 117, 129

Naima, 42
natural catastrophes, 48
New Julfa, 16, 54, 234
　merchants, 179–81
Nichanian, Marc, 18
Nshanean, Mesrop, 148–9, 168, 198, 204, 209, 211, 212, 289

Ohanjanyan, Anna, 244
Öntuğ, Mustafa Murat, 128
Ōrmanean, Malak'ia, 204
Orthodox Church, 93, 188–9
Oskean, Hamazasp, 33, 34, 36
Ostan, 172
Ottoman Empire
　Armenian culture, destruction of, 3
　bureaucracy, 61–2, 63
　military practices, 10, 12, 63–4
　Seventeenth-Century Crisis, 9–12
Özel, Oktay, 11

P'ach'achean, Sargis P., 92, 127
Parker, Geoffrey, 10
Papademetriou, Tom, 93, 183
Paron, 150–3, 156–7, 165
Patriarch of Constantinople *see* Armenian Patriarchate of Constantinople/Istanbul

Patriarchal History of Constantinople, 183
Pērperēan, Hayk, 168, 170
pilgrims/pilgrimage, 46–7, 71, 201–3
Piromalli, Paolo, 183–5
poetry and verse, 29, 38, 43, 44, 51–3
　Armeno-Turkish, 262
　aşıks, 262
　and causes of the Celali Revolts, 60–2
　Celali Revolts descriptions of, 51–3, 57–9, 221–2
　K'eōmurchean, Eremia, 199, 216, 218, 219–24, 229, 235–6, 237–8, 239, 244–7, 264–5, 267
　testimonies of the Great Armenian Flight, 64–5, 67–70
Pohl, Walter, 5
Poland, 15–16; *see also* Simēon of Poland
priests *see* clergy
printing, 238–9, 263

relics, 164, 167, 202–3, 234
religion, 6, 20–1, 88–9, 203
　Armenian holy sites, destruction of, 31–3
　Celali disruption of, 46–7
　conflict in Istanbul, 206–7, 208
　conversions, 96, 99, 100, 101–5, 118, 119, 185, 241
　fake priests, 175–7
　heresy, 177–9
　missionaries, 183–5, 240
　vardapets, 171–5, 205, 232–3, 270
　in Western Anatolia according to *Chronicle* of Grigor Daranałts'i, 175–86

Rodosto (Tekirdağ), 4, 14, 18, 19–20, 67, 73, **84**, 126, 133, 157–8, 164, 166, 190, 249
  Armenian communal leadership, 92–3
  Armenian converts to Islam, 101–5, 118, 119
  Armenian sartorial violations, 105–7, 119
  Armenians' arrival according to Daranałts'i, 87–94
  Armenians' arrival according to Islamic court records 1595–1611, 94–119
  Celalis, 111–13
  churches, 88, 92, 122–3, 124, 167, 188, 202–3
  community diversity, 85–6
  court records of 1620–2 and 1627–32, 119–24
  demographic change, evidence for, 124–9
  demographic information in court records, 121–2
  economic activities of Armenians, 119–20
  economic importance, 84–5
  first Armenian neighbourhood, 122
  first Kemah Armenians at the Rodosto court, 96–101
  Greek-Armenian animosity, 90–1, 94–5
  migration of Armenians from Kemah, 83–144
  occupations and housing of Armenians, 110–11
  population, 85
  surety documents and eviction notices for Armenian refugees, 107–10, **109**
  taxation, 113–18, 120–1, 123–4, 127–8, 129
  at the turn of the seventeenth century, 83–7

Safavid Persia, 15
Sahakyan, Hasmik, 198, 211, 244–5
St Grigor the Illuminator Church, Tophane, Istanbul, 236–7, **237**
St Karapet Church, Candia, 227
St Makar Monastery, Cyprus, 165–6, **165**
St Nicholas Church, Edirnekapı (later Kefevi Mosque), 156, **157**
St Step'anos Monastery, Vahanashēn, 173
Sanjian, Avedis K., 198, 267
Schütz, Edmond, 198
Selim I, 13–14, 38, 39
Sepulchre of the Nine Saints, T'ordan Village, Monastery of, 36, **37**
Sevan, Sevda, 85
Shahname, 38
Simēon of Poland, 15, 45–7, 66, 125–6, 127, 130
Sis, 170, **171**, 197
Sivas, 45, 117, 130, 131
sof (mohair wool), 46
Srapion, 153, 154
Sruandzteants', Garegin, 72
Step'anos Dashtets'i, 57–8, 67–8, 69, 213, 214, **217**
Step'anos of Tokat (poet), 57–8
Step'anyan, Hasmik, 262, 263

Strabo, 33
Süleyman (sultan), 13–14, 39

taxation, 38–9, 113–18, 120–1, 123–4, 127–8, 129, 160–1
Tekirdağ *see* Rodosto (Tekirdağ)
Ter-Ḷevondyan, A. N., 279–80
Terzioğlu, Derin, 241
Tezcan, Baki, 10
Thomson, Robert W., 278–9
Tietze, Andreas, 198, 267
Tokat, 45, 57–8, 68–9, 150
tombstones, 34, **35**, 85–6, 167
Topal Osman Paşa, 49
Tʻordan (village), 31, 36, 38–9, 71, 234
Tʻorgomean, Vahram Y., 198
torture, 49–50
translation movement, Armeno-Turkish, 261–87
  Armeno-Turkish, history of, 262–4
  concept of translation, 267–8
  devotional translations, 268–72
  Eremia's original works in Armeno-Turkish, 264–7
  Eremia's translations, 267–82
  Muslim readers, 274–5, 279–80, 282
  'secular' translations, 273–82
  sermons, 270–2
travelogues, 29, 41, 44, 45–50, 66, 125–6, 127, 230
Trdat III, King, 5

urbanisation, 8, 11, 86, 129, 263, 288

Vâdî-i Vank (Valley of Monasteries), 39, 40, 151, 190

and the Celali Revolts, 70–2
Vahanshēn Monastery, 154–5
Vahanshēn Village, 154, **155**
Van, 40, 172
Vardan Areveltsʻi, 39
vardapets, 171–5, 205, 232–3, 270
Vaslı Monastery *see* Monastery of the King
Verneuil, Henri, 85

Warner, Levinus, 270
White, Sam, 10
women, 103, 104, 108, 112, 120

Xenophon, 83

Yakob, bishop of Rodosto, 87–8, 93
Yakob of Tokat (poet), 57–9, 68–9
Yakob Karnetʻsi, 39, 55–7
Yazıcı, Kara, 47, 49, 51–2, 53–4, 58, 60–1
Yerevan, 49
Yohannēs Erznkatsʻi, 38
Yovhannēs Kamenatsʻi, 15
Yovhannēs Khul, 182–3
Yovhannēs Muḷnetsʻi, 205, 206

Zakʻaria Aguletsʻi, 233–4
Zakʻaria Kʻanakʻeṙtsʻi, 15
Zevi, Sabbatai, 245–7
zhoḷovatsoy (manuscript collection), 39
Zoroastrianism, 31, 74n
Zuhab, Treaty of (1639), 14, 16, 48
Zulalyan, M. K., 12, 52

EU representative:
Easy Access System Europe
Mustamäe tee 50, 10621 Tallinn, Estonia
Gpsr.requests@easproject.com

www.ingramcontent.com/pod-product-compliance
Lightning Source LLC
Chambersburg PA
CBHW052045220426
43663CB00012B/2445